BBQ PETER HOWARD'S COLLECTION

NEW HOLLAND

CONTENTS

01 Intro 07

02 Starters 10

03 Mains 124
    Meat 124
    Poultry 182
    Seafood 206

04 Salads 270

05 Desserts 312

DEDICATION

To Lyndey Milan, Gastronomique Goddess of the Australian food and wine scene and a true friend for nearly three decades.

INTRODUCTION

The worldwide renaissance of barbecuing is in full swing!
For that reason and my absolute love of barbecuing, I decided to write my fourth book on this delicious way of eating with family and friends—a ritual that is known as being Australian but in reality is a worldwide fascination and is embraced everywhere. How well I remember having a barbecued pike on the Isle of Wight and yes, it was cold and drizzling with misty rain, but for us the umbrella meant scrummy fish from the wood barbecue.

Peter Howard's Barbecue Collection is a combination of the best recipes from the first three books, *Barbecued!*, *Licence to Grill* and *Barbecue Seafood* along with many more new recipes. Pizza, soufflés, roasting and wok frying on the side burner are a few of the additional recipes I have included.

The influence of the barbecue is being felt everywhere and, funnily enough, the advent of the hooded barbecue has meant a renewed roasting. To that end, I have enclosed a roasting chart that you will find extremely useful—I have found roasting in my fabulous Sunbeam barbecue quicker than the conventional oven. A cheap and not to be missed internal meat thermometer must be included in your barbie kit these days.

The first book, *Barbecued!* was written 10 years ago and went on to be a great seller in Australia, the USA and the UK. It had a modern approach to the art of barbecue cooking. It was meant to guide us all from sacrificed sausages, cremated chicken and continued disappointment from the charred remains left lingering on the barbecue plate. It achieved its goals.

Barbecue Seafood was the publisher's inspiration. She said: 'Everyone is afraid of cooking seafood on the barbie—can you please do something about that?' and so we did—I wrote fantastic (so modest!) recipes that New Holland Publishers put into a sensational book that has been acclaimed by all who use it. Thanks Fiona to you for the idea and to your staff for the beautiful book that it became.

The 'Collection' continues in the same way the previous books have—to be of constant use. To that extent, I have expanded on meatless meals and included more salads that are not only accompaniments but also complete dishes. There is an increased demand for these types of dishes and you'll find them delicious. And the desserts are tantalising.

During my many demonstrations of cooking of all styles, I have been heard to say that there isn't too much one cannot do on a barbie…perhaps soufflés and sponges were the two remaining kitchen-bound dishes—not anymore now that I have shown how easy it is to do both sweet and savoury soufflés. Bring on the sponges!

Remember, he or she who holds the tongs rules the barbie!
Be happy and eat well.

Peter Howard

ROASTING CHART
INTERNAL TEMPERATURE GAUGE

Medium Rare to Medium   55°C – 60°C (130°F–140°F)
Medium to Medium Well   65°C – 70°C (150°F–160°F)
Well Done   75°C – 80°C (167°F–176°F)

Rest for at least 10 minutes before carving

OVEN TEMPERATURE CONVERSION CHART

Celsius	Fahrenheit
170	325
180	350
200	400
220	425

	RARE	MEDIUM	WELL DONE
Beef fillet (Tenderloin)	Temp 220°C | Mins 12–15	Temp 220°C | Mins 15 - 20	Temp 220°C | Mins 20–25
Rump	Temp 200°C | Mins 12–15	Temp 200°C | Mins 15–20	Temp 200°C | Mins 25–30
Striploin (sirloin)	Temp 220°C | Mins 12–15	Temp 220°C | Mins 15–20	Temp 200°C | Mins 25–30
Lamb leg	Temp 200°C | Mins 15–18	Temp 200°C | Mins 18–22	Temp 200°C | Mins 25–28
Lamb boned leg	Temp 220°C | Mins 10–15	Temp 220°C | Mins 15–18	Temp 200°C | Mins 20–25
Lamb Loin (Boneless)	Temp 220°C | Mins 12–15	Temp 220°C | Mins 15–20	Temp 200°C | Mins 20–25
Lamb shoulder		Temp 200°C | Mins 18–20	Temp 200°C | Mins 20–25
Rack of Lamb (7–8 cutlets)	Temp 220°C | Mins 15–17	Temp 200°C | Mins 17–20	Temp 200°C | Mins 20–25
Veal leg	Temp 180°C | Mins 15–8	Temp 180°C | Mins 18–22	
Veal Loin (Boneless)	Temp 180°C | Mins 20–25	Temp 180°C | Mins 25–30	
Pork leg		Temp 200°C | Mins 25–30	Temp 180°C | Mins 30–35
Pork Rack		Temp 200°C | Mins 25–30	Temp 200°C | Mins 30–35
Pork loin		Temp 170°C | Mins 30–32	Temp 170°C | Mins 32–35
Scotch fillet Beef	Temp 200°C | Mins 12–15	Temp 200°C | Mins 15–20	Temp 200°C | Mins 20–25
Whole Chicken			Temp 200°C | Mins 15–20

Time given is approximate and per 500g (1.1lb)

LAWS OF THE BARBECUE

1. Always start with a clean barbecue plate. After you finish cooking clean it ready for next time.
2. Heat your barbecue to the required temperature well before use.
3. Always practise good hygiene: don't leave raw ingredients sitting in the sunshine; never let raw meat come into contact with cooked meat and never use leftover marinade as a sauce without cooking it first.
4. Don't mask the natural flavours of your ingredients with too many additions—let their flavours shine through.
5. Concentrate on your cooking so that you never end up with a cremated mess.
6. Use the recipes as a guide and alter the ingredients to suit your personal taste.
7. Have the appropriate tools on hand—tongs or whatever implements suit your needs.
8. Ensure that the gas tank is filled—this saves you from the ultimate embarrassment of running out of 'puff' before the meal is cooked.
9. As the barbecue is a centre for family entertainment, be aware of any children around when you are cooking.
10. The last law always is to enjoy yourself. A barbecue seems to attract good humour and great friends so with careful preparation there is nothing left for you to do but cook and enjoy.

48 freshly shucked small Pacific oysters,
    on the shell
1 cup Semillon Sauvignon Blanc wine
2 tablespoons chives, chopped
1 teaspoon pink peppercorns,
    rinsed and roughly crushed
250g (9oz) salted butter, in 2cm (1in) cubes

SEMILLON SAUVIGNON BLANC OYSTERS

THIS WINE SAUCE IS SIMILAR TO A 'BEURRE BLANC' AND YOU CAN USE IT OVER BARBECUED WHITE FISH. YOU CAN ADD CITRUS TO IT TO MAKE IT APPROPRIATE TO THE OCCASION.

Check the oysters are grit free—try not to rinse under running water as you lose that lovely saltwater flavour of freshly shucked oysters.

Boil the wine and simmer for 2 minutes; add the chives and peppercorns and simmer for a minute. Remove from the heat and swirl in the butter to melt and add the peppercorns—combine well.

Put the oysters, shell-side down, onto the open grill about eight at a time—spoon over some of the sauce. When the liquid is bubbling, the oysters are ready to serve.

Lift from the barbecue and onto either heaped rock salt on platter to keep the oysters upright or on finely shredded outer lettuce leaves for the purpose. Leave to cool so they can be picked up and slipped out of the shell and into your mouth around the barbie.

SERVES 4

300g (10oz) piece of tuna,
   completely trimmed
Spray vegetable oil
Sea salt
16x1cm (½in) thick slices Telegraph
   cucumber, on kitchen paper towelling
2 tablespoons salmon roe

SEARED TUNA SLICES ON CUCUMBER WITH SALMON ROE

Cut the tuna into log size if possible, about 3cm (1½in) square. Ultimately, the idea is to be able to cut slices about 1–2cm (½–1in) thick to sit on the sliced cucumber.

Spray the tuna well with oil and sear on hot plate—turn so you get even cooking on each side of the log. You need cook no more than 30 seconds on each of the sides—lift and put on kitchen paper towelling. Cool and refrigerate.

With a very sharp, thin knife slice the seared tuna into 1–2cm (½–1in) thick slices. Top each slice of cucumber with the tuna slice and equally top with the salmon roe. Serve as a pass-around with cocktail napkins.

Serves 4

16 large oysters out of shell
16 pieces of bacon, rindless,
 8cm long x 3cm wide (3in x 1in)
Toothpicks
Worcestershire sauce

ANGELS ON HORSEBACK

Wrap each oyster in a piece of bacon and secure with a toothpick.

Spray a hot plate with a little oil and cook the angels at high temperature until bacon is crisp. Brush a little Worcestershire sauce onto the oysters as they cook.

Serve the angels on suitable plate with a little Worcestershire sauce on the side—these are great served around the barbie as guests arrive.

Serves 4

20 scallops on shell
Spray vegetable oil
3 tablespoons green spring onions, minced
1 tablespoon thick soy sauce (Kepak Manis)
1 teaspoon green ginger, finely minced
1 teaspoon lemongrass, white only
    and minced
1 tablespoon lime juice
1 small green chilli, seeds removed
    and minced
½ tablespoon water

ASIAN-FLAVOURED SEA SCALLOPS

Check each scallop to see it is clean and grit free—lift each scallop and give the shell a film of oil with the spray and return the scallop. Repeat for all the scallops and refrigerate until ready to cook.

Mix the remaining ingredients and spoon a little over each scallop on the shell.

Lift onto medium hot grill—cook a few at a time as they cook quickly. Turn the scallops carefully if you can on the grill, otherwise lift from grill and turn over. Spoon over a little more sauce, cook further and serve when all are done to your liking.

SERVES 4

500g (16oz) chicken thigh fillets
1 red capsicum, finely chopped
2 red chillies, chopped
2 cloves garlic, chopped
1 tablespoons ginger, minced
1 stalk of lemon grass, tender part only, chopped
2 lime Kaffir leaves, ribs removed and shredded

1 tablespoon fish sauce
½ cup coconut milk
1 whole egg
125g (4oz) beans or snake beans, cut into 3mm slices
1 cup fresh breadcrumbs
Vegetable/peanut oil
Sweet chilli dipping sauce

THAI CHICKEN CAKES

Cut chicken thigh fillets into small pieces.

Combine capsicum, chillies, garlic, ginger, lemon grass, Kaffir leaves and fish sauce into a food processor and blend to a smooth paste. Add chicken pieces, coconut milk and egg and blend well. Place mixture in a bowl and add sliced beans. Chill for at least 1 hour and then stir in the breadcrumbs (you may not need them all but you need a firm dough—not sloppy) to take up some of the excess moisture.

Pour oil onto a medium hot plate and shape a half tablespoon of the chicken mixture into a small cake as you place it on the barbie—do not overload as the chicken cakes cook quickly. I normally do six at a time. Ensure the plate is oiled where you are going to turn the half cooked cakes, then flip them over to cook through. Drain on plate lined with kitchen paper and keep warm. Repeat until all the mixture has gone.

Serve on a platter with the dipping sauce on the side.

Makes 15–20

16 large sea scallops
16 x 2cm (1in) thick slices blood sausage
Spray vegetable oil
2 cups creamy mashed potatoes, hot
Fresh dill sprigs
4 x 1cm (½in) thick slices of prawn and lime butter

For the Prawn and Lime Butter
250g (9oz) salted butter, room temperature
60g (2oz) cooked prawn meat, finely minced
1 tablespoon dill, finely chopped
1 tablespoon lime juice
1 teaspoon lime zest, finely grated

SCALLOPS, BLOOD SAUSAGE, PRAWN & LIME BUTTER

Trim the black membrane from the side of each scallop.

Cook the sausage slices very quickly on hot plate sprayed with oil. Lift and keep warm.

Spray scallops on both sides and cook very quickly on hot plate on both sides—1½ minutes on the first side and no more than a minute on the second side - to overcook them is to turn them tough.

Spoon 16 dollops of potato mash around well perimeter of four individual plates—top with a slice of sausage and then a scallop on top of the sausage. Decorate the plates with sprigs of chervil in the middle and top each scallop with a quarter slice of the prawn and lime butter—serve immediately.

For the Prawn and Lime Butter
Mash all ingredients together in a bowl and when well combined, spoon onto a piece of cling wrap and shape into a log/sausage. Roll, chill and freeze to keep. Slice when needed.

Serves 16

200g green lip Abalone or cocktail Abalones
Ground black pepper
2 tablespoons peanut oil
Sea salt

For the sauce
1 teaspoon white sugar
2 tablespoons lime juice
1 tablespoon fish sauce
2 small red chillies, deseeded and minced
1 large clove garlic, minced
1 tablespoon rice vinegar
2–3 tablespoons water

ABALONE STRIPS WITH VIETNAMESE DIPPING SAUCE

Sometimes, depending on the abalone and its shape, it is best to put it into a freezer for about 15 minutes to get the flesh really set, but not frozen. Use a very sharp thin knife to do the slicing

Slice the abalone into fine slices about 5mm thick and sprinkle with a little ground black pepper to taste and with the oil–toss to coat and let sit for 15 minutes.

Whisk the sauce ingredients and pour into a serving bowl.

Lift the strips onto a hot plate and cook in batches so as to not overcook. The strips really only need to be on the plate for about 15 seconds each side or until the flesh is firm but not rock hard. Lift from barbecue and serve around the bowl of sauce with toothpicks to lift pieces and dip.

Serves 4

4 x 300g eggplants (aubergine), roasted
    and peeled
Spray olive oil
4 garlic cloves, crushed
1 teaspoon salt
½ cup tahini
1 teaspoon ground cumin
50ml lemon juice, fresh
Olive oil
Sourdough bread slices, 2cm (1in) thick
    or the traditional pita bread

BABA GANOUSH

If you use pita bread, it is served either cut into triangles or whole so pieces can be ripped from it. You can also serve the spread on a flat plate with olive oil drizzled over the top in which case you drag it through the pita to eat.

Cut the eggplants in half lengthwise and score the flesh into diamonds. Spray the cut side of the eggplants with oil and cook on the grill for 25–30 minutes, turning regularly.

Lift the eggplants from the barbecue and allow to cool for 10 minutes before peeling the skin away from the flesh. Alternatively, scoop/scrape the flesh from the charred skin with a spoon.

Blend the cooked eggplant, garlic, salt, tahini, cumin and lemon juice to a smooth paste.

Grill the sliced bread or pita bread, sprayed with oil, until marked and serve warm with room temperature Baba Ganoush.

Makes 2½ cups

16 scallops, roe on
¼ cup good mayonnaise
1 tablespoon lemon juice
1 tablespoon cold water
4 anchovy fillets, mashed
16 small sprigs dill

SCALLOPS & ANCHOVY SAUCE

Trim the scallops by removing the black membrane from the side of the scallop.

Make the anchovy sauce by blending the mayonnaise, lemon juice, water, anchovies and dill to a smooth consistency.

Spray the scallops with oil and cook on a very hot plate for 1–1½ minutes. Turn and cook for no more than 1 minute on this side.

Spoon a small amount of the sauce into the base of Chinese spoons or dessert spoons. Place a scallop on top and spoon over a little of the sauce. Decorate with the dill sprig.

Serve on a platter with the handles facing to the rim.

SERVES 4

32 Kinkawooka black mussels, (these are already scrubbed and debearded)
2 tablespoons tandoori paste
3 tablespoons natural yoghurt
2 tablespoons mint, finely chopped
Tiny mint sprigs, for decoration

MUSSELS & TANDOORI DRESSING

Put the mussels onto a medium-hot open grill and soon they will start to open. Lift from grill into a large bowl and cool; lift the top shell from the mussel and set to one side. Reserve any juices that come from the mussels.

Mix the paste, yoghurt, mint and any reserved mussel juice. Dob half a teaspoon onto each mussel. You may need more for larger mussels but remember in the cooking it will melt and ooze a little.

Put the mussels back on the medium-hot open grill and cook until they bubble around the side of each mussel. Lift and serve immediately. We eat these around the barbecue so it's not necessary to add the mint leaves but if you want to plate them and serve as a sit-down starter, you can decorate with the mint sprigs.

Serves 4

400g (14oz) basic risotto (see below)
16 x 1cm (½in) cubed pieces of salami
Breadcrumbs

For the Risotto
60g (2oz) butter
1 small onion, chopped
1 clove garlic, chopped
1½ cups arborio rice
4 cups boiling chicken stock
2 teaspoons salt
½ teaspoon white pepper
3 tablespoons parmesan cheese, grated
2 tablespoons parsley, finely chopped

TINY ARANCINI

Leftover risotto will store in the refrigerator for up to four days. A cooked risotto can be turned out into a springform tin and allowed to set overnight. It can then be cut into wedges and char-grilled or pan-fried.

The arancini will not look cooked on the side but that is okay because the flavour and texture will be set by the flat sides of each one. I have made these with a cube of mozarella in the middle, replacing the salami.

Melt 30g (1oz) of the butter in a large heavy saucepan and cook onion and garlic. When onion is soft and golden, add the rice and fry for 2 minutes, stirring constantly, then pour in 1 cup boiling stock and cook gently, while stirring, until it is absorbed.

Continue cooking gently, adding stock a cupful at a time and stirring constantly for 15–20 minutes or until rice is tender and all liquid is absorbed. Season with salt and pepper, stir in remaining butter and the cheese. Cover with hood and leave risotto to sit for 3 minutes before serving. This will make 900g (2lb) of risotto.

To make the arancini, divide the 400g (14oz) of required risotto into 16 equal portions. Put one cube of salami into the middle of the mixture and roll/shake the rice into a ball. Flatten into a round of 4cm (1.7in) in diameter and 2cm (1in) thick, then roll in breadcrumbs. Make sure all excess breadcrumbs are removed.

To barbecue, spray a medium-hot plate with oil and shoode on the arancini. Cook for 1 minute. Spray liberally with oil and turn and cook for another minute on the other flat side. Lift the browned arancini onto a plate and leave for 2 minutes before service.

Makes 16

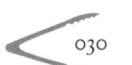

¼ cup burghul (cracked wheat)
1 tablespoon olive oil, plus extra to brush
1 small onion, finely chopped
2 garlic cloves, crushed
1 x 3cm (1in) piece ginger, peeled, finely grated
2 teaspoons ground coriander
½ teaspoon ground cinnamon
500g (1lb) ground lamb, no fat
1 egg yolk

2 tablespoons pine nuts, chopped
2 tablespoons freshly chopped coriander, plus extra coriander leaves to serve
Sea salt
Freshly ground black pepper
8–12 wooden skewers, soaked in cold water for 30 minutes
Spray oil
Pita bread, yoghurt and mint leaves, to serve

LAMB KOFTAS WITH PITA BREAD, YOGHURT & MINT

When cooking items like this on the grill, be aware that the bamboo skewers catch light very easily. The alternative to using metal skewers is better and also better environmentally too.

Soak the burghul in cold water for 30 minutes, drain and squeeze dry.

Cook onion in heated oil for 3 minutes or until onion is soft. Add the garlic, ginger and spices and stir for a further minute. Allow to cool.

Place the burghul, onion mixture, lamb, egg yolk, pine nuts and coriander in a large bowl. Using clean hands, mix until all ingredients are well combined. Season with salt and pepper to taste.

Wet your hands and shape the mixture around the skewer tip (the pointy end) in a small sausage shape. Refrigerate for at least 2 hours before use.

To cook, brush with a little olive oil and put onto a medium-hot plate. Cook the koftas for 5 minutes, turning occasionally until golden brown. Move to hot grill to crisp and brown even more. Serve with pita bread, yoghurt, mint and coriander.

Serves 4

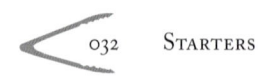

6 slices fresh white or brown bread
4–6 bacon rashers, rinds removed
    and cut into equal pieces
Peanut butter
Spreadable chilli jam (see recipe below)
Thick toothpicks
Spray oil

For the chilli jam
300g (11oz) red shallots, fried
150g (5oz) garlic, fried
50g (2oz) prawns, dried
50g (2oz) roasted large Thai dried chillies
1 cup palm sugar
120g (4oz) tamarind paste
½ cup water

BACON, CHILLI JAM & PEANUT BUTTER ROLLS

This gutsy side serve will give most barbecue dishes a real zing. However if your version is particularly feisty, make sure you tell everyone at the table.

To alleviate a chilli burn, use a milk product. For example, if you have a chilli burn on your lip, apply some yoghurt. If your tongue is burning up, rinse your mouth with some milk.

Cut the crusts from the bread, spread with peanut butter and smear with chilli jam (if the jam is not all that spreadable, flash it through the microwave for 5–10 seconds). Then cut the slice in two even rectangles. Roll them and then roll a piece of bacon around the bread; secure with a toothpick and repeat the process until all done

Spray the bacon-wrapped rolls with oil and toss onto a medium-hot plate. Turn regularly so as to crisp the bacon and heat the rolls through.

When lightly browned, serve with napkins around the barbie when they have cooled a little.

For the chilli jam
Blend in processor or in mortar and pestle. Simmer over medium heat, stirring constantly because the jam cooks in 5 minutes. Spoon into sterilised jar and cover with hood when cooled.

16 medium green king prawns, peeled
   and de-veined
Bamboo skewers, soaked in water for
   30 minutes or metal ones
4 lemon cheeks
Olive oil
Salt and pepper to taste

SKEWERED PRAWNS, BARBECUED LEMON

Insert the skewer into tail of the prawn and thread the meat on so that the flesh is kept straight. Arrange on a flat plate and drizzle over light olive oil. Rotate the prawns to coat them with oil.

Put the lemon cheeks onto the medium-hot grill, cut-side down, and cook for 1 minute.

Place the prawns on a medium-hot plate and cook for 3 minutes. Turn the prawns constantly and drizzle with the oil they have been sitting in. Sprinkle with salt and pepper.

To serve, remove the skewers from the prawns and put onto individual plates with a little side salad. Decorate with lemon cheek showing the barbecue marking. Alternatively, you can leave the skewers in and put on a platter, decorated with the lemon cheeks, and serve around the barbie as guests are assembling.

Serves 4

16 asparagus spears
8 slices prosciutto
Spray oil
Extra virgin olive oil
Cracked black pepper (optional)

Asparagus in Prosciutto

Trim the asparagus spears. Breaking them where the spears turn pale is the best.

Cut prosciutto slices into halves and wrap each half around an asparagus spear, starting from the bottom and winding up to the top. Refrigerate until ready to use.

Spray oil the prosciutto-wrapped asparagus lightly and put on the medium-hot plate; turn constantly until the prosciutto is starting to go crisp and pale. It really only takes a minute or two. Flash them onto a hot grill for a few seconds before serving.

Serve while standing around the barbie drizzled with a little extra virgin olive oil and sprinkle cracked pepper if you like.

Serves 4

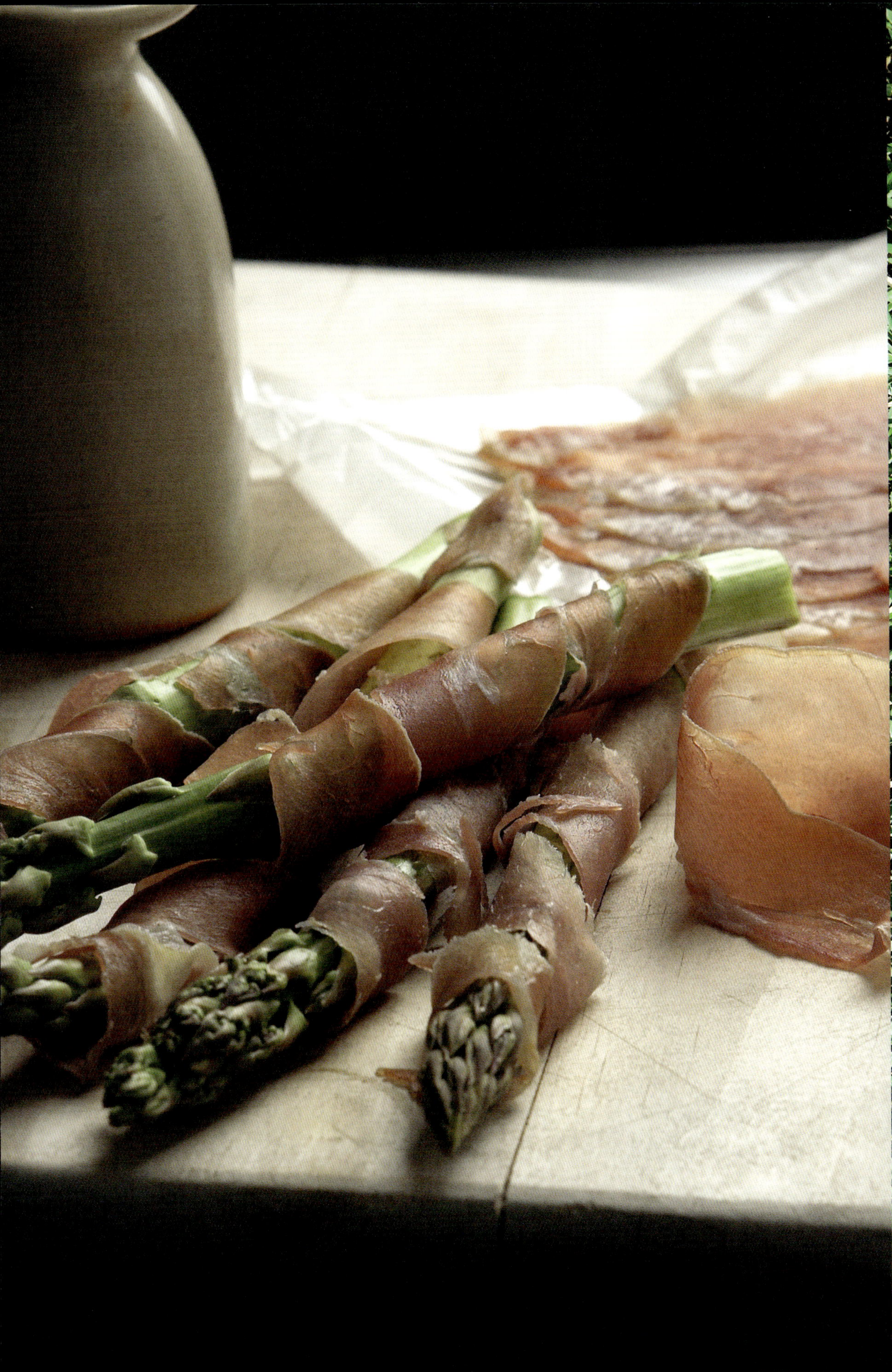
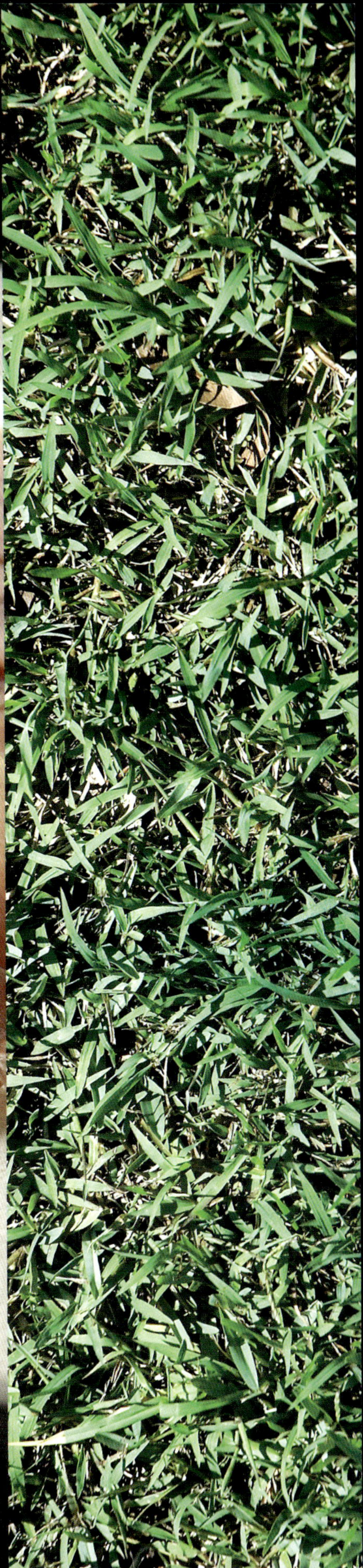

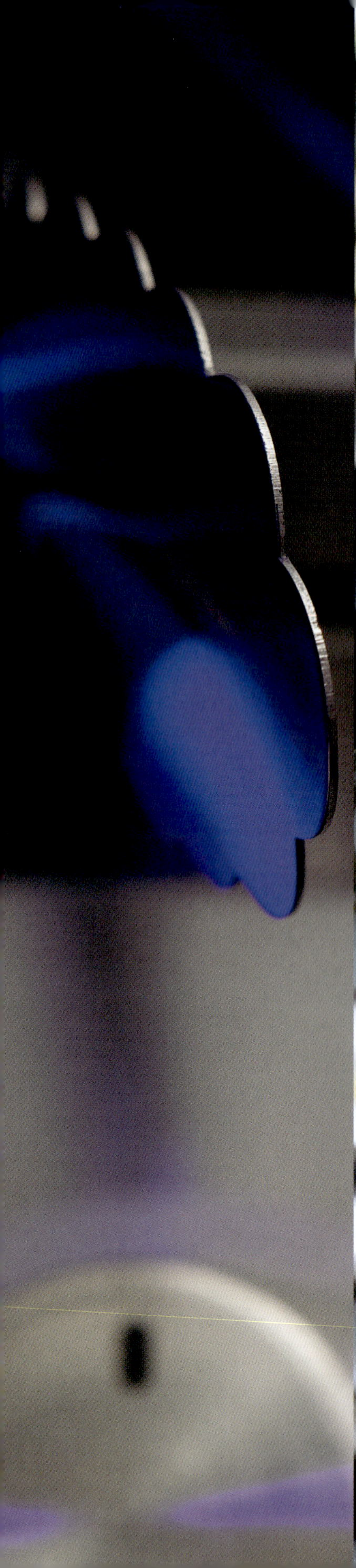
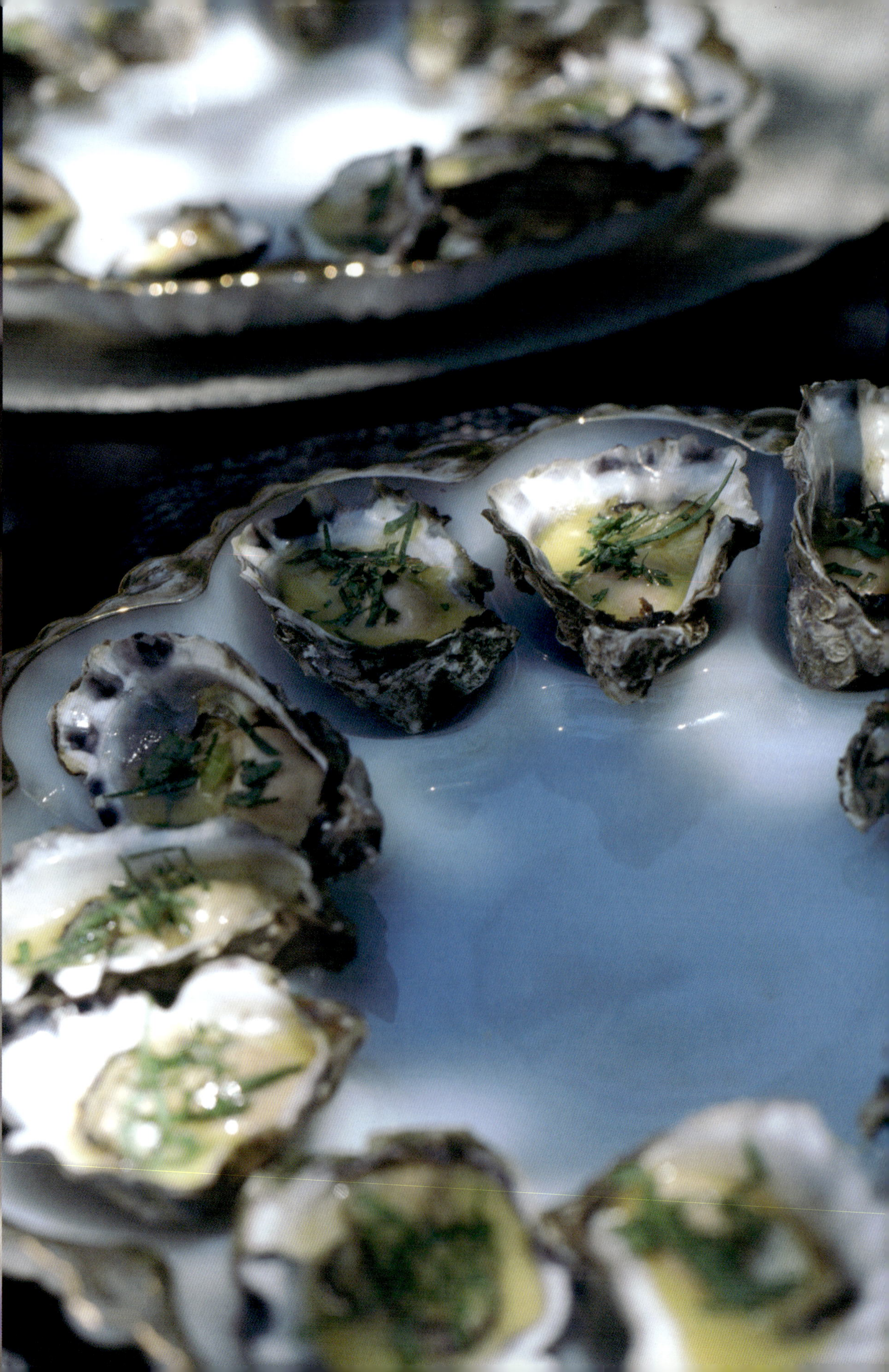

48 opened oysters, on the shell
1 cup chardonnay wine
2 green spring onions
1 teaspoon ground black pepper
200g (7oz) unsalted butter
Chopped parsley

CHARDONNAY BUTTER OYSTERS

IF YOU HAVE ANY BUTTER LEFT OVER, IT WILL STORE AND CAN BE USED OVER FISH OR CHICKEN AT ANY TIME. REHEAT IN A SAUCEPAN OR MICROWAVE.

Pour the wine into a saucepan and bring to the boil. Meanwhile, trim and finely mince the spring onions. Add to wine and simmer for 2 minutes. Remove from the heat and dice in the butter and swirl to let the butter melt and combine with the wine.

Put the oysters on a hot grill about 6 to 8 at a time. Spoon on some of the butter and sprinkle over the chopped parsley. The liquid around the edge of each oyster needs to be just bubbling to indicate the oysters are ready to serve. Do not boil or overcook as they shrink easily.

These are best served around the barbecue. Lift onto a plate filled with rock salt to 'secure' them. To eat, slip out of the shell and into your mouth and have a container to take the empty shells.

SERVES 4

16 x 30g (1oz) pieces ocean trout, skinless
    and bones removed
16 small bamboo or stainless steel skewers
½ cup thick satay sauce
¼ cup coconut cream
Spray vegetable oil
Coriander leaves for decoration

OCEAN TROUT BROCHETTES WITH SATAY DIPPING SAUCE

Thread one piece of the fish onto the tip of each skewer. Refrigerate until ready to cook.

Heat the satay sauce and coconut cream until warmed and combined. Pour into dipping bowl.

Spray the ocean trout with a little oil (remembering that this fish has naturally good oil in it) and cook on a medium-hot flat plate for 30 seconds each side. Serve on a plate with the dipping sauce in the middle and decorate with coriander leaves.

Makes 16

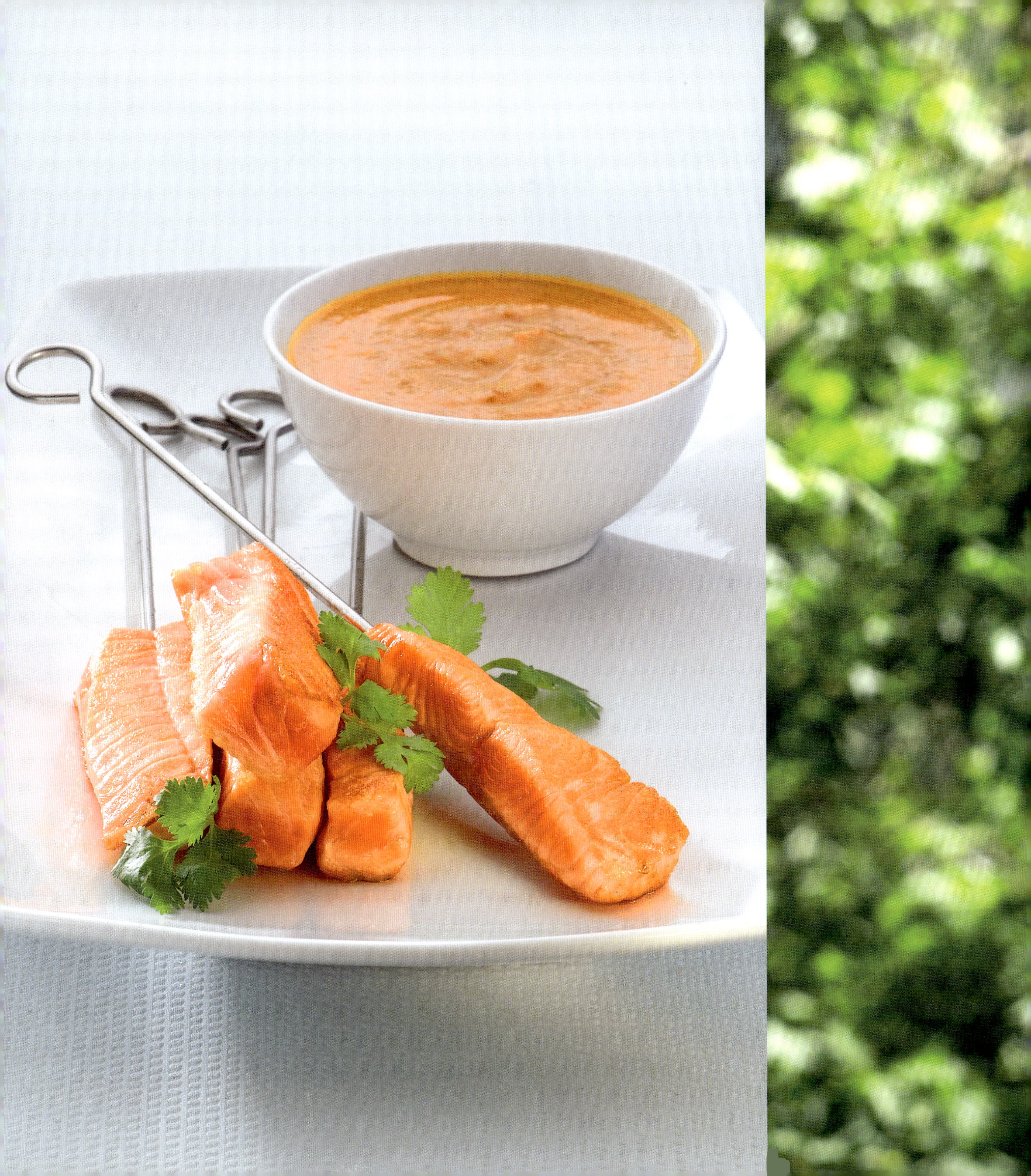

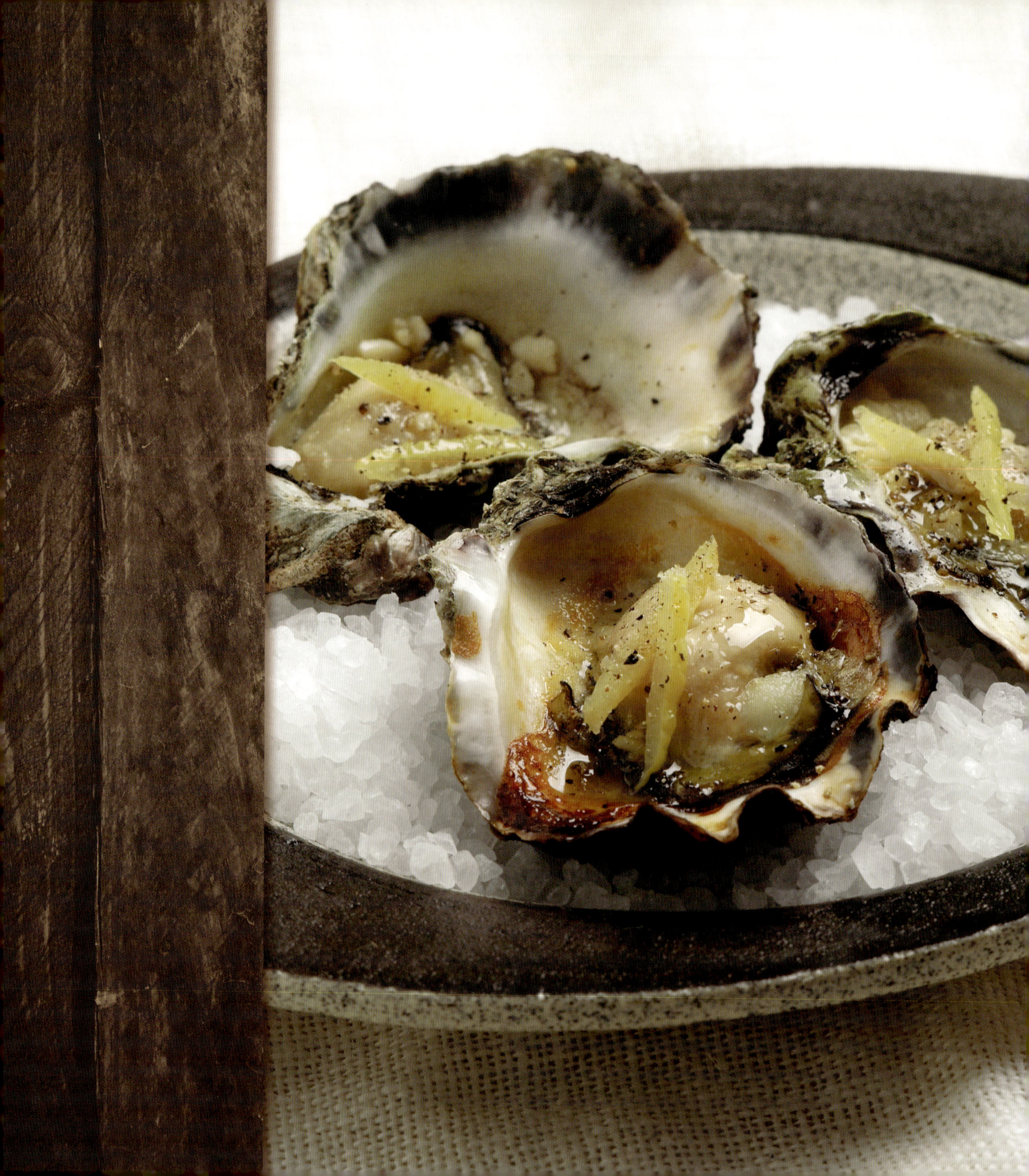

24 large Coffin Bay oysters or Sydney
　　Rock oysters, freshly shucked
Garlic oil (see Beef Sausages and Barbecue
　　Vegetable Stir Fry recipe, page 135)
Rock salt
Preserved lemon rind to taste, washed
　　and minced or very finely sliced
Cracked black pepper

OYSTERS WITH GARLIC OIL & PRESERVED LEMON

PRESERVED LEMON CAN BE VERY STRONG IN FLAVOR SO USE SPARINGLY.

Place the oysters onto a hot grill and drizzle with a little garlic oil. Cook for 1–2 minutes. The rim of the oyster flesh should start to bubble, which indicates the oysters are ready to serve.

Serve the oysters on a bed of rock salt (to stop them slipping) on individual plates. Top with preserved lemon and sprinkle with cracked pepper. Be mindful that the shells are very hot to handle and will continue cooking for a couple of minutes after they have been removed from the heat.

SERVES 4

1kg (2.2lb) starchy potatoes
    (Pontiac or Sebago), peeled
1 medium onion, peeled
1 cup frozen/fresh peas
1 tablespoon plain flour
½ cup fresh tarragon, chopped
Salt and pepper to taste
Olive oil
8 slices smoked salmon
4 teaspoons light sour cream
4 teaspoons salmon roe

POTATO, TARRAGON & PEA CAKES WITH SMOKED SALMON & SALMON ROE

Wash the potatoes and grate them and the onion into a bowl. Add the peas, flour, tarragon and salt and pepper. Mix well.

Spoon on some olive oil onto a medium-hot plate. Make four cakes from the mix by taking a small handful and squeezing out the liquid. Shape into a flatish, round pattie/cake and place onto the oiled plate. Repeat until all the mixture is used.

When the base of the cakes is set, drizzle some oil onto the top of the cakes and flip over. Press down on each cake with the back of the spatula and ensure the shape of the cakes is kept roundish. Do not add any more oil but turn until cooked through. Remove from the barbecue onto a paper towel-lined plate and keep warm.

Put a small dob of sour cream onto the centre of individual serving plates, top with a cake (sour cream stops the cakes from shooding). Curl on equal amounts of smoked salmon, spoon on equal amounts of sour cream and top with a teaspoon of the salmon roe, sometimes referred to as salmon caviar.

Serves 4

½ cup finely minced ham
1 tablespoon green spring onions, minced
2 cloves garlic, minced
2 cups rehydrated cous cous
1 teaspoon cumin powder
1 egg, beaten
1 tablespoon plain flour
1 teaspoon salt
1 tablespoon parsley, chopped
Spray oil
Sour cream (optional)
Parsley sprigs for decoration

HAM, CUMIN & COUS COUS CAKES

Mix all the ingredients together except for the oil, sour cream and parsley. Refrigerate for at least 1 hour before use.

Using wet hands, take a tablespoon of the mixture and roll into a ball, then flatten slightly so as to allow even cooking.

Spray the cakes well with oil and cook on both sides until browning and starting to crisp.

Put the cakes onto a plate or platter and allow to cool before passing around. They must be quite cool if you are serving the sour cream with them which is a half a teaspoon (if that) on top of each cake. If too hot, the cream will melt and run.

Makes 16–18

24 Pacific oysters, freshly shucked
6 x 1cm (½in) thick slices of Café de Paris butter, cut into quarters
Rock salt for serving
4 lemon cheeks

Café de Paris Butter
250g (9oz) unsalted butter, room temperature
1 teaspoon capers, rinsed
1 clove garlic, roughly chopped
1 tablespoon tomato paste
1 tablespoon smooth French mustard
1 teaspoon parsley, chopped
1 teaspoon tarragon leaves, chopped
¼ teaspoon paprika
1 anchovy fillet, drained
1 tablespoon lemon juice
1 teaspoon green peppercorns

OYSTERS & CAFÉ DE PARIS BUTTER

Sit the oysters on a medium-hot grill. Ensure they sit as upright as possible and cook 6–8 at a time. Put a quarter piece of butter on top of each one. Drop the hood and cook until the sides of the oysters are just bubbling and butter melting.

Meanwhile, heap the salt onto individual dinner plates. Lift equal quantities of oysters from the grill and sit firmly into the salt so they sit upright and serve with a lemon cheek.

For the Café de Paris Butter
Put all the ingredients into a food processor and work to combine. Lift out onto large piece of cling wrap and shape into a sausage/log. Roll and secure the end and chill to set or freeze. Slice when needed directly from the freezer and with a warmed knife.

Serves 4

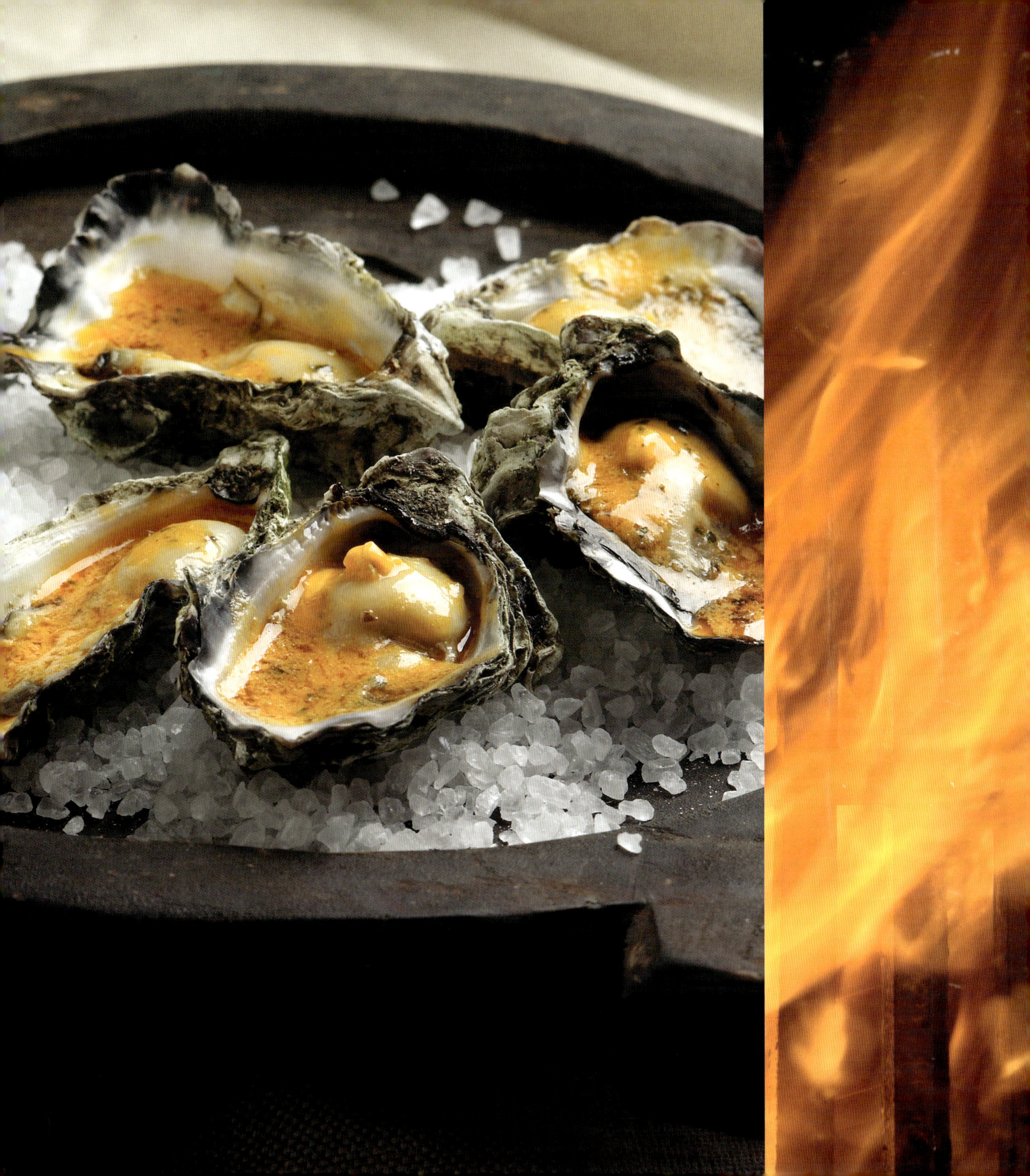

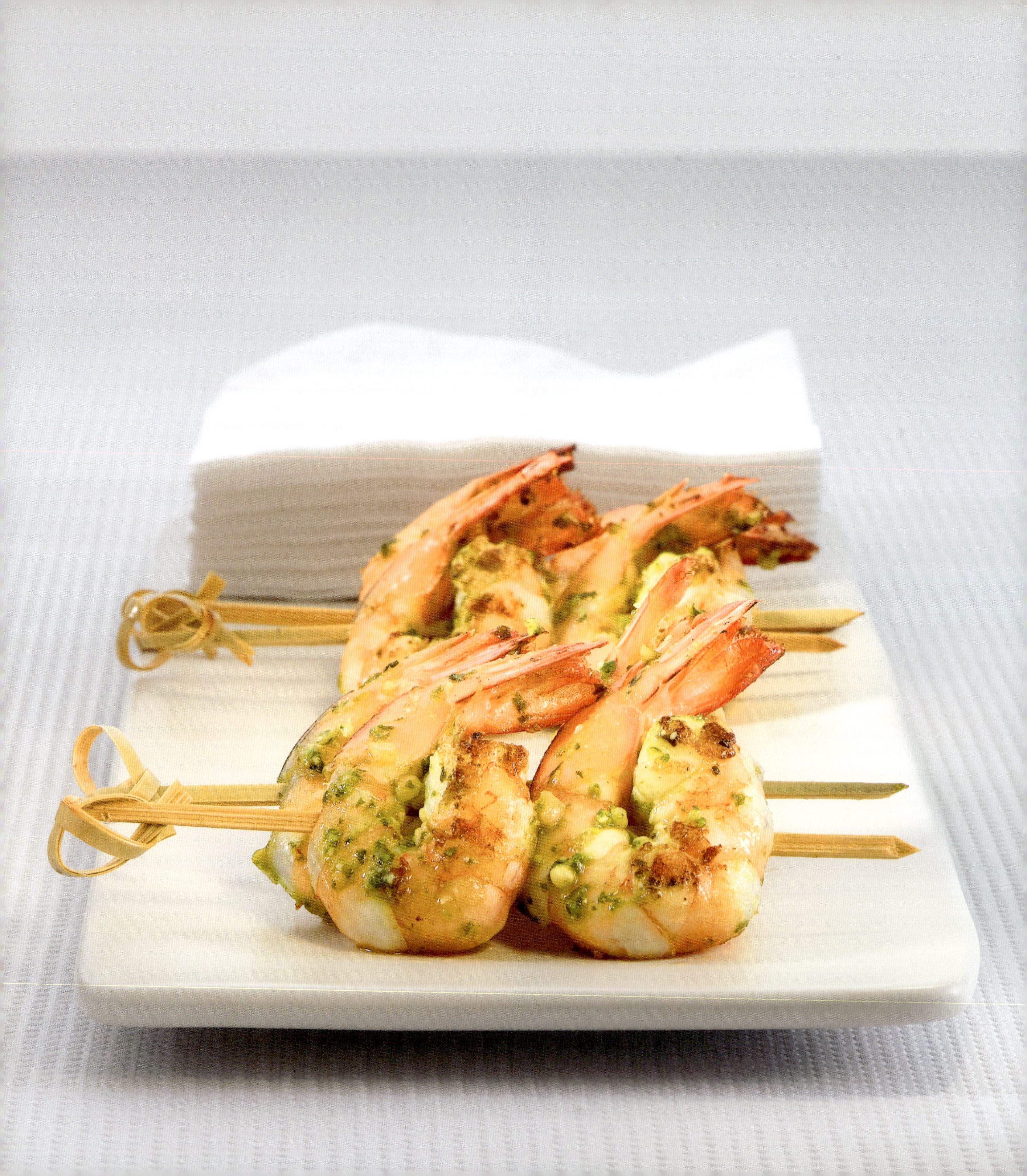

16 green king prawns, completely
    peeled and deveined
8 small bamboo skewers, soaked in
    water for 30 minutes (or metal ones)
200g bottled pesto, pre-prepared
    from the supermarket
Spray olive oil
Ground black pepper

PESTO-INFUSED PRAWN SKEWERS

Mix the prawns and pesto in a large bowl, coat well and refrigerate for 1 hour. Thread two prawns onto each skewer and sit on cling wrap-lined plate. Spoon the pesto over, cover with cling wrap and refrigerate for 2–3 hours.

Spray a medium-hot plate with oil. Add the prawns and cook. Sprinkle on black pepper and baste once with the pesto. You can turn these twice during the cooking and serve on a platter with cocktail napkins to have as a starter around the barbecue.

Serves 4

500g (16oz) lean minced beef
3 tablespoons green spring onions, chopped
1 teaspoon pre-prepared curry powder
½ cup cous cous, hydrated
1 teaspoon oregano, chopped
1 egg
½ cup barbecue sauce (see Barbecued Beef and Mushroom Kebabs recipe, page 132)

MEATBALLS & HOMEMADE BARBECUE SAUCE

To make it easy to roll the meatballs, dip your hands into a bowl of cold water and then start the rolling process.

Combine all the ingredients, excluding the sauce, and mix well using your hands.

Roll into 3cm (1in) diameter meatballs (around 25g/1oz each). Cover and refrigerate for 2 hours.

Spray a hot plate with oil. Add the meatballs and turn regularly to cook for 5–7 minutes.

Place meatballs on a platter and serve with the sauce to one side.

Makes 20–24

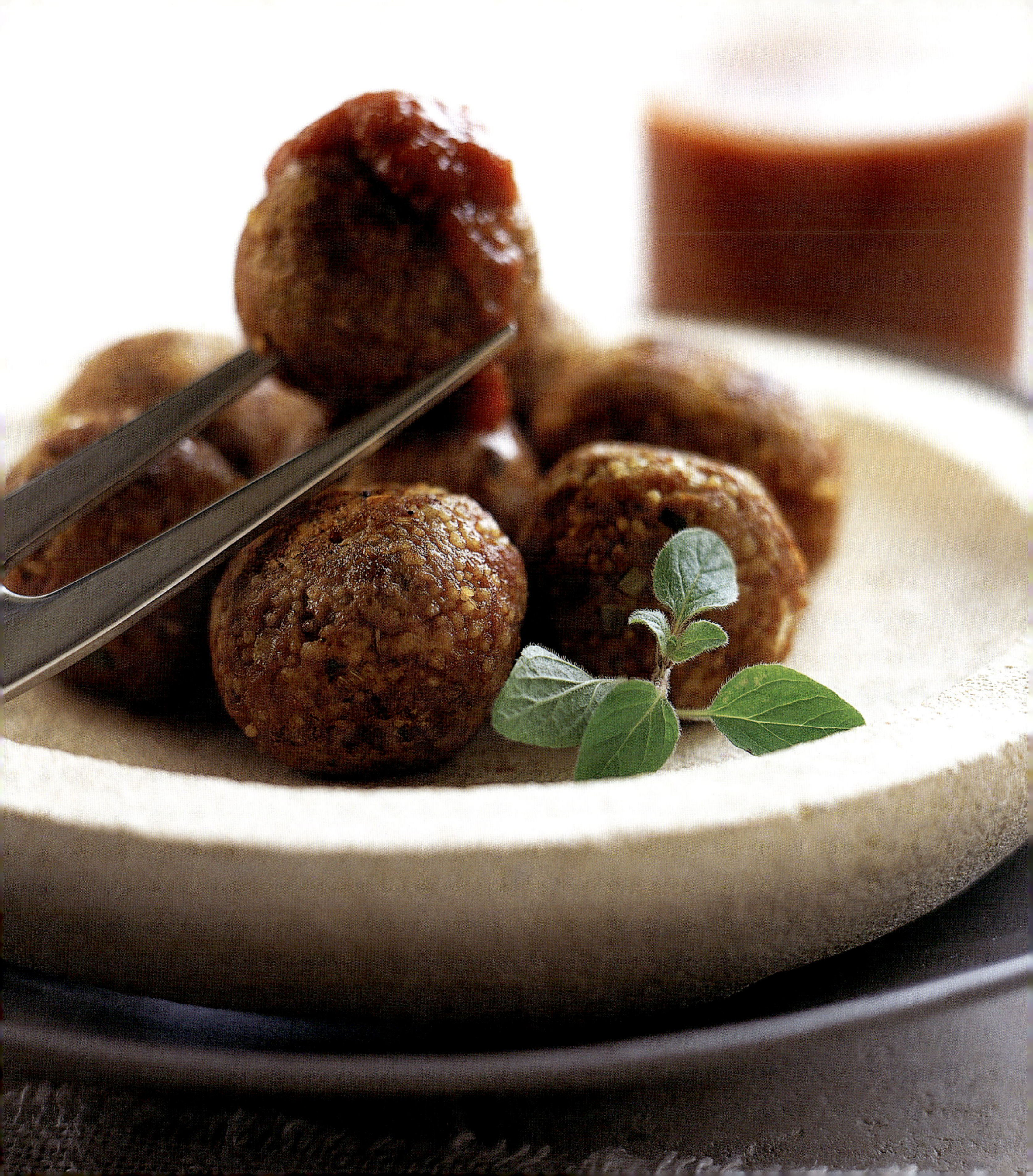

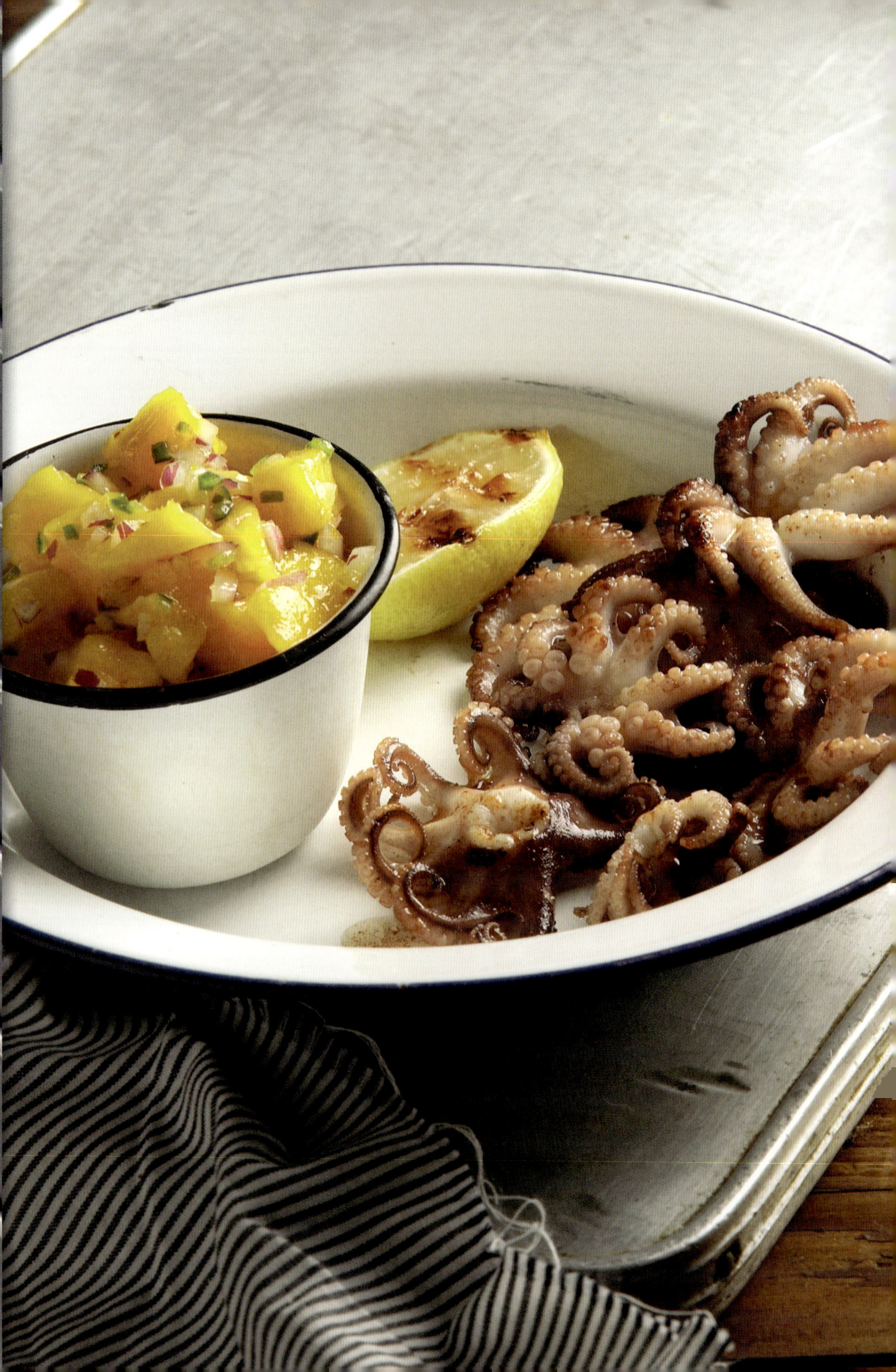

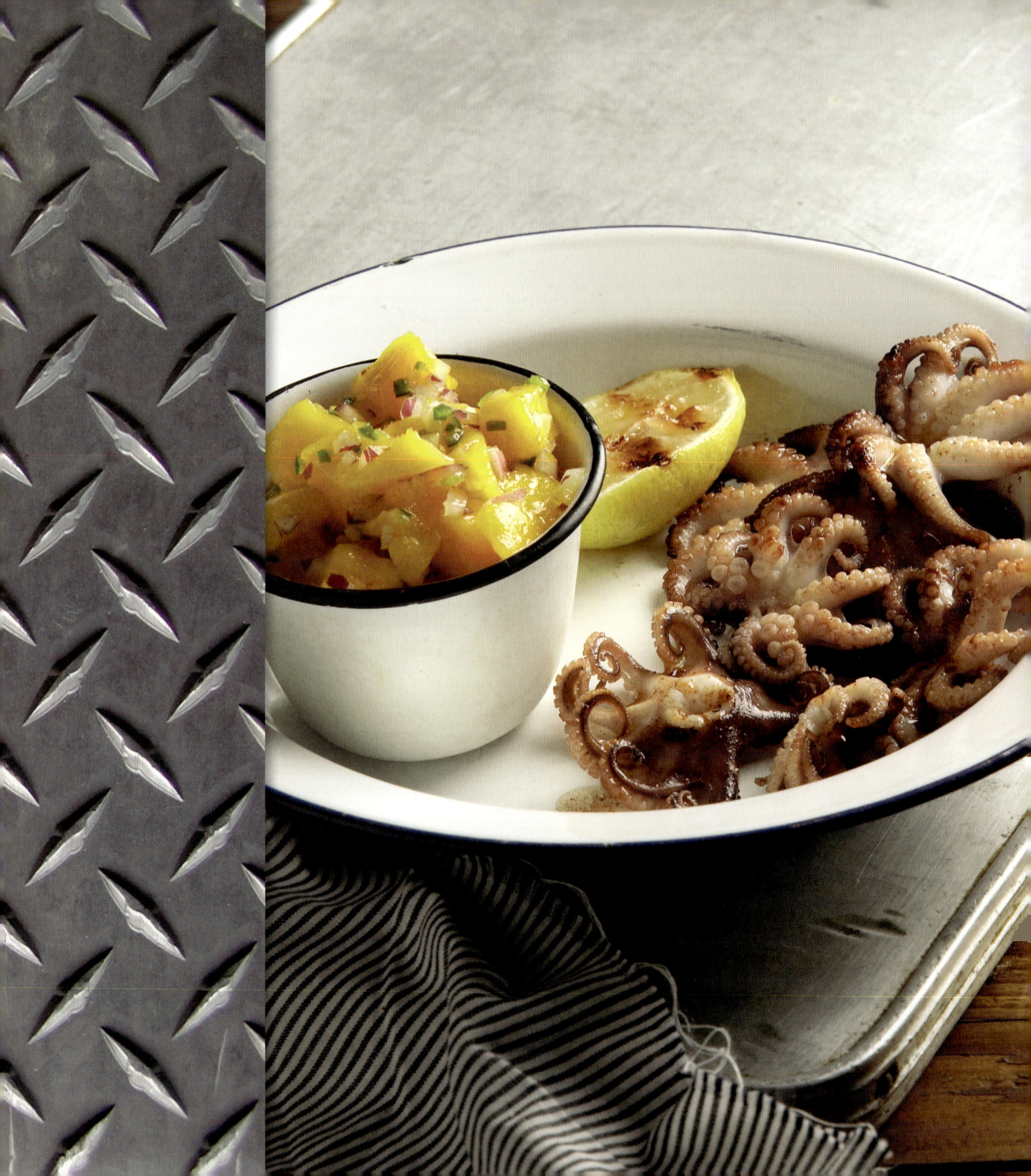

20 baby octopus, cleaned and tenderised
2 tablespoons vegetable oil
¼ teaspoon sea salt
500g (16oz) mango flesh, diced into 1cm cubes
100g (4oz) red onion, finely diced
1 large green fruity chilli, deseeded and finely chopped
2 tablespoons orange juice
1 tablespoon orange zest, finely grated

CHARGRILLED BABY OCTOPUS WITH MANGO SALSA

Put the octopus in with the oil and salt and toss; let sit for 10 minutes. This eliminates the need to oil the barbecue plate when cooking.

Mix the mango, onion, chilli, juice and zest; sit for 10 minutes.

Cook the octopus on a very hot plate and toss to cook evenly. Do not overcook as they go tough—once firm they are ready to go. Put the salsa into the middle of a large plate and place the octopus around the salsa. Serve with a good green salad for a more substantial starter.

Serves 4

12 fingers pide bread, roughly 4cm
    (1.5in) wide
Spray oil

For the beetroot hummus
2 cups cooked pinto beans
200g (7oz) cooked beetroot, chopped
2 tablespoons lime juice
2 tablespoon organic tahini
1 teaspoon white sesame seeds
½ teaspoon ground white pepper
1 teaspoon powdered cumin
½ cup olive oil

GRILLED PIDE & BEETROOT HUMMUS

Spray pide fingers with oil and crisp/brown on the hot grill. Serve the hummus in a bowl surrounded by the warm pide fingers.

Serves 4

For the beetroot hummus
Puree all ingredients to a rough paste in a processor or with a hand blender. Store in airtight container in the refrigerator for up to 7 days.

Makes 2½ cups

Starters

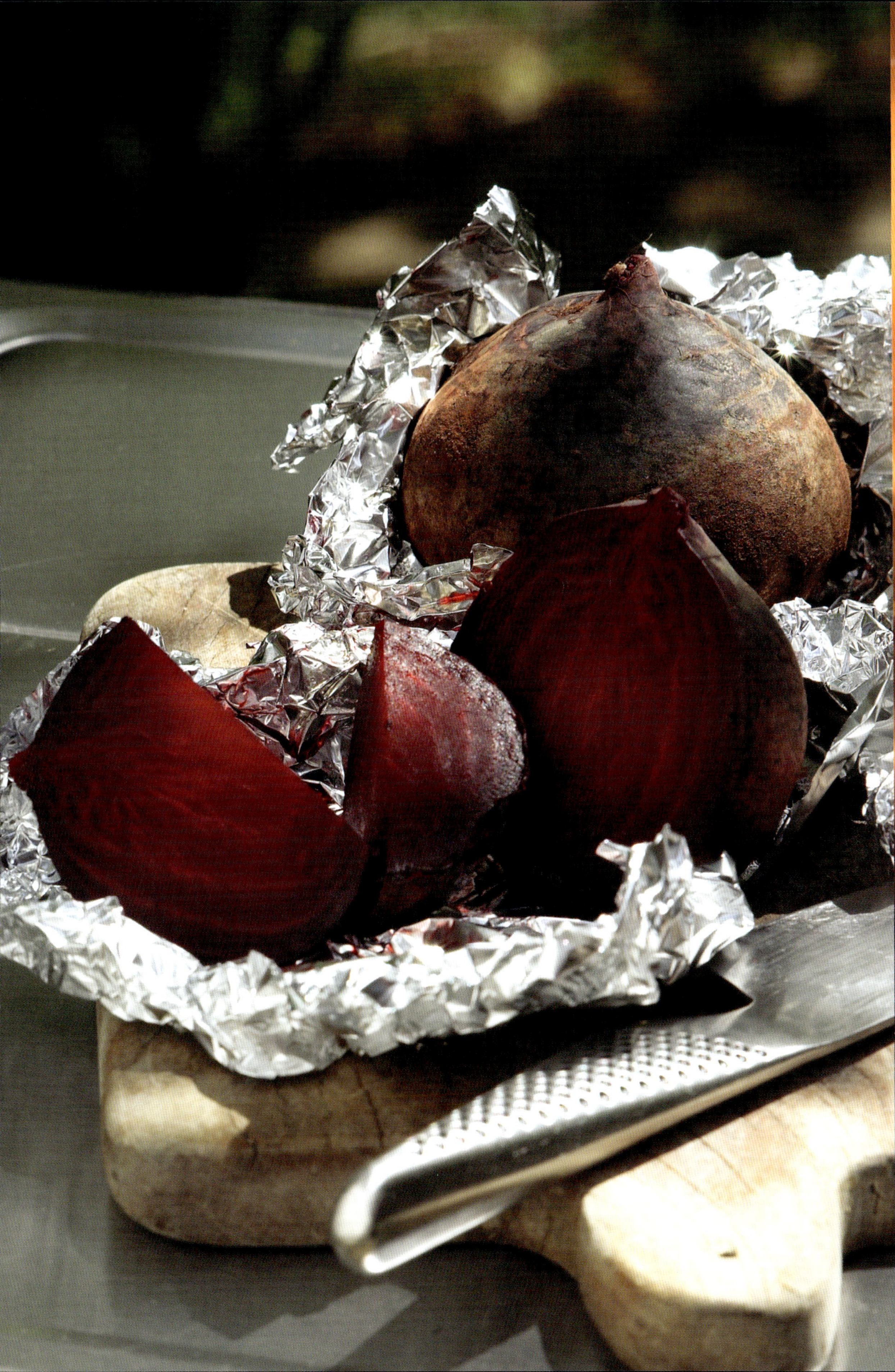
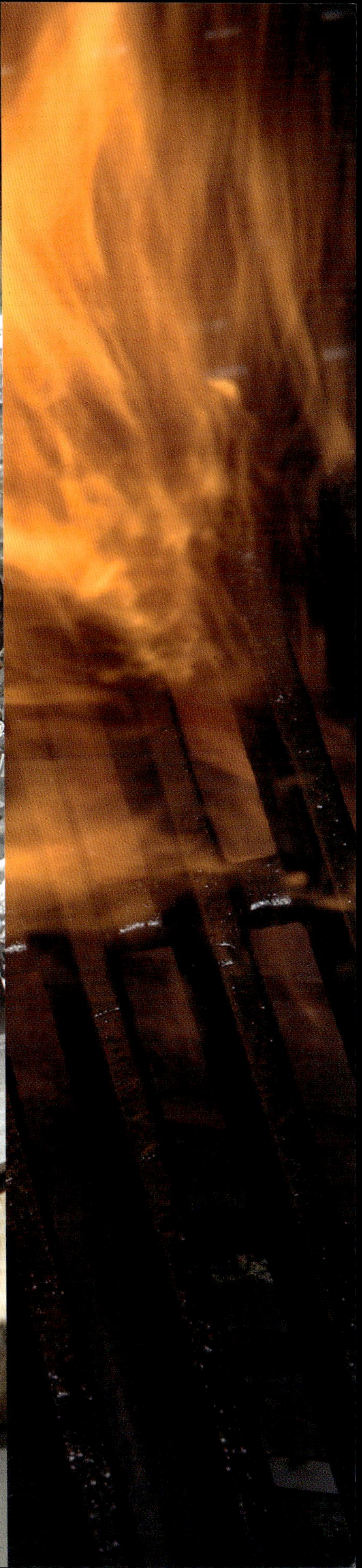

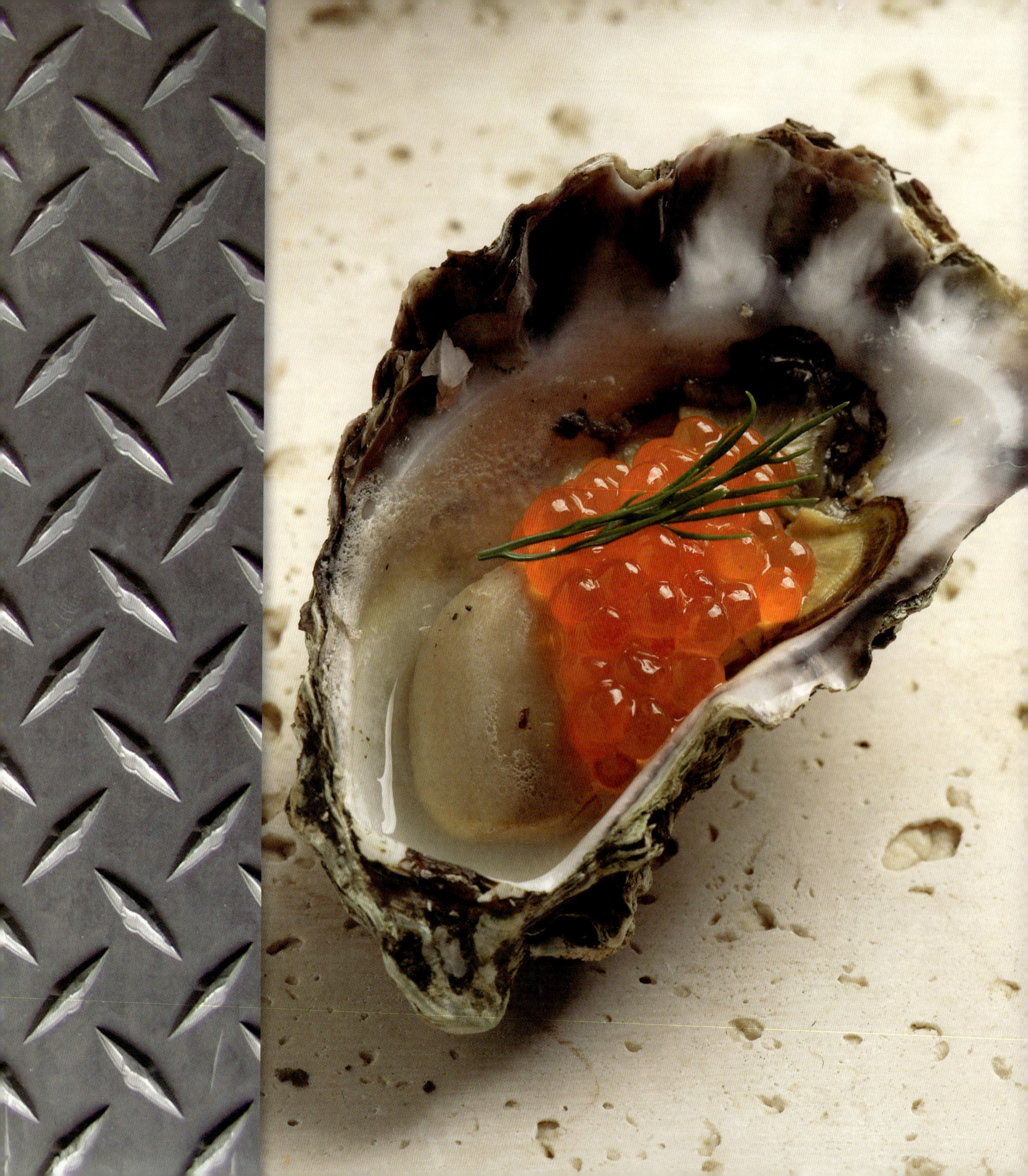

24 Pacific oysters, freshly shucked
Stolichnaya vodka
Rock salt
Salmon roe
24 tiny dill sprigs

DRUNKEN OYSTERS

Put the oysters onto high-heat grill with the flesh up and cook for 2 minutes.

During the cooking, splash a little vodka onto the oysters with a spoon. Do not pour from the bottle or the jug because the vodka can ignite easily.

Carefully lift oysters onto service platter filled with rock salt (to keep the oysters upright) or onto individual plates. Top with ½ teaspoon of salmon roe and a sprig of dill.

SERVES 4–6

8 medium eggs, free range if possible
Salt to taste
Ground black pepper, to taste
240g (9oz) crab meat, chopped
Spray oil
4 teaspoons butter

Spicy Cucumber Salsa
4 tablespoons coconut/rice vinegar
3 tablespoons white sugar
1 small red chilli, deseeded and minced
1 Lebanese cucumber, seeds removed and finely diced
1 red shallot, finely diced
1 tablespoon ginger, grated
1 clove garlic, crushed
1 tablespoon coriander leaves, chopped
1 tablespoon vegetable oil
1 tablespoon fish sauce

CRAB OMELETTES WITH SPICY CUCUMBER SALSA

Beat the eggs well with salt to taste, in four separate containers. I use teacups.

Divide the crab into four even batches.

Spray a low-heat, very clean barbecue plate with oil in a circle about 22cm (9in) in diameter. Add a teaspoon of butter and, as it melts, spread around that circle with a spatula. Tip on the first two beaten eggs and very quickly pull/push the eggs into a circular shape and let the eggs start to set. Cut holes into the setting egg mixture to let the uncooked egg move through and set.

When firm, which will take about a minute, spoon the crab mixture down the centre and fold each side over the crab meat. Flip the omelette over and let sit for 30 seconds or until set.

Lift from the barbecue, keep warm and repeat with the other three batches.

When all have been cooked, serve at room temperature onto individual plates. Spoon a little drained cucumber salsa on the side of each omelette.

For the Spicy Cucumber Salsa
Mix the vinegar and sugar together and stir to dissolve. Add all the ingredients and marinate for 1 hour before serving.

Serves 4

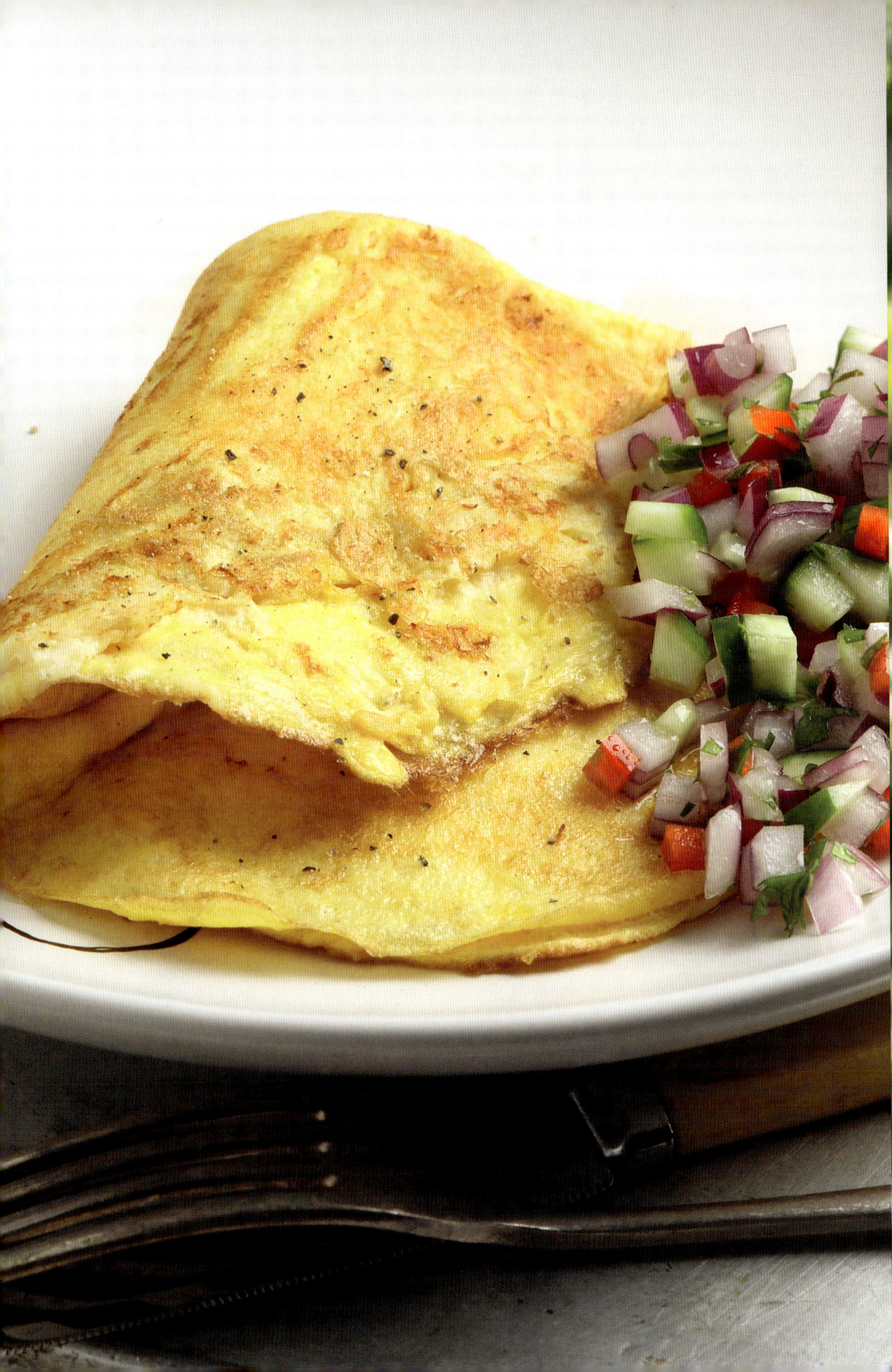

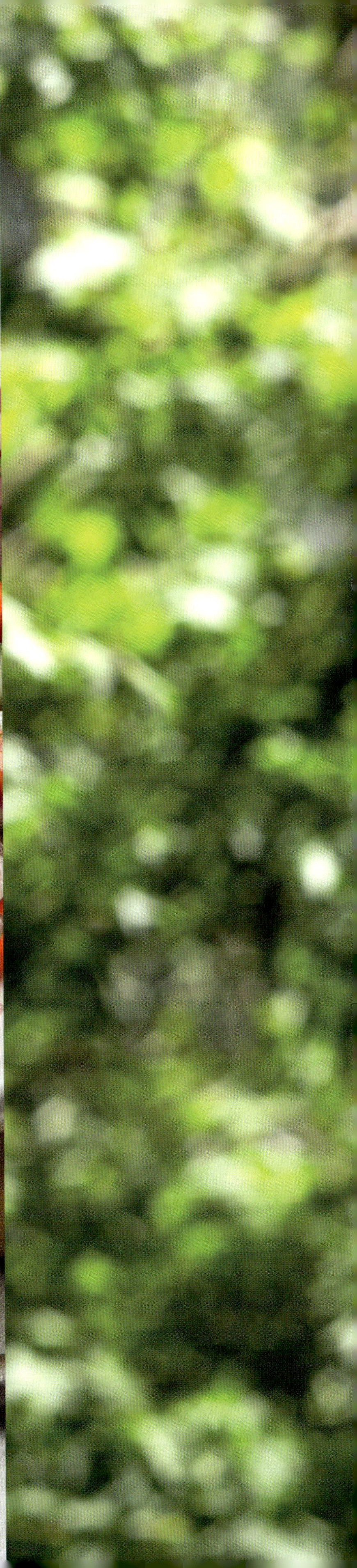

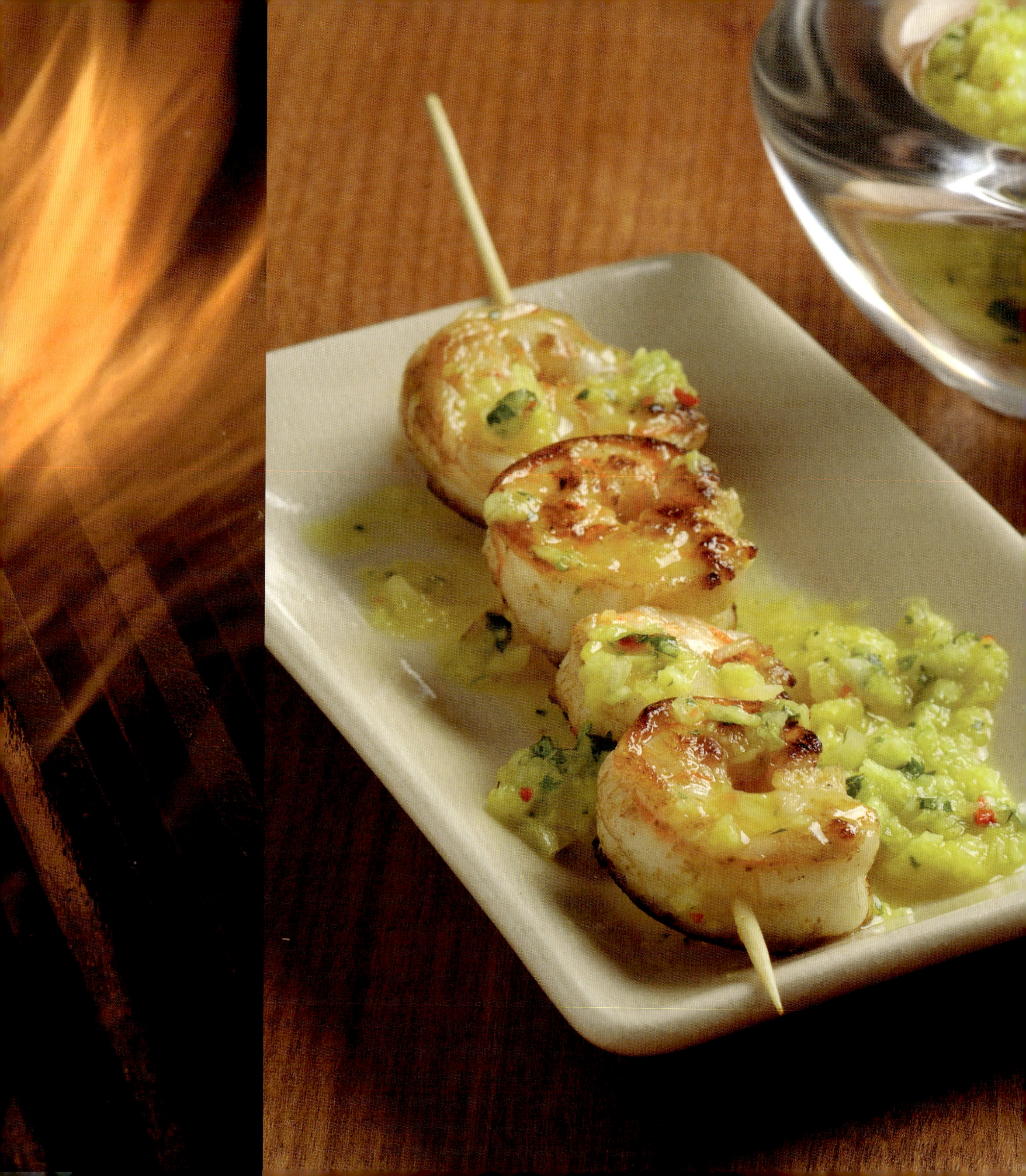

16 green king prawns, peeled completely and de-veined
3 tablespoons pineapple juice
1 tablespoon vegetable oil
1 teaspoon Thai green curry paste
4 stainless steel skewers or bamboo skewers soaked in water for 30 minutes
Spray vegetable oil

Pineapple Coriander Salsa
60g (2oz) white onion, roughly chopped
150g (5oz) pineapple, peeled and roughly chopped
1 small red chilli, flesh only and chopped
1 cup coriander leaves, loosely packed

PRAWN KEBABS WITH PINEAPPLE CORIANDER SALSA

Toss the prawns with the juice, oil and curry paste. Let sit for 15 minutes. Thread the prawns onto the skewers so you have four on each one. This is best done by curling the prawns in their natural form and then pushing the skewer through so as to get four horseshoe shapes in a row.

Spray with oil and cook on medium-hot plate for 1 minute; spray with oil and turn again and cook through. Baste with the pineapple marinade at least once.

Serve on large platter with pineapple salsa spooned over.

For the Pineapple Coriander Salsa
Put all ingredients into a food processor and pulse to a rough paste. This salsa is quite runny and is best served immediately.

Serves 4

2 x12cm (5in) square pieces focaccia
Garlic spray oil
1–2 cups Spicy Eye Bean spread
   (see recipe below)
1 medium Lebanese cucumber,
   finely sliced into rounds
½ cup sundried tomatoes,
   roughly chopped
2 cups rocket leaves, crisped
½ cup Romano cheese, grated/shaved
Extra virgin olive oil
Ground black pepper

Spicy Black Eye Bean Paste
250g (9oz) dried black-eye beans, soaked
4 cloves garlic, poached
2 tablespoons lime juice
1 teaspoon powdered cumin
1 teaspoon powdered nutmeg
½ teaspoon ground white pepper
¼ teaspoon powdered chilli
½ teaspoon salt
2 tablespoons virgin olive oil
1 tablespoon parsley, chopped

CRISPY FOCACCIA WITH SPICY BLACK EYE BEAN SPREAD & ROCKET

Cut the focaccia through the middle to give four even squares/rectangles. Spray the cut side with garlic oil. Brown and crisp both sides on a medium-hot grill.

Spread the paste thickly onto the cut side of focaccia. Evenly distribute cucumber slices and tomatoes and top with rocket leaves on top of the spread—don't worry if some of them slip off—and add the cheese. Drizzle over a little oil and sprinkle the pepper. Serve immediately.

For the Spicy Black Eye Bean Paste

Cook the beans at a simmer until starting to break down. Strain and reserve a cup of the cooking liquid.

Put all the ingredients except for the oil and parsley into a food processor and work into a paste. You may need to add some cooking liquid to make the paste the consistency you like but it should be smooth and creamy.

Tip from the processor bowl and smooth over the top. Spoon over the olive oil and sprinkle with the parsley. Serve as it is or keep refrigerated for up to five days.

Serves 4

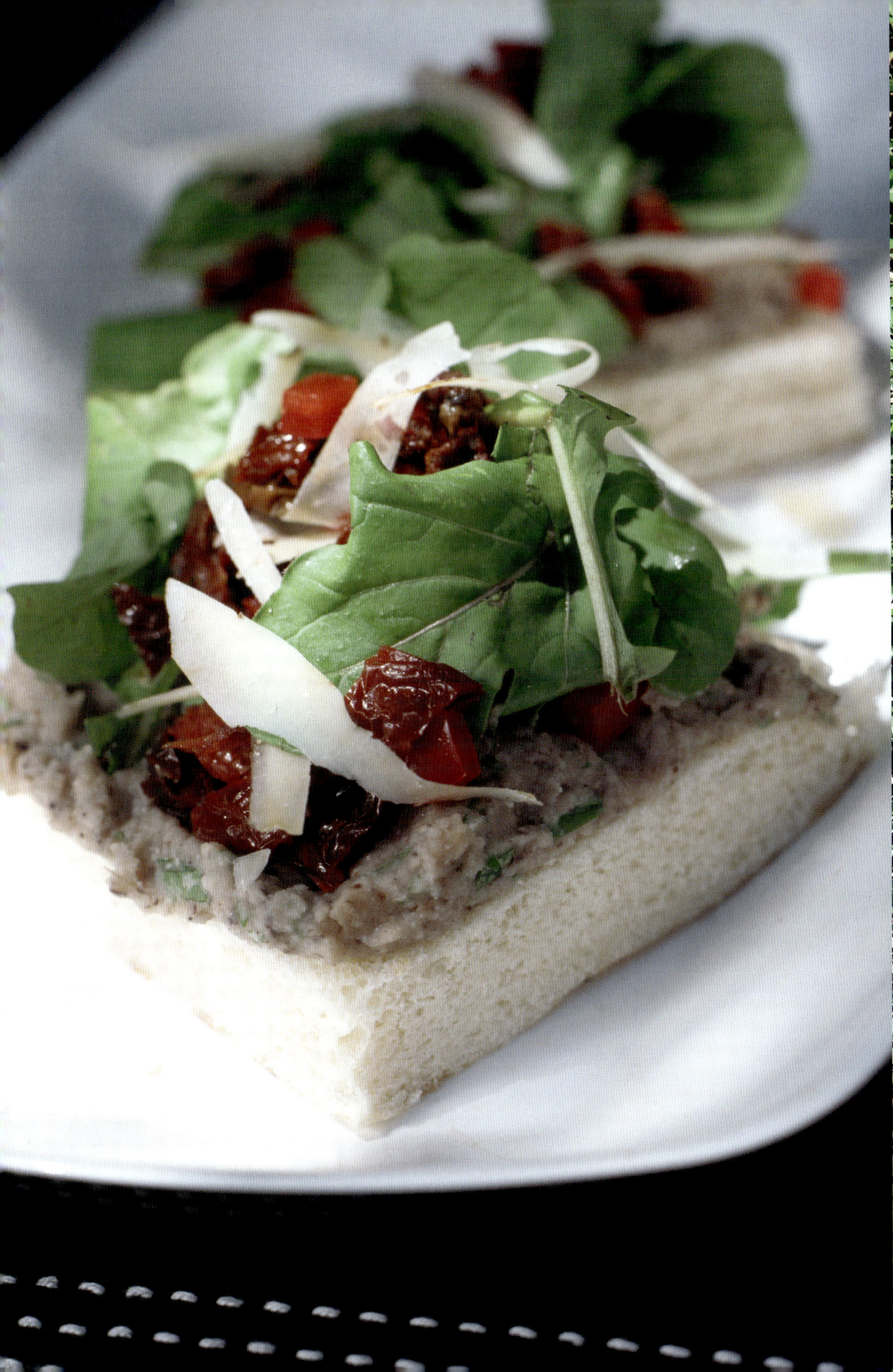
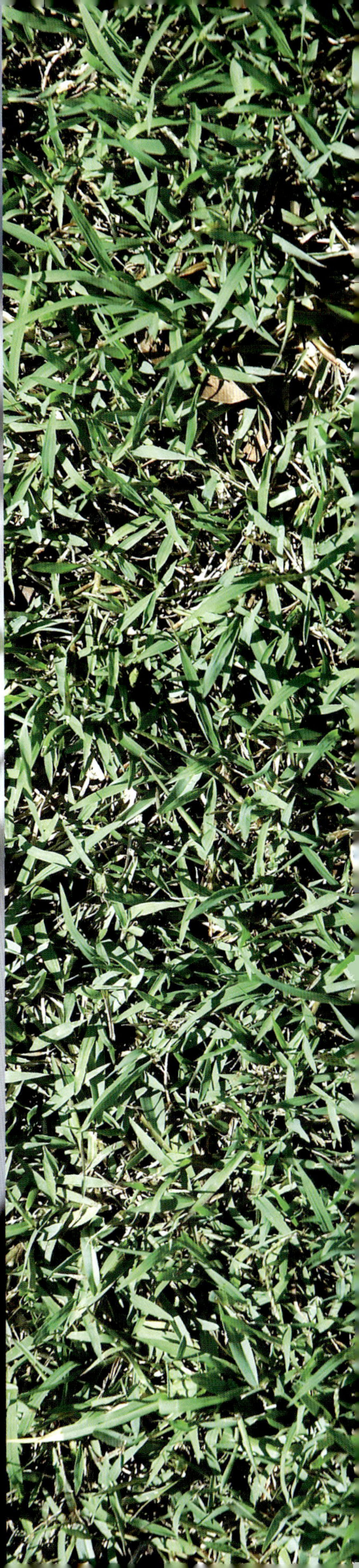

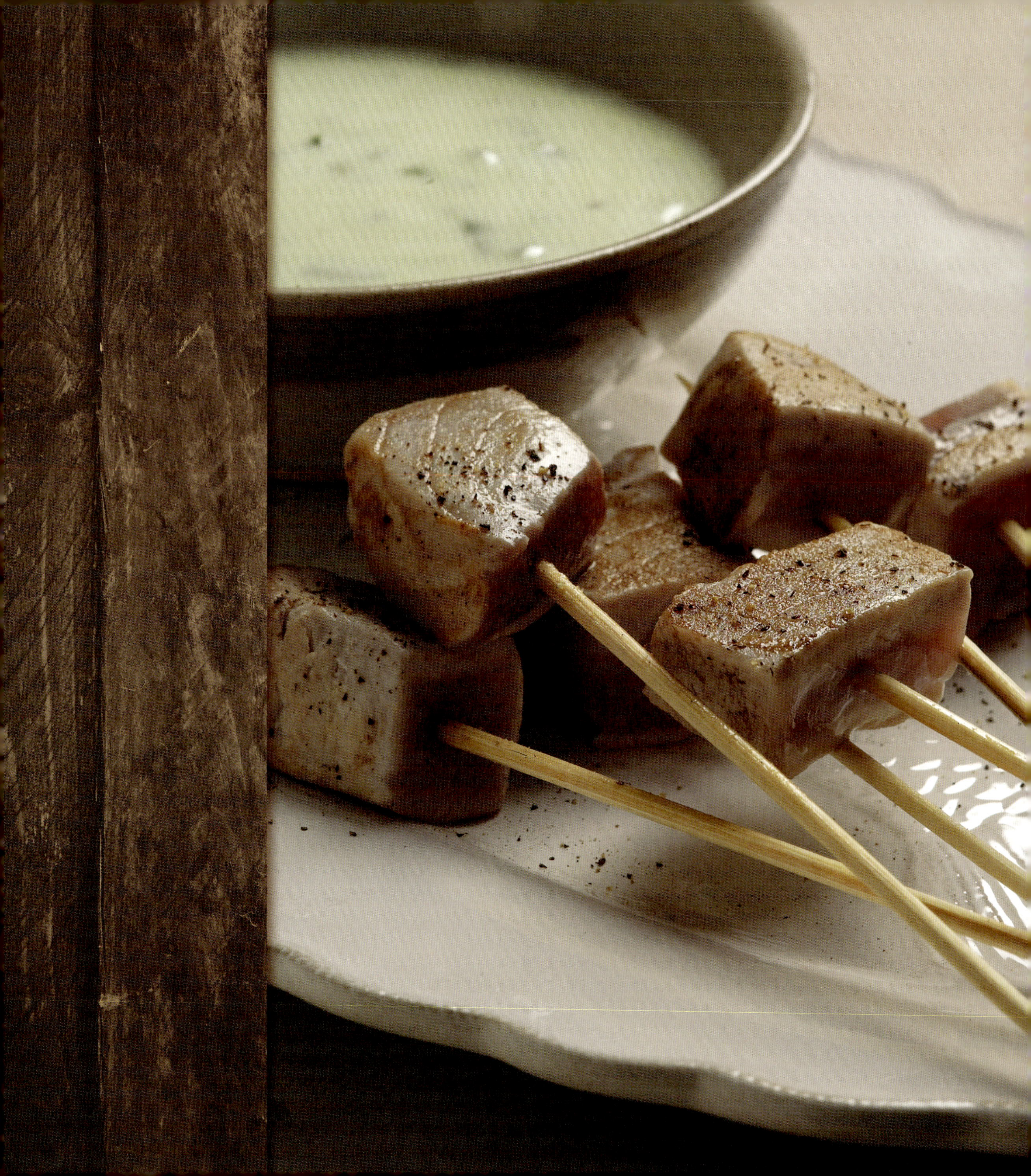

400g (14oz) fresh tuna
12–16 bamboo skewers soaked in water
    for 30 minutes, or metal skewers
60g (2oz) plain yoghurt
2–3 tablespoons wasabi paste
1 tablespoon rice vinegar
1 tablespoon finely shredded mint
Spray vegetable oil
Sea salt

SKEWERED TUNA & WASABI CREAM

Cut the tuna into even pieces to get 12–16 pieces. Thread one piece only onto a suitable skewer (don't leave the tip exposed) and refrigerate until ready to cook.

Mix the yoghurt, wasabi paste, vinegar and mint well and pour into dipping bowl.

Spray the tuna with oil and cook on medium-hot plate–sprinkle with a little salt and spray with oil before turning to cook the other sides.

Tuna loves to be undercooked so when you see the sides of the cubes going whitish, turn. Lift when all sides have been exposed to the plate and serve on a platter with the wasabi sauce. The tuna will be rare to medium.

Serves 4

For the salad

120g cos lettuce, inner whitish leaves, washed, crisped and cut into bite-sized pieces
2 hard-boiled eggs, shelled and roughly chopped
4 tablespoons crisp bacon bits
50g shaved parmesan cheese
Garlic croutons to taste
24 medium green king prawns, peeled, deveined and with tail on and butterflied
spray oil

For the dressing

3 anchovy fillets, well drained of oil
2 egg yolks
2 large cloves garlic, minced
1 teaspoon Worcestershire sauce
1 tablespoon white vinegar
120 ml olive oil

Garlic Croutons

4 slices day-old sourdough bread
1 tablespoon garlic, crushed and mixed with 2 tablespoons olive oil

KING PRAWN CAESAR SALAD

Make the dressing in the bowl you will serve the salad in by mashing the anchovies with the back of a fork. Add the egg yolks, garlic, Worcestershire sauce and vinegar—combine until lighter in colour and thickening. Whisk in the oil slowly to make a thickish dressing.

Spray the prawns with oil and cook on medium-hot flat plate—toss to cook through; remove and keep at room temperature.

Add the cos lettuce, eggs, bacon and prawns to the dressing and toss to coat—sprinkle on the cheese and croutons.

Serve in the middle of table.

For the Garlic Croutons

Cut the bread into 2cm (1in) squares. Heat the garlic oil to medium-hot in a pan. Toss in the bread cubes and coat with the oil mixture. Cook on the wok burner until browned, turning regularly. Tip onto a plate lined with kitchen paper when done.

Serves 4

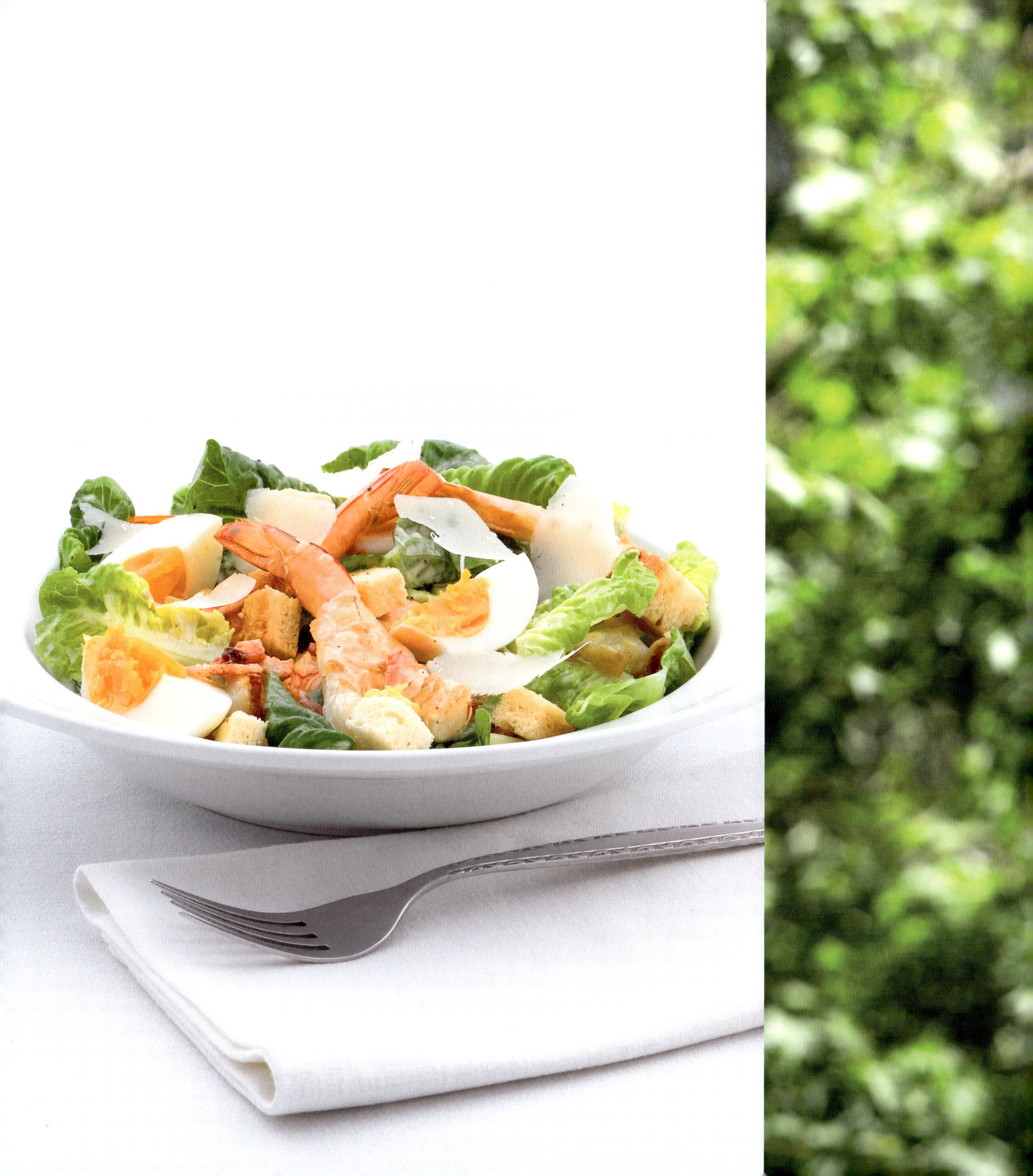

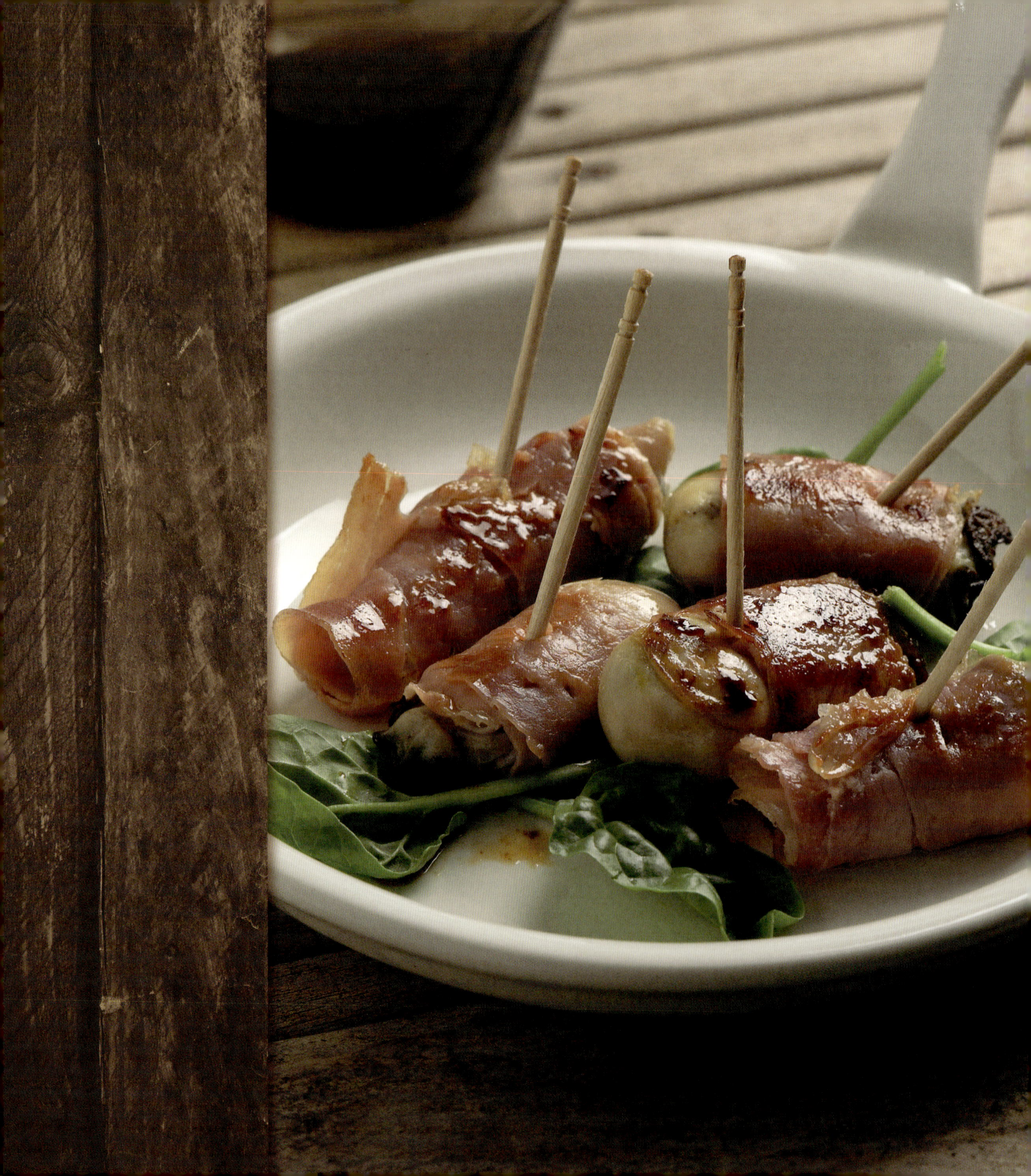

24 large oysters, out of shell
24 x 10cm (4in) prosciutto
Toothpicks
Olive oil spray
2 lemon cheeks

OYSTERS IN PROSCIUTTO

Wrap each oyster loosely in a piece of prosciutto and secure with a toothpick.

Spray a medium-hot plate with a little oil and cook on medium-temperature flat plate until crisping, about 2–3 minutes.

Arrange on a platter, squeeze with lemon and pass around as you barbecue.

SERVES 4

12 large sea scallops, roe optional
Spray oil
200g (7oz) canned cannellini beans, drained
1 clove garlic
Salt and cayenne
¼ cup good olive oil
8 slices panini
1 very ripe red tomato, halved
Ground black pepper
Extra virgin olive oil
Fresh basil leaves

SCALLOPS, WHITE BEAN PUREE & PANINI BRUSCHETTA

Trim the scallops of the vein that runs around the side of each one; refrigerate until ready for use.

Cover the beans with water. Add the garlic, salt to taste and add a pinch of cayenne. Simmer for 5 minutes, drain and tip into a food processor bowl. Start processing and pour the oil down slowly to make a smooth paste. Remove from the bowl.

Spray the panini slices with oil and brown both sides on a hot grill. Remove and rub with the cut part of the tomato halves ensuring you squeeze the flesh so some will stick to the brioche.

Spray the scallops with oil and flash-cook them on a very hot plate. These cook extremely quickly and so turn after 1–1½ minutes and turn to cook for another minute on the other side to see that they are sealed and browned. Remove immediately.

Spoon equal amounts of the warm bean paste onto the centre of each plate and place the scallops around. Drizzle with a little extra virgin olive oil, decorate with fresh basil leaves and serve immediately with the panini on the side.

SERVES 4

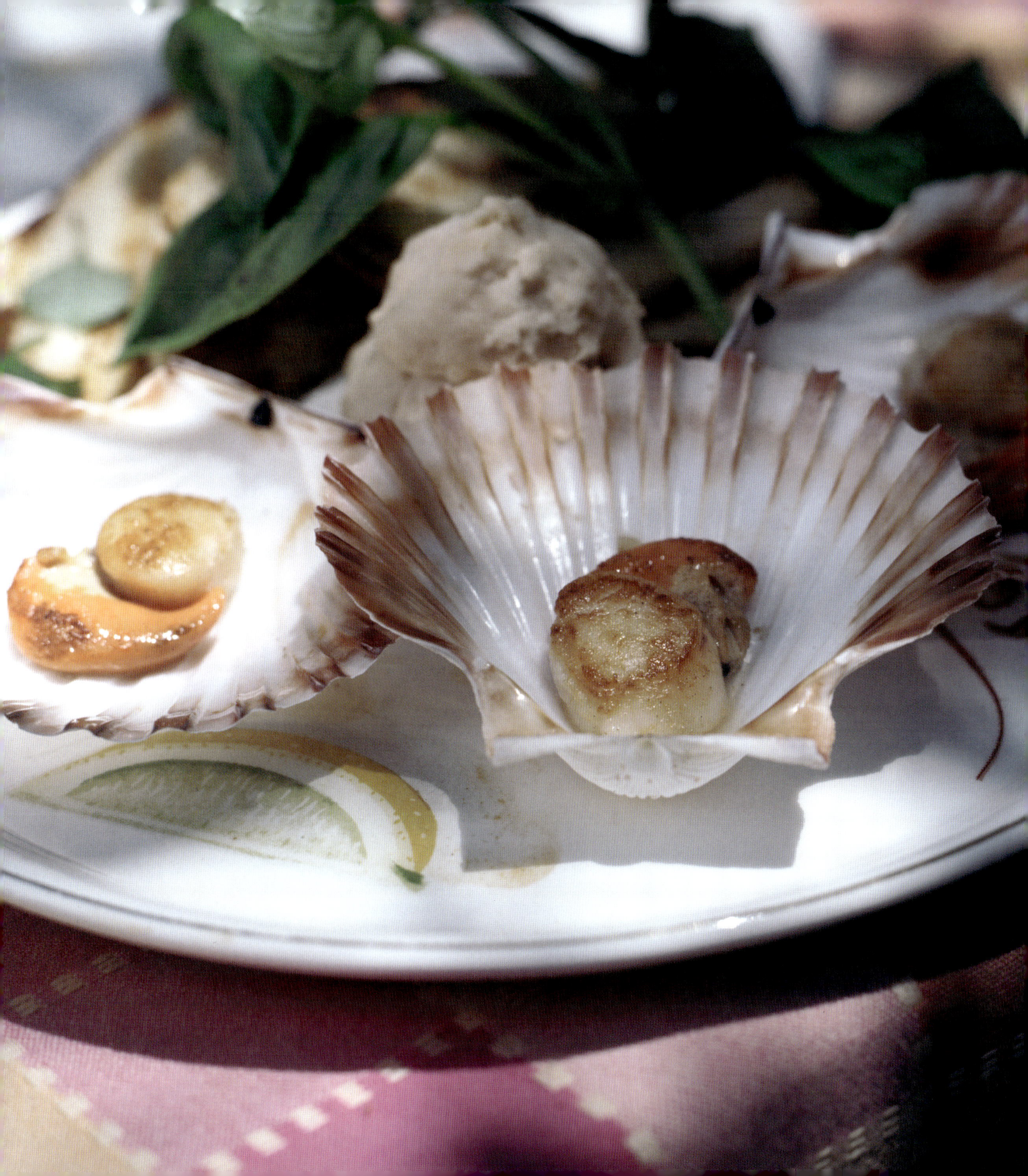

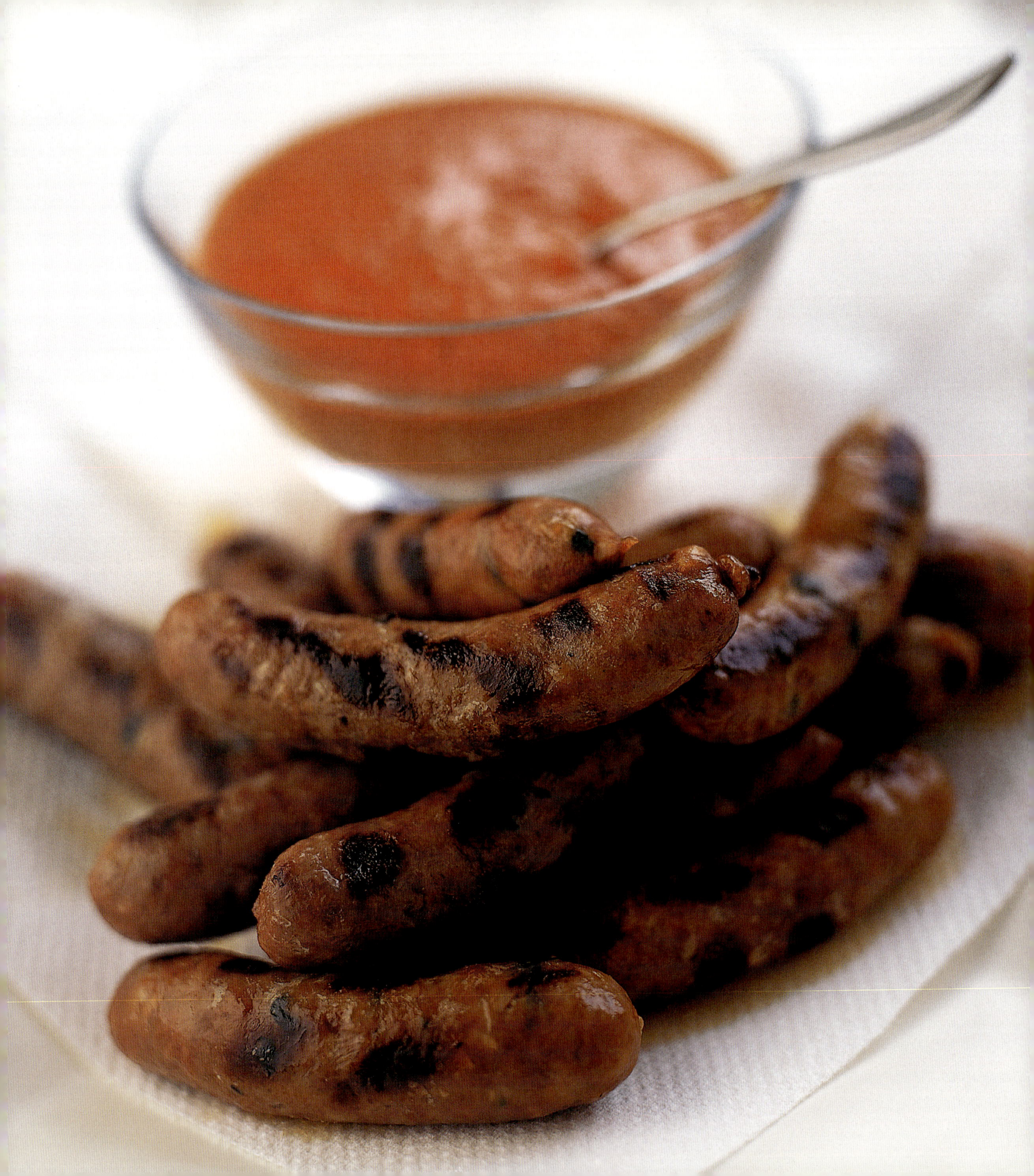

16 tiny sausages/chippolatas
150ml (5fl oz) roasted red bell pepper sauce (see recipe below)
Spray oil

Red Bell Pepper Sauce
5 medium red bell peppers/capsicums, deseeded and roughly chopped
2 medium onions, roughly chopped
4 large cloves garlic, crushed
2 tablespoons thyme
1 cup white wine
1 cup cider vinegar
½ teaspoon salt
½ teaspoon cayenne pepper
1 cup olive oil

TINY SAUSAGES & RED BELL PEPPER SAUCE

This sauce is great as a base for pizza instead of the usual tomato sauce and is sensational with barbecued lamb chops.

Spray and cook sausages on a hot plate for 3–4 minutes or until done. Lift onto some paper towelling. Serve the sausages with a bowl of the sauce at one end of the platter.

For the Red Bell Pepper Sauce

Put the red bell peppers/capsicum, onions, garlic, thyme, wine and vinegar into a large pot. Simmer for 45 minutes. Lift the hood for the last 10 minutes of cooking to allow evaporation. You should have about ½ cup cooking liquid left when you finish the cooking. Add the salt and cayenne pepper.

Blend red bell pepper/capsicum mixture in processor or blender. When finely pureed, slowly pour in the oil as you blend. Strain (optional) and test for seasoning.

Pour into sterilised jar and refrigerate when cool. It will store for up to 7 days.

Serves 4

16 sea scallops
Spray olive oil
Sea salt
2 cups iceberg lettuce, finely shredded middle leaves only
1 cup ripe Roma tomatoes, flesh only and finely diced
1 tablespoon dill, finely chopped
4 tablespoons parsley & macadamia pesto
Ground black pepper

Parsley & Macadamia Pesto
1 cup parsley sprigs, washed and tightly packed into the cup
1 tablespoon macadamia nuts, roughly chopped, roasted, unsalted
1/3 cup macadamia nut oil
1 large clove garlic, crushed
30g (1oz) parmesan cheese, finely grated

SEA SCALLOPS, PARLSEY & MACADAMIA PESTO

Trim the scallops of the black membrane on the side. Spray each one and cook on hot flat plate for 1–1½ minutes each side depending on the thickness of each scallop. Turn and cook for no more than 1 minute on the other side.

Scallops must not be overcooked and prefer to be seared rather than cooked through as they go very tough when overcooked. Sprinkle with salt only as you cook.

To serve, put equal amount of the finely shredded lettuce in small piles around the perimeter of individual dinner plates. Top with scallops, sprinkle on the tomato dices that have been mixed with the dill.

Spoon an equal amount of pesto onto the centre of each plate. Grind black pepper over the plate and serve immediately.

FOR THE PARSLEY AND MACADAMIA PESTO
Put all ingredients into a processor bowl. Pulse the processor until the ingredients start to break down then leave the engine to run to form a smooth paste. Adjust the consistency of the pesto with more oil if needed.

SERVES 4

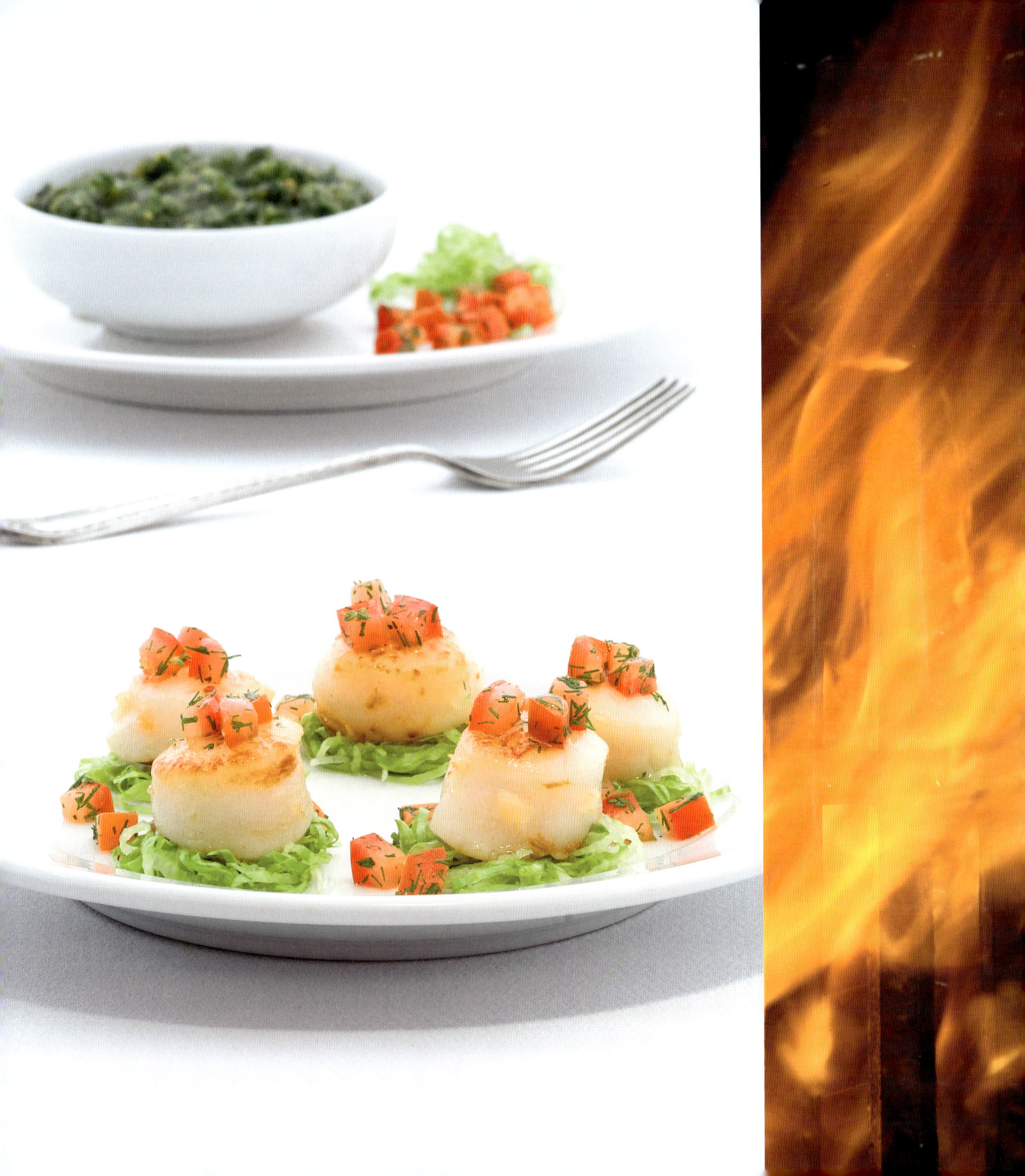

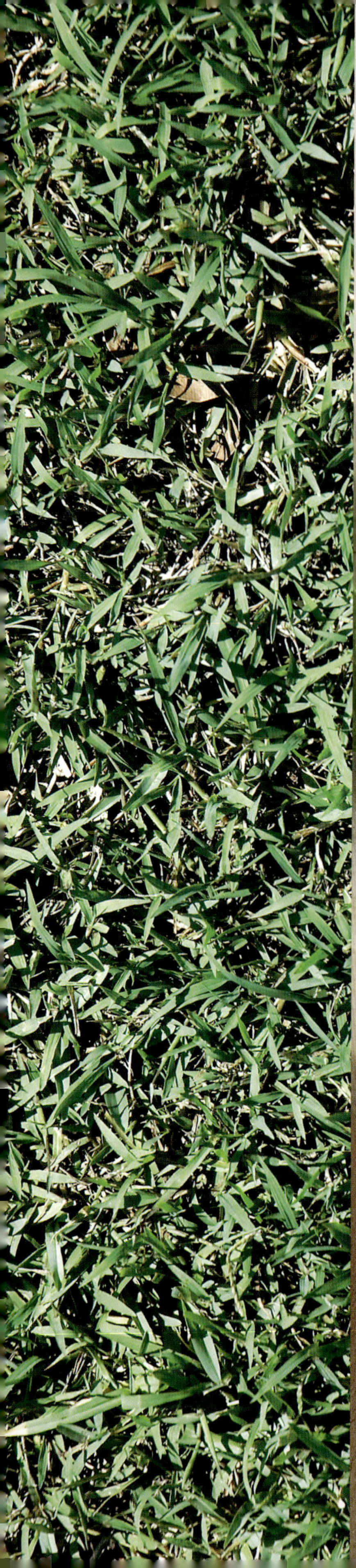
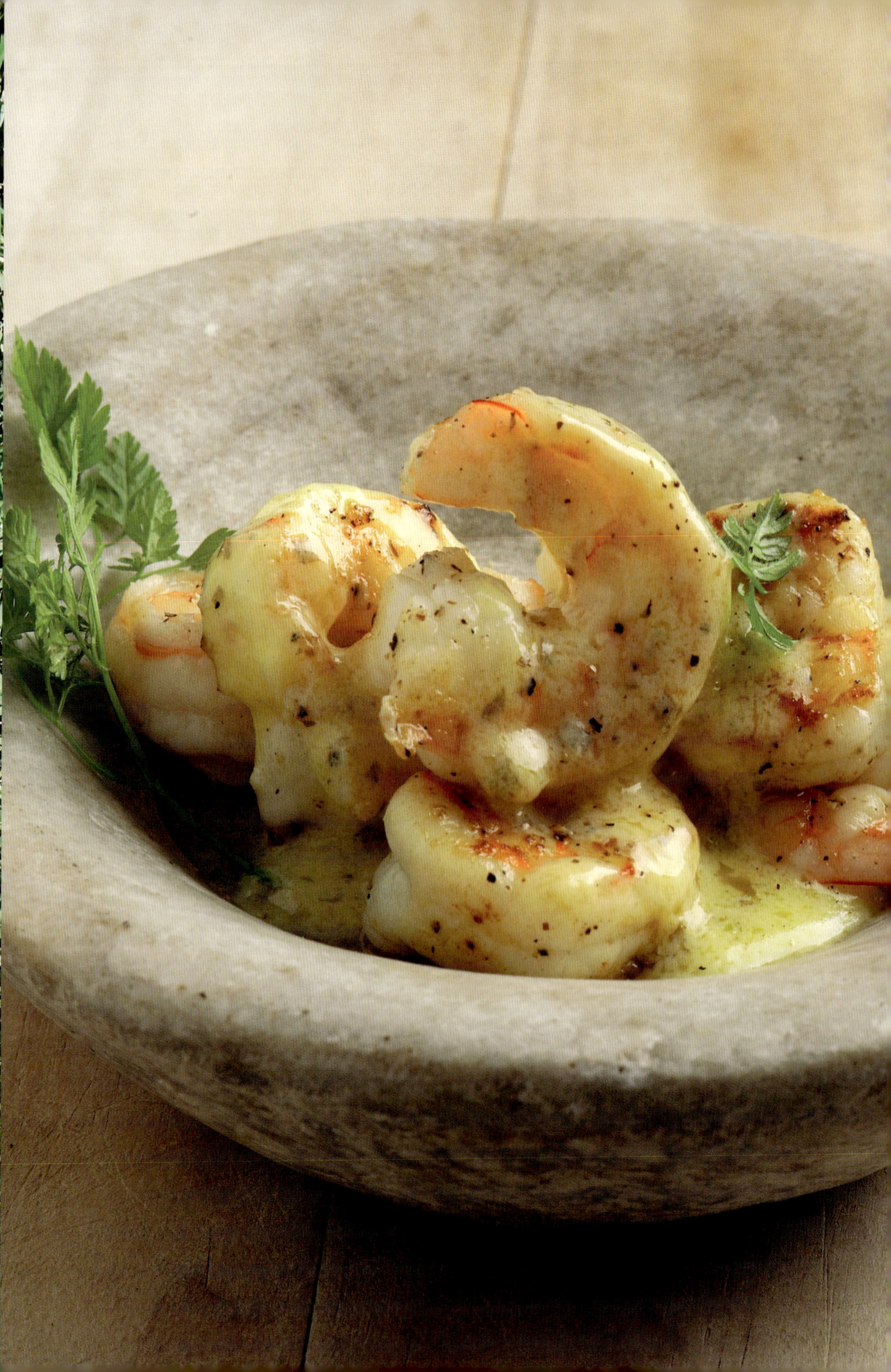

16 medium king prawns, completely peeled and deveined
2 tablespoons oil
½ teaspoon each of salt
½ lemon cracked pepper
Mint and Chervil Sauce (see recipe below)

Mint and Chervil Sauce
1 tablespoon eschallots, finely chopped
2 tablespoons fresh mint, chopped
1 tablespoon fresh chervil, chopped
1 small sprig fresh thyme
2 tablespoons white vinegar
2 tablespoons white wine
2 egg yolks
120g (4oz) firm butter, cut into cubes
½ teaspoon lemon juice
Salt and cayenne to taste
1 tablespoon fresh mint, finely sliced
1 tablespoon chervil, finely chopped

KING PRAWNS, MINT & CHERVIL SAUCE

Toss the prawns in oil, salt and lemon pepper. Sit for 15 minutes. Cook the prawns on a hot plate and turn regularly to cook through—they will take only a couple of minutes. Remove from the heat.

Serve the prawns on individual plates and with the sauce spooned over. Sprinkle with a little more cracked pepper to decorate.

For the Mint and Chervil Sauce

Make the sauce by putting the eschallots, mint, chervil, thyme, vinegar and white wine into a saucepan and boil down by two thirds. Remove from the heat and tip into the top of a double boiler. Cool and add the egg yolks and whisk.

Put over the top of simmering water and whisk until the mixture thickens. As it does, start to whisk in the butter until all is used. Remove from heat and pour in the lemon with salt and cayenne to taste. Strain and stir in the mint and chervil.

Serves 4

30g (1oz) butter, melted
2 tablespoons dry breadcrumbs, finely grated
60g (2oz) salted butter
60g (2oz) plain flour
500ml (17fl oz) milk, heated not boiled
3 large eggs, separated
300g (11oz) steamed pumpkin (Jap is good), finely mashed and cooled
2 tablespoons parmesan cheese, grated
1 teaspoon nutmeg, finely grated
Salt and white pepper to taste
4 teaspoons sour cream (optional)

PUMPKIN & PARMESAN SOUFFLE

Preheat barbecue to 180°C (350°F).

Brush 4–5 1-cup soufflé dishes with the melted butter. Line the inside with breadcrumbs. Make sure you shake out any excess crumbs and refrigerate the soufflé bowls. Remove 10 minutes before use.

Melt the salted butter in a saucepan. Stir in the flour and stir over medium heat until the mixture is going sandy in colour. Stir or whisk in the milk over medium heat in three batches. Stir or whisk quickly to ensure no lumps. Stir for three minutes once all the milk is incorporated. Remove from heat and let cool for 5 minutes before the next step.

Fold in the egg yolks, pumpkin, cheese, nutmeg and salt and pepper. Whisk the egg whites until they are light and fluffy. Not firm peaks, just soft.

Spoon 1 large tablespoon of the egg whites into the warm pumpkin mixture. Fold in the rest of the whites. Do this gently so as not to lose the trapped air in the egg whites. Spoon equal amounts into the individual soufflé dishes and cook for 18–20 minutes or until firm to touch and browned on top.

Serve immediately with a dressed green salad. If you use the sour cream, break open the top with a spoon and drop the sour cream inside.

SERVES 4

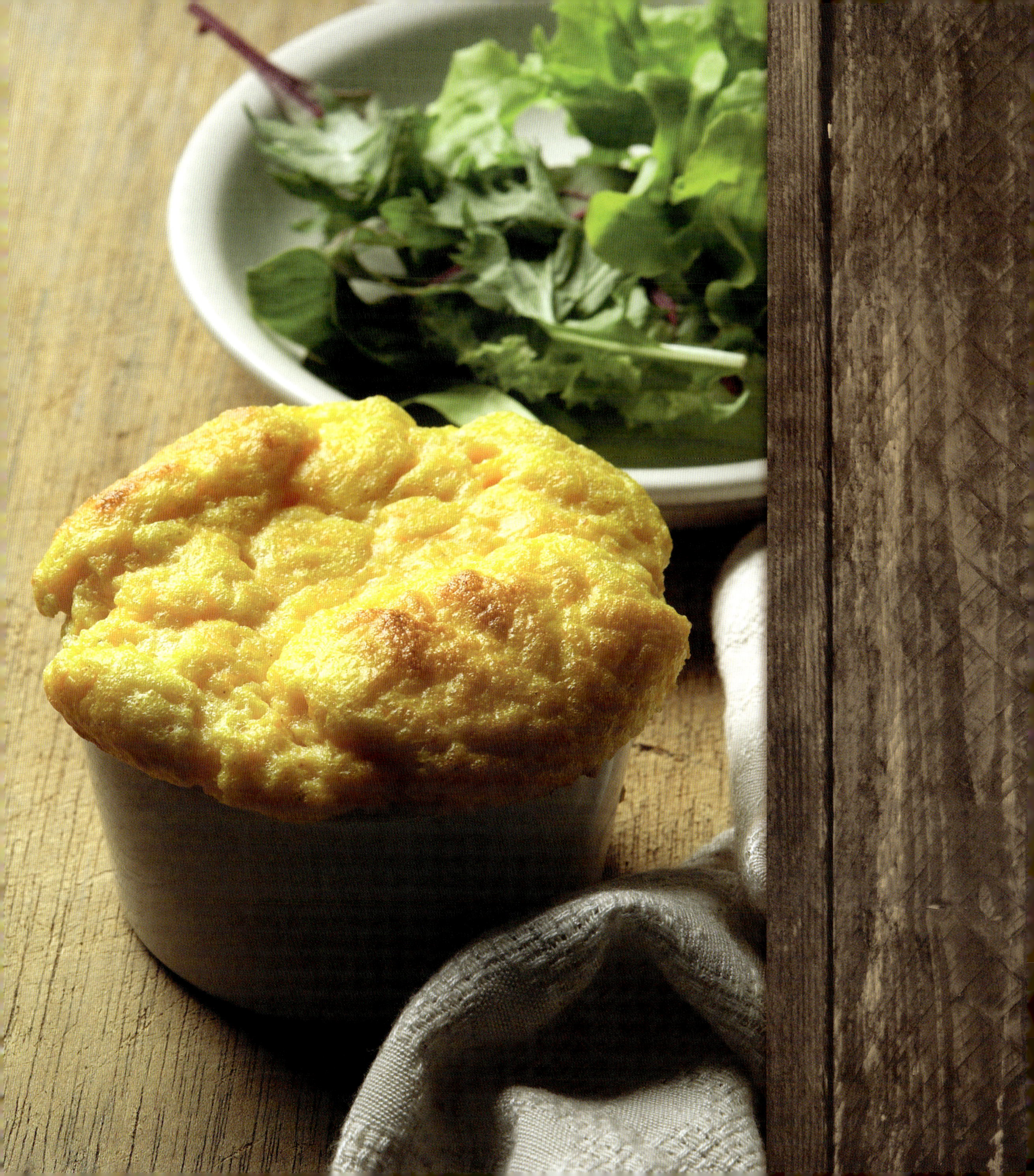

16 slices white bread, crust removed, approximately 10cm (4in) square
butter at room temperature
English mustard
16 fresh asparagus spears, approximately 15cm (6in) long and blanched
16 toothpicks
Spray oil

GRILLED ASPARAGUS ROLLS

Lay the bread out and roll it flattish with a rolling pin, smear with a little butter and spread a tiny amount of mustard.

Lay the asparagus on the buttered bread 3cm (1.2in) in from one point and roll from point to point. Secure with toothpick.

Spray the bread rolls with oil and cook for 4 minutes on a medium-hot grill, turning regularly.

Serve these as soon as they come from the barbecue.

Serves 4

20 green king pawns, peeled and deveined, tails on
2 kaffir lime leaves, rib removed and finely shredded
1 lime, juiced
Coriander leaves for decoration
Spray oil

Sweet Chilli Sauce
2 tablespoons peanut oil
5 long red chillies, deseeded and roughly chopped
2 coriander roots, washed, trimmed and roughly chopped
3 garlic cloves, roughly chopped
1 teaspoon fish sauce
1 cup coconut vinegar
1 cup palm sugar, roughly grated

Kaffir Lime Prawns with Sweet Chilli Sauce

Soak the prawns in with the shredded leaves, lime juice and oil for 15 minutes.

To barbecue the prawns, drain from liquid and toss onto an oiled hot plate and move around to cook through.

Pour some chilli sauce into a bowl for dipping and place in the centre of a large plate surrounded by the prawns. Decorate with the leaves.

For the Sweet Chilli Sauce

Pulse the chillies, coriander roots, garlic and fish sauce to a fine pulp in a food processor.

Pour the chilli mixture into a small saucepan with the vinegar and sugar. Boil and then simmer for 15 minutes. The sauce will thicken, then let it cool. What you don't use will keep in the refrigerator for at least seven days.

Serves 4

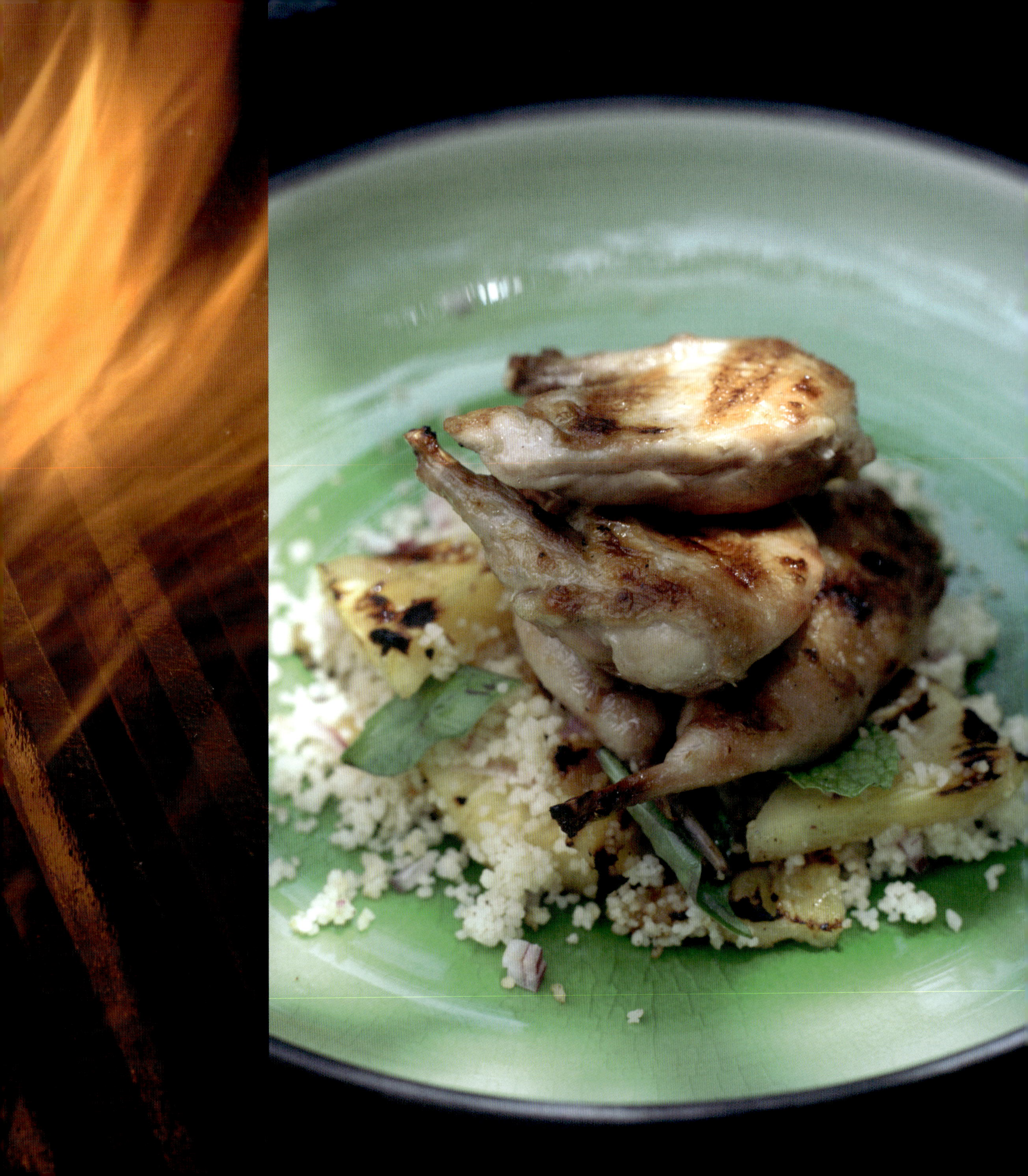

4 large quails
Olive oil
4 x 2cm thick slices fresh pineapple,
    core removed and cut in large dices
1 small red onion, finely chopped
1 cup dried cous cous
1¼ cups boiling water
1 tablespoon extra virgin olive oil
1 teaspoon Baharat spice
¼ cup basil leaves, ripped
¼ cup mint leaves, ripped
Salt and powdered black pepper
2 tablespoons toasted sesame seeds

QUAIL & PINEAPPLE SCENTED COUS COUS

Cut the quails into quarters and remove the winglets. Put into a bowl and drizzle over some oil. Toss to coat the quail and refrigerate until ready for use.

Rehydrate cous cous by pouring on boiling water in a large bowl. Leave to sit for 30 seconds, then then add diced onion and extra virgin olive oil. Fork through to stop the grains sticking together.

Remove the quail from the refrigerator 10 minutes before use. Drain the quarters of the oil and cook on a medium-hot plate. Turn regularly until done—quail is best not over-cooked.

Flash cook the pineapple on a very hot plate so the dices are lightly browned. Remove and toss with the Baharat and salt and pepper. Add to the cous cous with the herbs and mix thoroughly.

Serve the cous cous in the middle of the table with the quails on another platter.

SERVES 4

24 Pacific oysters, freshly shucked
30–40ml (1–1.4fl oz) Mandarin Vodka
Rock salt
6–8 mandarin segments, drained
　　from can and cut into small pieces
Chervil sprigs

Mandarin Vodka Chervil Oysters

Ensure the oysters are clear of visible shell grit and sit on hot grill in batches, say 6 at a time.

Spoon some vodka from a jug (do not pour from the bottle) onto each oyster. They will sit okay but do not overfill them with vodka as they will ignite if spilt over the edge of each oyster. They are ready to go when there is a little bubbling around the edge of the oyster flesh. Do not overheat!

Lift from the barbecue onto a large plate packed with rock salt so the oysters will sit upright. Top with a piece of mandarin segment and some chervil sprigs and serve, while warm, with cocktail napkins.

Serves 4

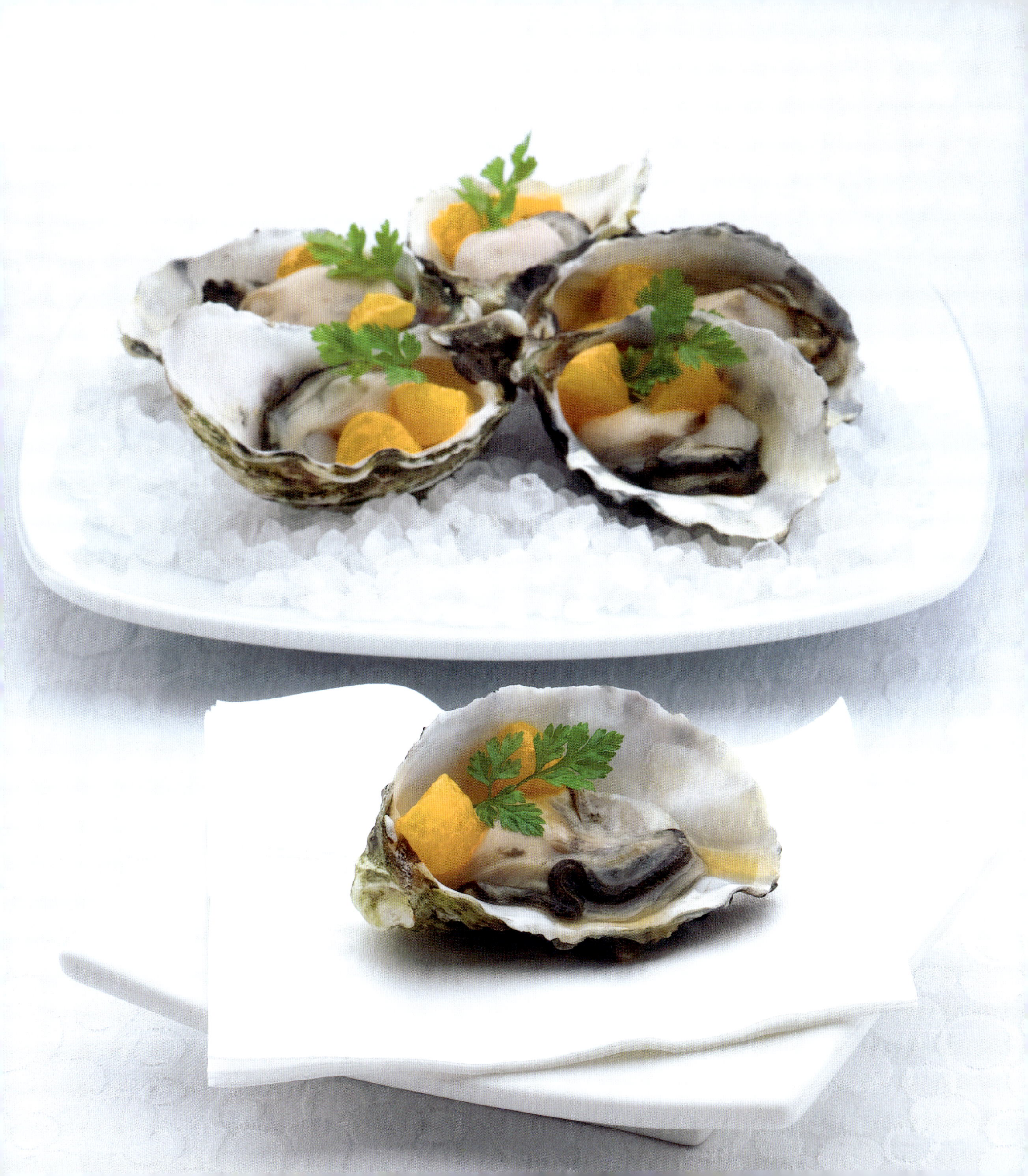

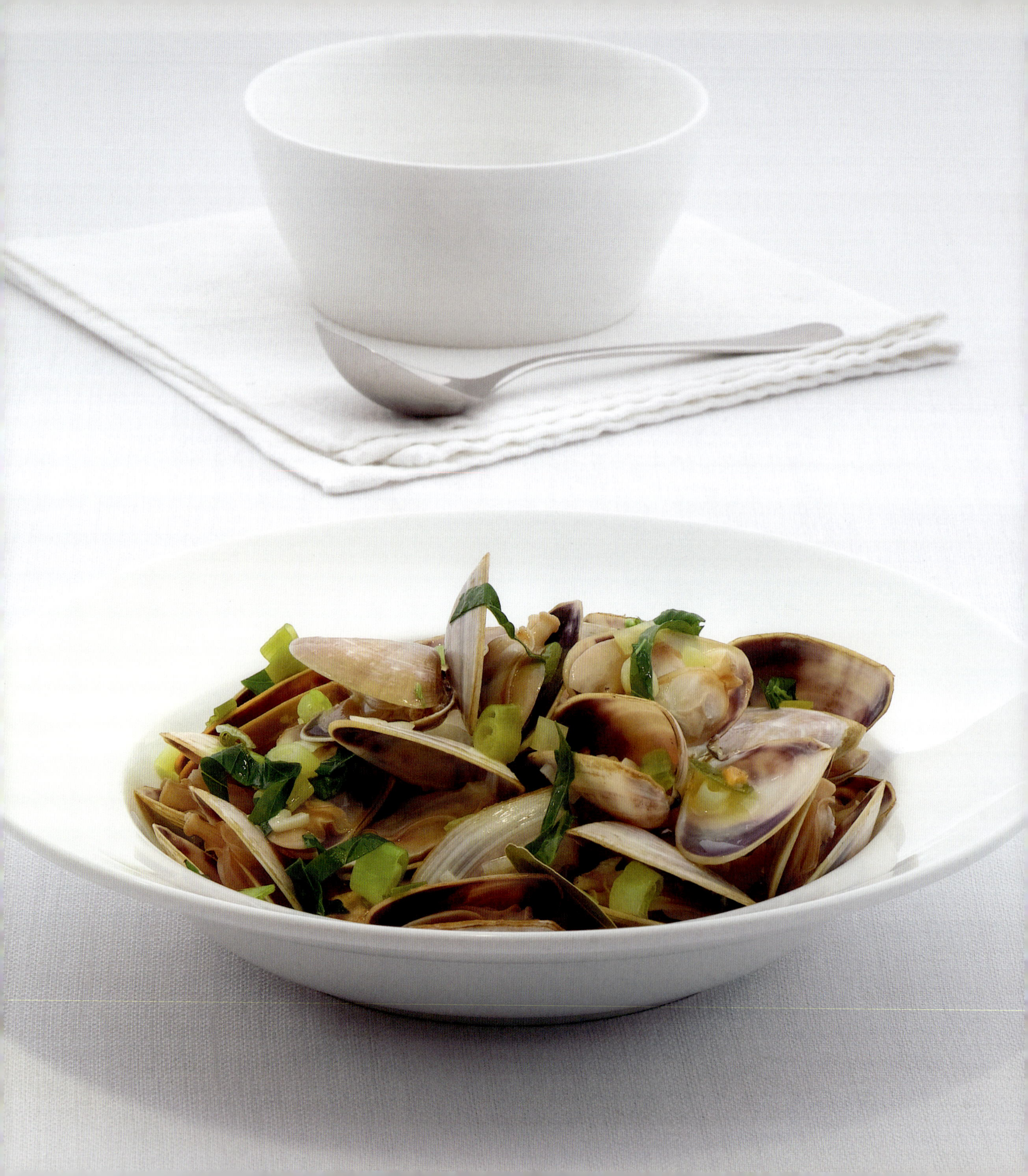

48 Boston Bay clams
2 spring onions, roughly chopped
2 cloves garlic, roughly chopped
2 bay leaves
12 peppercorns
1 cup dry white wine
2 cups fish stock
2 tablespoons Italian basil, chopped
3 tablespoons salted butter, very cold and in 3cm (1in) dices
4–8 slices garlic bread

BOSTON BAY CLAMS WITH BASIL & WHITE WINE

Make sure the clams are cleaned and ready for cooking.

Put the onions, garlic, bay leaves and peppercorns into a stainless steel frying pan or similar that will go into the barbecue. If you have a domed hood for it, all the better.

Add the clams, wine and fish stock. If you have a hood, fit it on now and put onto a very hot grill. If no hood, drop the hood and cook. If there is no hood, cover with stainless steel bowl or similar, bring to the boil and then simmer for 5 minutes. These can be done on the wok burner provided the container has a hood.

Lift from the barbecue and distribute the clams into large individual bowls. Return pan to heat. Add the basil and cook for 30 seconds. Remove from the heat and swirl in the butter. Pour equal amounts over the clams and serve with garlic bread.

Serves 4

16 green king prawns, peeled and deveined, tails left on
16 asparagus spears, trimmed
Spray vegetable oil
4 mint sprigs

Mint Hollandaise
1 tablespoon eschallot, finely chopped
1 teaspoon mint, dried
2 tablespoons fresh mint, chopped
2 tablespoons white vinegar
2 tablespoons white wine
2 egg yolks
120g (4oz) firm butter, cut into cubes
1 teaspoon lemon juice
Salt and cayenne pepper to taste
2 extra tablespoons mint, finely shredded

PRAWNS, ASPARAGUS & MINT HOLLANDAISE

Butterfly the prawns by nearly cutting through back and open out, slightly flatten.

Spray the asparagus with oil and cook on medium-hot plate. Turn regularly for 3–4 minutes. Spray the prawns and cook on medium-hot open grill until done.

Lift both from the barbecue and serve by placing the spears together in the centre of individual plates. Top with four prawns each and spoon over a little sauce. Decorate with a sprig of mint.

Serves 4
For the Mint Hollandaise

Make the sauce by putting the eschallots, dried mint, fresh mint, vinegar and white wine into a saucepan and boiling down by two thirds. Remove from the heat and tip into the top of a double boiler. Cool, add the egg yolks and whisk.

Place over the top of simmering water and whisk until the mixture thickens. As it does, start to whisk in the butter until all is used. Remove from heat and pour in the lemon with salt and pepper to taste. Strain and stir in the extra mint.

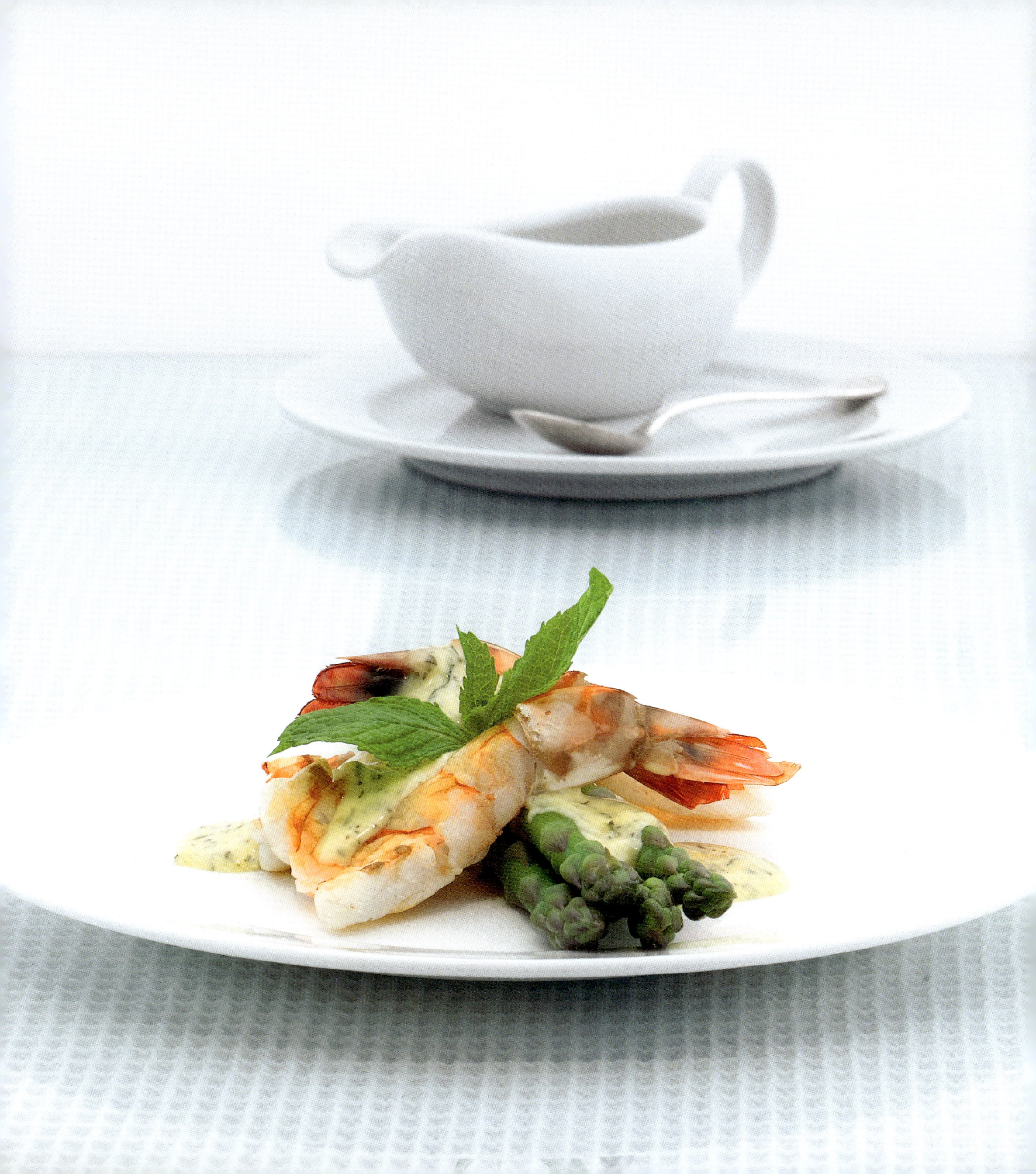

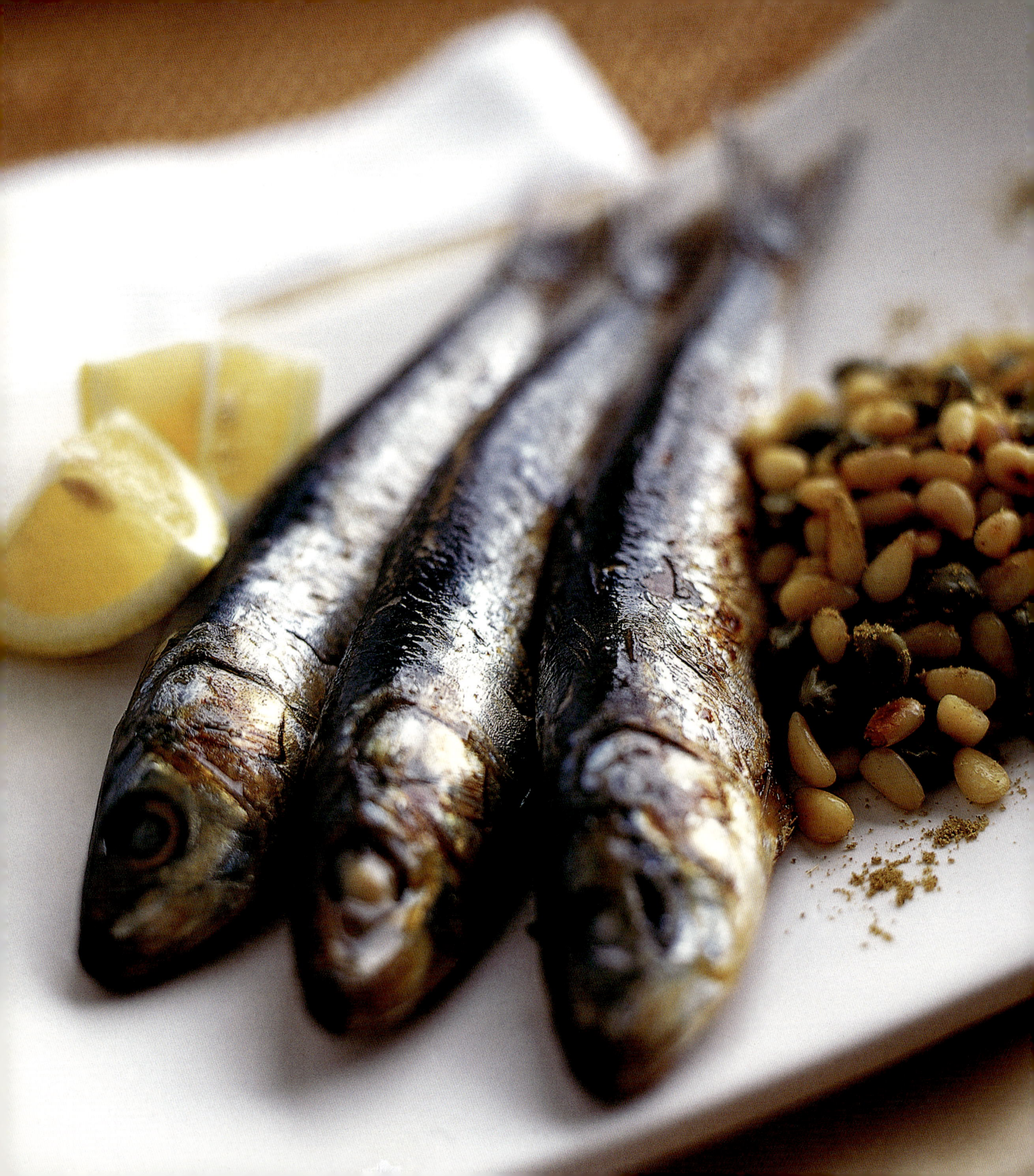

12 sardines, fresh and cleaned (gut removed)
¼ cup capers, drained and washed
¼ cup pine nuts
¼ teaspoon cumin powder
Spray olive oil

WHOLE SARDINES, CAPERS & PINE NUTS

The sardines are eaten whole, bone and all, or you can bone them as you eat. While the capers have a big taste, the flavour of the sardines will match it. Lemon wedges can be served too.

Wash and pat dry the sardines. Spray with oil and cook on a medium-hot plate for 1½ minutes.

Combine the capers and pine nuts. Tip onto the plate; toss and move the capers and nuts around but keep them in a concentrated area.

Spray the sardines with oil. Turn to cook for a further 1½ minutes.

The capers and pine nuts will be done in 2 minutes; sprinkle on the cumin and toss. Remove when the nuts are lightly browned and the capers warmed through.

Plate the sardines, either onto individual plates or a platter, spoon over the pine nuts and capers and serve with a green salad and crusty bread.

Serves 4

500g (18oz) basic risotto, cooled (see below)
1 tablespoon lemon zest, finely grated
100g (4oz) Atlantic salmon, boneless, skinless and finely chopped
2 eggs
½ cup plain flour
1 teaspoon powdered dill
Breadcrumbs
Spray olive oil

Basic Risotto
30g (1oz) butter
3 tablespoons onions, finely chopped
2 cloves garlic, chopped
1 cup Italian arborio rice
4 cups boiling fish/prawn stock
3 tablespoons parmesan cheese, finely grated
1 teaspoon salt
½ teaspoon white pepper

ATLANTIC SALMON RISOTTO CAKES

The basic mixture with the salmon added is quite sticky so it is best to divide the mixture into the 24 portions using a small ice-cream scoop or a spoon dipped in water. Dip your hands in water too before you roll and flatten the balls. I sometimes don't use the breadcrumbs and the cakes still cook nicely.

For the Basic Risotto

Melt butter in a large heavy saucepan and fry onion and garlic until soft and golden. Stir in the rice and fry for 3 minutes, stirring constantly, then add 1 cup boiling stock and cook, while stirring, until it is absorbed. Add stock a cupful at a time and stir constantly for 15–20 minutes or until rice is tender and all liquid is absorbed and the risotto is creamy and white.

Stir in cheese, salt, pepper and dill. Cover with hood and leave risotto to sit for 3 minutes before serving.

Mix the room-temperature risotto with the zest, salmon, eggs, flour and dill and stir well. Divide the risotto into 24 equal portions and roll into balls. Flatten into patties of 4cm (2in) in diameter, then coat in breadcrumbs. Make sure all excess breadcrumbs are removed and refrigerate until ready to use.

Spray the flat plate liberally with oil, add the cakes and cook for 1 minute. Spray liberally with oil, turn and cook for another minute on the other flat side. Serve as pass-round or in the middle of the table with a tossed salad.

Makes 24

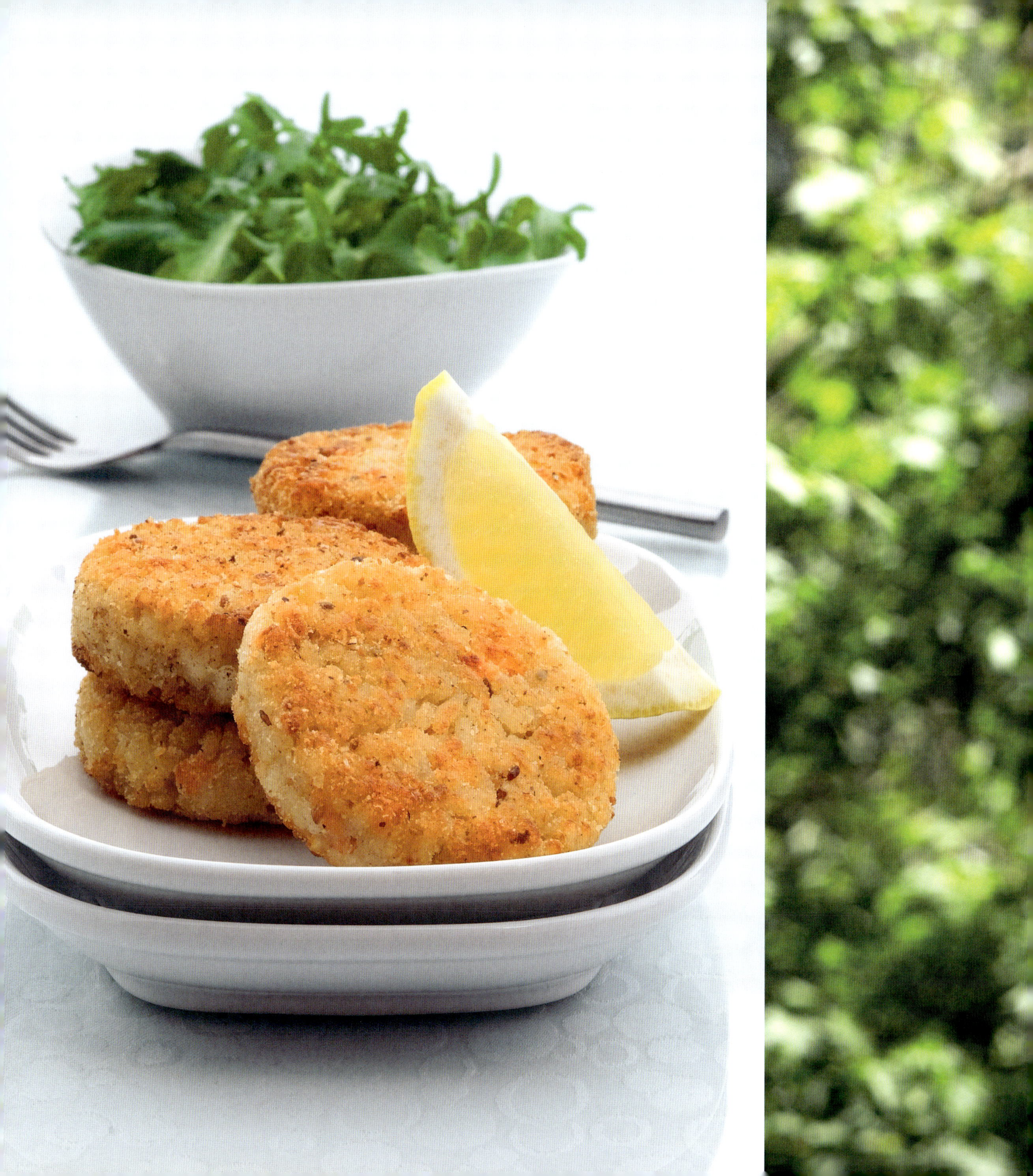

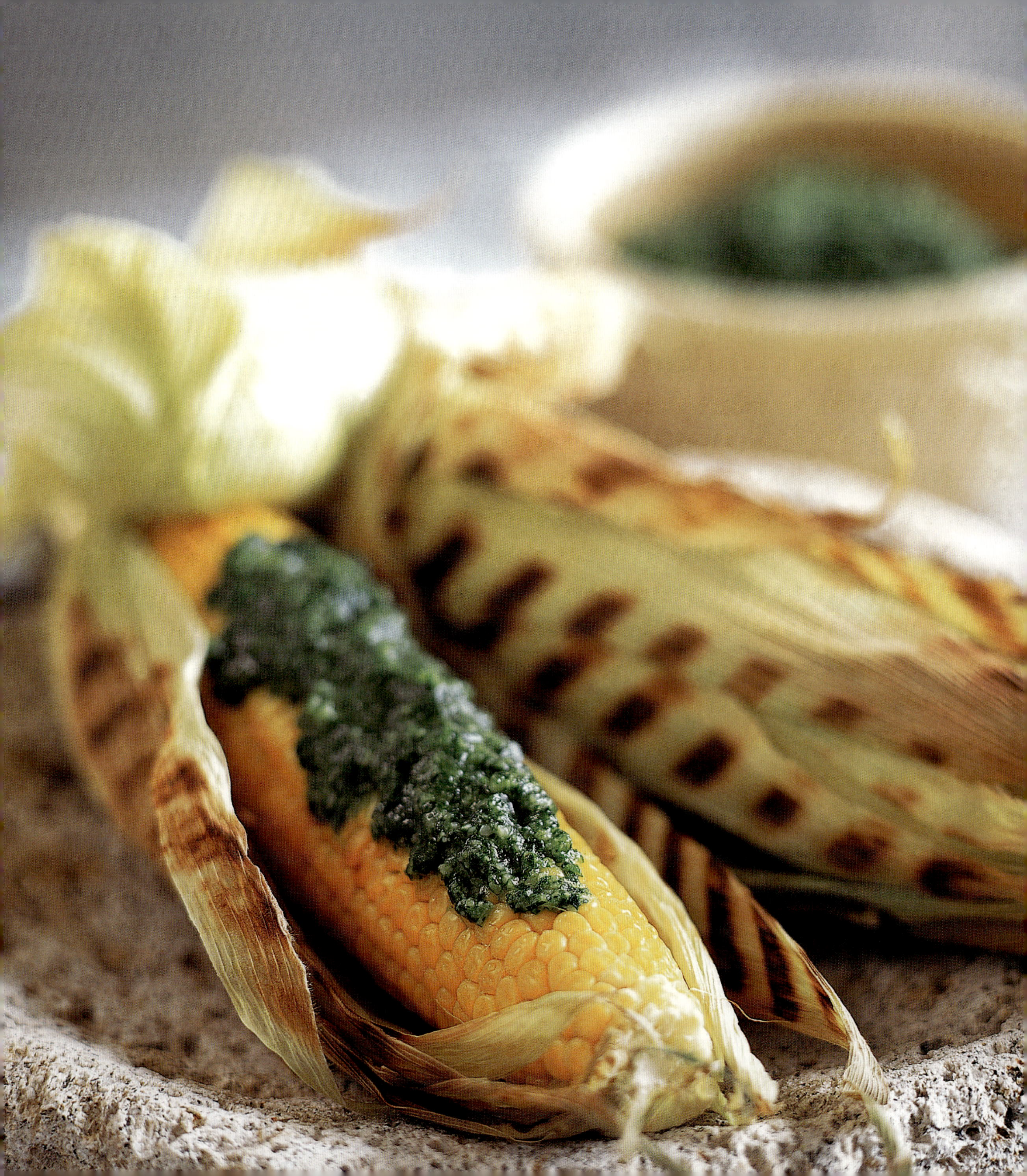

4 complete corns on the cob, husk on
1 cup parsley sprigs, washed
   and tightly packed
1 tablespoon unsalted, roasted macadamia nuts, roughly chopped
1 large clove garlic, crushed
60g (2oz) Australian cheddar cheese, grated
$1/3$ cup macadamia nut oil
Salt and pepper to taste

CORN ON THE COB WITH PARSLEY PESTO

FOR THE PESTO

Put the parsley, nuts, garlic and cheese into a processor bowl and pulse the processor until the ingredients start to break down, then leave the engine to run as you pour the oil in to form a smooth paste.

Pull back the husk from the corn kernel (but do not pull off) and remove silk. Replace the husk back over the corn.

Grill the whole corn cobs over a medium-hot grill for 30 minutes, turning at least every 5 minutes. Spray with water if it looks as though the husks are drying out too much although it doesn't matter if the husks are browning. Remove from barbecue and allow to cool for five minutes.

Serve on platter in the middle of the table. To eat, pull husks back from the corn. Be careful here because the steam can build up inside the husk. Spread some pesto over the corn and eat.

SERVES 4

16 sea scallops, roe removed
16 parsley leaves
16 x 10cm (4in) pieces bacon, rind removed
16 stainless steel skewers or bamboo
   skewers, soaked in water for 30 minutes
4 lemon cheeks
Spray oil

SCALLOP & BACON KEBABS

Remove the little black membrane from the side of each scallop.

Sit each scallop on the end of each piece of bacon. Top with a parsley leaf and roll the bacon around each scallop. Thread four wrapped scallops onto each skewer.

Cook on medium-hot flat plate, sprayed with oil, for 2–3 minutes each side and serve with the lemon cheeks.

Serves 4

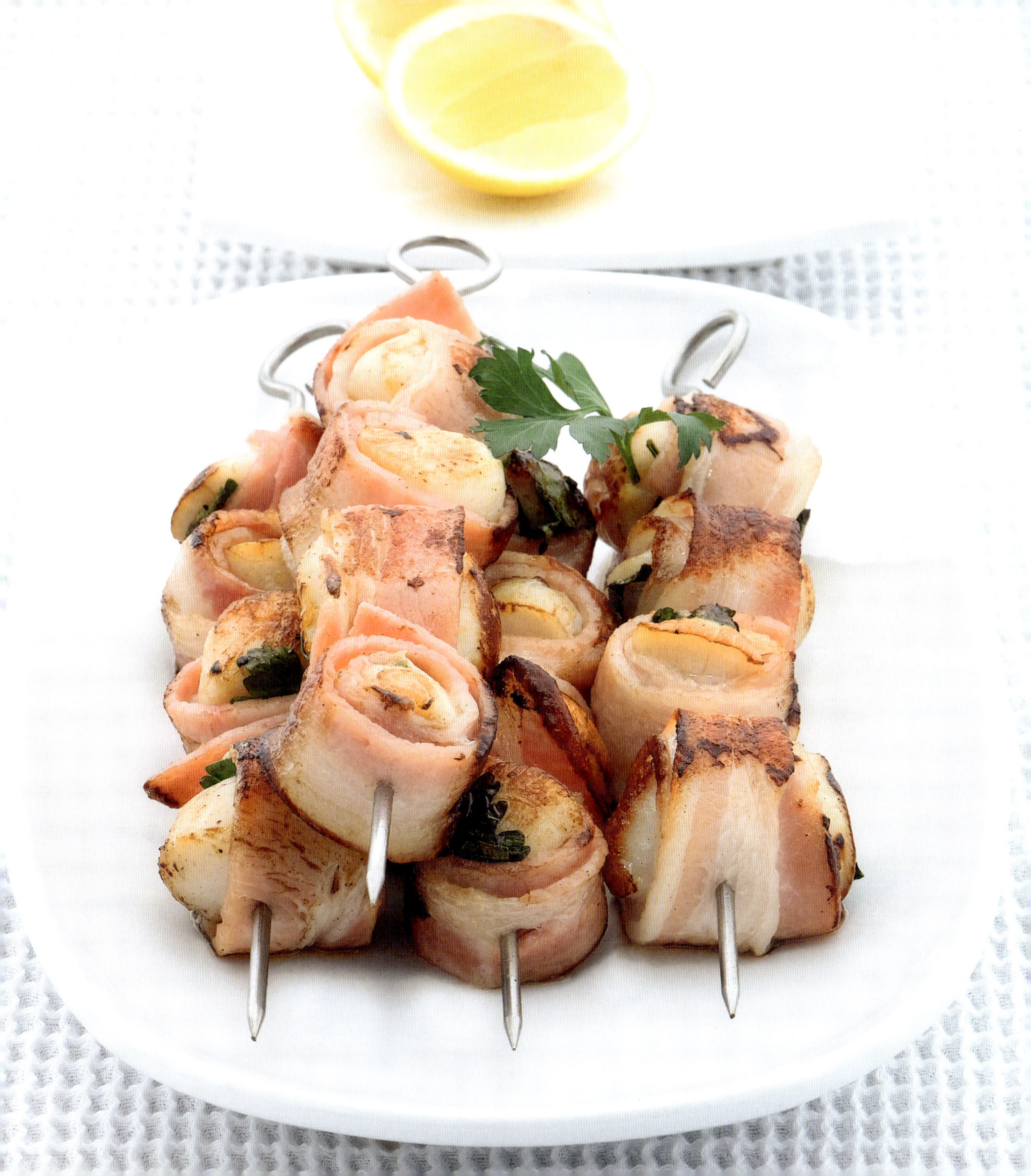

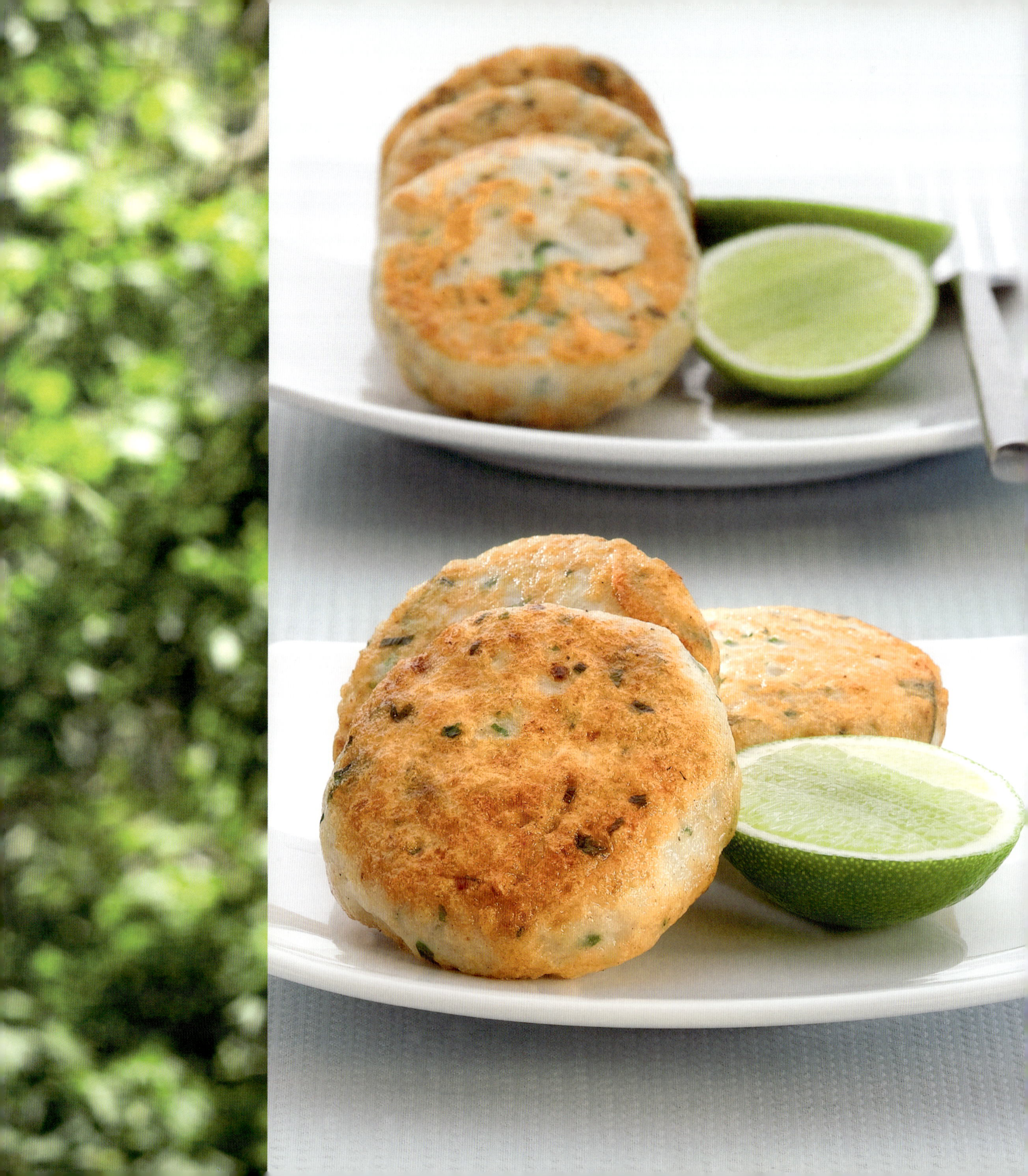

- 500g (1lb) white fish, such as snapper, skin removed
- 2 tablespoons garlic chives, washed and finely chopped
- 1 clove garlic, finely minced
- 1 tablespoon lemongrass, white part only and finely chopped
- 2 egg whites, lightly beaten
- 4 candle nuts (or blanched almonds), roughly chopped
- ¼ teaspoon nutmeg, grated
- ½ teaspoon dried shrimp paste
- 1 kaffir lime leaf, fresh and shredded
- 10 large coriander leaves, roughly chopped
- 1 tablespoon fish sauce
- 1 tablespoon rice flour
- Spray vegetable oil
- 4–8 lime cheeks

THAI-INSPIRED FISH PATTIES

YOU CAN SERVE SOME LIGHT SOY SAUCE FLAVOURED WITH A LITTLE SWEET CHILLI DIPPING SAUCE. A SQUEEZE OF LIME JUICE IS JUST PERFECT.

Finely mince the fish by pulsing in the food processor or putting through a mincing machine. Either way, the fish must be finely minced.

Combine all ingredients except for spray oil and lime cheeks with the minced fish and mix well using your hands. Cover and refrigerate overnight.

After dipping your hands in cold water and leaving wet, shape the fish patties into the size you desire. I like mine around 6cm (2in) in diameter and around 2cm (1in) thick. Place onto a cling wrap-lined plate, cover and refrigerate for 1 hour.

Spray the fish cakes liberally with oil and place them on a medium-hot plate oiled side down. Cook for 2 minutes. Spray the patties with oil and turn to cook for a further 2 minutes.

MAKES 12–15

300g (11oz) cuttlefish tubes
¼ cup olive oil
2 tablespoons dill, chopped
100g (4oz) baby rocket leaves
100g (4oz) ripe tomatoes, diced

For the Salsa Verde
2 cloves garlic, roughly chopped
2 cups parsley, tightly packed
1 tablespoon fresh oregano
1 tablespoon capers, rinsed
2 tablespoons white wine vinegar
1 tablespoon Dijon mustard
2 anchovy fillets
½ cup extra virgin olive oil

CUTTLEFISH WITH SALSA VERDE & BABY ROCKET

For the Salsa Verde

Put all ingredients, except for the oil, into a food processor and start the motor. After 15 seconds or so, start pouring in the oil. You will have to stop once or twice to scrape the mixture down the side with a spatula. Work to a good paste. You may need extra olive oil or vinegar. Check the seasoning and spoon into a stainless steel or glass bowl.

Cut the cuttlefish open to form large pieces and score the flesh side into diamond shapes with a very sharp knife. Cut into bite-size pieces and tip into a bowl with the olive oil and dill. Toss to coat and let sit for 10 minutes.

Lift and drain the cuttlefish and cook on a hot plate until done. Move it constantly so that all flesh is exposed to heat. When done, lift into the salsa verde bowl and coat the cuttlefish. Allow to cool.

To serve, put equal amounts of rocket and diced tomato onto individual plates and top with the salsa verde-coated cuttlefish.

Serves 4

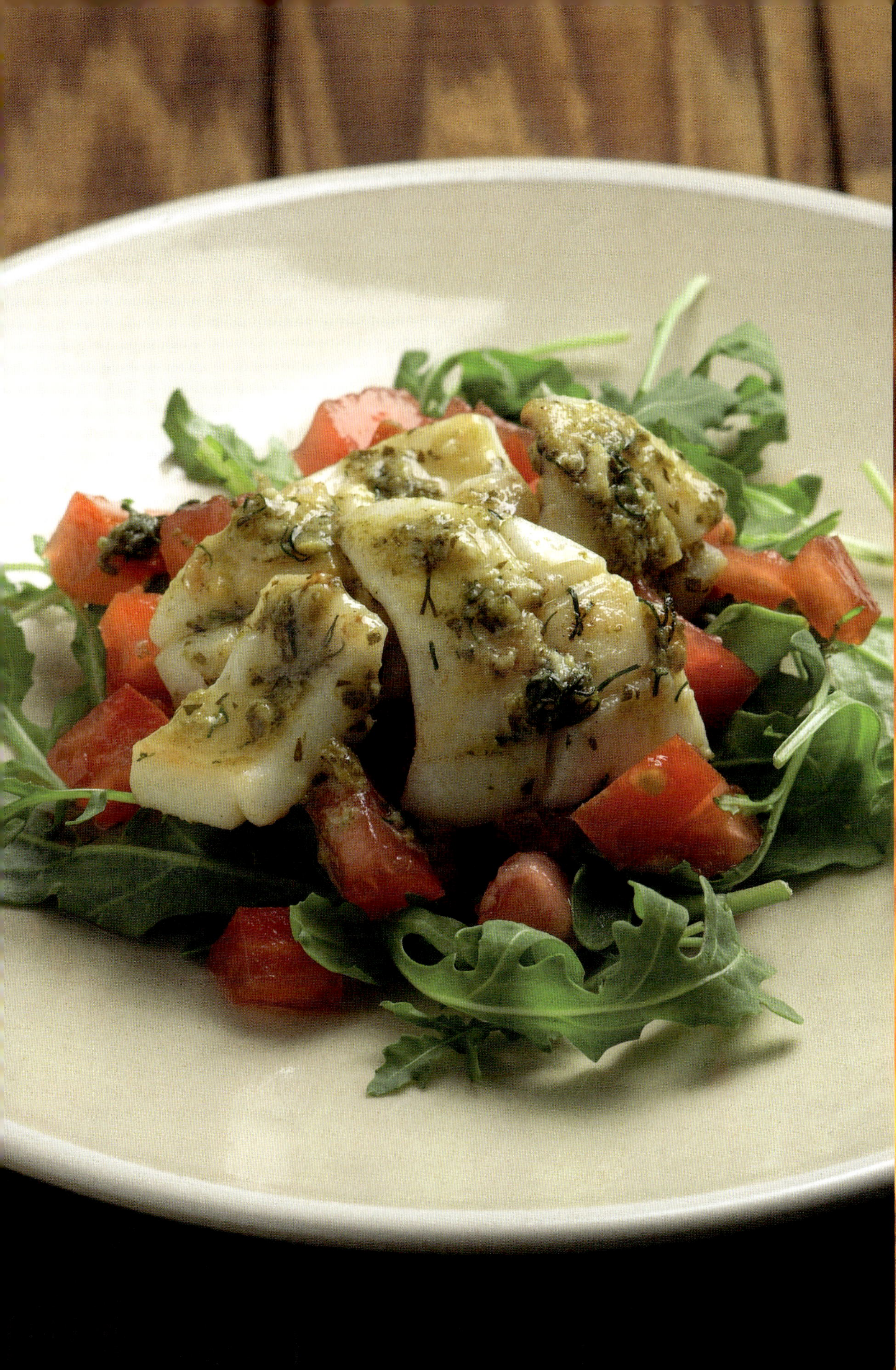
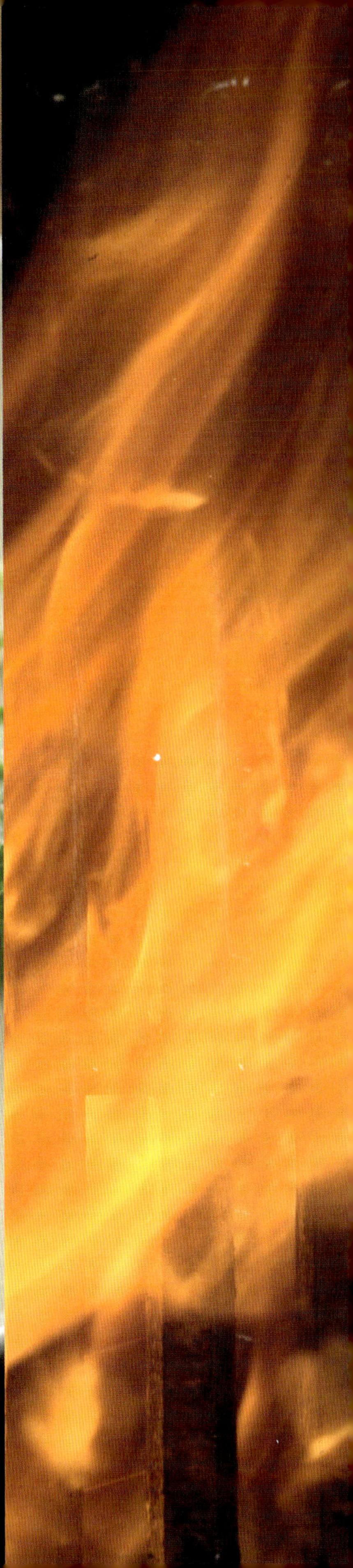

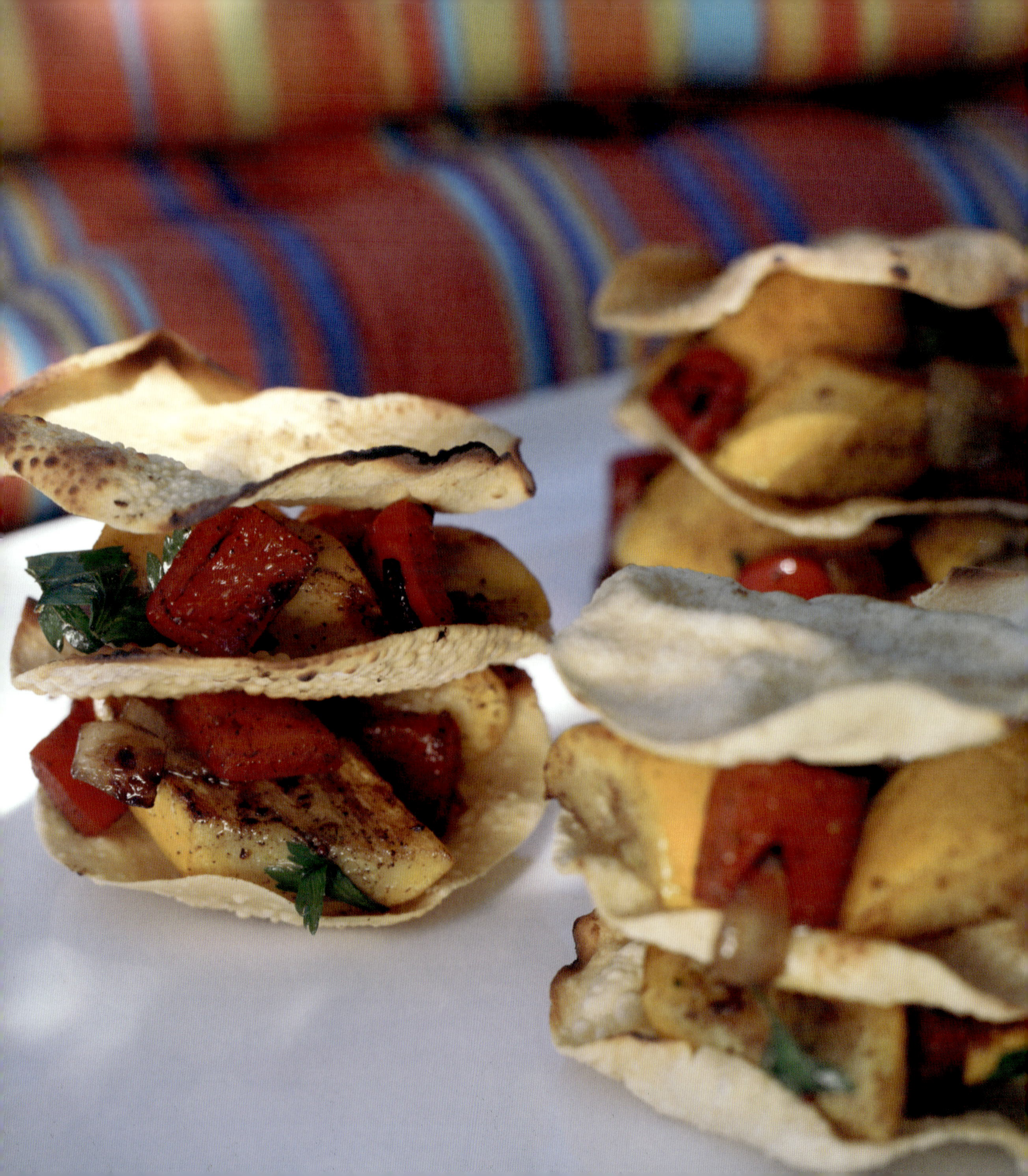

4 medium yellow or green zucchinis or both
3 tablespoons vegetable oil
1 teaspoon black mustard seed
1 tablespoon Indian curry powder
1 red capsicum, cheeks only
1 small onion, peeled
Salt to taste
12 small pappadums
Spray oil
200g (7oz) natural yoghurt
Indian mango pickle

CURRIED ZUCCHINI PAPPADUM STACK

Trim the zucchinis and cut down the centre lengthwise. Cut these halves into half moons around 2cm (1in) long. Pour the oil into a bowl and mix in the mustard seeds and curry powder. Dice the flesh of the capsicum and onion and add to the oil mixture. Now add the zucchini and toss to coat. Leave to sit for 1 hour before cooking

Spray both sides of the pappadums liberally with oil and put onto a hot grill. Do only a couple at a time so you can turn them quickly. They crisp and sizzle very quickly so be ready to turn. Drain on kitchen towelling.

Tip the zucchini mixture onto the flat plate. Allow to cook through, turning regularly; sprinkle with salt to taste. The zucchini is cooked more quickly by dropping the hood. When soft, remove from barbecue with as much of the cooking juices as possible.

Put some natural yoghurt into the centre of the individual plates and place a pappadum. Spoon over some zucchini mixture and add another pappadum. Spoon over a little more of the zucchini and top with a pappadum. Repeat until the four plates are done.

Serve with the Indian mango pickle and yoghurt on the side.

Serves 4

24 black mussels, cleaned and beard removed
1 cup garlic and red wine butter
1 large baguette or ciabiatta

Garlic and Red Wine Butter
250g (9oz) salted butter, room temperature
2 large cloves garlic, roughly chopped
2 tablespoons parsley, roughly chopped
3 tablespoons red wine
½ tablespoon black pepper, freshly ground

Black Mussels with Garlic & Red Wine Butter

For the Garlic and Red Wine Butter

Combine all ingredients together in a processor or by whipping with a fork or whisk. This will keep in an airtight container if you don't use it all and you'll be surprised how you can use it.

Put the mussels onto a medium-hot grill. Very shortly they will start to open. Lift each one into a bowl as they do.

When all are removed and cool enough to handle, remove the empty top shell of each mussel. Dot each mussel with some butter (don't overload as the butter will melt and spill onto the flames).

Put back onto the grill and lower the hood for 1 minute. Lift to check that the mussels are bubbling and the butter is melting.

Serve on individual plates with more melted garlic and red wine butter and plenty of good bread for dunking into the juices.

Serves 4

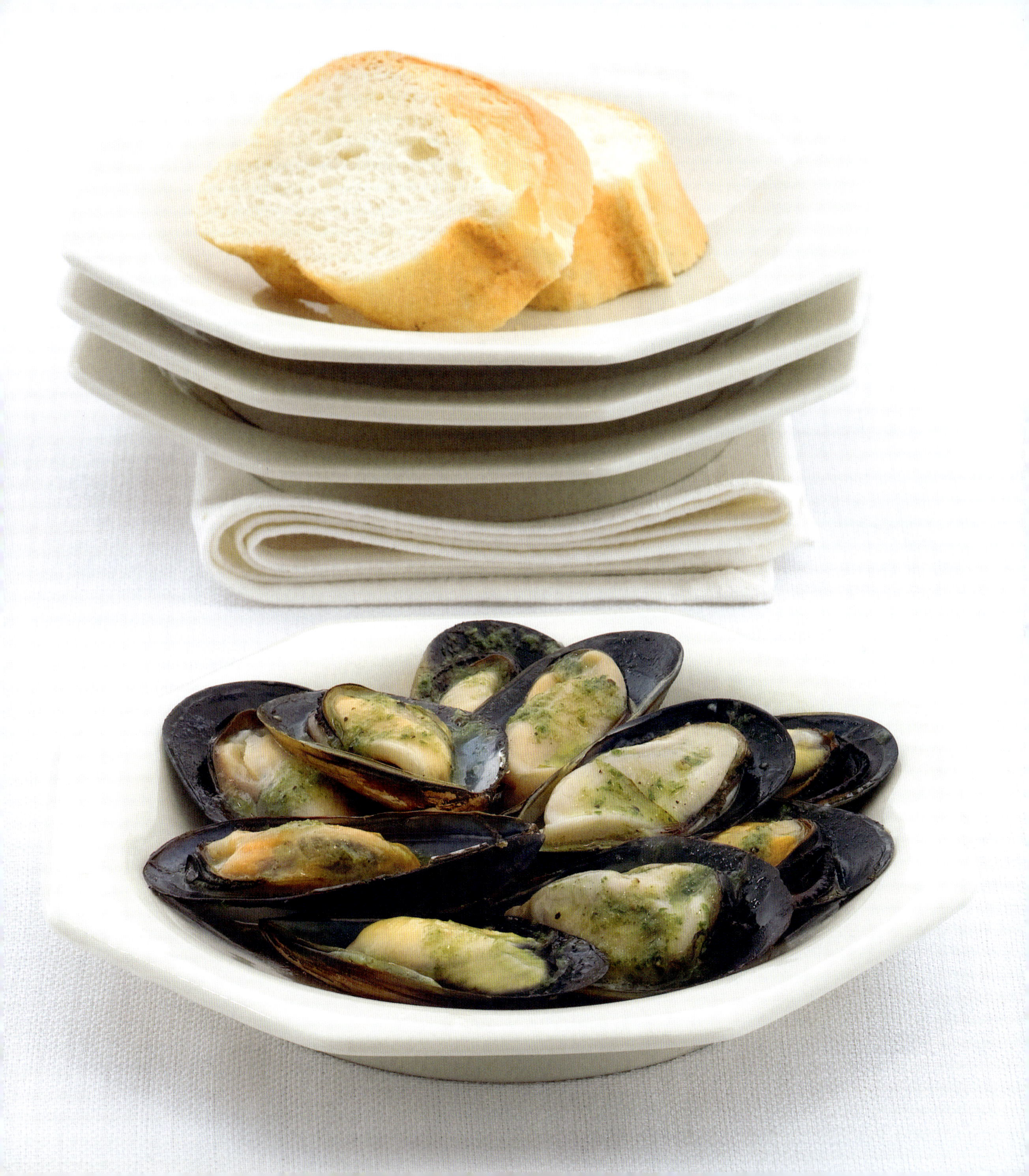

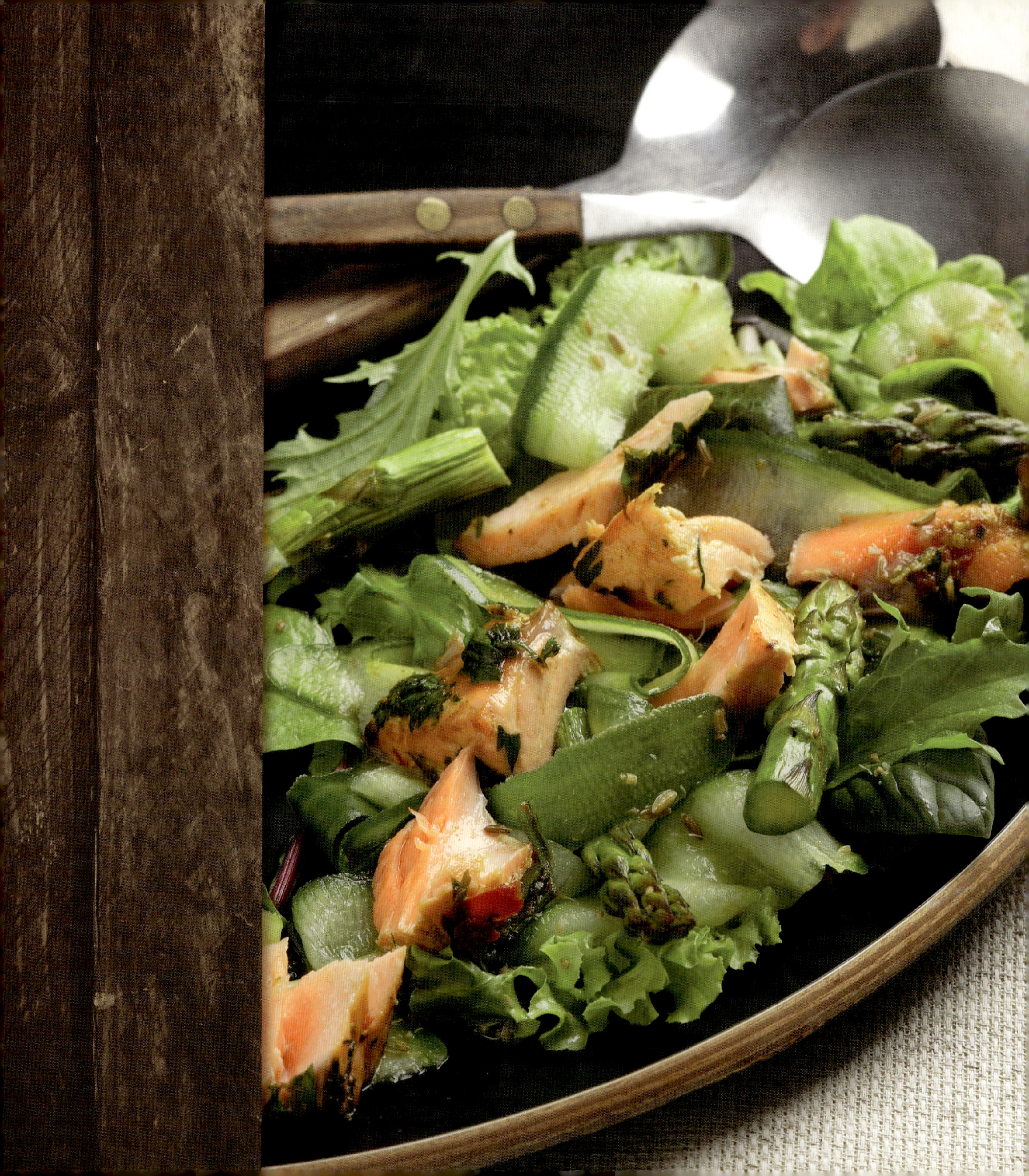

500g (1lb) Atlantic salmon fillet,
    skin removed and cut into strips 3cm
    (1in) wide
½ cup Chermoula (see recipe below)
300g (11oz) Lebanese cucumber, deseeded
1 teaspoon salt
1 teaspoon sugar
¼ white vinegar
2 tablespoons fennel seeds, crushed
1 x 100g (4oz) bag mixed lettuce leaves
8 asparagus spears, trimmed
Spray oil

My Chermoula
1 small onion, very finely chopped
2 teaspoons fresh coriander leaves, finely chopped
4 teaspoons parsley, finely chopped
2 cloves garlic, minced
1 small red chilli, finely chopped
4 teaspoons ground cumin seeds
2 teaspoons mild paprika
1 teaspoon powdered tumeric
¼ teaspoon cayenne pepper
4 tablespoons olive oil
¼ teaspoon salt
¼ ground black pepper

CHERMOULA RUB ATLANTIC SALMON SALAD

For the Chermoula

Mix all the ingredients together in a bowl or you can process them into a paste if you prefer. Use as required.

Pat the salmon strips with the Chermoula and let sit for 10 minutes.

Using a vegetable peeler, cut the cucumber into longish ribbons and put into a bowl. Add the salt, sugar, vinegar and fennel. Stir, cover and refrigerate for 1 hour.

Lift the salmon strips from the Chermoula, shake off excess and spray well with oil. Cook on hot plate until medium, turning often. Remove from the plate when done and cool.

Spray the asparagus and cook on a hot grill for 2–3 minutes. Remove, cool and cut into bite-sized pieces.

Place the mixed leaves onto a large platter and scatter the cucumber strips across the top of the leaves. Break/flake the fish onto the leaves and sprinkle cucumber liquid over the top. Serve with good bread.

Serves 4

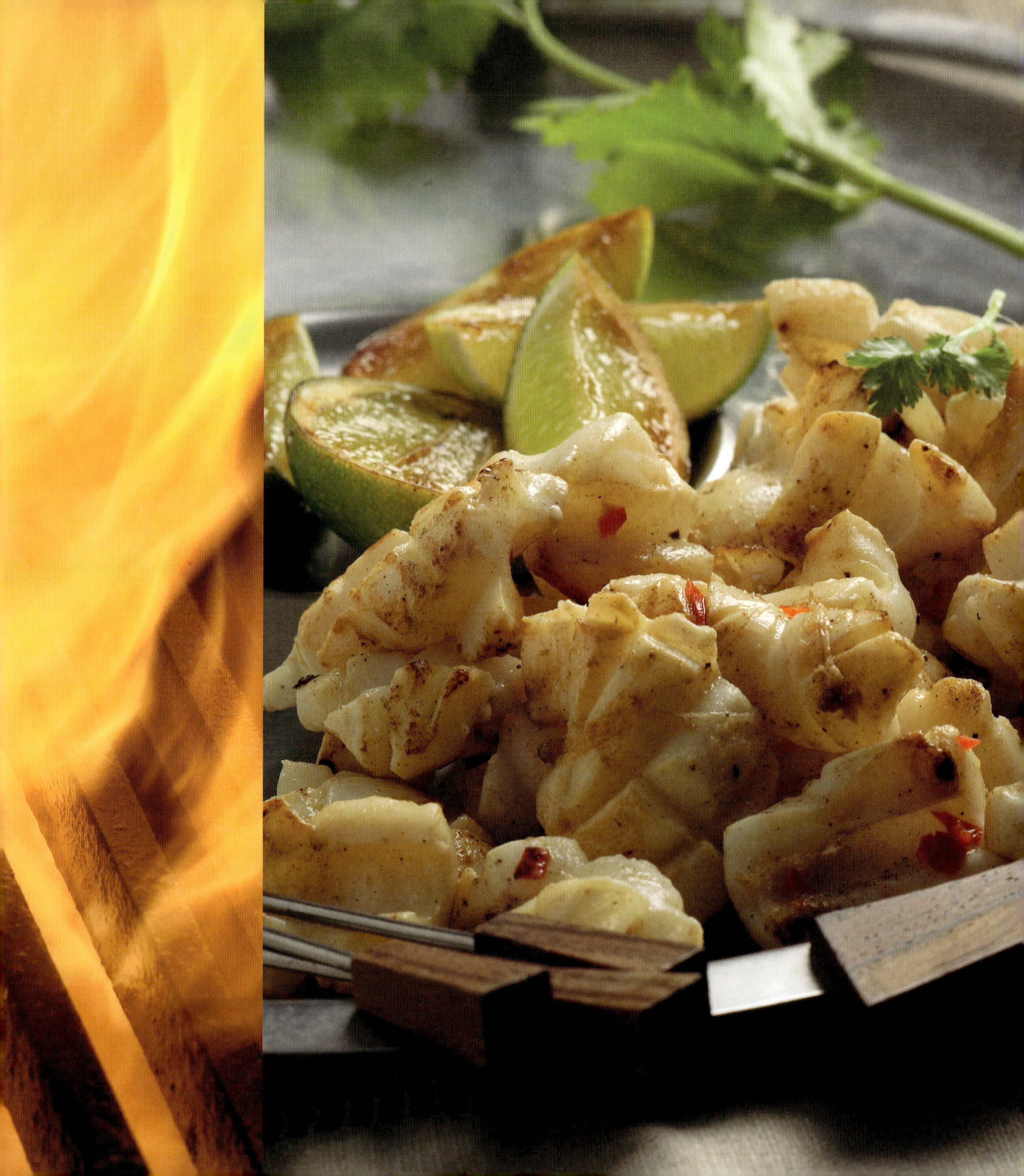

6 medium calamari tubes, cleaned
3 fresh tablespoons lime juice
1 tablespoon peanut oil
1 small red chilli, de-seeded and minced
1 root coriander, washed and minced
3 teaspoons fish sauce (Nam Pla)
1 teaspoon palm sugar
Spray oil
Sprigs of coriander, washed
　and crisped in refrigerator

CALAMARI WITH LIME JUICE & CORIANDER

Slit the tubes down one side and open to lay flat, skin side down, and score finely. Cut into bite-sized pieces.

Make a marinade by combining the lime juice, peanut oil, chilli, coriander root, fish sauce and sugar. Mix well. Soak the scored calamari in this marinade for 15 minutes.

Lift the calamari from the marinade and drain off any excess juices.

Spray a hot plate with oil and put the calamari onto it. Cook in small batches.

Tumble and turn the pieces, cooking for no longer than 2 minutes.

Decorate with scattered torn coriander leaves and serve.

Serves 4

500g (1lb) chicken, finely minced
1 onion, finely chopped
1 chilli, seeded and chopped
2 tablespoons fresh mint, chopped
½ teaspoon salt
1 teaspoon garam masala
½ teaspoon coriander powder
½ teaspoon cumin powder
½ cup dried bread crumbs
Bamboo skewers
Spray oil
Mint sprigs for decoration

CHICKEN KOFTAS

Mix chicken with onion, chilli, mint, salt, garam masala, coriander, cumin and breadcrumbs. Knead mixture until stiff and smooth.

Shape the chicken mixture into a small sausage size around one end of the bamboo skewer. The meat mixture should be around 3cm (1in) in diameter and 8cm (3in) long.

Lay the koftas on a cling wrap-covered plate. Cover and refrigerate for 1 hour.

Spray the koftas with oil and cook on a medium-hot plate. Turn every minute until cooked, 8–10 minutes.

Serve on platter decorated with mint sprigs.

SERVES 4

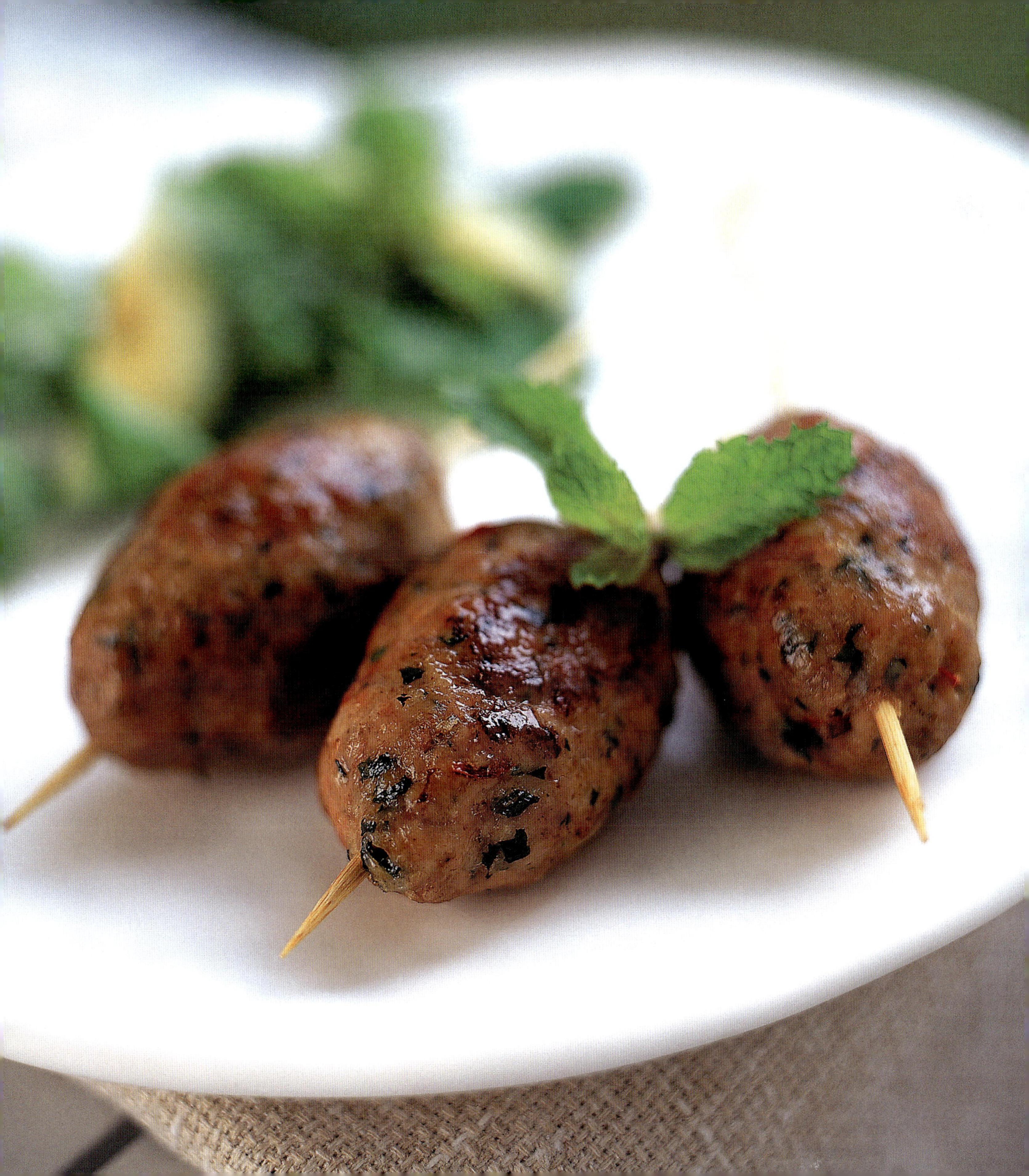

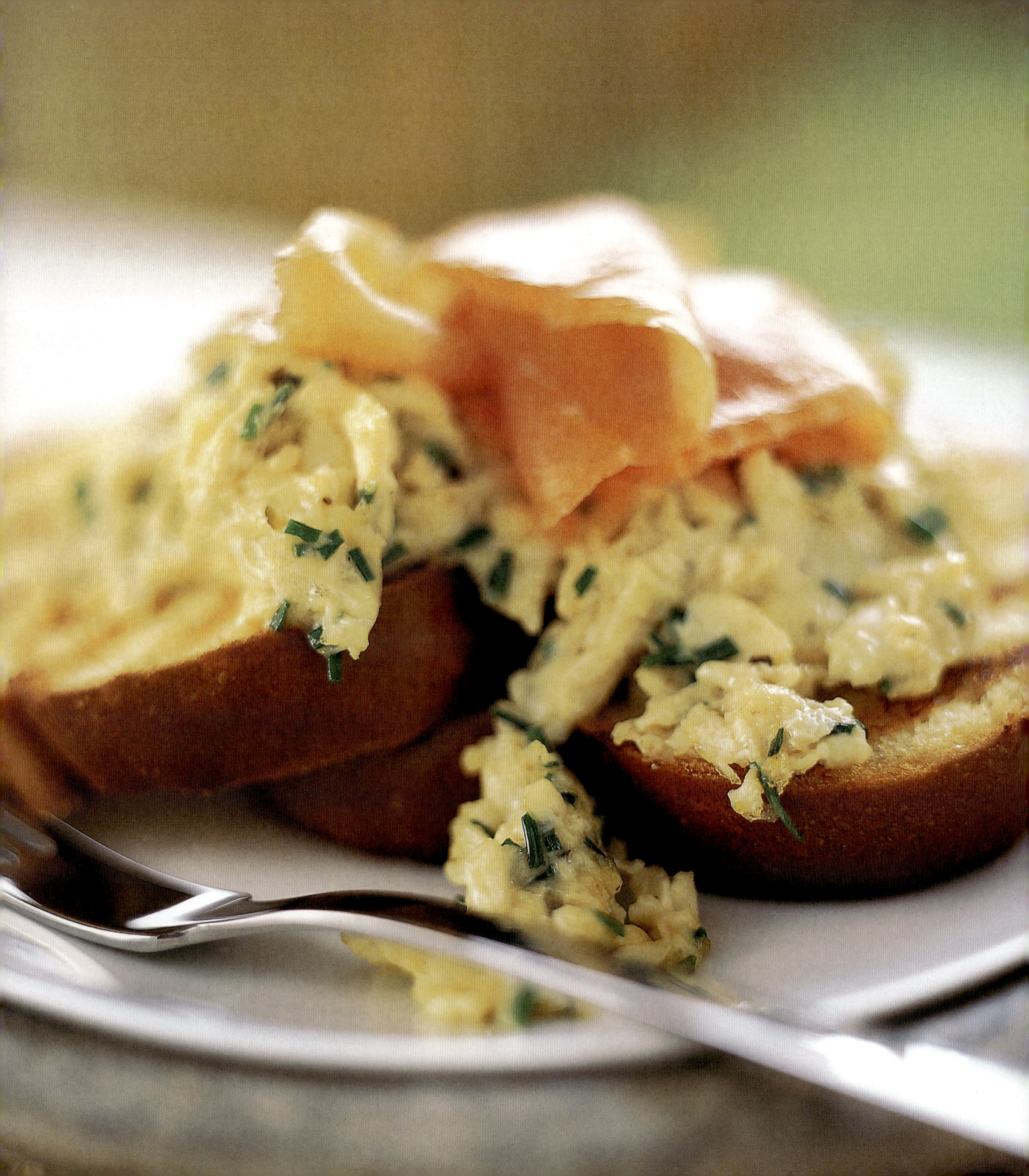

8 medium eggs, free range if possible
3 tablespoons chives, chopped
1 tablespoon butter, melted
   and at room temperature
¼ teaspoon ground black pepper
4–8 slices brioche
8 slices smoked salmon
Spray vegetable oil

CHIVED EGGS, SMOKED SALMON & BRIOCHE

IT IS ESSENTIAL THAT YOU HAVE A VERY CLEAN FLAT PLATE ON WHICH TO COOK THESE EGGS.

Beat the eggs well into batches of four. Stir in equal amounts of chives, butter and ground black pepper.

Spray the brioche lightly with oil and toast on both sides on the grill. Place the slices onto individual plates.

Liberally oil the flat plate and pour the eggs on using a spatula to keep them from running all over the plate. This is like making eggs in a frying pan, not a saucepan, so you need to keep the egg mixture constantly moving around a concentrated area on the barbecue plate. Each batch will take 45–50 seconds to cook. When done, lift equal amounts of the scrambled eggs onto the brioche, top with the salmon slices and serve immediately.

SERVES 4

8 small calamari tubes
2 tablespoons olive oil
1 tablespoon parsley, chopped
Sea salt
Spray oil

Green Lentil Salad
2 cups cooked green lentils, drained and washed (I use canned, cooked green lentils)
1 small Spanish onion, roughly chopped
½ cup red capsicum, diced
1 cup mint leaves
½ cup mayonnaise
2 tablespoons Spanish sherry vinegar
1 teaspoon salt
½ teaspoon powdered tumeric

CALAMARI WITH GREEN LENTIL & MINT SALAD

Cut the tubes open and score the flesh with a very sharp knife to form diamond shapes. Do not cut through the calamari tubes and let the weight of the knife be enough pressure—the finer the diamonds, the quicker the calamari cooks. Cut the calamari into bite size pieces and tip into a bowl. Add the oil and parsley and toss to coat. Let sit for 10 minutes before use.

Lift from the bowl onto an oiled, hot flat plate and cook quickly, moving the calamari around to expose all the flesh to the heat. Sprinkle with sea salt and the calamari cooks very quickly. Remove from barbecue and keep warm.

Scoop lentil salad into the centre of individual flattish bowls, top with calamari and serve.

For the Green Lentil Salad
Combine the lentils, onion and capsicum. Tear the mint leaves into pieces as you add them to the lentils. Whisk the mayonnaise, vinegar, salt and tumeric. Pour over the lentils and stir well to combine flavours. This salad is best done the day before use and stored in the refrigerator.

Serves 4

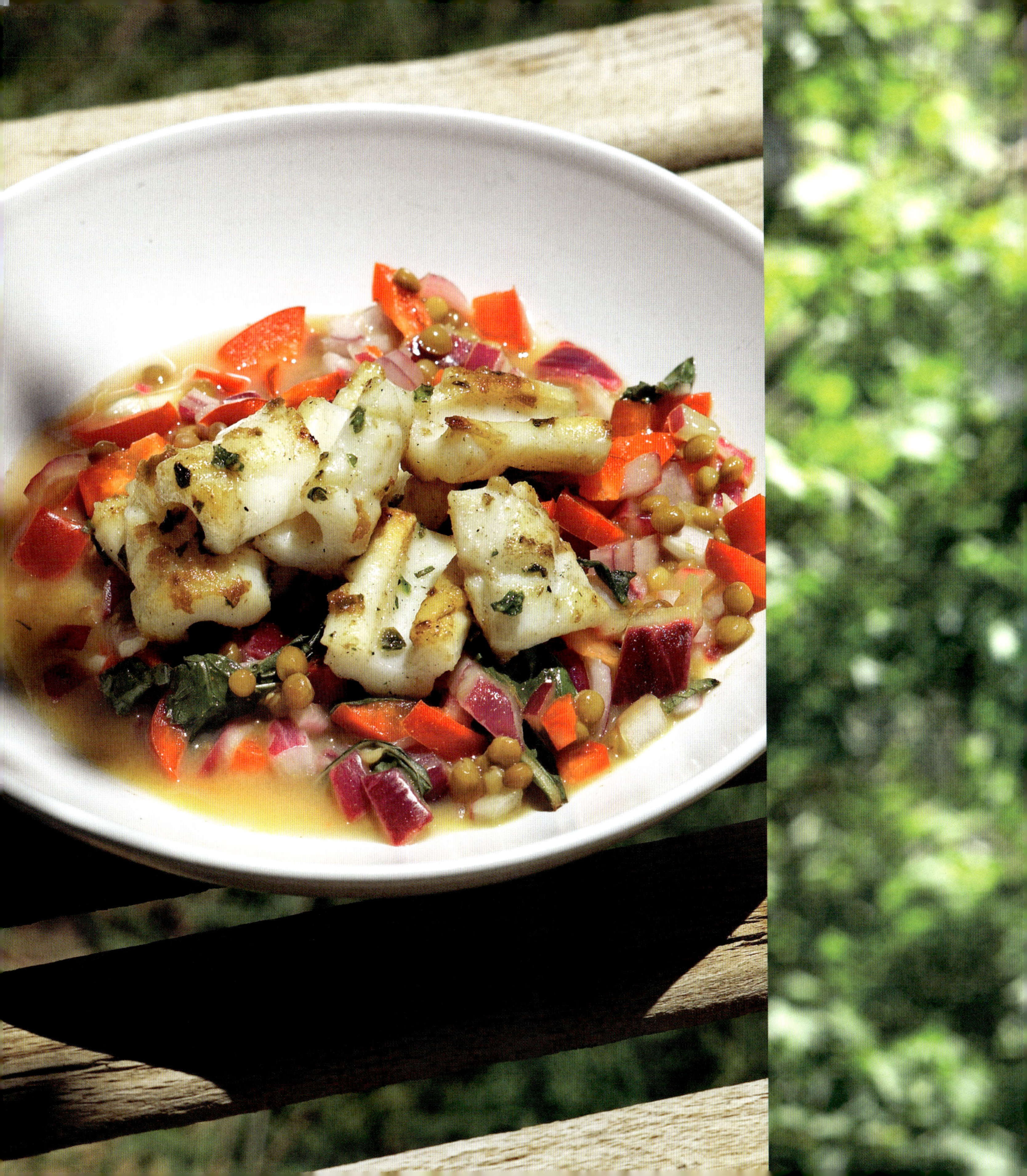

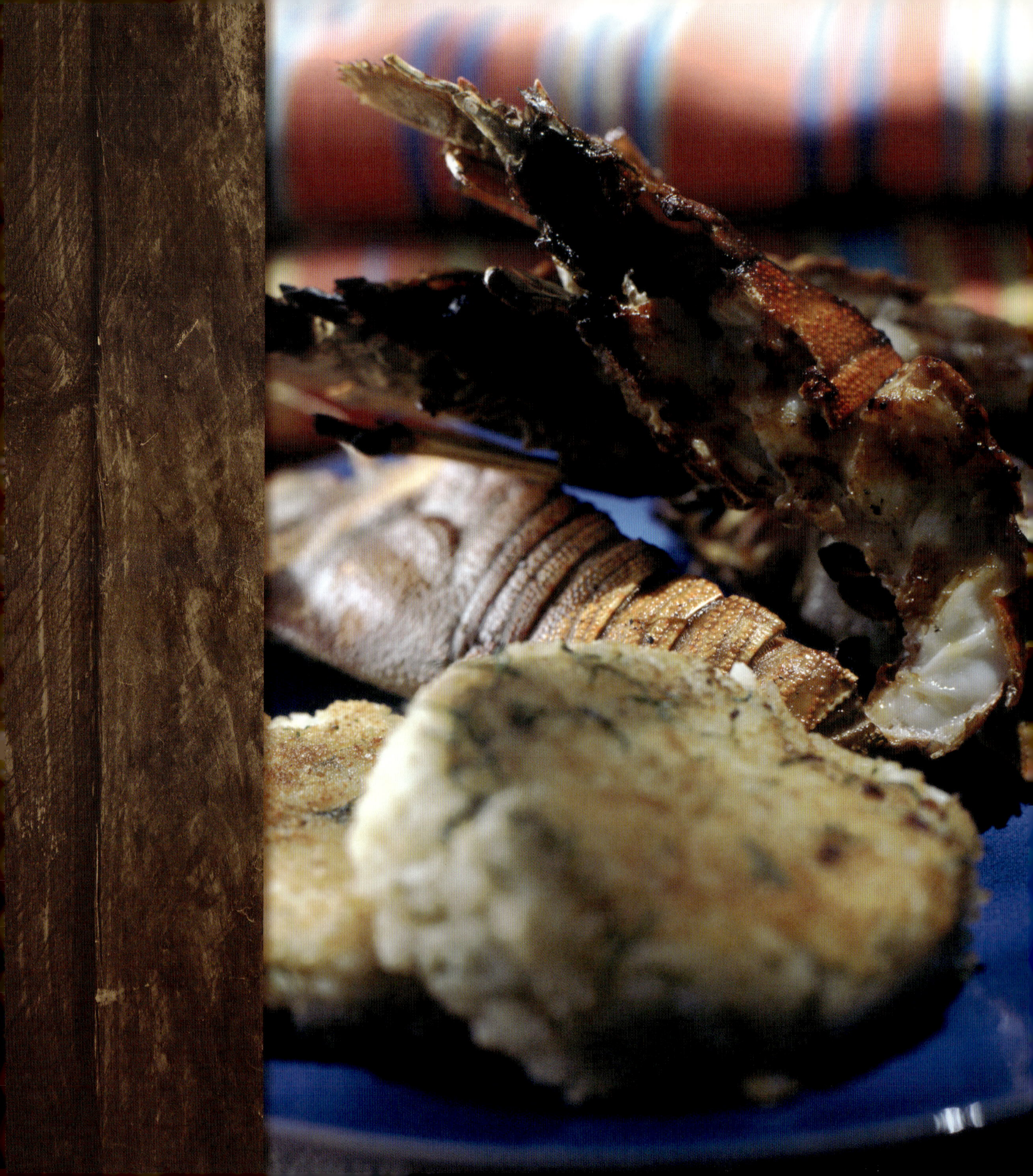

8 green Moreton Bay/Balmain Bug tails
Spray garlic oil
400g (14oz) basic cooked risotto (see Tiny Arancini recipe, page 30)
3 tablespoons chopped dill
½ teaspoon lemon essence
Breadcrumbs
1 cup garlic, white wine and anchovy cream sauce (see recipe below)

Garlic, White Wine Anchovy Cream
2 cloves garlic, crushed
½ cup white wine
450ml (15fl oz) pouring cream
1 x 45g (2oz) can anchovies, drained
1 tablespoon parsley, coarsely chopped
¼ teaspoon cayenne

BUG TAILS & DILL RISOTTO CAKES WITH GARLIC, WHITE WINE & ANCHOVY CREAM

Any leftover sauce stores well in an airtight container in the refrigerator and when cooled it thickens and can turn into a spread for crackers or be used to spoon over grilled meats.

Cut the bugs in half lengthwise and rinse clean or buy them already split down the middle. Refrigerate until ready to use.

Mix the risotto with the dill and lemon essence. Divide into 8 even amounts and roll into balls with wet hands. Roll in breadcrumbs and flatten slightly to allow for even cooking on the barbecue. Cover and refrigerate for at least 1 hour before use.

Spray the flesh of the bugs with the oil and cook on a medium-hot grill, turning regularly. If you put the flesh side directly onto the grill, make sure it is well oiled.

Cook the risotto cakes on a well-oiled medium-hot plate and cook slowly to allow the heat to penetrate. Turn regularly and allow to brown.

Serve the bugs on a platter with the cakes on another plate and the heated sauce alongside. A green salad completes this meal.

For the Garlic, White Wine Anchovy Cream
Place all ingredients into a saucepan and simmer until the mixture reduces to half the volume.

Serves 4

1 cup self-raising flour
Salt and white pepper to taste
1 egg
1–1¼ cups beer, at room temperature
1 cup roasted or boiled beef, finely diced
2 tablespoons seeded mustard
2 medium onions, finely diced
1 tablespoon chives, chopped
Spray oil
Tomato Relish (see recipe below)

Tomato Relish
6 large, semi-ripe tomatoes, roughly diced
1 large onion, finely chopped
3 garlic cloves, finely chopped
2 tablespoons raw sugar
¼ cup apple juice
1 tablespoon mustard powder
2 tablespoons curry powder
½ cup Worcestershire sauce
1 tablespoon tamarind pulp
1 bay leaf
6 whole cloves
1 cinnamon curl
1 teaspoon salt

BEEF, ONION & CHIVE PANCAKES WITH TOMATO RELISH

Sift the flour, salt and white pepper into a bowl. Mix the egg with the beer and stir into the flour. Tip in the beef, mustard, onion and chives. Stir well and leave to rest for 15 minutes.

Spray oil a medium-hot plate and make the pancakes by dropping the beef batter onto the plate. Do as many as you like, ensuring you have room to flip the pancakes.

You can vary the size if you want. Smaller ones are great as pass-rounds at the barbie with a small dollop of relish while the large ones make a great starter when served with a good salad.

Makes 8–10

For the Tomato Relish

Put all ingredients, except the salt, into a suitable pot and simmer until the onion is cooked and the flavours combined for about 20 minutes, stirring constantly. Add the salt and cook a further 10 minutes, stirring all the time. The constant movement in the pan will aid evaporation or you can cook in a large open pan, if you prefer. At this time, the relish can stick and burn on the bottom of the pan.

Remove from the heat and cool before storing in sterilised, airtight containers. Store in the refrigerator for at least four weeks.

Makes 4 cups

12 medium chicken livers
100g (4oz) breadcrumbs, dry
1 tablespoon ground marjoram
Medium skewers, bamboo
    (soaked in water for 30 minutes) or metal
1 tablespoon lemon juice
1 teaspoon marjoram, fresh and finely chopped
½ tablespoon olive oil
Spray olive oil
150g (5oz) cooked basmati rice

CHICKEN LIVERS, LEMON & MARJORAM BASTE

Trim the livers well. Mix the breadcrumbs and dry marjoram together, skewer three chicken livers onto skewers and roll into the breadcrumb mixture.

Mix the lemon juice, fresh marjoram and olive oil together.

Liberally spray a medium-hot plate with oil. Add the chicken livers and cook for 2 minutes. Spray the chicken livers with oil and turn to cook for another 2 minutes for rare to medium-cooked livers. If you need them well done, cook them longer.

In the last minute of cooking, baste with a little of the lemon, marjoram and oil mixture.

When done to your liking, remove from the barbecue and rest for 2 minutes. Serve on a bed of rice with the remainder of the lemon mixture on the side.

Serves 4

1 pizza base (either purchased or made from recipe below)
Spray oil
3 tablespoons tomato cumin pizza base sauce
100g (4oz) mixed Mediterranean grilled vegetables (from supermarket), roughly chopped
100g (4oz) Chorizo, finely sliced into rounds
100g (4oz) goat's curd, from small log
1 tablespoon parmesan cheese, finely grated

CHORIZO, MEDITERRANEAN VEGETABLES & GOAT'S CURD PIZZA

Heat pizza stone on grill to high heat for 20 minutes

Put the pizza base on a lightly oil-sprayed pizza tray. Spoon over the tomato cumin sauce.

Evenly spread the vegetables over the tomato topping. Spread the sausage over and around the pizza. Cut the goat's curd into 6 rounds (can be difficult if the cheese is not really firm enough to do this, so you can add dollops if it is easier).

Cook on the pizza stone in the barbecue at 220°C (425°F) for 7–8 minutes or until the crust is crisp around the edges. Remove from the barbecue and tip onto cutting board. Grate on the parmesan using a microplane or very fine grater; cut into 6–8 wedges and serve on its own as a pass-round or with a salad as a light lunch.

SERVES 2–4

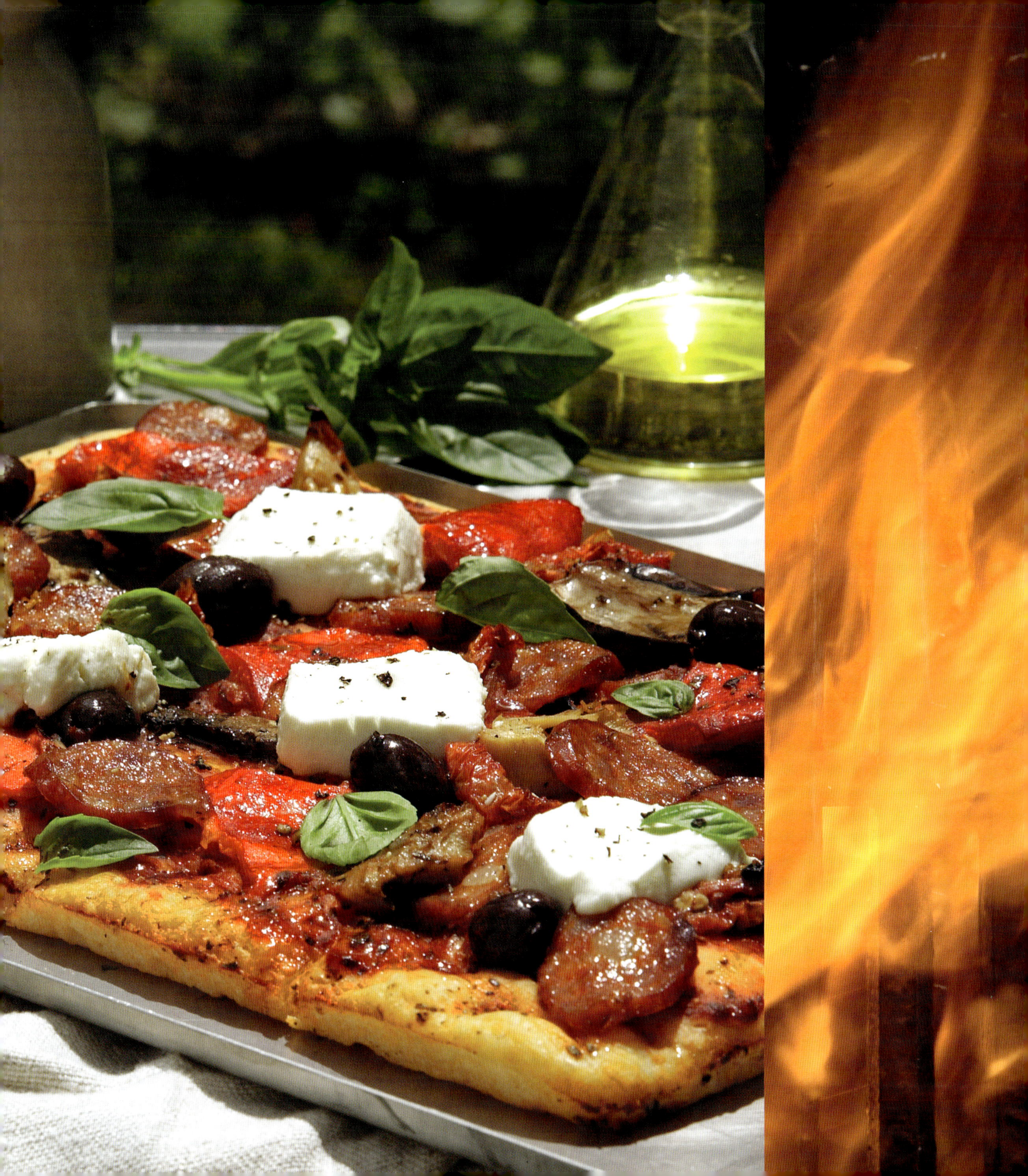

Basic Pizza Dough
8g (¹/₃oz) instant dried yeast
½ teaspoon caster sugar
¾ cup warm water
2 cups plain flour, sifted
1 tablespoon olive oil
½ teaspoon salt
Extra flour

For the Basic Pizza Dough

Place the yeast into a small bowl with the sugar and a ¼ cup of the warm water and stir to dissolve. This is ready to use when it starts to foam.

Make a well in the middle of the flour in a suitable bowl or you can heap the flour on a cool bench top and make a well in that. Put the oil and salt into the well, along with the dissolved yeast mixture, and begin stirring in the flour with spoon or using your hands as a whisk.

Add the remaining water, a little at a time, until all of it is absorbed and the mixture resembles dough. Knead for 8–10 minutes or until the dough is smooth and elastic.

Sprinkle a little flour into a large bowl, add the dough and sprinkle a little more flour on top. Put a damp tea towel over the top of the bowl and leave to rise in a draught-free, warm spot for an hour or until doubled in size.

Punch the dough down and knead for a few more minutes, then divide into three equal parts. Roll or stretch the dough to fit a 25cm lightly oiled pizza tray.

MAKES 3 X 23–25CM (9–10IN) PIZZA BASES OR ROLL OUT TO SUIT WHATEVER SHAPE PIZZA TRAYS YOU WANT TO USE.

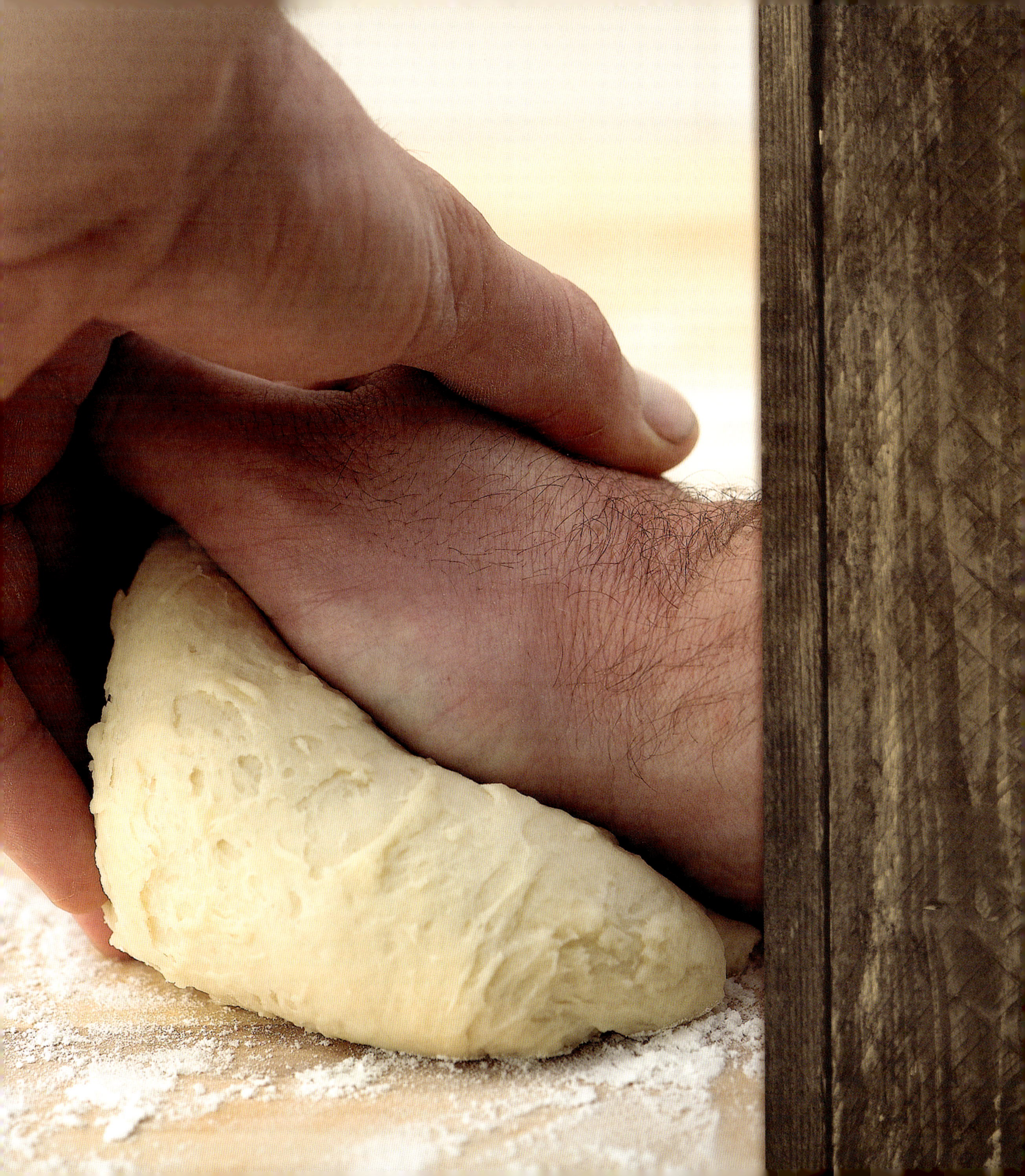

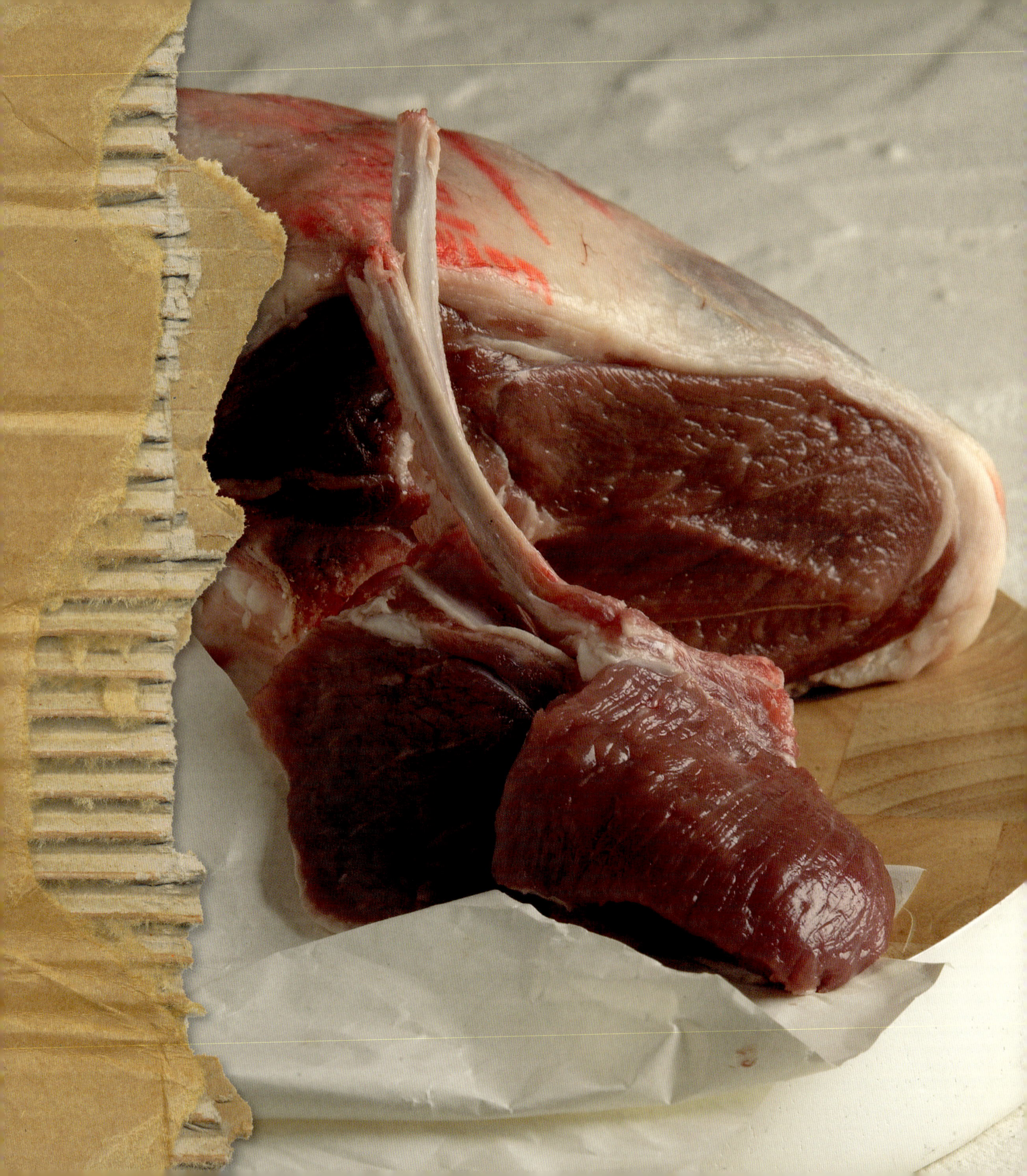

MAINS
MEAT

4 x 150g (5oz) lamb steaks
1 tablespoon cracked lemon pepper
4 large cos lettuce leaves, crisp and roughly sliced
16 pieces semi-roasted tomatoes
2 bocconcini, sliced into flat rounds
Flat bread such as ciabatta, sourdough or focaccia,
    cut into 4 equal pieces to suit size of steaks
Spray oil

BARBECUE LAMB SANDWICH WITH CHILLI CHIVE MAYO

This versatile sauce can be made by using a food processor or blender. Simply put the first five ingredients into the bowl. Work the machine until the mixture is light in colour and drizzle in the oil as for handmade mayo. If you add the olive oil too quickly, the mayonnaise will curdle. Should this happen, beat in 1 teaspoon of hot water and continue to add a little more oil to the mixture. A good thing to remember is that when using egg yolks in cooking, they cook very quickly so if you are doing a warm egg yolk sauce, such as a hollandaise, and the egg yolks look as though they will curdle, drop an ice cube into the mixture and whisk away from the heat.

Sprinkle the lamb steaks on both sides with the cracked lemon pepper.

Spray the lamb steaks with oil and cook for 2 minutes on one side, turn, cook one further minute, then lift to plate and let rest for 1 minute before assembling the sandwich.

Slice the flat bread pieces into halves and spray with oil to grill cut-side down. When charred, turn and mark/brown the other side of the bread.

To assemble the sandwich, take the base piece of bread and spread some of the mayonnaise mixture and put on individual plate. Equally distribute the cos and semi-roasted tomatoes on top of the base.

Serves 4

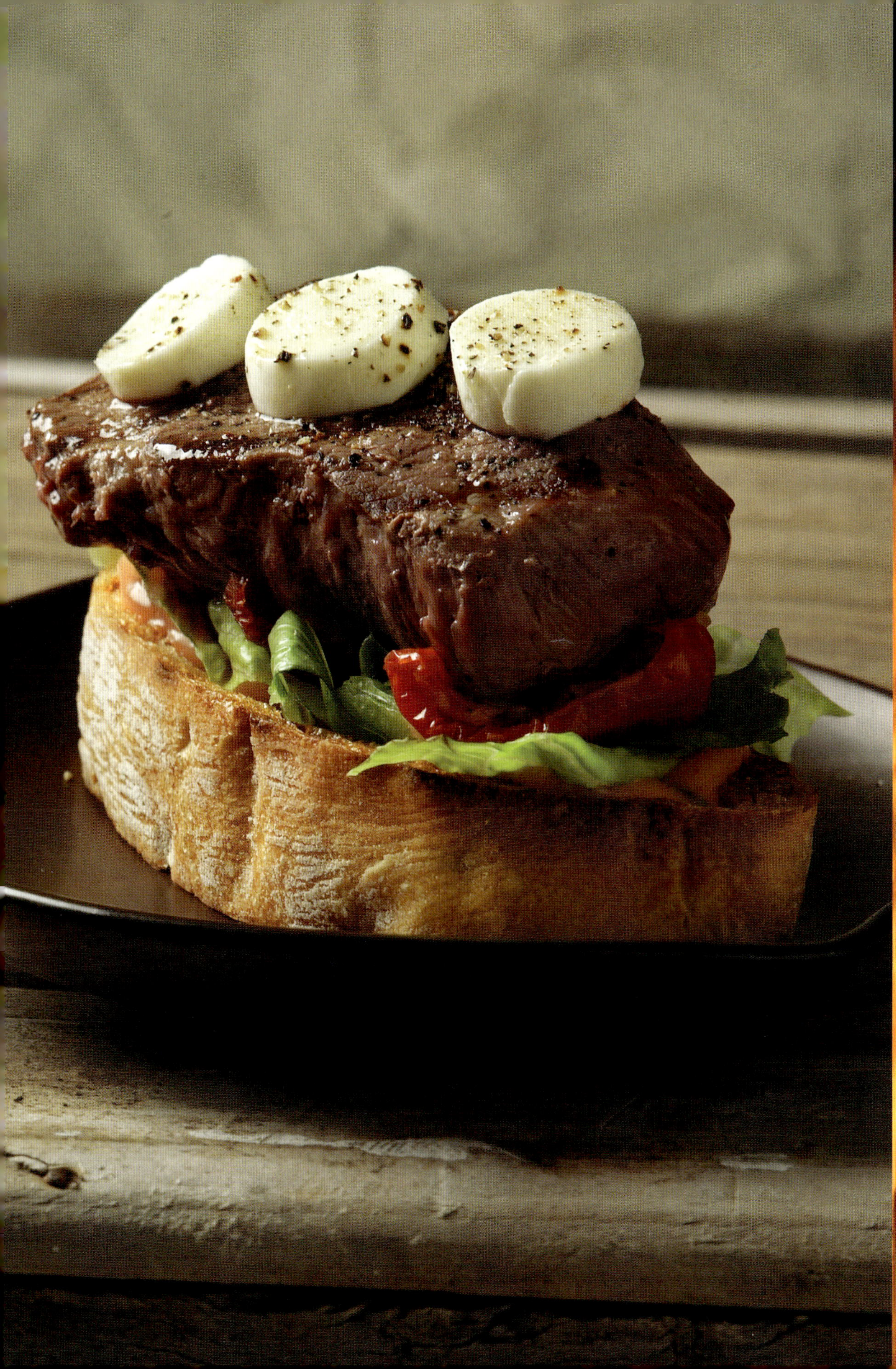

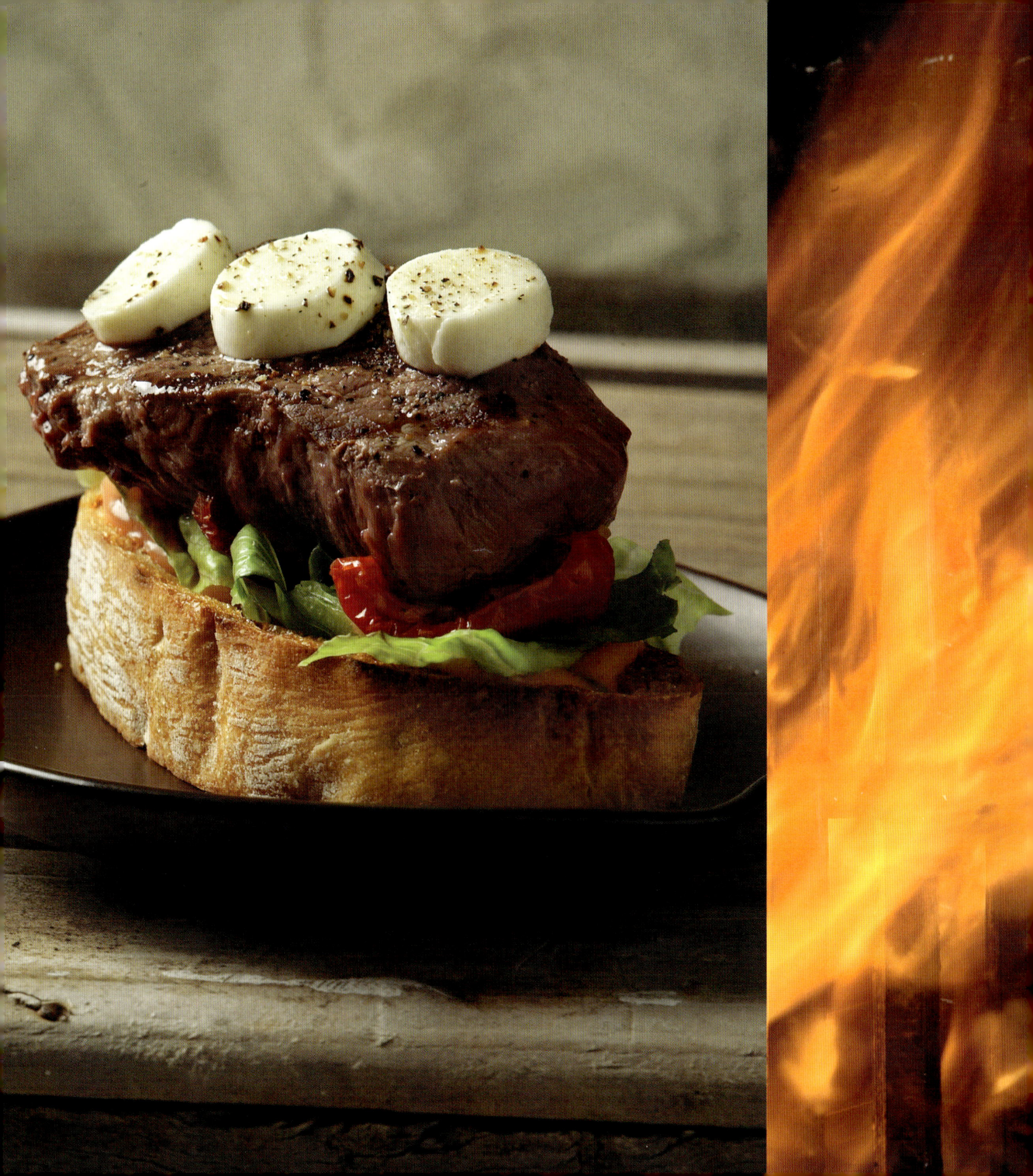

Chilli Chive Mayo

1 cup mayonnaise (a good supermarket one or handmade—see below)
¼ cup garlic chives, finely chopped
1 tablespoon hot chilli sauce
Mix all ingredients together.

Basic Handmade Mayonnaise

2 large egg yolks at room temperature
¼ teaspoon salt
Pinch white pepper
½ teaspoon prepared mustard (smooth Dijon is best)
1 teaspoon white vinegar
1 cup light olive or vegetable oil

Place the lamb on top of the tomatoes and spread the bocconcini evenly over the lamb. Spread some mayonnaise mixture on the top piece of bread and sit that on the bocconcini. Press each sandwich gently and then cut each sandwich on the diagonal.

For the Basic Handmade Mayonnaise

Place the egg yolks, salt, pepper, mustard and vinegar into a clean, warmed mixing bowl.

Secure the bowl by wrapping a damp tea towel around the base of the bowl–this will keep it steady.

With a balloon whisk, whisk the egg yolks and other ingredients until lightly golden. Whisk in the oil almost drop by drop until you have a third of the cup added. Slowly increase the flow of oil to a steady thin stream until all oil has been incorporated.

The mayonnaise will refrigerate for up to 5 days in an airtight container.

Serves 4

750g (2lb) sirloin steak, in one piece with all fat and connective tissue removed
Spray oil
½ cup coconut milk
½ cup green curry paste, prepared or made to recipe below
½ cup roasted peanuts, no skins and roughly chopped

2 cups coconut cream
1 tablespoon raw sugar or palm sugar
1 teaspoon salt or fish sauce
3 long green chillies, seeded and cut into fine strips
3 kaffir lime leaves, vein removed and cut into fine strips
Fresh coriander leaves

BARBECUED SIRLOIN & GREEN CURRY DRESSING

Make sure the beef is completely trimmed—refrigerate until ready to cook.

Make the dressing by bringing the coconut milk to the boil in a wok and cook for a minute–the milk will separate—then add the green curry paste and stir for 2 minutes. The liquid will become very fragrant.

Add two-thirds of the peanuts and the coconut cream and cook until heated through. Tip in the sugar and salt/fish sauce and stir. The liquid should now be heated, salty and sweet so adjust the flavours to your liking. Add the chillies and kaffir lime leaves, then remove from heat and stir for a minute.

Remove the beef from the refrigerator 10 minutes before use. Spray the beef with oil, put onto the very hot plate and seal for a minute on all sides. Then lift onto medium-hot grill and cook for 5–10 minutes on each side or until medium rare. This will depend on the thickness of the beef. Remove and let sit in a warm place for 20 minutes.

When the beef is ready, thinly slice and pack onto a shallow plate. Pour over the curry sauce, sprinkle in the remaining peanuts and rip the coriander leaves over the beef and sauce. Serve with steamed fragrant rice.

Serves 4

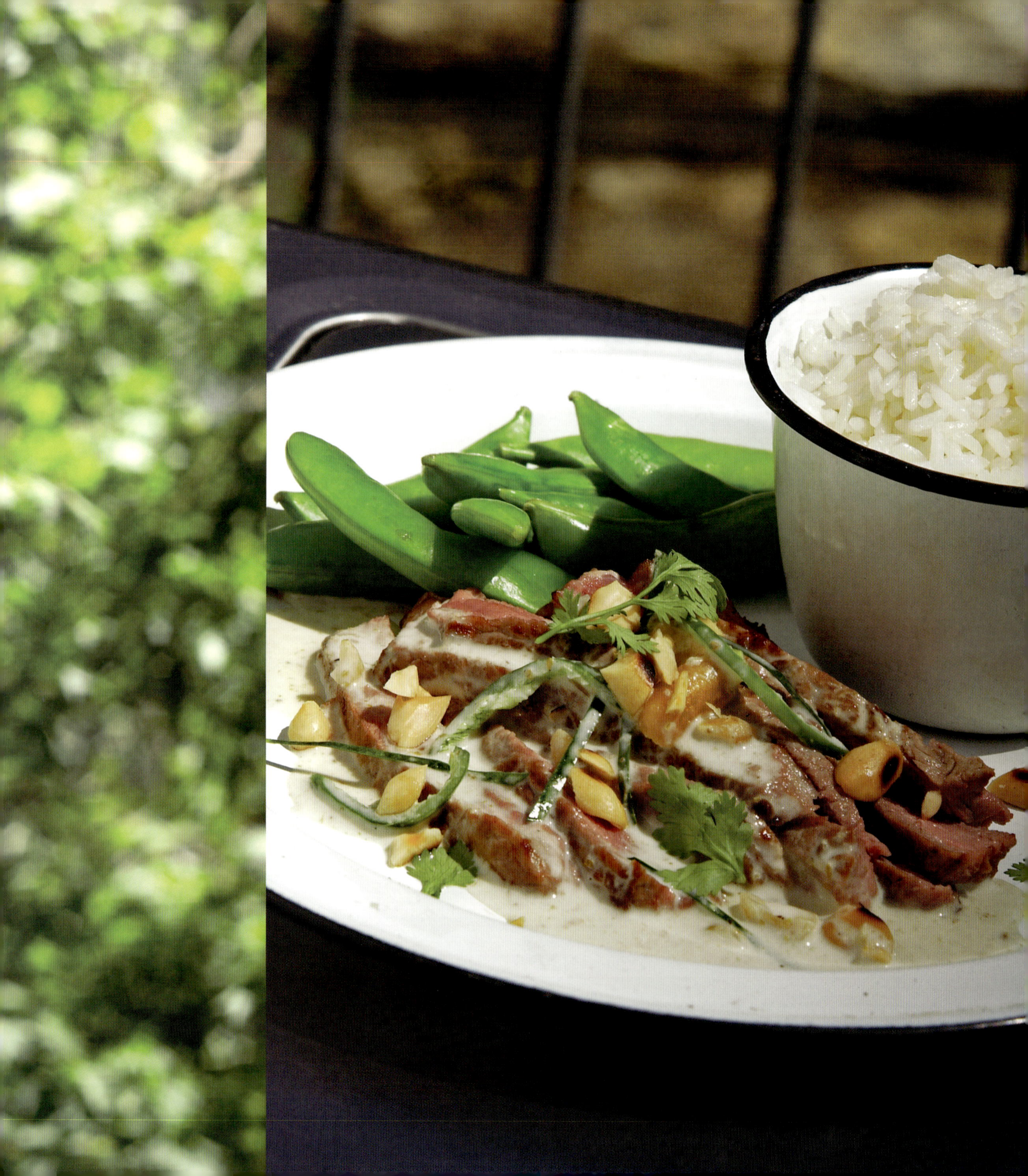

Green Curry Paste

1 teaspoon cumin seeds
2 teaspoons coriander seeds
2 green spring onions, trimmed, washed and finely sliced
3 cloves garlic, peeled and roughly chopped
1 red eschallot, peeled and chopped
3cm (1in) piece ginger, peeled and roughly chopped
1 tablespoon fish sauce
6 small green chillies, seeded and roughly chopped
3 kaffir lime leaves, vein removed and finely chopped
1 teaspoon roasted shrimp paste
1 tablespoon raw peanuts, roughly choppe

FOR THE GREEN CURRY PASTE

Dry fry the cumin and coriander seeds over medium heat for 1 minute or until lightly browned. Cool and then grind into a powder using a mortar and pestle or a special spice grinder.

Combine the green spring onions, garlic, eschallot, ginger, and fish sauce into a food processor or pound using a mortar and pestle. When a paste is forming, add the remaining ingredients including the cumin and coriander powder and work into a paste.

Keep in airtight container in the refrigerator for no longer than two days.

MAKES 1–2 CUPS

Homemade Barbecue Sauce
1 cup orange juice
1 cup ketchup
1 cup red wine
½ cup golden syrup/maple syrup
¼ cup malt vinegar
¼ cup onion, chopped

600g (21oz) rump steak, cut into cubes of 2cm (1in)
16 button mushrooms, stem removed and wiped clean
8 pickled onions, small, cut into halves
Bamboo or metal skewers—if using bamboo, soak in water for at least 30 minutes
Salt
Spray oil

BARBECUED BEEF & MUSHROOM KEBABS WITH HOMEMADE BARBECUE SAUCE

It is recommended by the mushroom growers of Australia to not ever wash mushrooms unless they are to be used immediately. The best way to clean mushrooms if they are to be cleaned at all is to wipe them individually and gently with a damp cloth.

Thread the different ingredients onto the skewer starting and finishing with a beef cube. Alternate with the mushrooms and the onion halves. Refrigerate until ready to use and then remove for 10 minutes before cooking.

Spray the kebabs with oil and cook on a hot plate for 2 minutes before turning to continue cooking. Sprinkle with salt as you turn.

Lift kebabs from the barbecue and serve with a good potato salad and the sauce on the side.

For the Homemade Barbecue Sauce
Make the sauce by blending all ingredients. Pour into a saucepan and simmer to reduce to a consistency of commercial tomato sauce, for about 15–20 minutes.

Serves 4

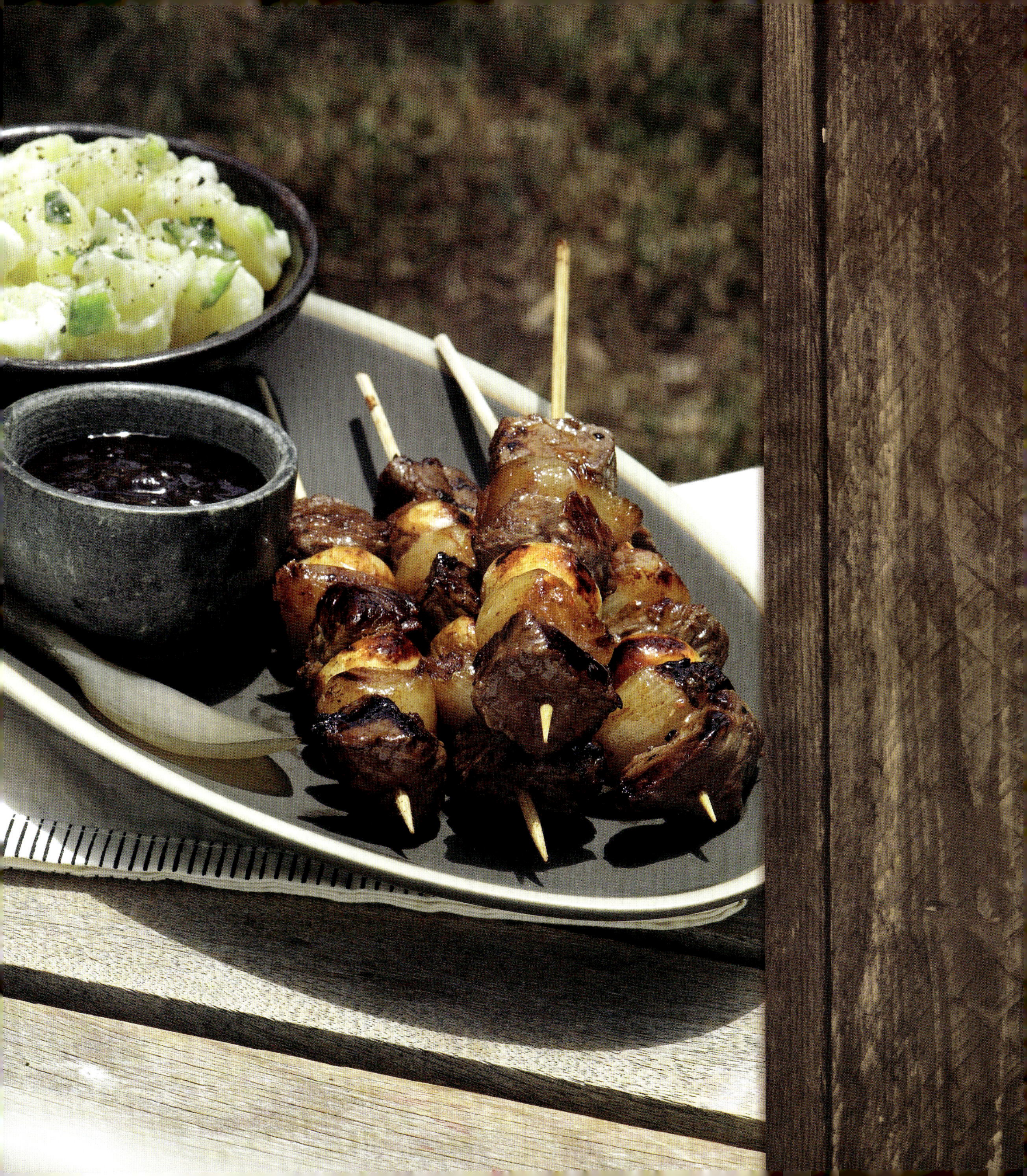

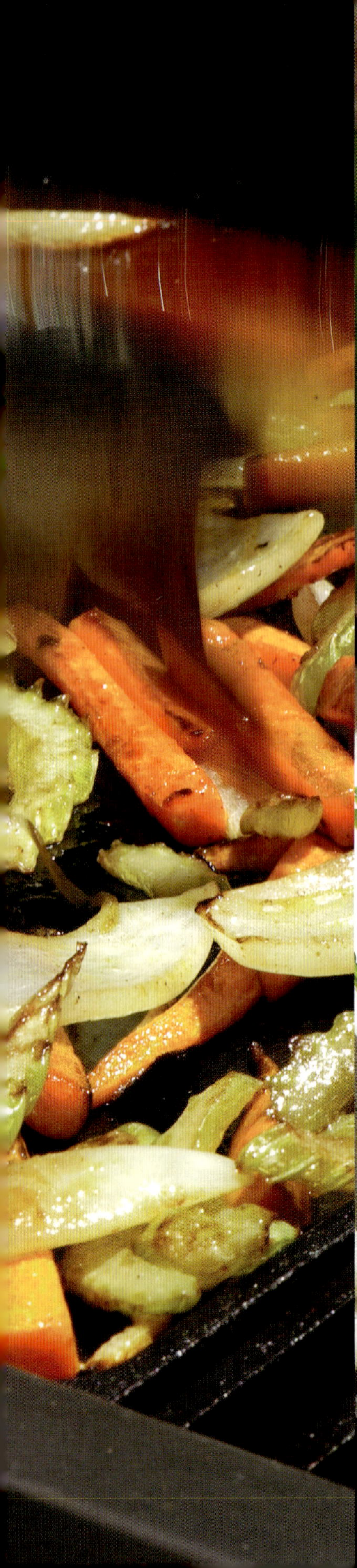
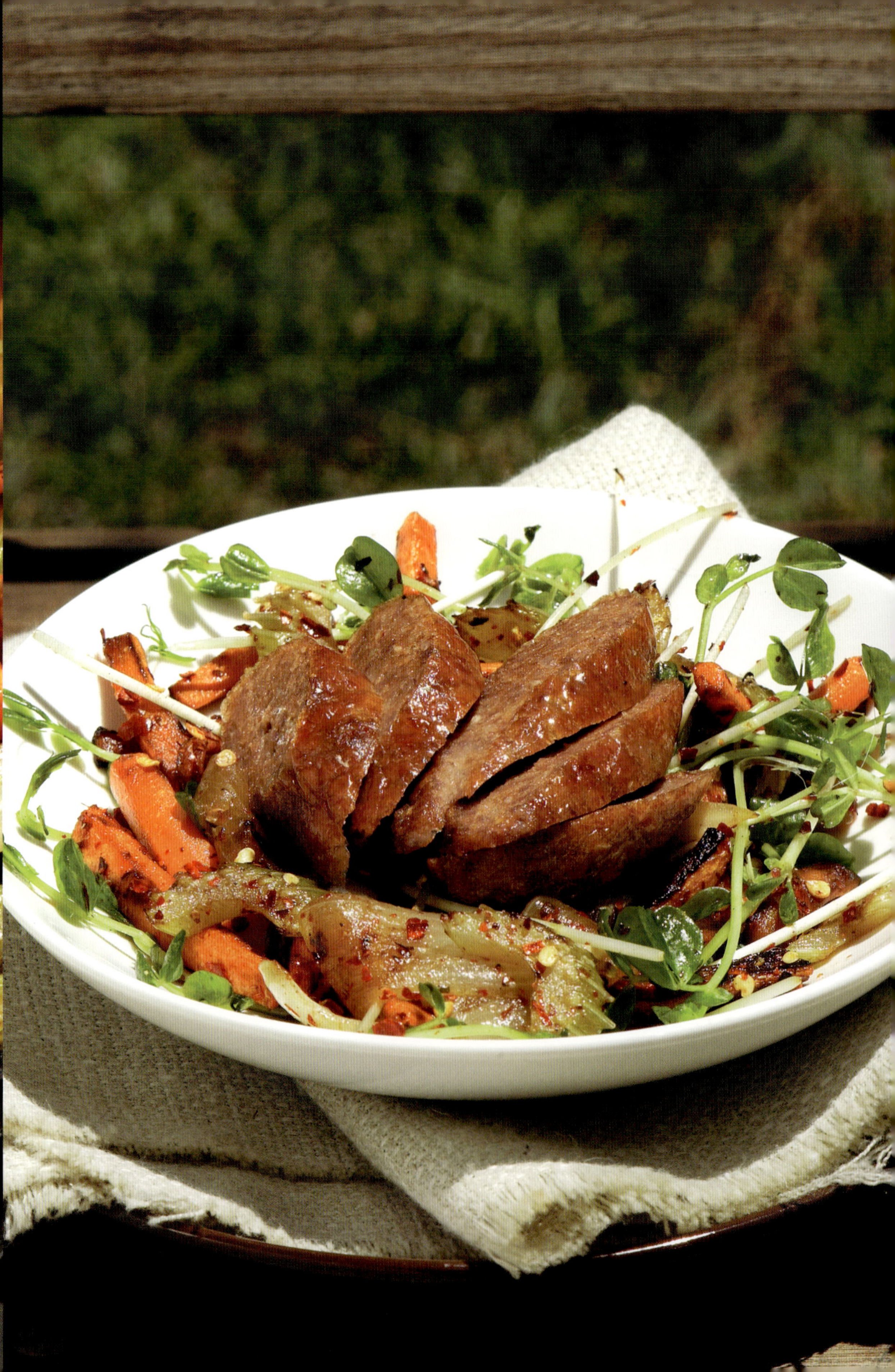

Garlic Oil
2 large heads of garlic
500ml (17fl oz) olive oil
Spray olive oil

8 good beef sausages,
¼ cup garlic oil (recipe below)
100g (4oz) celery, washed, finely sliced on the diagonal
100g (4oz) carrot, peeled and trimmed, cut into strips/batons
1 medium onion, peeled, halved and cut into wedges
½ teaspoon dried crushed chilli
1 cup of mung bean sprouts or snow pea sprouts
½ cup mirin

BEEF SAUSAGES & BARBECUE VEGETABLE STIRFRY

Put the sausages on a medium-hot grill and cook, turning regularly. If the sausages are really thick you are better to blanch them first to speed up the cooking. When the sausages are nearly done, start the stirfry.

The stirfry can be done in a traditional way in the wok on the barbecue or on the plate.

Pour half the oil onto the flat plate and add the celery, carrots and onion. With two spatulas, lift and move the vegetables around the plate. Cook for a minute and add the chilli. Continue to toss and cook a further 2 minutes. Add the sprouts, the rest of the oil and the Mirin and continue to cook for another 2 minutes. Be careful here as the Mirin will evaporate and cause steam which can cause burns.

Lift the cooked vegetables onto a platter and top with the sausages.

For the Garlic Oil
Cut the garlic heads across the middle to have two roundish halves. Spray the cut side of the garlic and place it, cut-side down, onto a medium-hot plate. Cook for 2–4 minutes so the garlic is browned.

Remove from the heat and put into airtight storage container. Cover with oil and leave to sit for three days before use. The oil will keep, refrigerated or in a really cool place, for 6–7 days and can be used in many other ways.

Serves 4

1.5kg (3lb) boneless leg of lamb, butterflied
½ cup fresh rosemary leaves only, roughly chopped
1 tablespoon celery salt
½ teaspoon black pepper, freshly ground
½ teaspoon coriander powder
½ teaspoon mild Indian curry
Olive oil
Pastry brush or similar

BONELESS LEG OF LAMB WITH ROSEMARY RUB

By leaving the meat to sit or rest, the juices settle and the meat carves easily. The juices in the base of the platter are delicious and best spooned over the sliced meat.

Lay the leg of lamb out as flat as possible and ensure that the meat has an even thickness. This can be difficult as the muscle structure varies and so you may have to slice the meat to flatten it. Skewer into place to maintain a flat appearance.

Mix the rosemary, salt, pepper, coriander and curry. With your fingers, sprinkle/spread half the rub ingredients over the cut side of the lamb and then massage it in.

Put the leg of lamb onto a medium-hot grill cut-side down. Cook for five minutes.

Lightly brush the skin side of lamb with oil and turn the leg over to cook for 10–15 minutes with the hood down.

Brush the partially cooked cut side with a little oil and sprinkle over the remaining rub. Turn the meat over again, drop the hood, and leave to cook on the skin side for 10 minutes.

Turn the leg one more time to the open flesh side and cook a further 10–15 minutes with the hood down. Remove from the barbecue and let rest for 5 minutes. Slice the meat and serve with salads or vegetables of your choice.

Serves 4

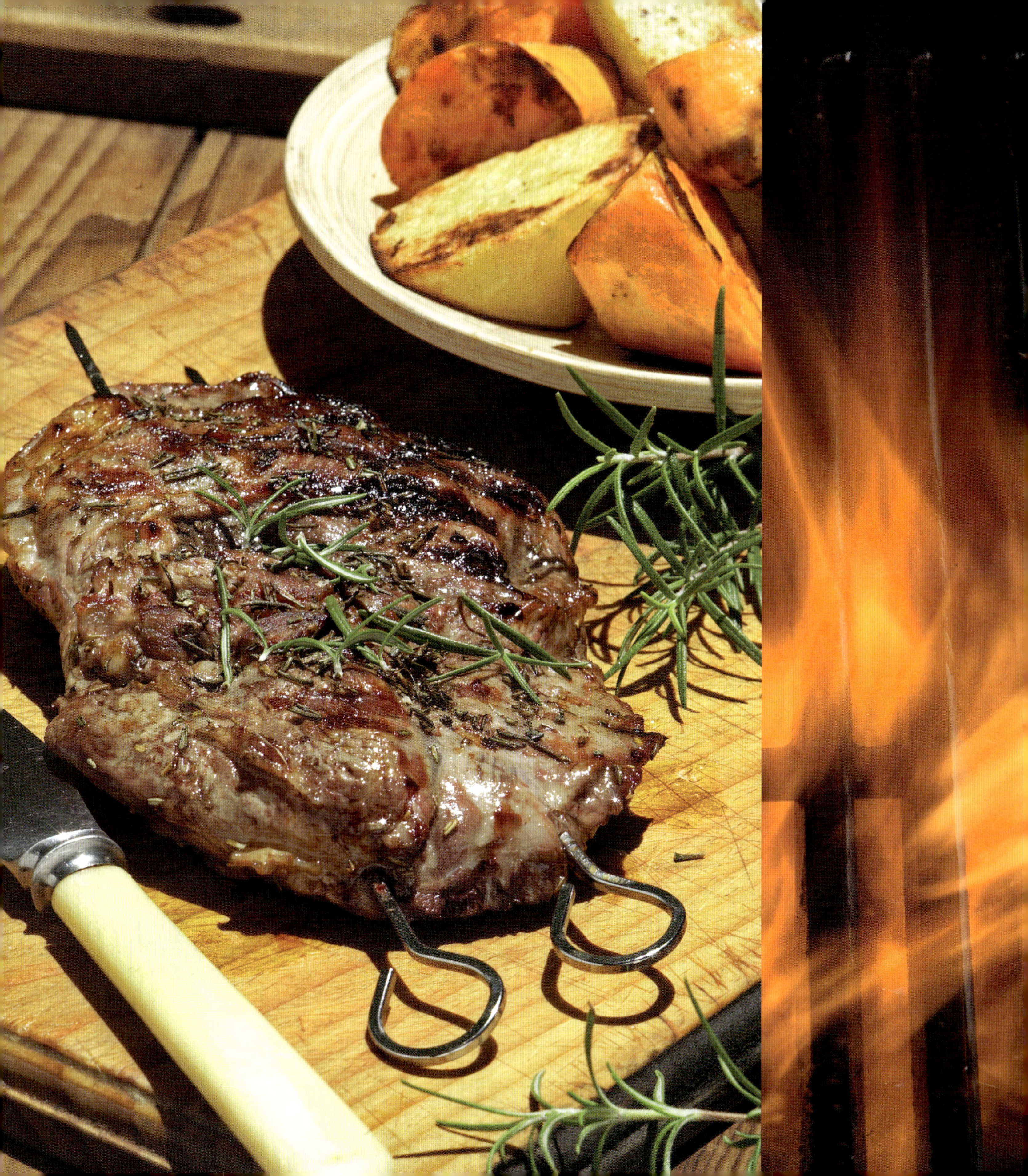

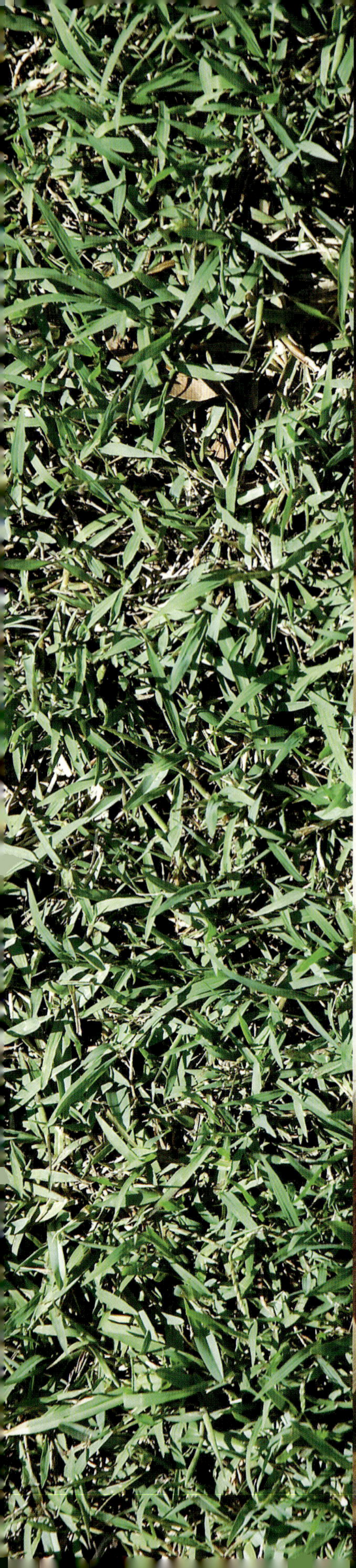

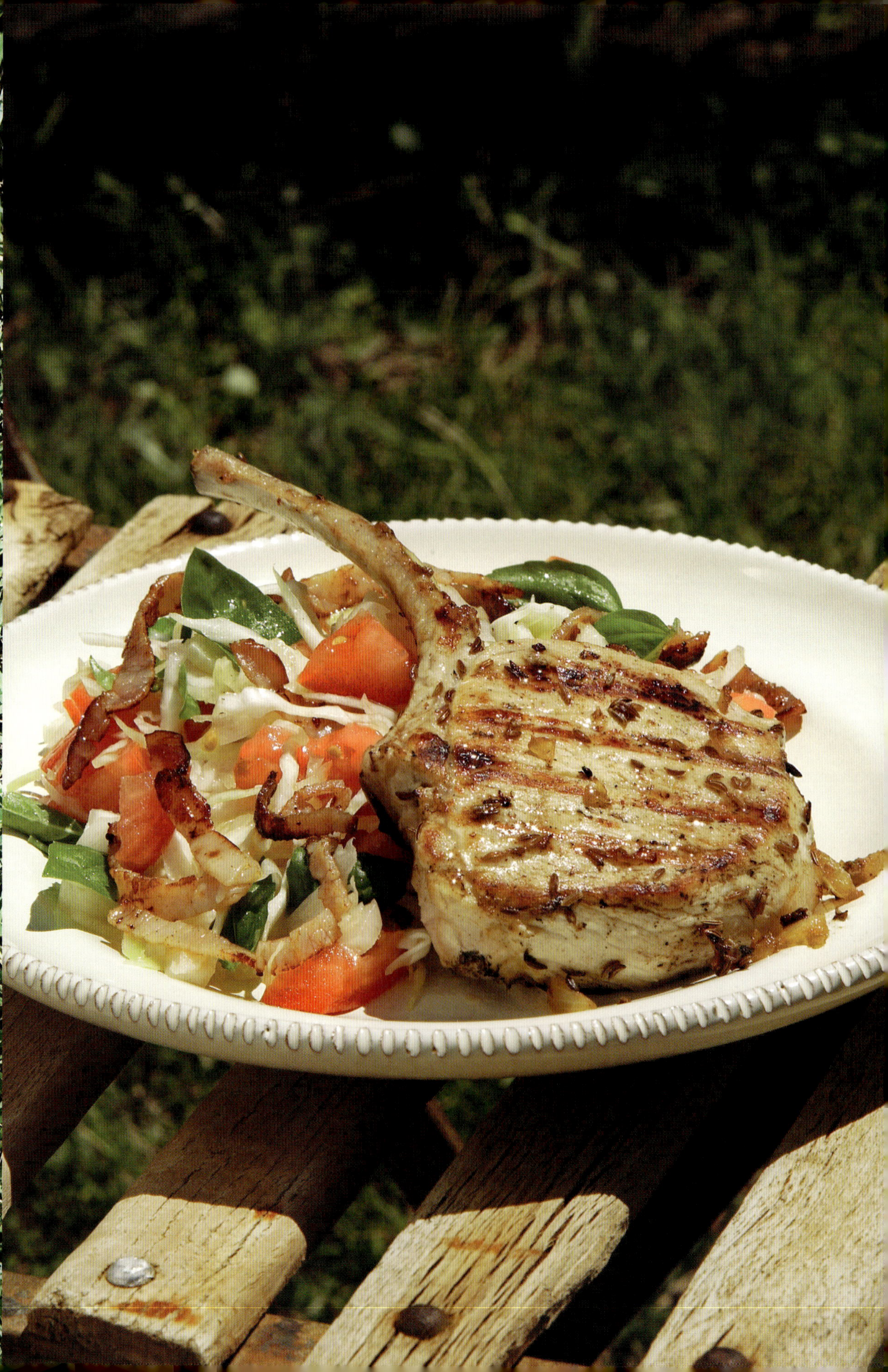

4–8 pork cutlets, depending on size
1 teaspoon caraway seeds
1 cup beer
2 tablespoons onion, finely diced
2–3 bay leaves
4 cups savoy cabbage, core removed and finely shredded

1 cup basil leaves
2 large ripe tomatoes, roughly chopped
1 small white onion, roughly chopped
¼ cup verjuice
2 tablespoons extra virgin olive oil
2 rashers bacon, rind removed and cut into fine strips
Salt to taste

CARAWAY PORK CUTLETS WITH BASIL & TOMATO SLAW

Trim any excess fat from the pork and place in glass bowl. Tip in the caraway seeds, beer, small diced onion and the bay leaves. Move the cutlets around to let them soak in the beer for 10 minutes.

Put the cabbage into a bowl and rip the basil leaves over the top. Add the tomatoes and onion. Pour in the verjuice and olive oil, add salt and tumble to combine.

Cook bacon pieces on a hot plate until crisp and when done, lift onto a paper toweling lined plate; cool before adding to the slaw and combine.

Put the cutlets onto the plate where the bacon has been and cook on each side for 2 minutes to seal the pork. Spoon a little of the beer and caraway seeds onto the pork as it cooks.

To finish the cutlets, flash them on a very hot grill on both sides.

Spoon some 'slaw' onto the middle of individual plates and sit the pork cutlets on top. Serve any remaining 'slaw' in the middle of the table.

SERVES 4

500g (1lb) rump steak
2 tablespoons light olive oil
2 tablespoons sherry vinegar
1 teaspoon Mexican chilli powder
½ tablespoon ground allspice
½ tablespoon oregano powder
1 teaspoon salt
2 cups lettuce, shredded
2 medium salad tomatoes, cut into wedges
1 large red onion, chopped
1 cup cheddar cheese, grated
2 tablespoons coriander leaves, chopped
8 tacos

CHILLI BEEF STRIPS TACOS

Cut the steak across the grain into 1cm (½in) wide strips and place in bowl.

Mix the oil, vinegar, chilli powder, allspice, oregano and salt. Pour over the steak strips and stir to coat the pieces. Cover and refrigerate for at least 2 hours.

Spray the flat plate with oil and tip on the strips. Spread over the plate and cook by tossing and lifting the pieces and allowing them to brown.

The meat will cook in 5–6 minutes and, when done, lift the strips onto a large platter with heaped lettuce, tomatoes, onion and cheese.

Heat 8 taco shells (Stand 'n Stuff are good) in the barbecue at 180°C (350°F).

Serve all the various components in the middle of the table so everyone can stuff their own tacos—meat first into the shell followed by lettuce, tomato, onion, cheese and coriander.

SERVES 4

600g (21oz) boneless loin of lamb
Large toothpicks
12 slices Desiree potatoes, 2cm (1in) thick rounds, par-boiled
200g (7oz) spinach leaves, washed and de-stemmed
½ cup croutons
Caesar dressing
1 large rasher bacon, rind removed and cut into 3cm (1in) lengths

BUTTERFLIED LOIN LAMB WITH GRILLED POTATO & CAESAR SPINACH SALAD

Cut the loin of lamb into 8 even pieces and then cut each piece almost through. Open out into butterfly shape about 2cm (1in) thick. Slip a large toothpick through to hold the butterflied piece of lamb in place.

Spray potato slices on both sides and grill over medium heat, turning regularly, on both sides until crisp and cooked through. Put the bacon pieces onto the medium-hot plate and cook until crisp.

Partially prepare the Caesar salad by placing the spinach and croutons in a bowl and refrigerate.

Spray each lamb butterfly with oil and place on a medium-hot plate for 2 minutes. Spray with oil and turn and cook for 2 minutes. It is important that as you turn each lamb steak, you hold it in place for a couple of seconds by pressing on top with a spatula which stops the lamb from curling.

Lift the bacon onto some kitchen paper toweling and drain.

To serve, place three slices of potato in the middle of individual plates and top with two lamb steaks with the toothpicks removed. Place the bacon into the spinach salad and add the dressing. Toss the leaves to coat and serve in the middle of the table.

SERVES 4

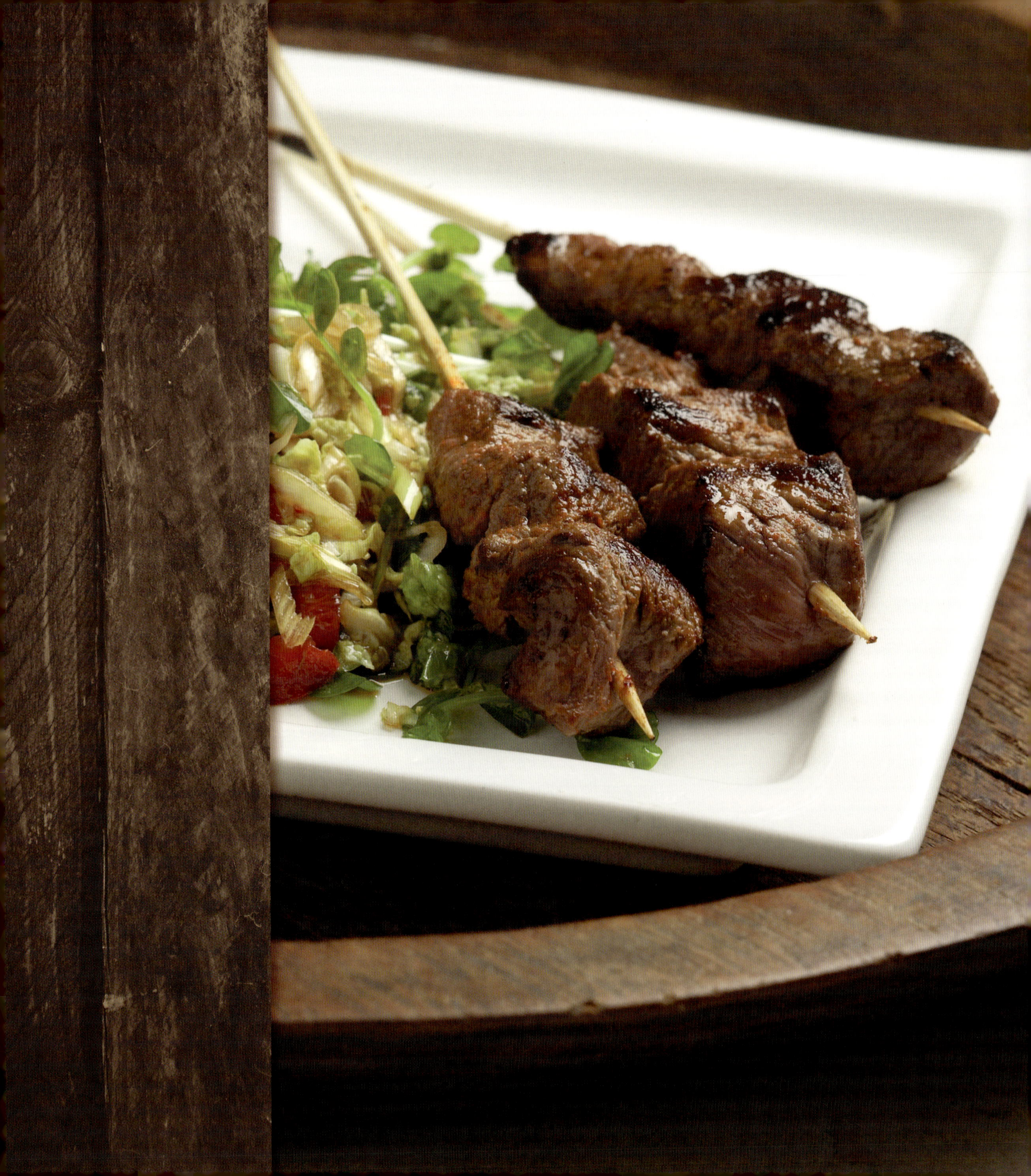

500g (1lb) lean lamb strips
4 stainless steel skewers (lightly oiled) or bamboo skewers that have been soaked in water for
   30 minutes
½ teaspoon chilli powder
4 lime cheeks

Asian Slaw
4 cups shredded Chinese cabbage
½ cup finely sliced spring onions
½ cup diced red capsicum
60g (2oz) snow pea sprouts
¼ cup low-salt soy sauce
1 tablespoon green ginger, minced
1 small red chilli, seeds in and minced
1 teaspoon sesame oil
1 teaspoon palm sugar
2 tablespoon lime juice

CHILLI LAMB SKEWERS & ASIAN SLAW

The addition of lemon to the lamb is an old favourite of lamb eaters—the Greeks love it with barbecued lamb. The acid (from the squeezed lemon juice) cuts down the fat in this recipe so the fat is almost non-existent.

I like to make the slaw and use immediately. It loses its crunch if you let it sit for any period of time with the dressing. If you are serving this to guests, you can have the cabbage partly done, covered with cling wrap and refrigerated, and the same for the dressing. Mix to combine as you need this delicious slaw.

Buy the lamb already in strips if you like; however it is best to cut them from lamb mini roasts which I use to get 2cm (1in) strips. Thread equal amounts on to skewers in an 'S' shape. Sprinkle evenly with the chilli and let sit for 5 minutes.

Asian Slaw
Make the slaw by combining the cabbage, onion, capsicum and snow pea sprouts. In a separate container, mix the soy, ginger, chilli, oil, sugar and lime juice. Stir well and pour over the cabbage mix and toss well.

Cook the oil-sprayed lamb on a medium-hot plate which will cook in 5 minutes or leave longer for well done. Serve each skewer of lamb on top of equal amounts of slaw and with a lime cheek on each plate.

Serves 4

400g (14oz) green beans
1 small Spanish onion, peeled and finely diced
½ cup vinaigrette dressing (see recipe below)
1 x 350g (12oz) kumara (sweet potato or yam)
8 x 100g (4oz) lamb loin chops,
    about 2cm (1in) thick
Spray oil

Traditional Vinaigrette
3 tablespoons olive oil
1 clove garlic, minced
½ teaspoon smooth Dijon mustard
2 tablespoons white wine vinegar
1 tablespoon parsley, finely chopped
½ teaspoon salt
¼ teaspoon white pepper

LAMB CHOPS WITH GREEN BEAN SALAD & KUMARA

For the Traditional Vinaigrette

For the very best results, this dressing must be done by hand. Put the oil, garlic and mustard in a large bowl and whisk until the mixture is creamy in consistency and light yellow in colour. The whisking aerates and blends extremely well.

Whisk in the vinegar and add the parsley and salt and pepper and continue stirring until well mixed.

Top, tail and wash the green beans, place in bowl and pour over boiling water to cover. Leave to sit for 30 seconds, drain and run under very cold water.

Trim the kumara if it has thin ends and cook in the microwave at 70 per cent for 4 minutes. Spray the kumara with oil, place on a medium grill and cook until done. Turn every 5 minutes.

Tip the green beans onto an oiled, medium-hot plate and turn regularly just to heat through—try not to brown. Put the reheated beans into a bowl, add the onion and vinaigrette and toss. Allow to cool.

Grill the chops over medium heat—note there is no need to spray. Cook for 3 minutes on each side or longer if you like.

To serve, slice the kumara into even rounds and equally distribute into the centre of individual plates. Top with equal amounts of green bean salad and add two lamb loin chops to each plates.

Serves 4

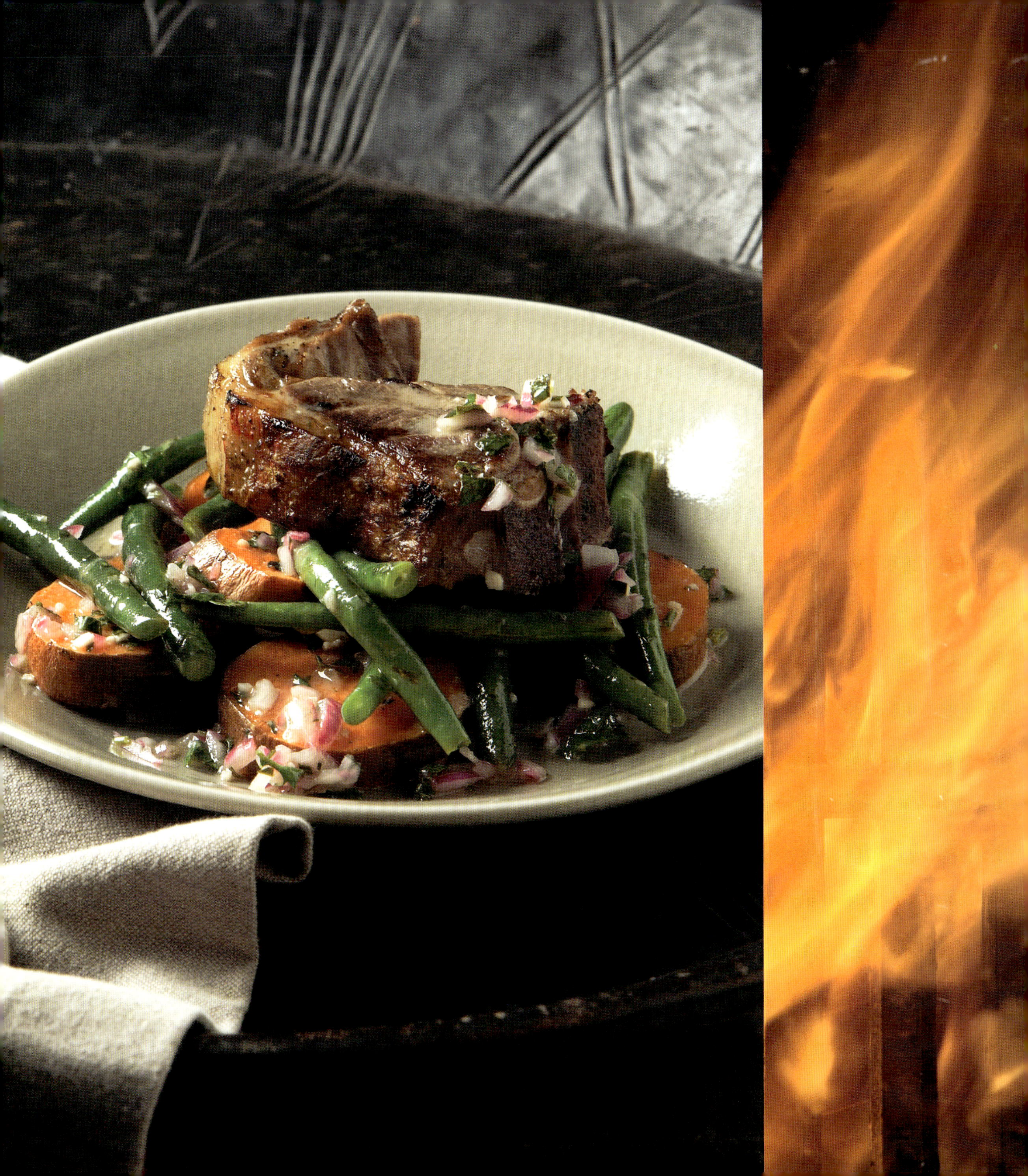

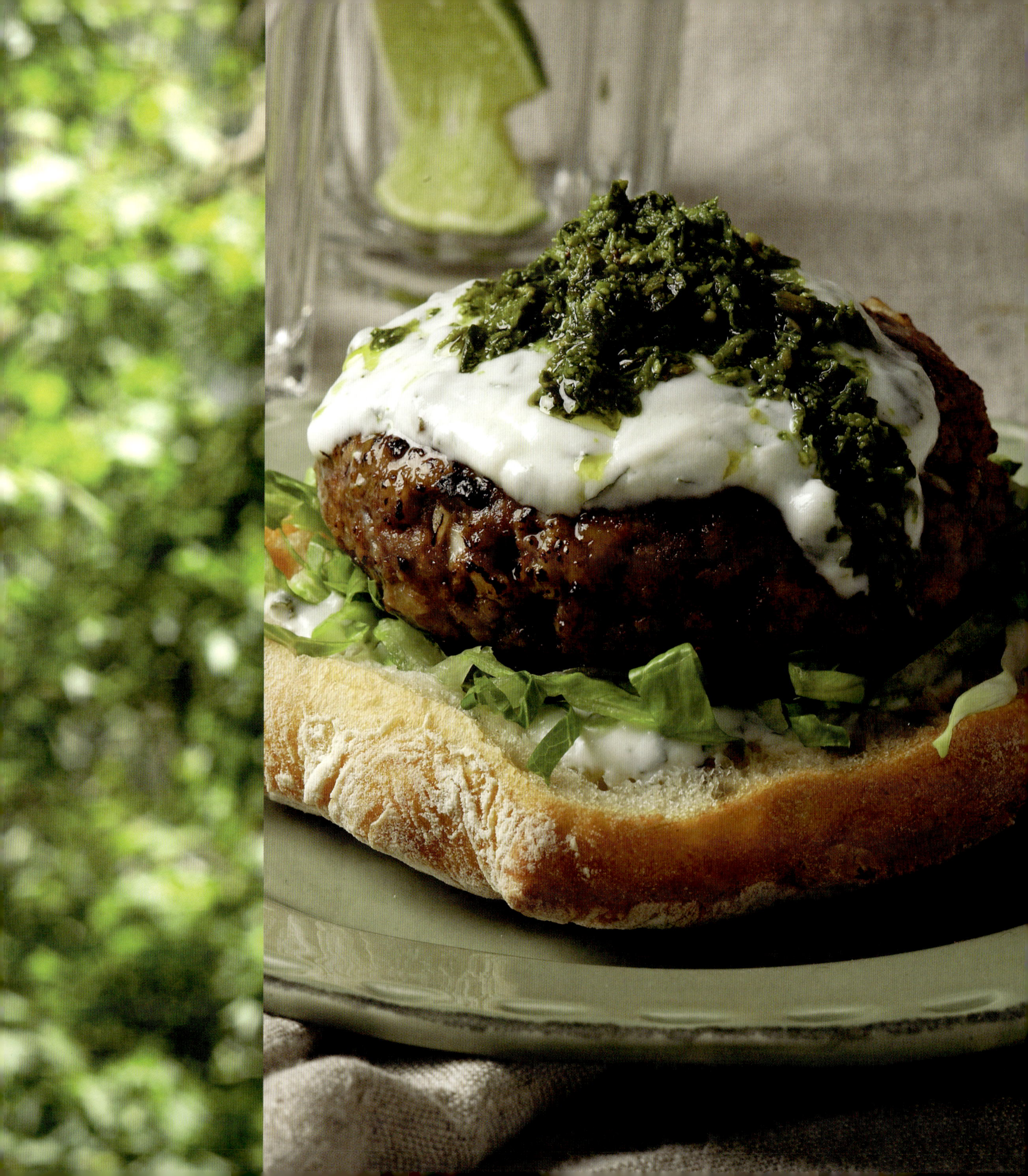

Mint Pesto
1 cup fresh mint, washed and tightly packed
1 tablespoon pinenuts, roasted to a light brown colour
1 large clove garlic, roughly chopped
⅓ cup walnut oil
30g (1oz) parmesan cheese, grated
Salt

4 large bread rolls
600g (1lb) lean lamb mince
2 eggs
1 teaspoon sweet chilli sauce
1 tablespoon Worcestershire sauce
60g (2oz) onion, finely diced
1 tablespoon extra virgin olive oil
½ teaspoon salt
2 cups shredded lettuce
300ml (10fl oz) plain yoghurt
½ cup mint, finely chopped

LAMB BURGERS WITH MINTED YOGHURT & MINT PESTO

Cut the bread rolls in half and pull out the centre of each half so that you have a well. Break the bread that you have removed into really small pieces and add to it the lamb, eggs, sauces, onion, oil and salt.

Mix well, using your hands. The bread you have used is enough to be the binder, however if your mixture is too moist, add enough dried breadcrumbs to take up that excess liquid. Shape into four even patties. Cover and refrigerate for at least 1 hour.

For the Mint Pesto
Put the mint, pinenuts and garlic into a food processor and blend for 30 seconds. Slowly add the oil and then the cheese and salt to taste and work to a smoothish paste. This pesto must be used as soon as possible because it darkens very quickly and does not store.

Spray the patties with oil and cook on a medium-hot plate and finish with a burst on the grill. Turn only once or twice. The juices coming out on top should be clear for well done.

Mix the yoghurt and mint and spoon some into the well of the bread roll base and top with equal amounts of lettuce, then add a cooked pattie and spoon over more yoghurt and finish with mint pesto.

Add the top half of the bread and press down to compress the fillings and to make it easier to eat.

Serves 4

500g (1lb) beef, lean minced
1 cup breadcrumbs, dry
1 small onion, chopped
1 tablespoon ginger, minced
1 tablespoon parsley, chopped
1 teaspoon salt
1 teaspoon white pepper, ground finely
1 tablespoon orange zest, finely grated, and juice of that orange
1 large egg, beaten
2 tablespoons seeded Dijon mustard
Olive oil

Mushroom Ragout
1½ tablespoons butter
60g (2oz) green spring onions, chopped
3 cloves garlic, minced
400g (14oz) assorted mushrooms, roughly chopped (use wild or exotic mushrooms such as shitake as well as regular ones)
300ml (10fl oz) demi-glace (from a good deli, butcher or supermarket or make it yourself see Blue Eye with Pea Mash and Cabernet Jus recipe, page 258)
¼ cup red wine
1 tablespoon fresh marjoram, chopped
½ teaspoon salt

ORANGE-SCENTED MEATLOAF & MUSHROOM RAGOUT

If the foil you have on hand is thin, use 2–3 sheets, shiny side in.

Combine all ingredients, except for the olive oil, and mix thoroughly. Take a large sheet of thick foil and brush with olive oil. Tip the mixture onto the foil and shape into a sausage shape, 23cm (9in) long by 6cm (2in) in diameter. Wrap the foil around to hold the meat in place and twist the ends to seal. Refrigerate for at least 1 hour and prepare the mushroom ragout.

Put onto a medium-hot plate, hood down and cook for 30 minutes, turning every 10 minutes to ensure even cooking. Remove from barbecue and rest for 10 minutes before peeling away the foil.

Slice and serve on top of the mushroom ragout in deep-welled individual plates with a green vegetable of your choice or seasonal salad.

For the Mushroom Ragout

Melt the butter in a saucepan and add the spring onions and garlic. Cook for 2 minutes. Add the mushrooms, demi-glace and red wine to bring to the boil, then simmer for at least 1 hour. Add the marjoram and salt and cook for a further 5 minutes.

Serves 4–6

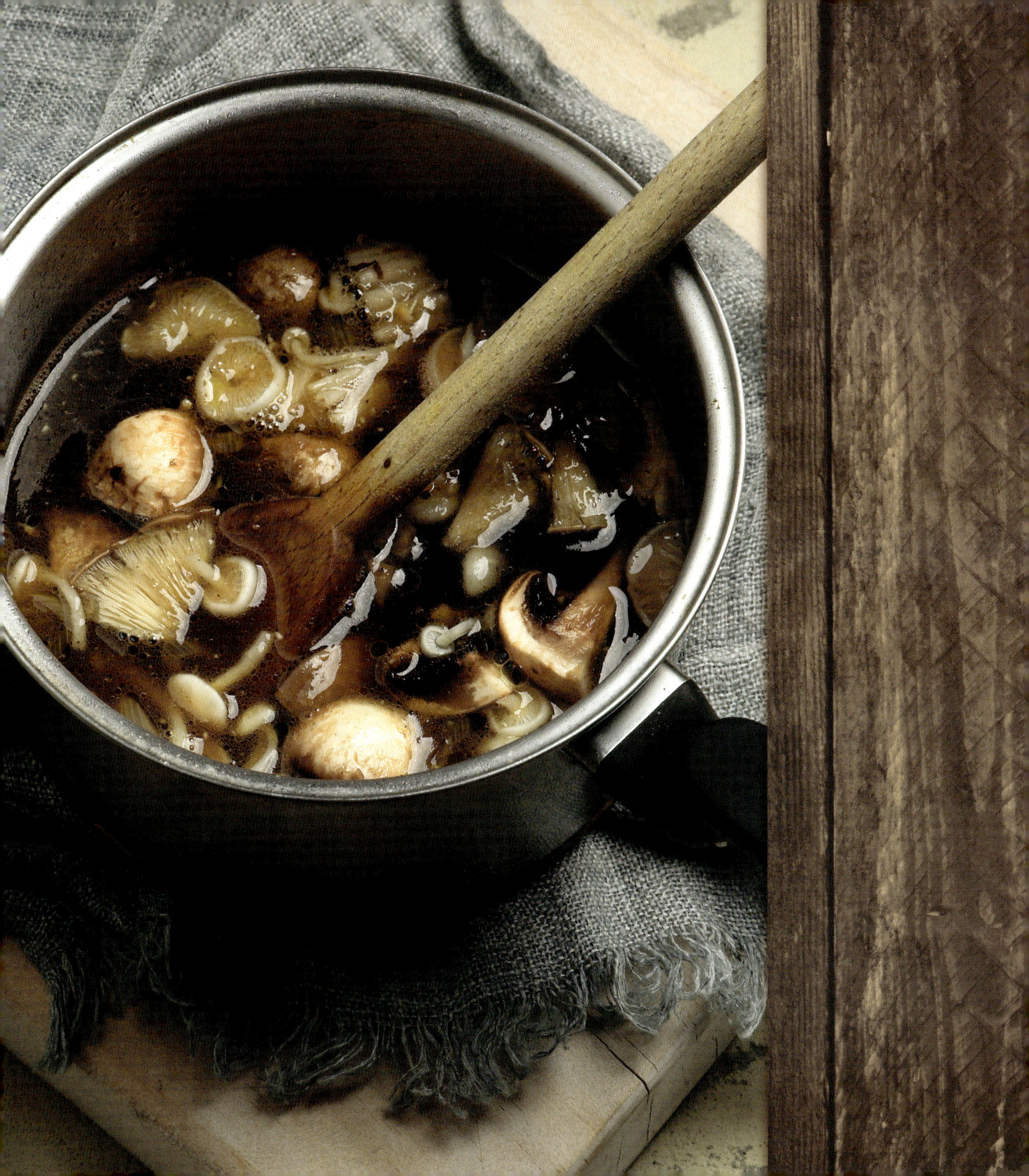

4–8 pork chops, depending on size
120g (4oz) blue cheese of your choice,
    crumbled
1 tablespoon white vinegar
1 tablespoon spring onion, finely chopped
1 cup mayonnaise
400g (14oz) mashed potatoes,
    at room temperature
4 tablespoons canned corn kernels, drained
1 egg, beaten
Salt and white pepper to taste
Dry breadcrumbs
Spray oil

PORK CHOPS WITH BLUE CHEESE MAYO & SWEETCORN POTATO CAKES

Trim the pork chops of the rind if you like. Set to one side.

Whisk the cheese and vinegar until the combined, stir in the onion and fold in the mayonnaise.

Make the potato cakes by mixing the potatoes, corn, egg and salt and pepper together. Add enough breadcrumbs to take up the moisture and to make a firm mixture. Evenly divide the potato mixture and shape into patties. Refrigerate if not using immediately.

Cook the chop/s on a hot plate and when nearly done, move to the hot grill plate to complete the cooking. Leave on the plate if thick and reduce heat to cook through.

Spray the potato cakes until lightly browned on each side of the hot plate.

Serve cakes with the pork chops; spoon sauce over the chops or serve on the side. Freshly steamed broccoli completes this dish.

SERVES 4

MAINS | MEAT

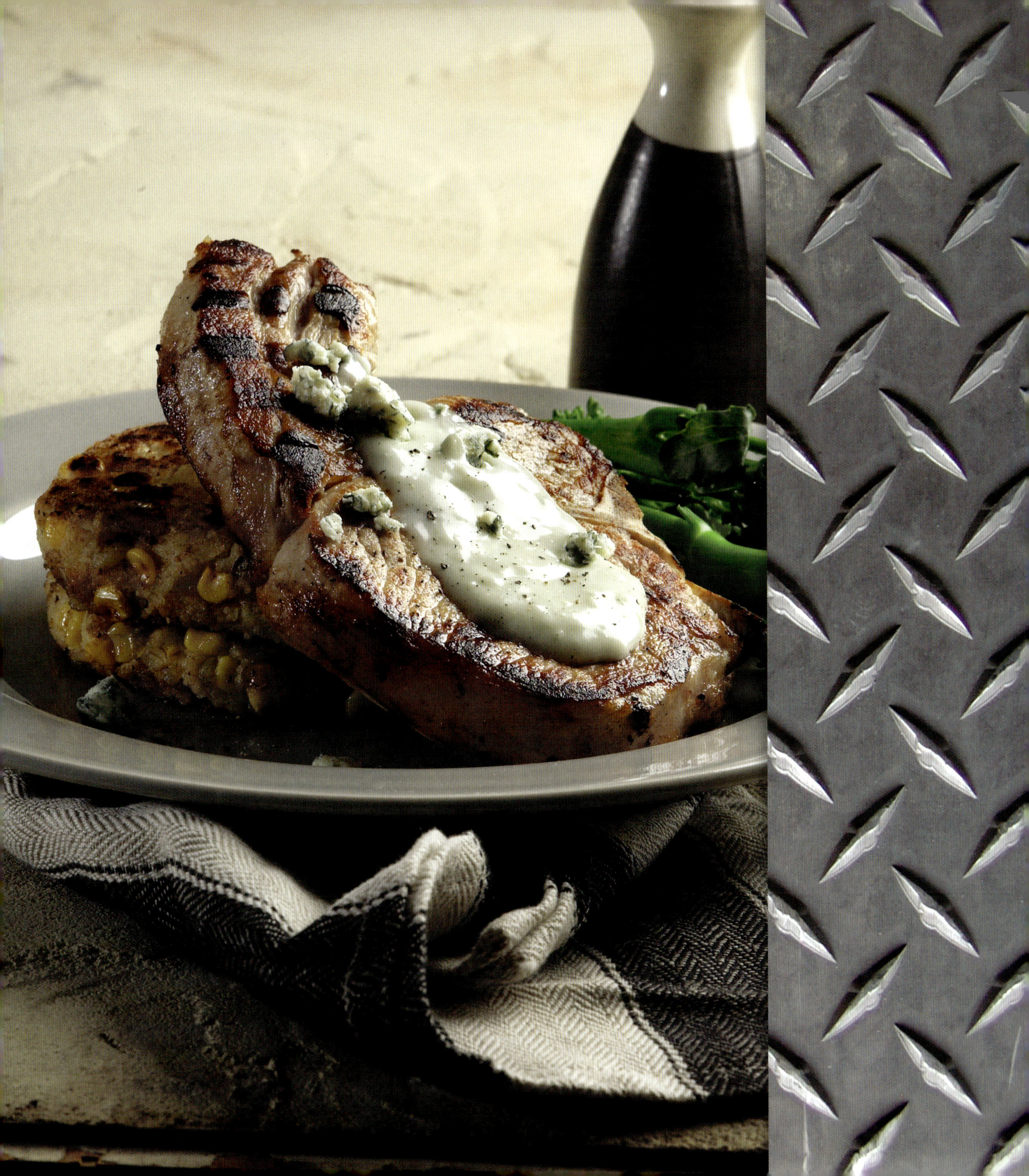

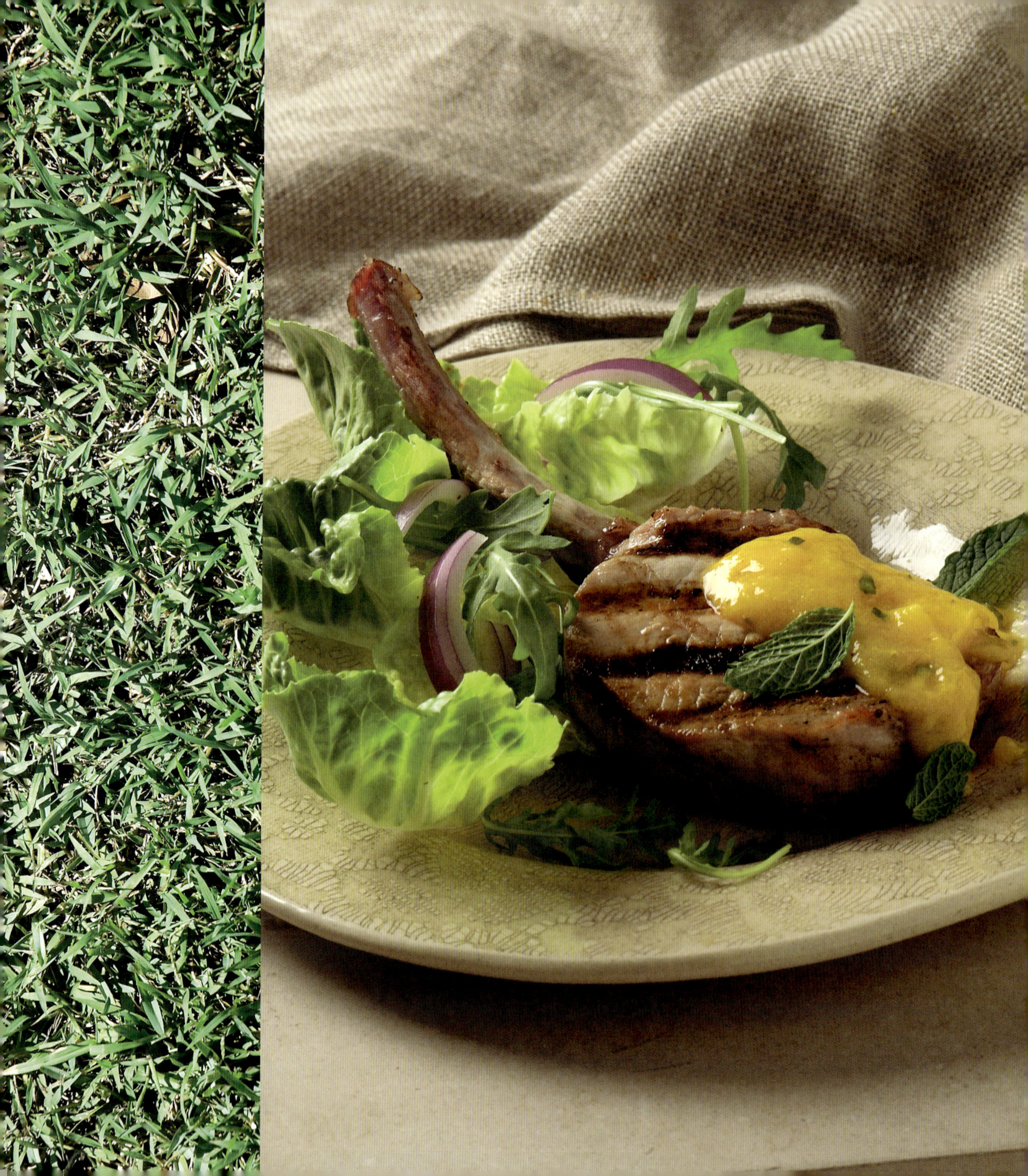

4 x 200g (7oz) pork cutlets
Spray olive oil
Cracked black pepper
1 large mango or two medium mangoes
¼ cup olive oil
1 small green chilli, seeds removed and roughly chopped
½ teaspoon cumin powder
6 sprigs of mint, leaves only
Salt and white pepper

PORK CUTLETS & MANGO MINT SAUCE

Trim cutlets if necessary and spray with oil when ready to cook on a medium-hot grill.

Remove the flesh from the mango carefully by cutting the cheeks from each side of the mango/mangoes. Score the flesh in the skins, being careful not to cut through the skin. Scoop out the flesh with a spoon and put into a food processor or blender. Add oil, chilli, cumin and mint leaves, breaking them up as you put them in. Work mixture to a smooth consistency and add salt and pepper to taste. Remove to a suitable bowl.

Barbecue the cutlets until done and serve with the mango sauce and salad of your choice.

SERVES 4

500g (1lb) pork fillet, trimmed
300g (11oz) spaghetti, dried
100g (4oz) zucchini, finely sliced into rounds
100g (4oz) white onion, finely sliced in rings
2 cloves garlic, crushed
1 glass white wine
1 tablespoon Italian parsley, chopped
1 teaspoon marjoram, chopped
½ teaspoon salt
½ teaspoon cracked pepper
1 tablespoon extra virgin olive oil
Spray oil

Pork Fillet with Zucchini & Herb Spaghetti

Slice the pork fillet into 3cm (1in) thick rounds and flatten with the heel of your hand.

Cook the spaghetti in plenty of boiling salted water. To cook al dente will take approximately 7–8 minutes. It is important that the pasta not be overcooked and it will be cooked again on the barbecue. When done, strain and run under warm water. If using it straight away there is no need to rub oil through the spaghetti.

Spray the pork fillet pieces with oil and cook on a hot plate for 2 minutes on each side. Remove and keep warm.

Lightly oil the plate and tip on the zucchini, onions and garlic. Continue to move the vegetables around the plate until done. Add the spaghetti, pork and pour over ½ glass white wine and with two spatulas, lift and combine the spaghetti with the pork and vegetable mixture.

Cook like this for a couple of minutes or until the spaghetti is heated through—you may need to add more wine if necessary.

Sprinkle on the parsley, marjoram, salt and pepper and lift and toss to spread those flavours through the spaghetti mixture.

Serve in a suitable bowl, drizzle with the extra virgin olive oil and serve with salads of your choice

Serves 4

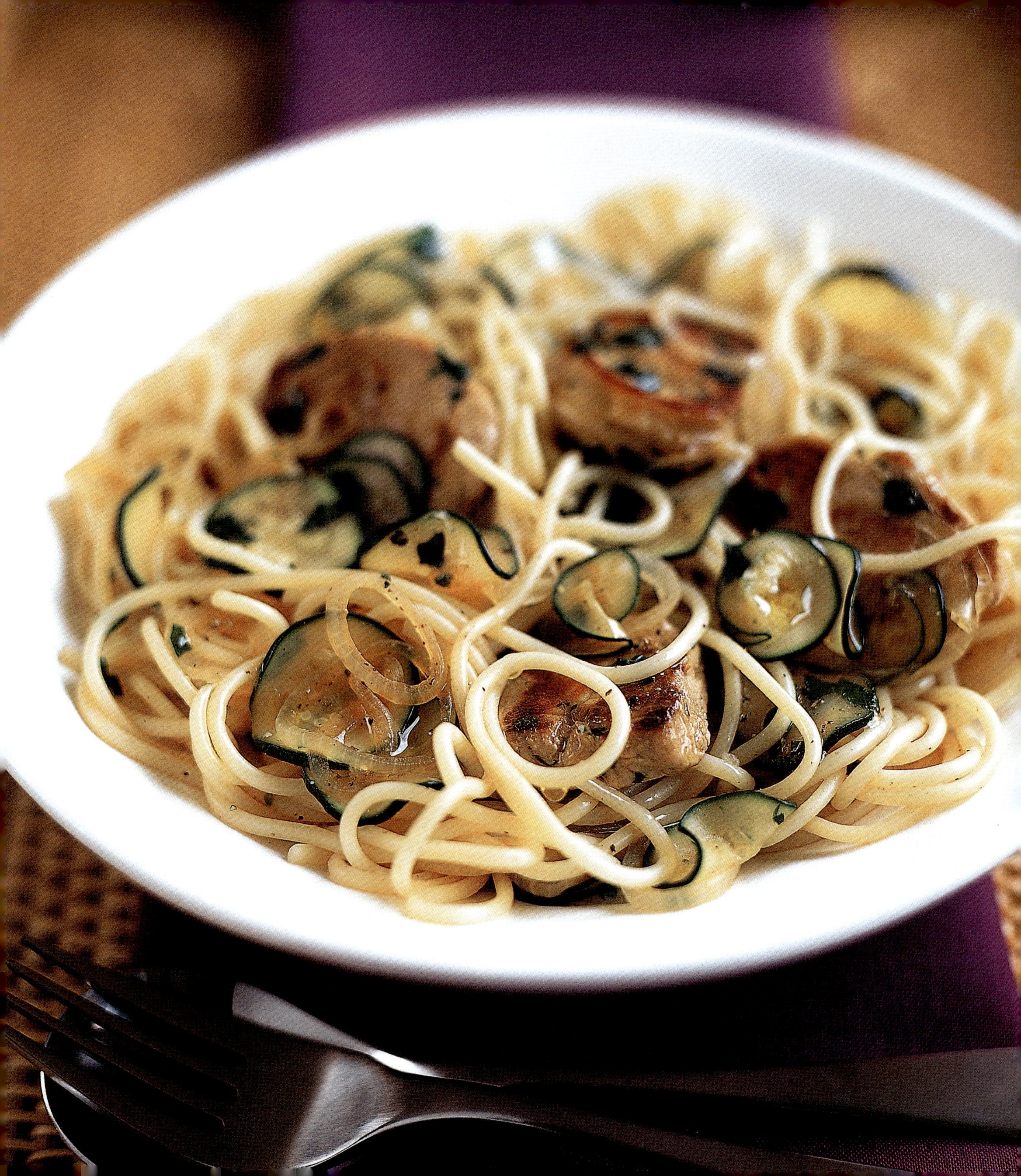

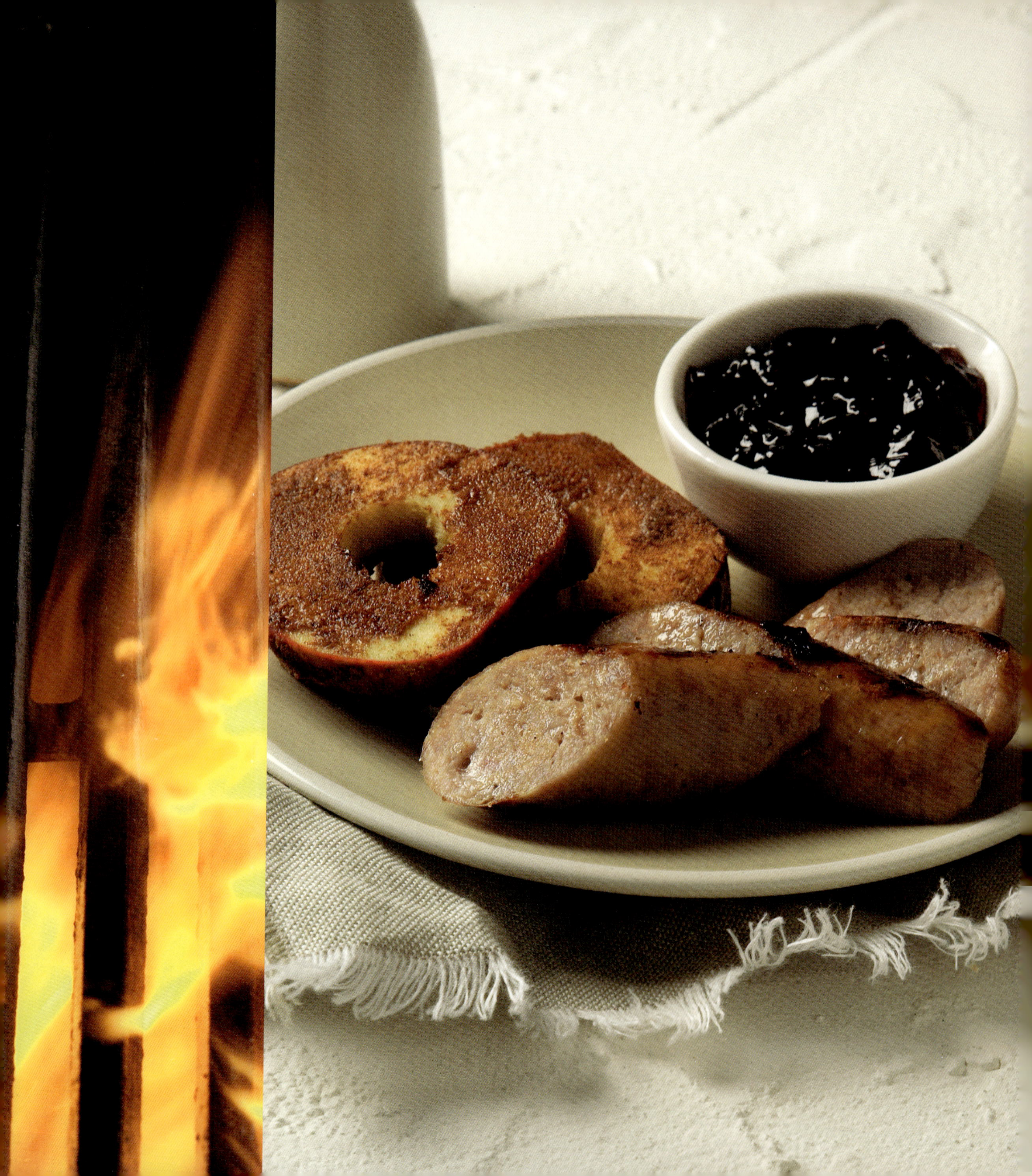

8 x 100g (4oz) good pork sausages
1 teaspoon powdered cloves
1 teaspoon powdered ginger
1 teaspoon cinnamon powder
1 teaspoon icing sugar
2 red apples, cored and sliced into 2cm (1in) rounds
2 tablespoons red currant jelly
Spray oil

PORK SAUSAGES WITH SPICED APPLE & RED CURRANT JELLY

Cook the pork sausages on a medium-hot grill for 8–10 minutes, turning regularly.

Combine the spices and the icing sugar and mix well. Press the apple slices into the spice mix on both sides. Spray the medium-hot plate with oil and add the apples. Cook for one minute, spray the uncooked apples and turn to cook a further 2 minutes on the other side.

Lift the apple slices off the barbecue and arrange around the outside of a platter. Take the cooked sausages off the barbecue and put into the centre of the platter, surrounded by the apple border. Put the jelly in a separate bowl on the table.

Serve in the middle of the table with a good potato salad and lots of good crusty bread, or even garlic bread would be delicious with this meal.

Serves 4

4 lamb rumps
Ground black pepper
Spray oil
4 lemon cheeks
200g (7oz) dried green lentils
1 large onion, roughly chopped
200g (7oz) sugar snap peas, trimmed
200g (7oz) green peas
½ cup chervil leaves

¼ cup olive oil
1 tablespoon lemon juice
   (from the lemons used for the cheeks)
Salt to taste
2 eggs, for omelette
2 tablespoons parsley, finely chopped

PEPPER-CRUSTED LAMB RUMP WITH LENTIL, SUGAR SNAP PEAS & CHERVIL SALAD

THE SIZE OF THE LAMB RUMPS VARIES ACCORDING TO YOUR SOURCE AND SO ADJUST THE COOKING TIME FOR THE LAMB TO SUIT THE SIZE YOU BUY—YOU MAY BE ABLE TO GET SOME THAT ARE SUITABLE TO SERVE TWO.

Trim the rump of all fat and roll in as much or as little ground black pepper as you like. Refrigerate until ready for use.

Soak the lentils in cold water for 20 minutes. Drain and put into saucepan with onion. Cover well with water and bring to the boil then simmer until the lentils are soft but disintegrating, about 15 minutes. Drain and rinse under cold water.

Blanch the sugar snap peas and the peas.

Make the 1-egg omelettes by beating 1 egg with 1 tablespoon water and parsley. Pour into a well-oiled non-stick small omelette (crepe) pan and let the mixture run all over the base of the pan. It should be very thin and look like a crepe. When set and lightly browned, shoode out of the pan and repeat for the other omelette. When cooled, roll into a sausage shape and cut into 1cm (½in) wide strips.

MAINS | MEAT

Take the lamb from the refrigerator 10 minutes before cooking on an oil-sprayed hot plate. Turn to seal by cooking for 2 minutes on each side. Lower the heat to medium and drop the hood. Cook all up for 4–5 minutes on each side (depending on the size of each rump). Remove and allow to rest for 10 minutes before slicing.

Sit the lemon cheeks, cut-side down, on a hot grill for 1 minute before serving with the lamb.

Assemble the salad by combining the lentils and onion, the two lots of peas and the chervil. Toss with the oil, lemon juice and salt.

Spoon the lentils into the centre of individual plates, slice each rump into four equal slices (refer to note below) to sit on top of the lentil salad with the lemon cheeks to one side.

SERVES 4

12 large sage leaves
12 trimmed medium lamb cutlets
12 thin slices parmesan cheese
12 slices prosciutto
Olive oil

400g (14oz) cooked linguine
120g (4oz) fresh or frozen peas
2 medium ripe tomatoes, diced
2 tablespoons pasta tomato sauce
Lamb or beef stock
Salt and ground black pepper

PROSCIUTTO SAGE LAMB CUTLETS WITH PEA & TOMATO LINGUINE

Place a sage leaf on top of each cutlet and an appropriate piece of parmesan cheese (so it covers the leaf and the meat); wrap in a slice of prosciutto.

Cook the lamb cutlets on a medium-hot plate until the cheese is starting to seep through the crisped prosciutto. Remove and keep warm.

Heat enough olive oil in a suitable pan or wok over medium heat. Add the linguine, peas, tomatoes and tomato sauce. Stir and pour in enough stock to make the peas and tomato cook and provide a good sauce for the linguine. Season with salt and pepper to taste.

Serve the linguine in the centre of bowls with the cutlets sitting on top or around the pasta.

SERVES 4

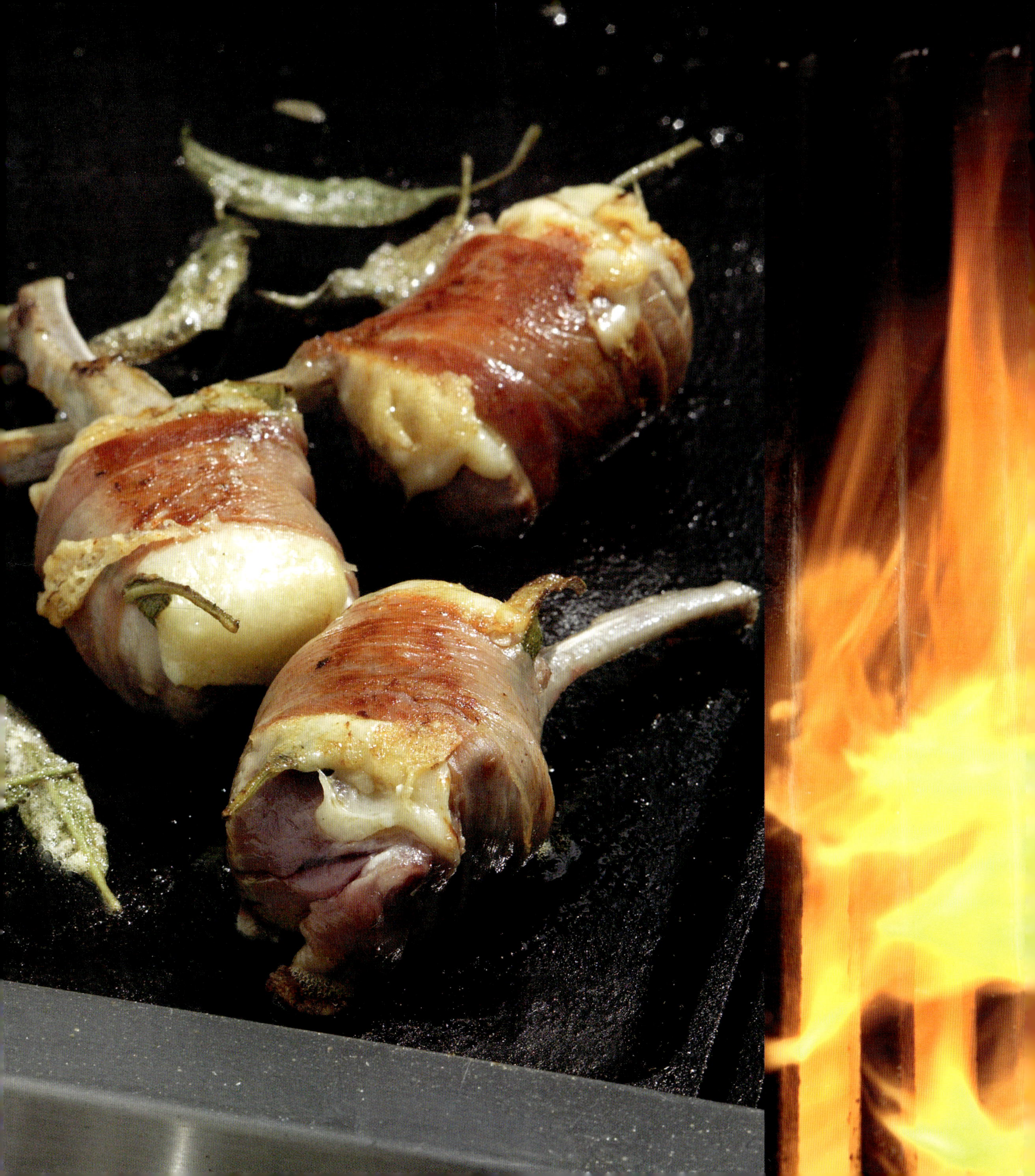

2 tablespoons vegetable oil
1 tablespoon butter
1 small onion, finely chopped
½ cup rolled oats
750g (2lb) beef, finely minced
2 tablespoons tomato ketchup
½ teaspoon tabasco sauce
2 eggs, large
½ teaspoon salt
1 teaspoon ground black pepper
Spray olive oil

RISSOLES & RATATOUILLE

Ratatouille is best made the day before it is to be used. Ratatouille keeps perfectly in a sealed container in the refrigerator for up to five days. It is great served as a starter with barbecued pita bread triangles.

Heat the oil and butter until foaming. Gently fry the chopped onion for two minutes.

Tip the onion mixture into a large bowl and add the rolled oats, beef, ketchup, tabasco, eggs, salt and pepper. Mix well—using your hands is the best way.

Refrigerate this mixture for 1 hour. Remove and shape into eight equal-sized patties that are 3cm (1in) thick.

Spray the rissoles with oil and cook on a medium-hot plate. Turn after they have cooked for one minute. Cook for another minute and then flip over onto a medium-hot grill. Cook a further two minutes on each side. The cooking time will vary depending on the thickness of each pattie.

Spoon required ratatouille into the centre of individual deep-welled plates and top with equal amounts of rissoles.

Serves 4

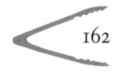

Ratatouille

500g medium eggplant (aubergine)
Salt
60ml (2fl oz) olive oil
1 Spanish onion, thinly sliced
1 capsicum, roughly diced
2 cloves garlic, roughly diced
2 tomatoes, ripe and chopped
2 medium zucchinis, roughly diced
2 teaspoons fresh thyme
1 teaspoon fresh oregano
60ml (2fl oz) vegetable stock
½ teaspoon black pepper, freshly ground
2 tablespoons fresh parsley or basil, chopped

For the Ratatouille

Roughly chop the eggplant, place in a colander, sprinkle with salt and allow to drain for 30 minutes.

Heat the olive oil in a large frying pan over medium heat. Add the onion and fry until soft. Add the capsicum, garlic, tomatoes and zucchini. Stir well. Mix in the thyme and oregano.

Rinse the eggplant under cold water and dry well with paper towels. Tumble into the cooking ingredients along with the stock. Cover and simmer over low heat, stirring occasionally for 20–30 minutes.

Season with the pepper and cook a further 10 minutes at a simmer.

Ratatouille

Vermicelli Noodles & Bok Choy

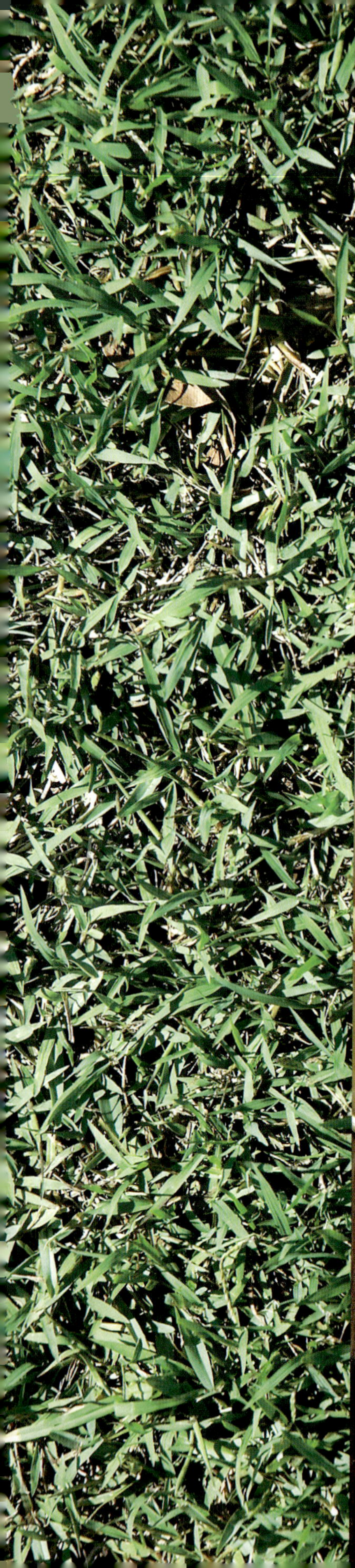
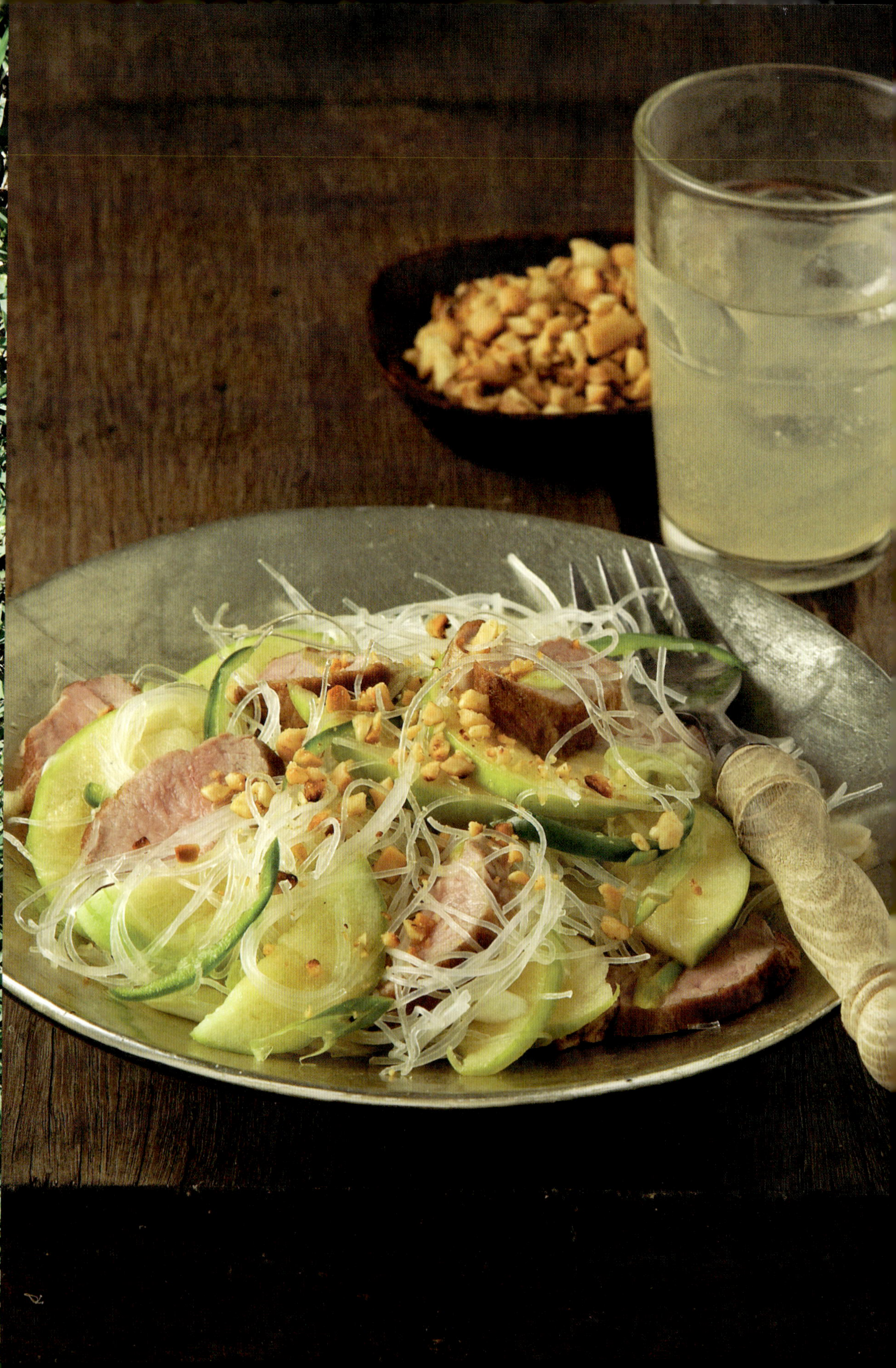

400g (14oz) pork fillet, in one piece
Spray oil
2 medium green apples or mangoes
½ teaspoon salt
1 tablespoon vegetable oil
2 cloves garlic, sliced
4 green spring onions, trimmed and sliced diagonally

1 tablespoon fish sauce
1 teaspoon palm sugar, finely grated
1 tablespoon lime juice
½ teaspoon ground white pepper
1 large green chilli, deseeded and finely sliced
1 cup vermicelli noodles, rehydrated
2 tablespoons roasted peanuts, crushed

PORK, GREEN APPLE & VERMICELLI NOODLE SALAD

Trim the pork to make sure all fat and silver tissue is removed.

If using mangoes, peel and slice from the seed—slice very finely into half-moon shapes. Place the mango or apple slices into a bowl and sprinkle with salt. Pour in oil and toss. Add the garlic and spring onions. Mix the fish sauce, sugar, lime juice and pepper and pour onto the mango/apple ingredients. Tip in the chilli and noodles and toss well.

Spray the pork fillet with oil and seal on a hot plate by rolling it around. When browned all over, lower the hood to cook to medium-to-well done. Do not overcook the pork fillet and remove to rest for 10 minutes.

Slice the pork finely into rounds and halve if large slices. Add to the mango/apple salad and toss gently. Serve heaped into the centre of individual bowls and sprinkled with the crushed peanuts.

Serves 4

400g (14oz) beef strips, of either rump or sirloin
¼ cup soy sauce
¼ cup rice vinegar
1 tablespoon peanut or vegetable oil
1 medium red chilli, de-seeded and finely chopped
1 x 10cm (4in) piece lemongrass, finely minced
1 tablespoon palm sugar
8 king prawns, completely peeled and deveined
1 small onion, cut into wedges
1 cup bean shoots
8 water chestnuts, finely sliced
2 cups cooked long grain rice
1 cup loosely packed coriander leaves
Spray oil

STIR-FRIED BEEF & PRAWNS

The strips of meat that you buy need to be tender so it can be cooked quickly and still remain tender. Sometimes lesser cuts of meat find their way into stir fries and they simply are not suitable. I always buy either the sirloin or the rump and cut it into strips around 1cm (½in) thick for use in a dish like this.

Make sure the meat is the same size. Add the soy, vinegar, oil, chilli, lemongrass and palm sugar. Mix well and sit covered for 1 hour.

To cook, strain the meat and reserve the soy mixture. Spray the very hot plate liberally with oil and tip on the meat strips immediately. Move around with a spatula. Cook the prawns on an oiled part of the plate and cook the onions on another part of the sprayed plate.

Add in the bean sprouts and water chestnuts and combine all cooking ingredients into a concentrated area on the barbecue.

Spoon over the marinade and lift and toss for another 2 minutes. Lift into a serving bowl, add the coriander and toss together gently. Serve with cooked rice.

Serves 4

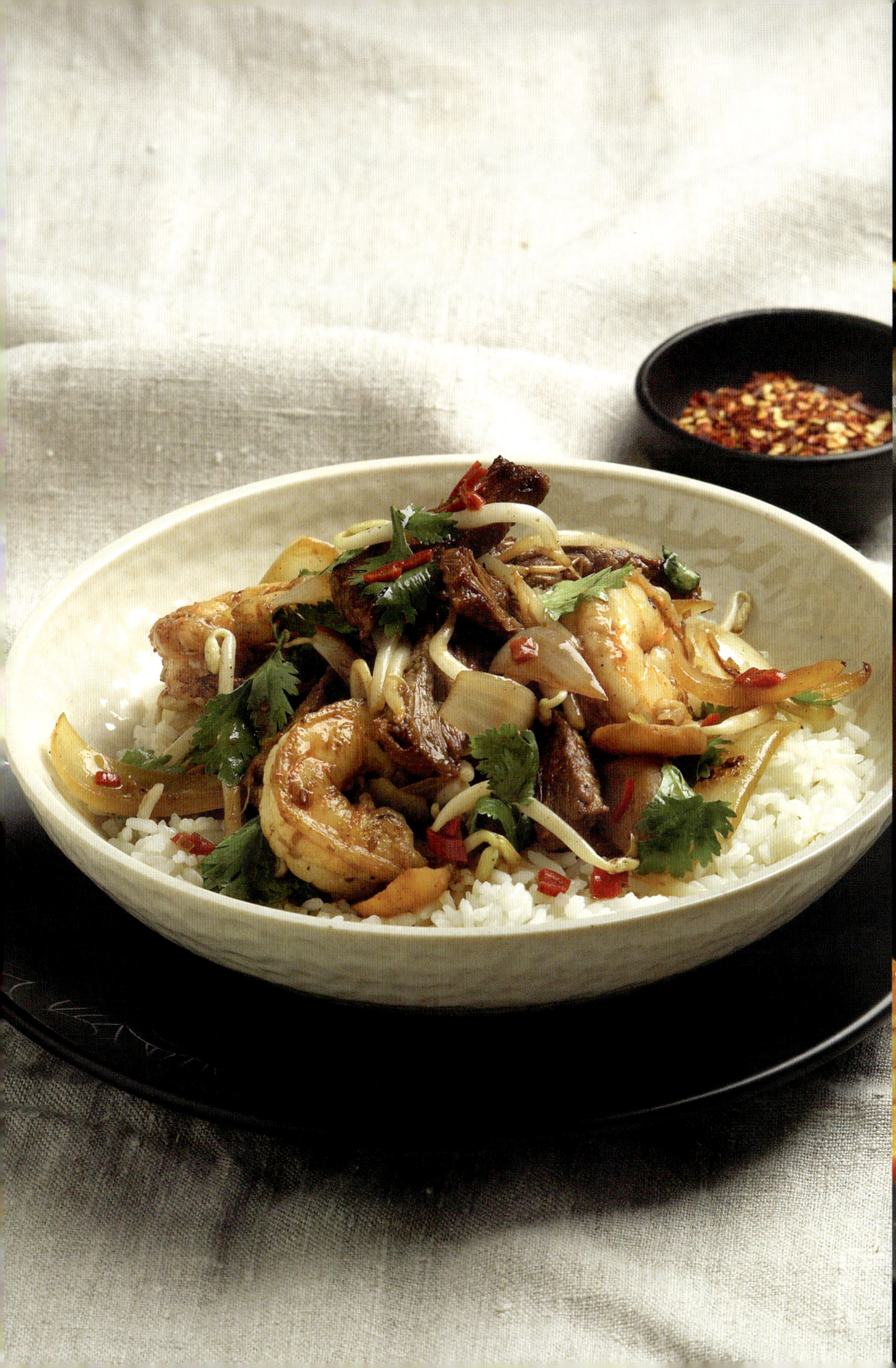
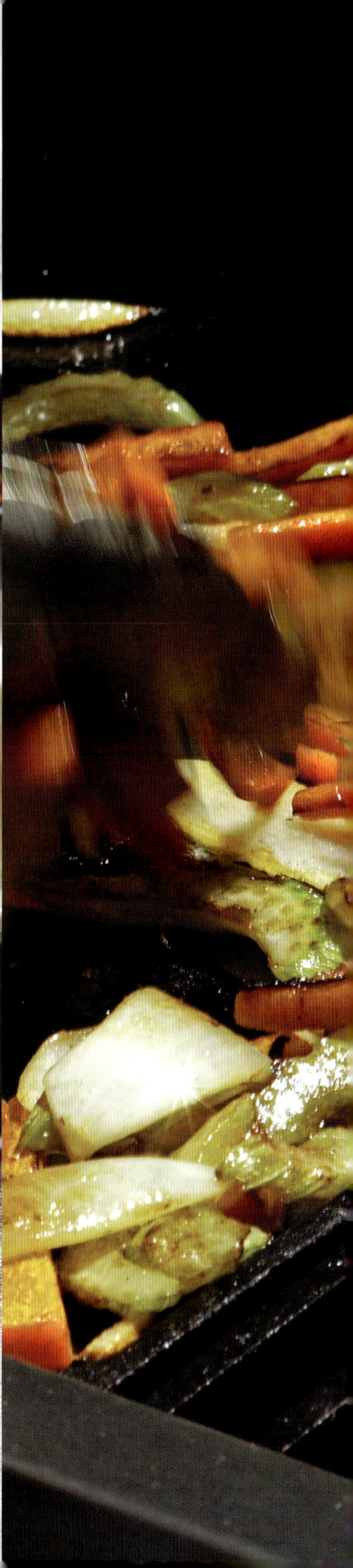

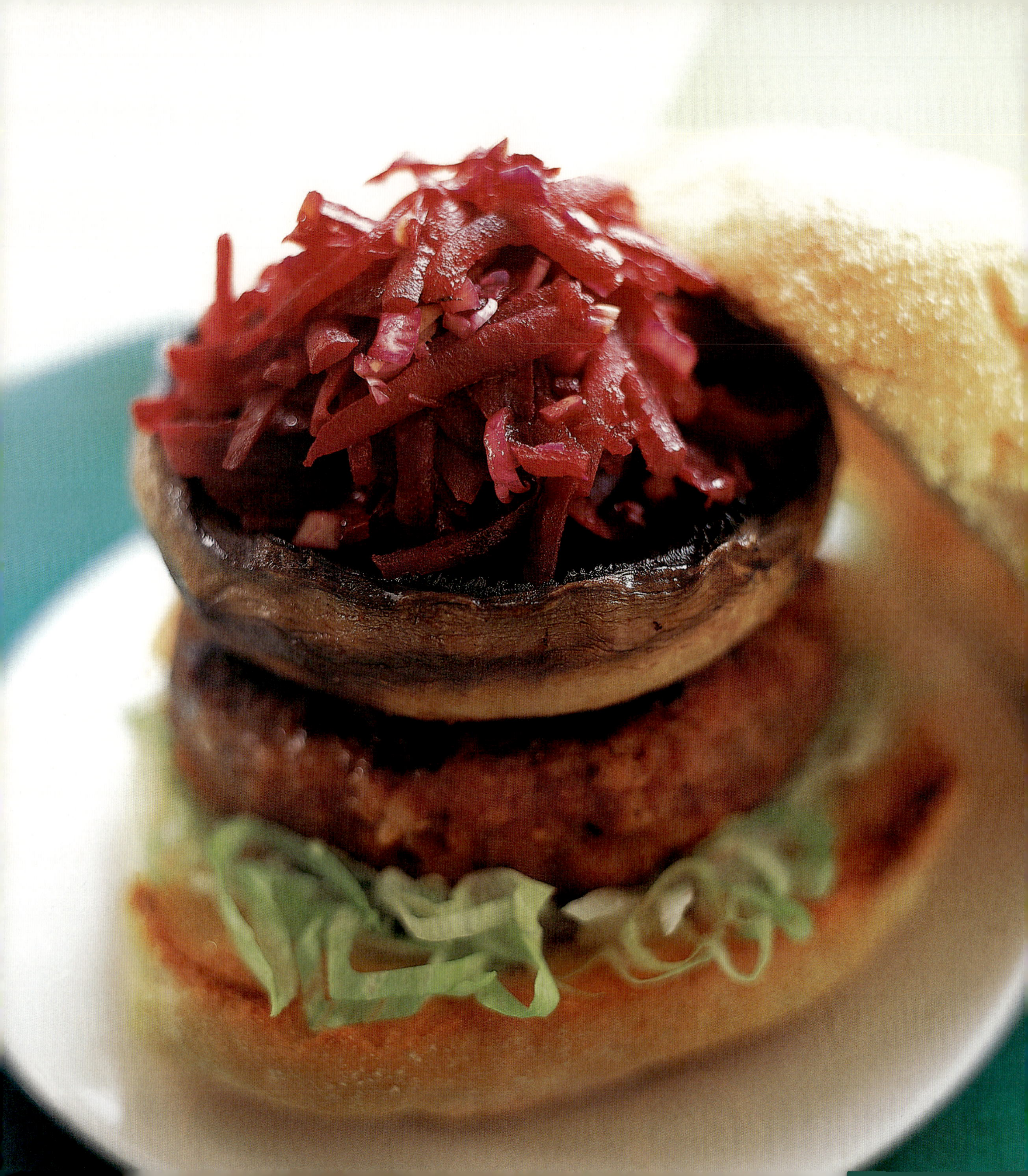

Beetroot relish:
200g (7oz) beetroot, cooked, cooled and grated
2 spring onions, finely minced
1 teaspoon anchovy sauce
1 tablespoon white wine vinegar
½ tablespoon truffle oil

4 large bread rolls
500g (1lb) veal mince
250g (9oz) minced ham
2 medium eggs
1 teaspoon tabasco sauce
1 tablespoon tomato sauce
60g (2oz) onion, finely diced
½ teaspoon salt
Spray oil
4 medium field mushrooms
2 cups shredded lettuce

VEAL & HAM BURGER WITH BEETROOT RELISH

I GOT INTO THE HABIT OF SCOOPING OUT THE CENTRE OF BREAD ROLLS AFTER I HAD SEEN SO MANY FILLINGS GO ALL OVER THE PLACE WHEN YOU LEAVE THEM FLAT. BY HAVING WELLS ON EACH SIDE YOU ARE ABLE TO BETTER CONTAIN THE FILLINGS.

Cut the bread rolls in half and pull out the centre of each half so that you have a well in both halves of the rolls. Break removed bread into tiny pieces and add to it the veal, ham, eggs, tabasco, tomato sauce, onions and salt. Mix well, using your hands. The bread you have used is enough to be the binder, however if your mixture is too moist, add enough dried breadcrumbs to take up that excess liquid. Shape into four even patties. Cover and refrigerate.

Make the relish by combining beetroot with the spring onions, anchovy sauce, vinegar and oil and mix well.

Spray the patties with oil and place on a hot plate. Cook for 1 minute. Spray the patties with oil and cook for a further minute. Barbecue the mushrooms on a medium-hot grill by spraying the gill side (the brown underneath) of the mushrooms. Cook for 2 minutes either side.

Place the hamburger patties on the grill. Cook a further 2–3 minutes each side to give you medium–well done patties. Spray the inside of the hamburger buns with oil and toast on the grill.

To serve, take all cooked items from the barbecue when done and assemble by putting equal amounts of the lettuce in the base part of the bread roll. Add a cooked pattie topped with a mushroom.

Spoon on beetroot relish to the top of the mushroom and add the hood. Press down to compress the fillings and make it easier to eat.

4 x 200g (7oz) veal cutlets
¼ teaspoon chopped fresh oregano
450g (1lb) waxy potatoes, Kipfler or Desiree
Spray oil
Salt and ground black pepper

Olive, Parsley and Lime Pesto
20 green olives, seeds removed
2 limes, grated zest only
1 lime, juiced
2 cloves garlic, peeled and halved
1 tablespoon pinenuts, toasted
1 cup tightly packed flat (Italian) parsley
$\frac{1}{3}$ cup extra virgin olive oil

VEAL CUTLETS WITH OLIVE, PARSLEY & LIME PESTO

Trim the veal cutlets if necessary and refrigerate covered with cling wrap until ready to use.

Wash potatoes and peel if desired. Cut into halves or quarters if big and boil in water for 3 minutes. Drain and cool. Refrigerate until ready to use.

Remove veal and potatoes from the refrigerator 10 minutes before use to bring them to room temperature.

Spray the cutlets with plenty of oil and seal on a hot plate by lightly browning both sides. Lower to medium heat to allow to cook to your liking. Sprinkle on some oregano and press onto each cutlet with the back of the cooking spatula. Turn only one more time and repeat the oregano on that side. Sprinkle with salt and pepper on the second turning only.

Spray the potatoes well and cook on a medium-hot plate. Sprinkle with salt and pepper and turn regularly until browned, crisped and cooked through.

When the veal is cooked to your liking, remove and rest for 5 minutes.

To serve, put equal amount of potatoes into the centre of each plate and top with the veal cutlets. Spoon over some of the pesto and serve with cooked broccoli or other green vegetables of your choice.

For the Olive, Parsley and Lime Pesto
Put the olives, lime zest, lime juice, garlic, pinenuts and parsley into a food processor bowl and start the motor. Gradually pour in the oil and work to a rough paste. Remove from processor bowl, cover and refrigerate.

Serves 4

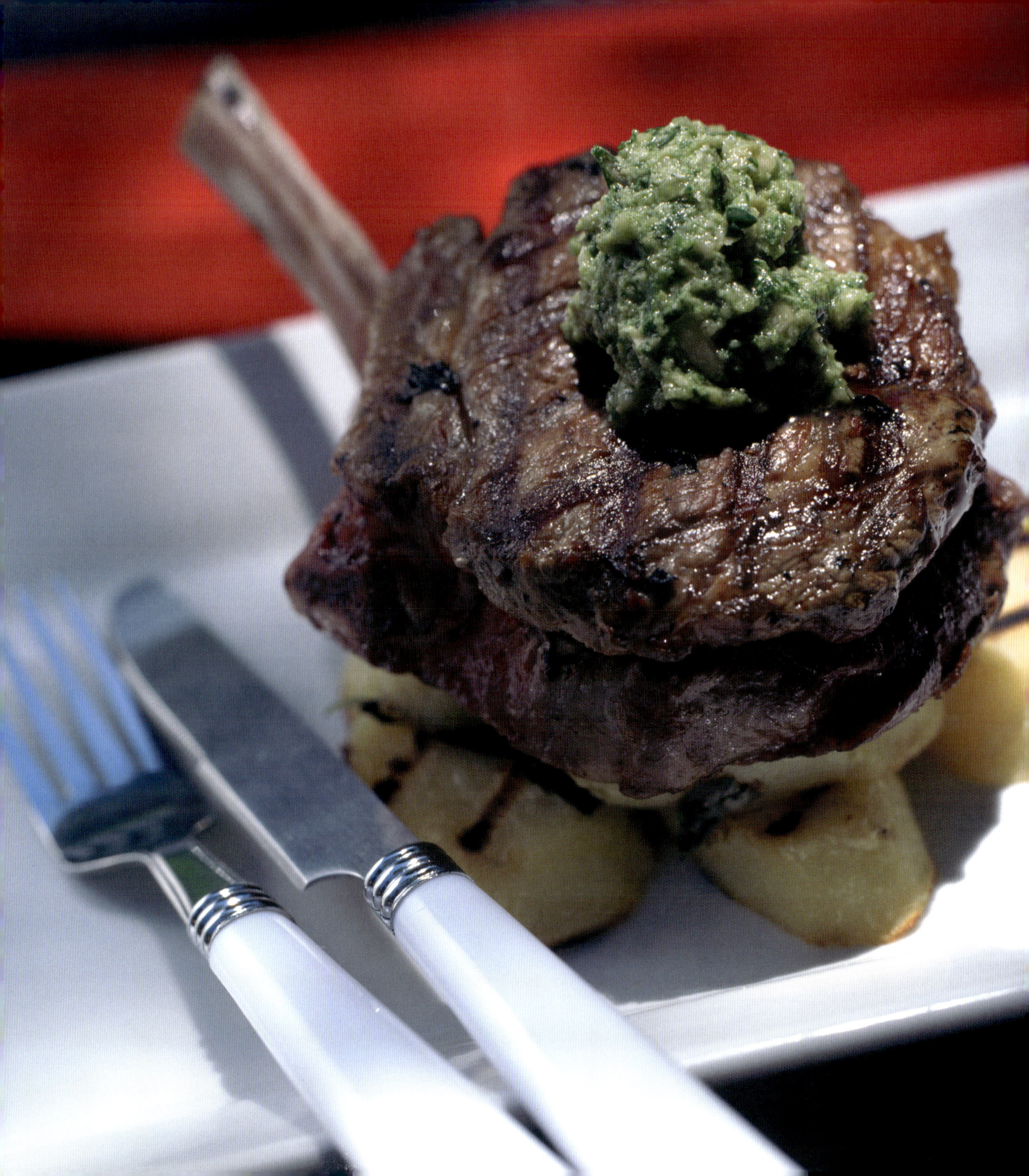

500g (16oz) calves liver, in 1½cm (½in) thick slices
4 small onions, peeled
Stainless steel skewers
8 small potatoes, cut into halves
Salt
Smoky paprika powder

Cashew Nut & Mustard Butter
250g (9oz) unsalted butter, room temperature
1 tablespoon seeded mustard
30g (1oz) roasted and salted cashew nuts, finely crushed
1 tablespoon fresh parsley, chopped
1 tablespoon white vinegar
¼ teaspoon freshly ground white pepper

CALVES LIVER WITH SKEWERED ONIONS & CASHEW NUT & MUSTARD BUTTER

For the Cashew Nut & Mustard Butter

Put the butter, mustard and crushed nuts into a bowl and start to mash them together. Add the parsley, vinegar and pepper and continue mashing until combined.

Roll into a sausage shape using clingwrap or wax paper and secure by screwing the ends together. Freeze until ready to use. Make sure the skin is removed from the outside of each slice of liver.

Cut the onions into 1½cm (½in) thick rounds and skewer the slices together on the flat.

Boil the potato halves in salted water for 4–5 minutes, drain.

Spray a medium-hot plate with oil and put the skewered onions on. Spray the potatoes and put them on the grill. Sprinkle both with salt and turn frequently to cook.

Once the onions are done, remove and spray the liver with oil and put onto a medium-hot plate. Sprinkle with a little smoky paprika and salt. Turn and do the same to the other side. Liver cooks quickly and it is important to serve it medium because well done makes the liver to dry and rubbery.

To serve, plate individually by putting four potato pieces into the centre of each plate and top with 1–2 slices of liver. Lay the onion rings beside the liver and potatoes and top the liver with a couple of slices of Cashew Nut & Mustard Butter. Serve as the butter starts to ooze over the liver.

Serves 4

400g (14oz) parsnips, peeled and core removed
100g (4oz) Pontiac potatoes, peeled and diced
100g (4oz) butter
½ teaspoon salt
8 large venison sausages

For the sauce
3 tablespoons red currant or quince jelly
1 tablespoon English mustard
¼ teaspoon ground ginger powder
1 teaspoon orange zest, finely grated

VENISON SAUSAGES & PARSNIP MASH WITH CUMBERLAND SAUCE

Chop the parsnips to a similar size as the potatoes. Bring to the boil and then simmer until tender. Strain and return to saucepan. Replace the hood and let sit for 3 minutes. Add the butter and mash the two together with the salt. Scoop out into microwave-proof bowl, cover and keep at room temperature.

Make the sauce by combining all ingredients and mix well. Cook in microwave on high for 30 seconds. Remove, mix thoroughly and let sit at room temperature.

Spray the venison sausages with oil and cook on a medium-hot plate. Cooking time will vary according to the size of your sausages. Turn regularly and finish the sausages on the grill for the last couple of minutes of cooking to crisp them up. Remove from barbecue and leave to rest for 2 minutes.

Reheat parsnip mash in the microwave and spoon equal amounts onto individual plates. Lean two sausages onto the mash. Serve the Cumberland Sauce separately with a cooked green vegetable of your choice.

SERVES 4

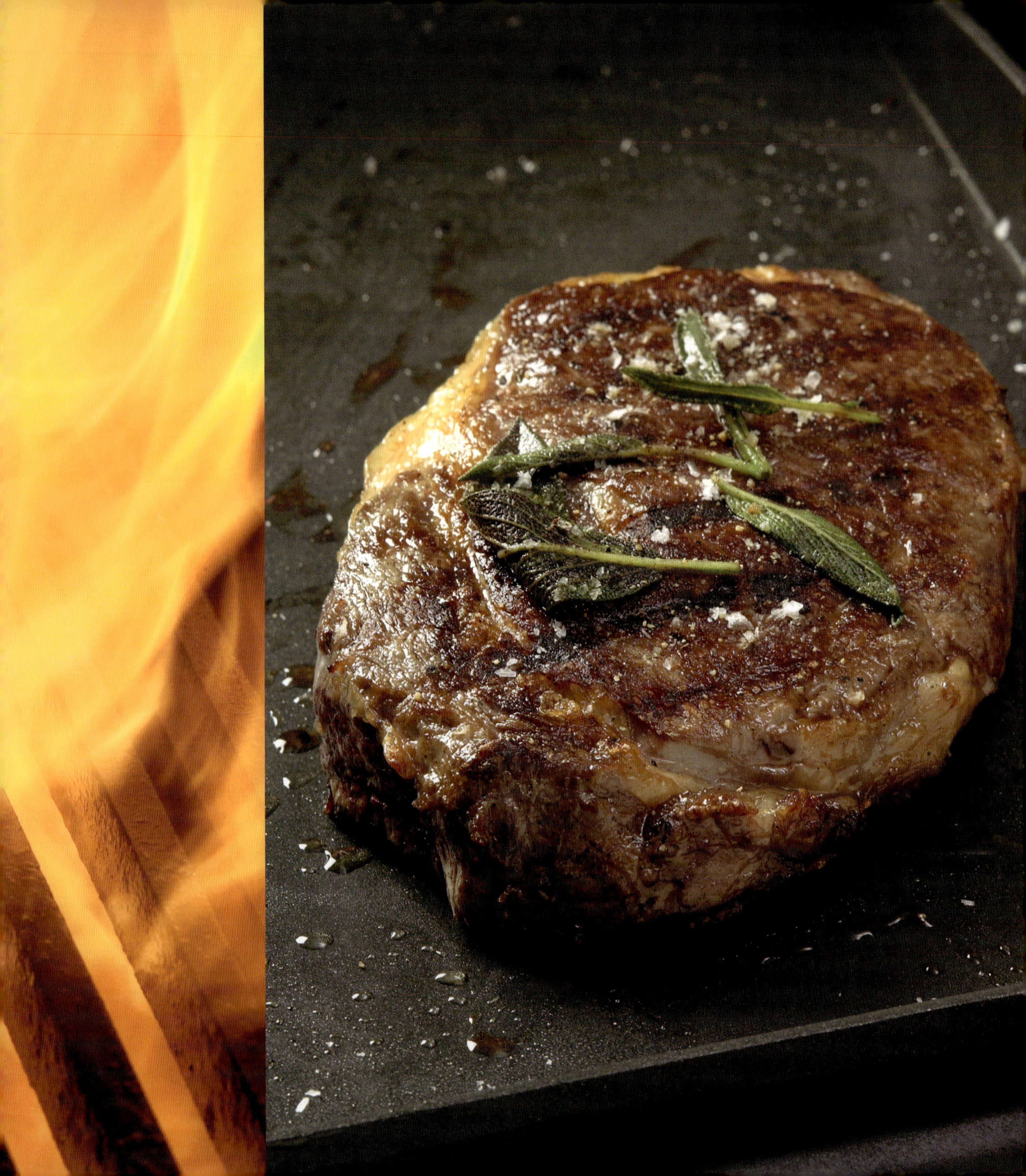

4 x 4cm (2in) thick sirloin steaks, well marbled
Salt and ground black pepper
Light olive oil

THE PERFECT BARBECUE STEAK

No barbecue book would be complete without a definitive steak recipe. Over the many years that I have cooked beef steak on the barbecue, I know this is the best method. Of course, choosing the correct beef cut is really crucial to the finished product. Cook your steak this way and never serve it any further cooked than medium.

You will have noticed that I have advised leaving some fat on the steak. This is essential for flavour complexity. If you prefer your meat without the fat, you may slice it off after the cooking has happened.

Marbled beef is identified by streaks of white through the red meat. These are thin lines of fat which melt in the cooking process and give that superb flavour of barbecue beef steak.

Trim as much fat from your steaks as you like but ensure that at least ½cm (¼in) is left. Importantly, always remove the meat you will barbecue from the refrigerator at least 10 minutes before use.

Spray the steaks with oil and place onto the very hot plate. Leave to sit for 2 minutes without disturbing the meat. Do not at any time puncture the steaks with forks or knives or you will release the vital juices of the meat.

Spray the steaks lightly with oil and turn onto another part of the very hot plate. If there is not enough room, lift each piece of meat and let the plate recover its heat so it can seal the meat on this side just as it did for the first side. Cook a further 2 minutes.

Flip the steaks again but this time onto the grill and cook for 2 minutes each side, sprinkling with salt and pepper as you turn them.

Remove and allow to rest for at least 5 minutes before serving. This gives the meat a chance to set and means that the red juices do not run all over the plate.

Serve the steak onto individual plates with vegetables or salad of your choice and at least one good mustard.

Serves 4

2 medium eggplants (aubergines), cubed
1 small onion, roughly chopped
1 teaspoon black mustard seeds
1 teaspoon Garam Masala
½ teaspoon chilli powder
2 medium green chillies, roughly chopped
4 tablespoons vegetable oil
2 medium tomatoes, roughly diced
4 large chapatis
Spray oil
300ml (10fl oz) natural yoghurt
Mint leaves

Lentil Puree
2 tablespoons vegetable oil
1 large onion, finely chopped
1 large clove garlic, roughly chopped
1 teaspoon green ginger, finely grated
1 teaspoon tumeric powder
250g (9oz) red lentils, washed and drained
3 cups boiling water
Salt to taste
½ teaspoon garam masala

SPICY EGGPLANT & LENTIL PUREE WITH CHAPATIS

Put the eggplant and onion into a bowl. Crush the mustard seeds in a mortar and pestle, then add the garum masala, chilli powder and chillies and pound really well. Combine the oil and mix well.

Pour the chilli mixture over the eggplant and onions. Toss well and let sit for 10 minutes. Tip the eggplant mixture onto a hot plate. Lift and toss to cook the mixture. When done, remove from the plate and keep warm. Spray the chapatis with oil and heat through on a medium-hot grill. Flip a couple of times to get them pliable and remove when lightly browned.

Put the eggplant into a bowl in the middle of the table with the chapatis, lentil puree, diced tomatoes, yoghurt and mint leaves. Let everyone assemble their own by spreading some of the puree over each chapatti, piling some of the spicy eggplant down the middle of the chapati, then some tomato, yoghurt and mint leaves. Roll and eat!

For the Lentil Puree
Heat the oil and lightly fry the onion, garlic and ginger. Add the tumeric and stir in. Tip in the lentils and stir for a minute. Pour in the boiling water and bring to the boil. Reduce to a simmer and cook for 15 minutes with the hood off. Add the salt and garam masala and continue cooking until mixture thickens and the lentils are breaking down. Continue stirring until all the water has evaporated and you have a paste. Tip into bowl or suitable airtight container.

Serves 4

Mains | Meat

4 lentil burgers
Spray oil
4 burger rolls
Spicy Black Eye Bean Paste
 (see recipe, page 62)
2 cups crisp lettuce, shredded
4 slices red onion
4–8 beetroot slices
1 cup alfalfa sprouts
Salt and ground black pepper to taste

Lentil & Beetroot Burger with Spicy Black Bean Paste

If the lentil burgers are frozen, thaw completely. If not, bring to room temperature at least 5 minutes before use. Spray with oil and cook on a medium-hot grill. Turn as they brown.

Cut the burger rolls through the middle to make two even disks. Spray with oil and brown on the grill.

Assemble the burgers by spreading desired amounts of the bean paste over each half of the rolls. Distribute shredded lettuce over the bottom of the burger rolls, top with a slice of onion and slices of beetroot. Add the cooked lentil burger and sprinkle over even amounts of sprouts. Put on the top and press firmly. Cut in half if you like and serve with potato salad or coleslaw.

Serves 4

2 x 8 cutlets rack of goat, trimmed
1 teaspoon ground cumin
½ teaspoon powdered ginger
½ teaspoon powdered coriander
½ teaspoon salt

4 x 100g (4oz) wedges butternut pumpkin
4 large ripe Roma tomatoes, halved lengthwise
12 asparagus spears, trimmed
Balsamic vinegar
Spray oil

CUMIN, GINGER & CORIANDER RUB GOAT RACK WITH ROMA TOMATOES, ASPARAGUS & BUTTERNUT PUMPKIN

Seal the racks of goat on a very hot grill, starting with the skin side down. Turn after 2 minutes and cook the other side for another minute. Remove and cool.

Mix the cumin, ginger, coriander and salt well and rub as much as you like into the cooled skin side of the racks. Turn over and rub into the meat part of the underside of each rack. Put into baking tray or aluminium foil tray and place on a cake cooling rack on the plate or put into the warming tray that hangs from the hood. Cook at 160°C (320°F) for 12–15 minutes to have an internal temperature of 65°C (150°F). Remove from barbecue and let rest for 5 minutes before cutting into individual cutlets.

Spray the pumpkin wedges and cook on hot plate until done. Turn regularly for about 10 minutes and remove when done.

Spray the tomatoes and asparagus to cook on hot plate until coloured and warmed through. Start on the plate and then finish the halves on the grill if you like. The asparagus cooks more quickly than the tomatoes so be ready to remove them before the tomato halves.

To serve, place the pumpkin wedges on individual plates first and top with equal amounts of asparagus and tomato halves. Arrange the cutlets around the vegetables or on top and sprinkle with a little balsamic vinegar to serve.

SERVES 4

Barbecued onions
600g (21oz) onions, peeled and sliced into rings
1 tablespoon oil
1 tablespoon butter
1 bottle beer, 375ml (13fl oz)
Salt, optional

2 x 8 cutlet racks of goat
3 large garlic cloves, finely minced
1 tablespoon lemon thyme or thyme, fresh and minced
1 teaspoon ground black pepper
1/3 cup vegetable oil
2 bunches broccolini, trimmed

CHAR-ROASTED GOAT RACK WITH GARLIC THYME BASTE, BARBECUED ONIONS & BROCCOLINI

Seal the racks on a hot grill, starting with skin side down, for 2 minutes; turn and cook another 2 minutes. Lift them onto a baking tray and let cool for 5 minutes.

Mix the garlic, thyme, pepper and oil. Baste the goat thickly with it and roast at 150–160°C (300°–320°F) with the hood down. I do mine by sitting the tray on a cooling rack on the plate with the two grill burners on medium. Cook for 5 minutes and then baste again to continue cooking for another 8–12 minutes. It should take about 12 minutes to reach 65°C (150°F) internal temperature but that time will vary depending on thickness of the racks.

Remove when cooked to your liking and rest for at least 5 minutes to set the juices.

Boil the broccolini until done, then drain and serve in the centre of individual plates. Top with barbecued onion and cut the cutlets to sit around and on the onions.

For the Barbecued onions
Sprinkle the onions with a little salt if you desire. Melt the oil and butter on a medium-hot plate and add the onions. Move around the plate with the spatula and let them lightly brown. Pour a third of the beer over the onions. Stir the onions around and drop the hood or cover with a large stainless steel bowl. Leave the onions to stew in their own juices and add the beer as they start to dry, still turning regularly. When done, remove from barbecue and keep warm until ready to serve.

Serves 4

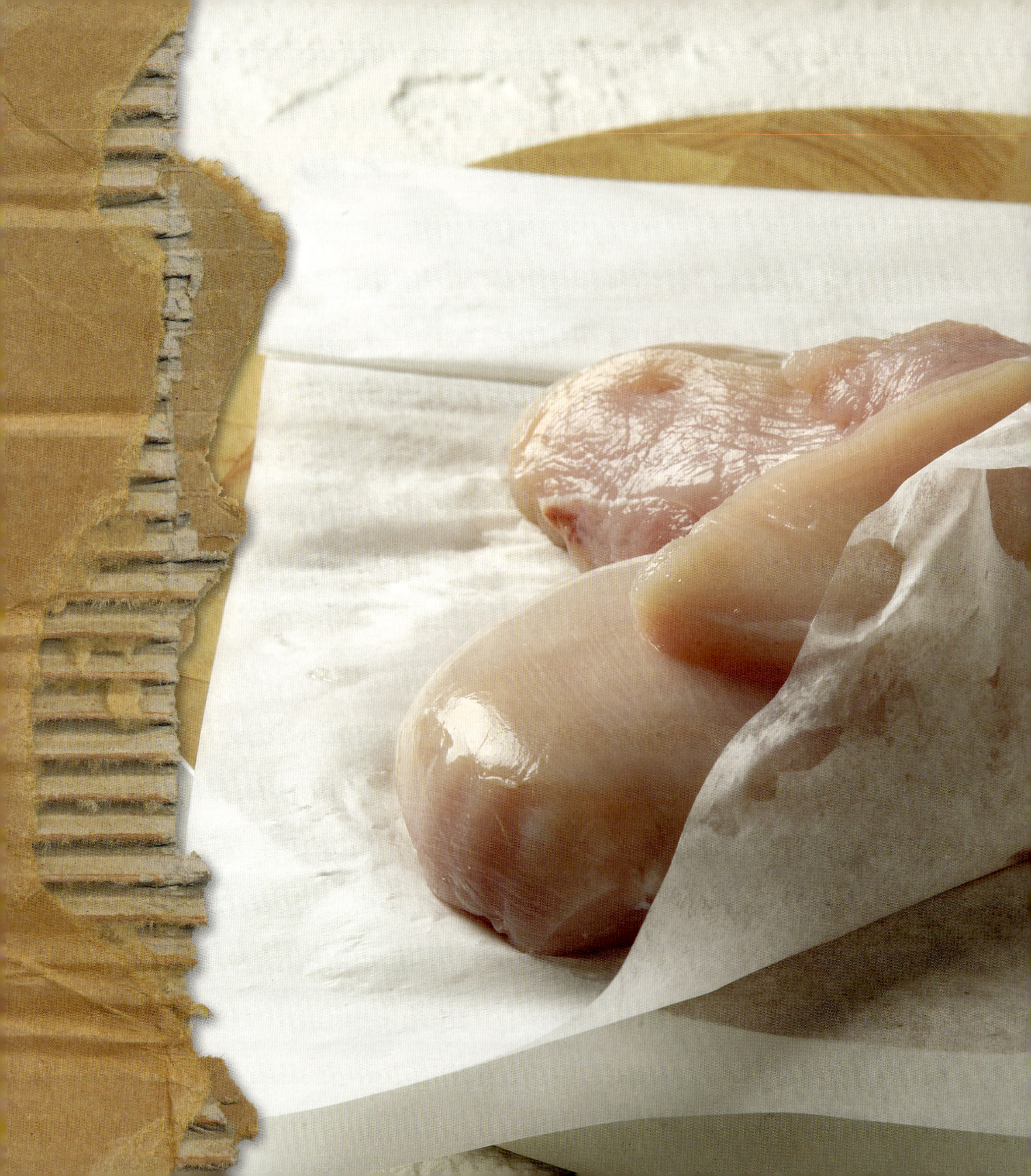

MAINS
POULTRY

4–8 duck sausages
400g (14oz) parsnips, peeled, quartered
   and core removed
Spray oil
200g (7oz) fava/broad beans, double peeled
1 small white onion, peeled and finely sliced
2 tablespoons marjoram, finely chopped
½ cup orange juice
2 tablespoons orange marmalade
½ teaspoon truffle-infused oil
Salt and white pepper to taste

DUCK SAUSAGES WITH PARSNIPS, FAVA BEANS & ORANGE DRESSING

Double peeled simply means that you have taken the beans out of the skin, blanched them in boiling water and refreshed them in ice water. Drain and peel the skin from the beans—the beans have brilliantly green flesh.

Cut the sausages into individuals if still linked.

Cut the parsnip into bite-sized pieces and blanch for two minutes—drain.

Heat the orange juice and marmalade over low heat and when the marmalade is melted, remove from the heat.

Spray a hot plate with oil and tip on the parsnip pieces. Cook through and only lightly brown—do be careful as the pieces brown very quickly. Lift into a bowl, add the onions and dressing, truffle-infused oil and salt and white pepper to taste. Toss together and allow to cool. Add the beans and marjoram and combine well.

Cook the duck sausages on a medium-hot grill until done.

Serve the parsnip mixture on the centre of individual plates and top with sausages.

Serves 4

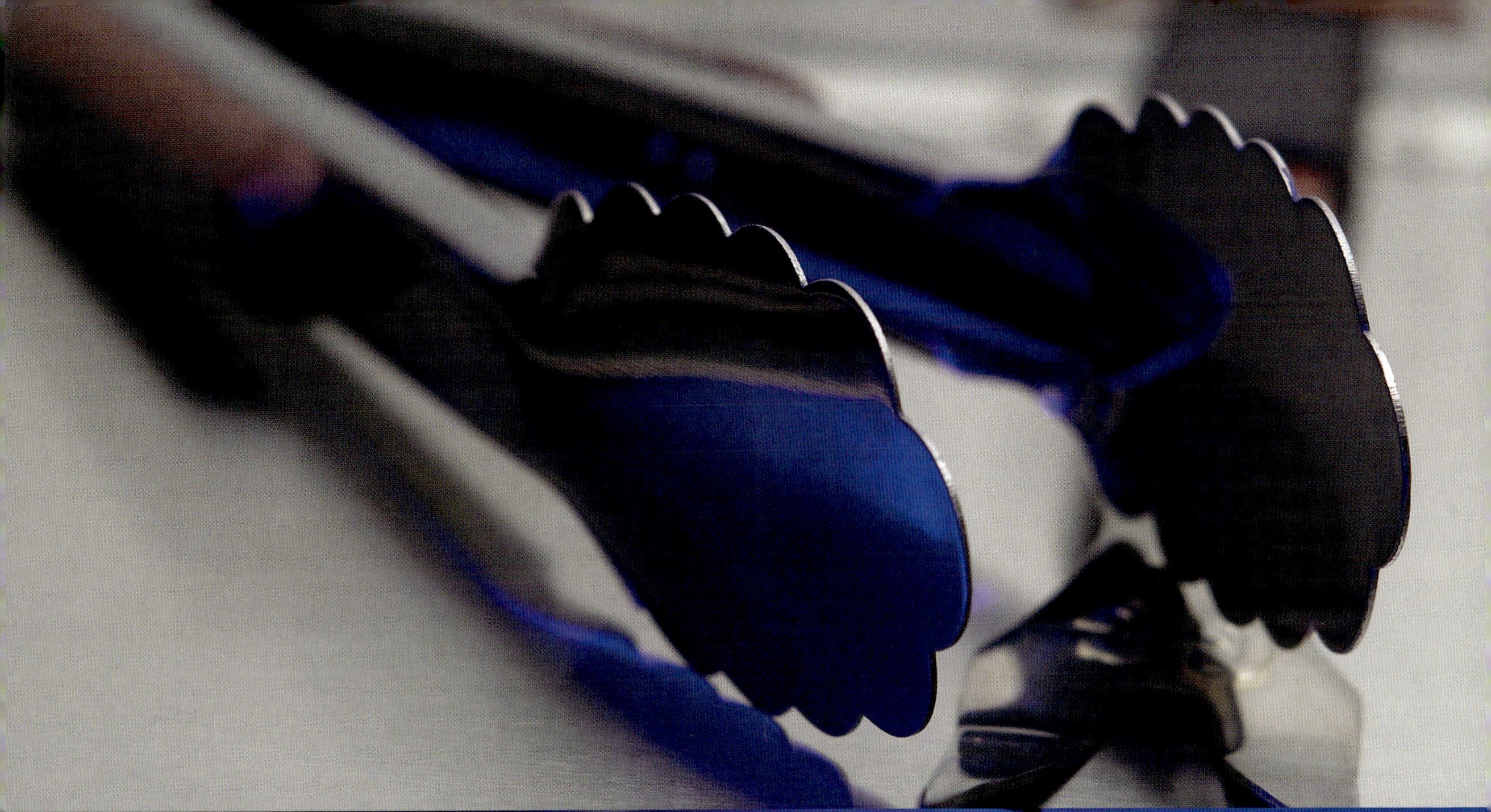

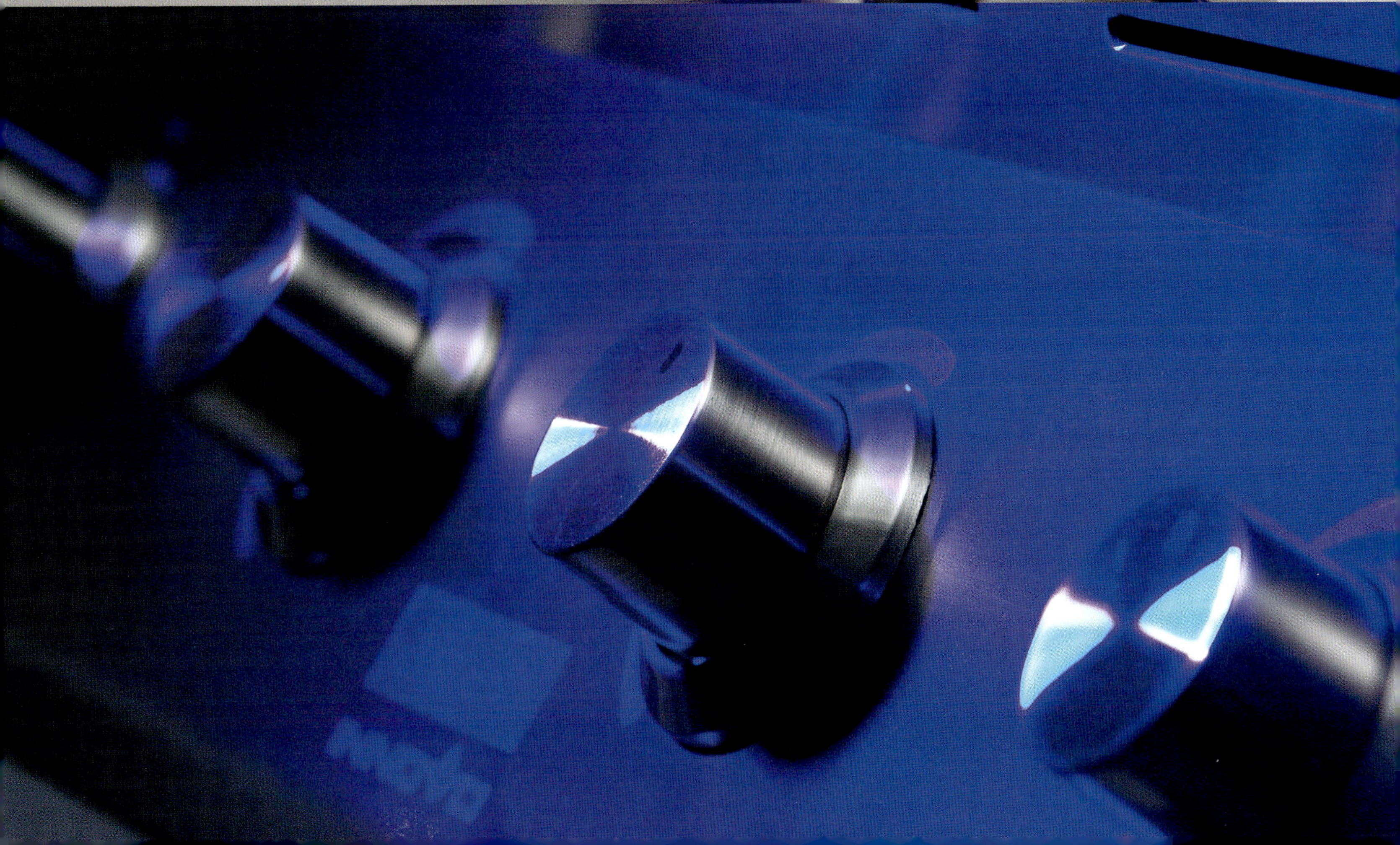

750g (2lb) boneless duck breasts
¼ cup sliced jalapeno chillies
¼ onion, finely chopped
¼ cup coriander leaves, rinsed and ripped
Salt to taste
1 cup cheddar cheese, grated
8 medium flour tortillas
Semi-roasted Tomato Salsa (see recipe below)

Semi-roasted Tomato Salsa
1 cup semi-roasted tomatoes, roughly chopped
¼ cup red onion, peeled and finely chopped
1 tablespoon Jalapeno chillies, minced
½ tablespoon brown sugar
1 tablespoon brown vinegar
2 tablespoons olive oil

DUCK QUESADILLAS & SEMI-ROASTED TOMATO SALSA

For the Semi-roasted Tomato Salsa

Make this delicious salsa at least four hours before use by mixing all the ingredients together—it will store in the refrigerator for five days. Trim the duck breasts of as much fat as possible. Leave the skin on and cut two diagonal slashes into the skin to let the fat escape during cooking.

Mix the chillies, onion, coriander leaves and salt together to make the salsa.

Put the duck on a medium-hot plate, skin-side down. Allow to cook and to brown very well—about 3 minutes—turn and cook for 5–7 minutes. Flip over onto a medium-hot grill to cook on the skin side for 2 minutes or until medium. Remove and let rest for 5 minutes. Slice into very thin strips when cool enough to handle.

Lay a flour tortilla out and spoon cheese over half of it. Top with some duck slices and then some of the chilli mix. Fold the empty half over the stuffing and tuck the folding edge in under some of the filling. Put to one side and repeat until all tortillas are filled.

Spray a medium-hot plate with oil and add the quesadillas, cheese-side-down first. Allow to cook for 1–2 minutes. Spray the top with oil and flip over quickly, holding the top as you do so the filling doesn't fall out. The cheese should have melted enough to grip most of the filling.

Lift the quesadillas off the plate when done—about 2 minutes on the second side will do it. Serve the quesadillas onto a large platter in the centre of the table, with the salsa in a separate bowl.

Serves 4

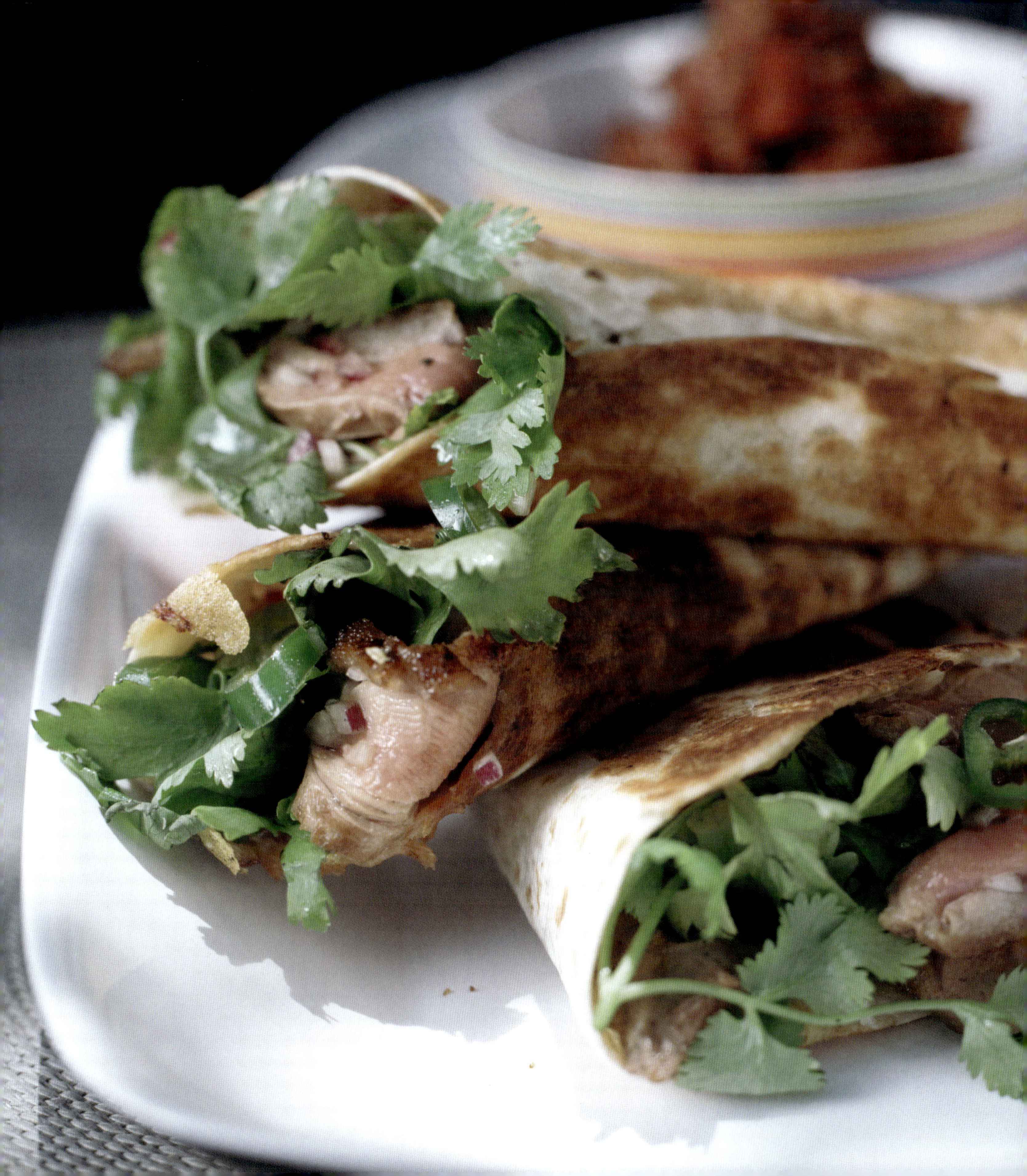

4 x 150g (5oz) chicken breast, boneless and skinless

For the salad
150g (5oz) curly parsley, washed and roughly chopped
20 Vietnamese mint leaves, torn into smaller pieces
60g (2oz) peanuts, roasted and crushed
1 green banana pepper, large, halved, de-seeded and roughly chopped
2 green spring onions, roughly chopped
1 tablespoon raw sugar
2 tablespoons fish sauce
2 tablespoons peanut oil
1 tablespoon rice vinegar
Spray oil

CHICKEN BREAST WITH ASIAN PARSLEY SALAD

Butterfly the chicken breast and slightly flatten.

Make the salad by combining the parsley, Vietnamese mint, peanuts, banana pepper and spring onions. Whisk the sugar, fish sauce, oil and vinegar until the sugar is dissolved and pour over salad ingredients. Toss well, cover and refrigerate.

Spray the open cut side of the chicken and place on a medium-hot plate. Cook for 1 minute and spray the uncut side with oil. Flip the chicken breast over and cook on this side for 1 minute. Lift the chicken breast onto a medium-hot grill and cook a further 1½ minutes on each side.

Remove the chicken breast onto paper towelling and return to the kitchen.

To serve, spoon an equal amount of salad into the centre of each plate. Cut the chicken breasts into halves along the existing cut line so that you have two pieces of chicken around the same size. Stack two pieces on top of each other and on the top of the salad. Repeat until each plate is completed.

SERVES 4

500g (1lb) chicken mince
1 egg
1 carrot, peeled and finely grated
1 medium orange, zest finely grated
1 tablespoon marjoram, finely chopped
Salt and white pepper
½–1 cup fresh breadcrumbs

4 medium field mushrooms, stem removed
Spray oil
8 slices sourdough rye bread
½ cup mayonnaise
    (for hand made see recipe page 242)
½ cup minced semi roasted tomatoes
1 x 100g (4oz) bag small salad leaves
White Balsamic vinegar

CHICKEN PATTIE & SOURDOUGH SANDWICH

Mix chicken, egg, carrot, zest, marjoram and salt and pepper to taste. Add enough breadcrumbs to take up the liquid and give you a firm mix. The mixture will come away from your hands easily when it is ready. Shape into even-sized patties and refrigerate for a few hours before use—done the day before use is even better.

Spray a medium-hot plate with oil and add the chicken patties and cook until done, turning regularly. You will know they are done when the juices that come out of the top of each pattie are clear.

Cook the oil-sprayed mushrooms on a medium-hot grill. Spray the bread and toast each side on the grill.

Spread each slice of bread with some mayo and on the bottom piece, sprinkle over some minced semi-roasted tomatoes. Top with the pattie, mushroom and the slice of mayonnaise-smeared grilled rye bread.

Slice through on the diagonal and serve with a little salad beside the sandwich and dress with a splash of white balsamic vinegar

Serves 4

500g (1lb) chicken breast meat, boneless and skinless
1 tablespoon corn oil
1 tablespoon sherry vinegar
1 tablespoon allspice, ground
½ tablespoon oregano, dried & ground
2 tablespoons onion flakes, pre-cooked
1 teaspoon salt
¼ teaspoon chilli powder
Spray oil
2 cups lettuce, shredded
1 cup carrot, grated
2 medium salad tomatoes, cut into wedges
½ cup sour cream
8 wheat flour tortillas

CHICKEN FAJITAS

Cut the chicken breast across the grain into 1cm-wide strips and place in bowl.

Mix the oil, vinegar, sherry, allspice, oregano, onion flakes, salt, and chilli powder and pour over the chicken. Stir to coat the pieces, then cover and refrigerate for at least 2 hours.

Liberally spray a hot plate with oil and tip on the chicken strips. Spread over the plate with a spatula and cook by tossing and lifting the pieces and allowing them to brown for about 5 minutes.

Spray the tortillas with oil and heat very quickly on the grill. They take about 15–30 seconds on each side. Stack on plate to keep warm and cover with foil if you like.

Lift the chicken onto a large platter and serve with heaped lettuce, carrot and tomatoes on another platter.

Serve the chicken, salad items, tortillas and sour cream in the centre of the table for people to share.

SERVES 4

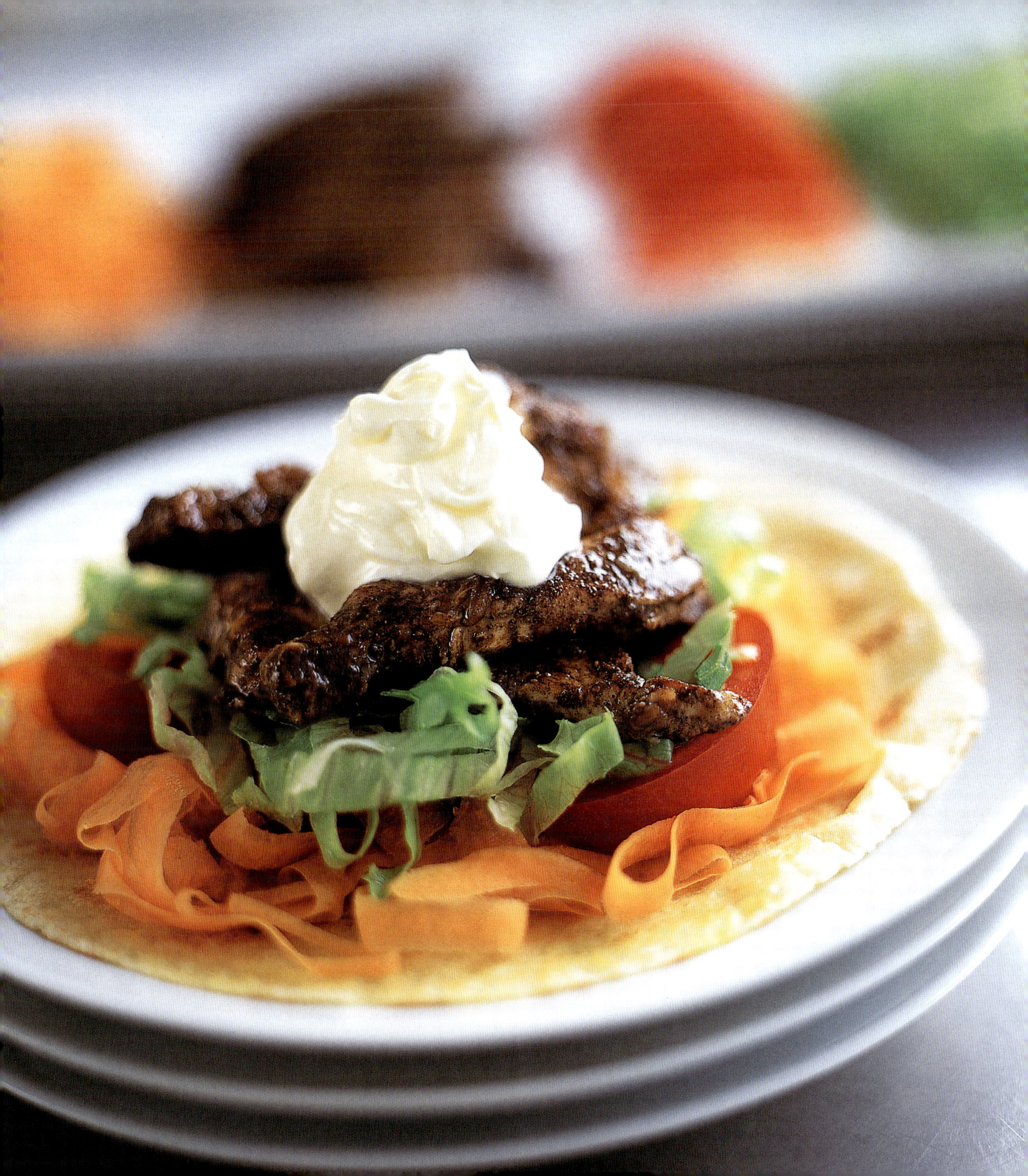

4 x 150g (5oz) chicken breast, skin on
2 tablespoons olive oil
Trim the chicken breast and drizzle with olive oil.

Ttzatziki
1 Lebanese or long green cucumber, about 25cm (10in) long
1 teaspoon salt
2 cloves garlic, crushed
1½ cups plain thick yoghurt
2 tablespoons mint, chopped
1 tablespoon extra virgin olive oil

Greek Salad
1 head regular lettuce, washed, crisped
2 medium tomatoes, cut into wedges
100g (4oz) feta cheese, diced
20 kalamata olives
2 tablespoons lemon juice
1 tablespoon extra virgin olive oil

Chicken Breast with Tzatziki & Greek Salad

For the tzatziki
Cut the cucumber in half lengthwise, scoop out the seeds using a teaspoon and peel the halves. Slice, very finely, into half moon shapes and put into a bowl, sprinkle on the salt and tumble. Leave to sit for 1 hour. Tip the cucumber pieces into a colander, run under cold water to rinse the salt and drain on paper towelling. With paper towelling, pat dry and tip into a serving bowl. Add the garlic, yoghurt, mint and olive oil and stir well. Refrigerate for 1 hour before serving.

For the Greek Salad
Break the crisp lettuce into bite size pieces into salad bowl. Add tomato wedges, tumble in the cheese and olives and leave the lemon juice and olive oil at room temperature. Drizzle the lemon juice and olive oil over the salad ingredients and serve so the salad may be tossed at the table.

Place the chicken on the medium-hot plate, skin-side down. Cook for 1 minute. Drizzle over a little of the oil the chicken has been sitting in and turn the chicken onto the flesh side. Cook for 1 minute and lift the chicken breast onto a medium-hot grill and cook for 2–3 minutes each side. Remove the chicken onto paper towelling and return to the kitchen.

To serve, spoon some tzatziki to one side of individual plates, slice the chicken across the grain and into rounds and fan around the tzatziki.

Serves 4

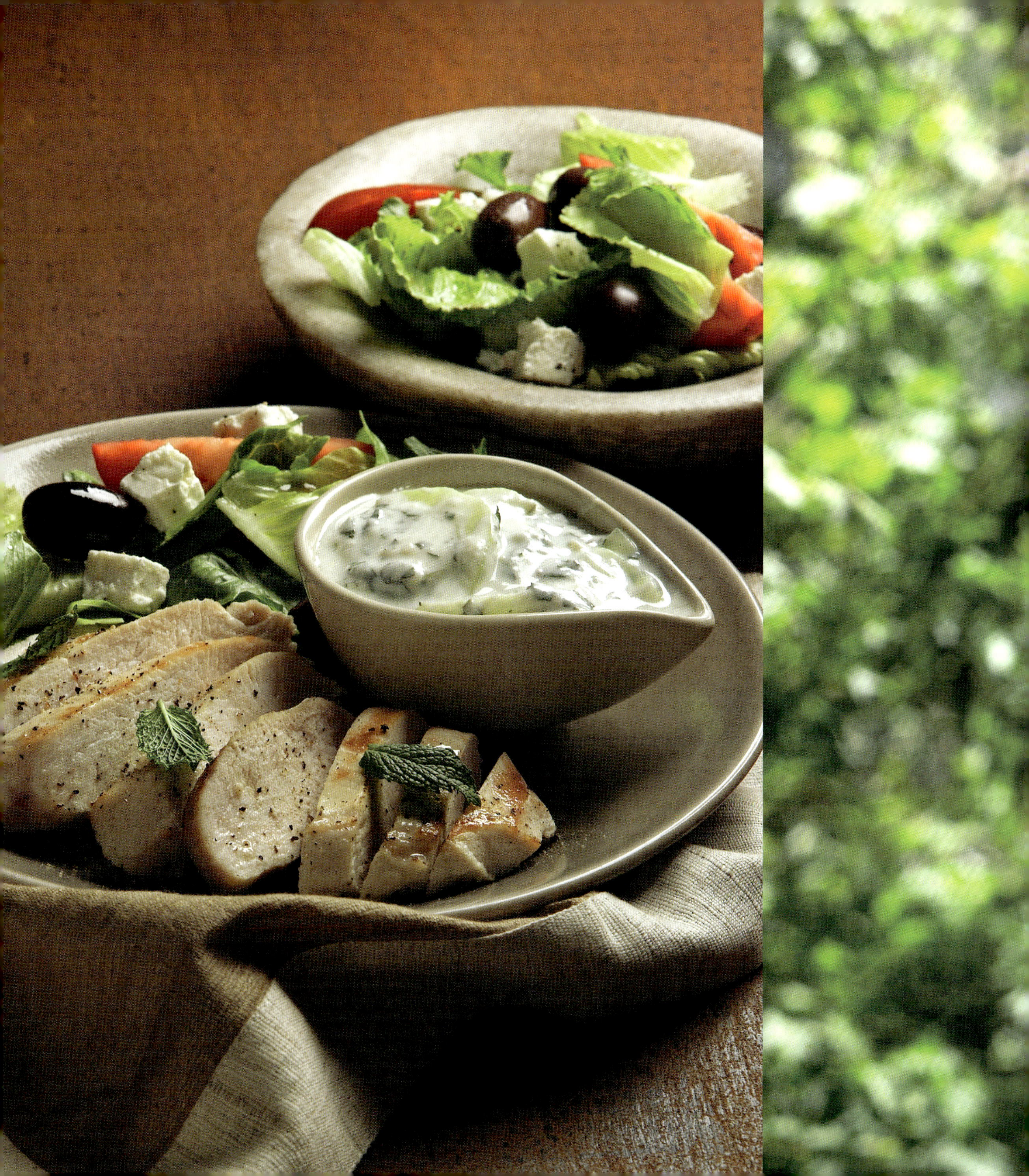

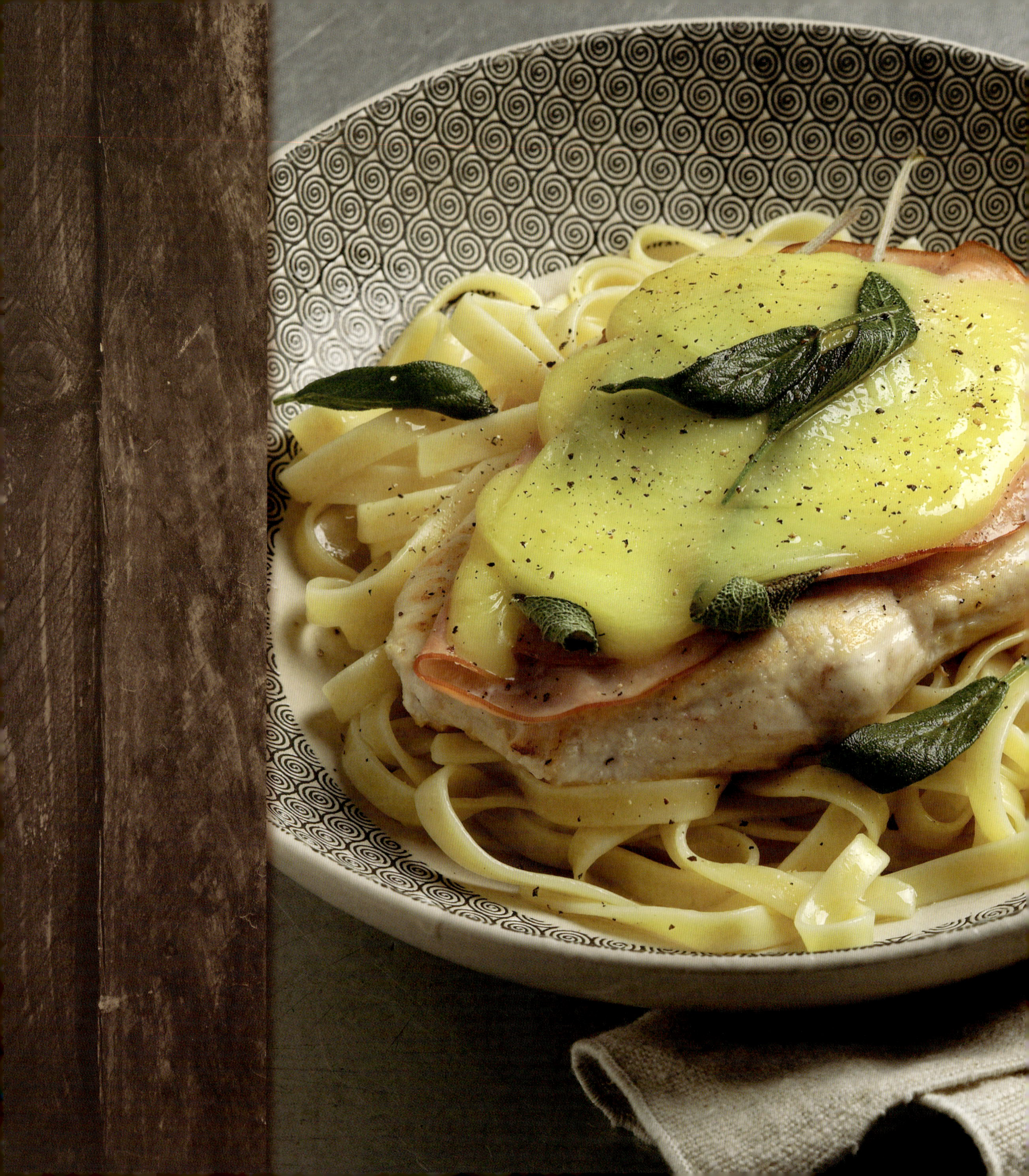

4 x 150g (5oz) chicken breasts, boneless
    and skinless
Spray oil
4 good slices ham, cut in half or enough to
cover the chicken
8 sage leaves
4 slices mozzarella cheese or enough
    to cover the chicken

CHICKEN BREAST SALTIMBOCCA

Put the single chicken breasts in between clingwrap and pound gently with a cooking mallet until evenly flat.

Spray the breasts with oil and seal each breast (for 30 seconds on each side) on a hot plate. Do not cook through as you have another cooking process to do yet and overcooking will dry out the chicken. Lift onto baking tray.

Cover each breast with ham and two sage leaves and cover with cheese. Sit tray on cake cooling rack and sit on plate (do not have burners on under the plate but the two burners of the grill going at high heat)—lower lid and cook until the cheese melts and is bubbling.

Serve on bed of cooked vegetables or pasta of your choice.

SERVES 4

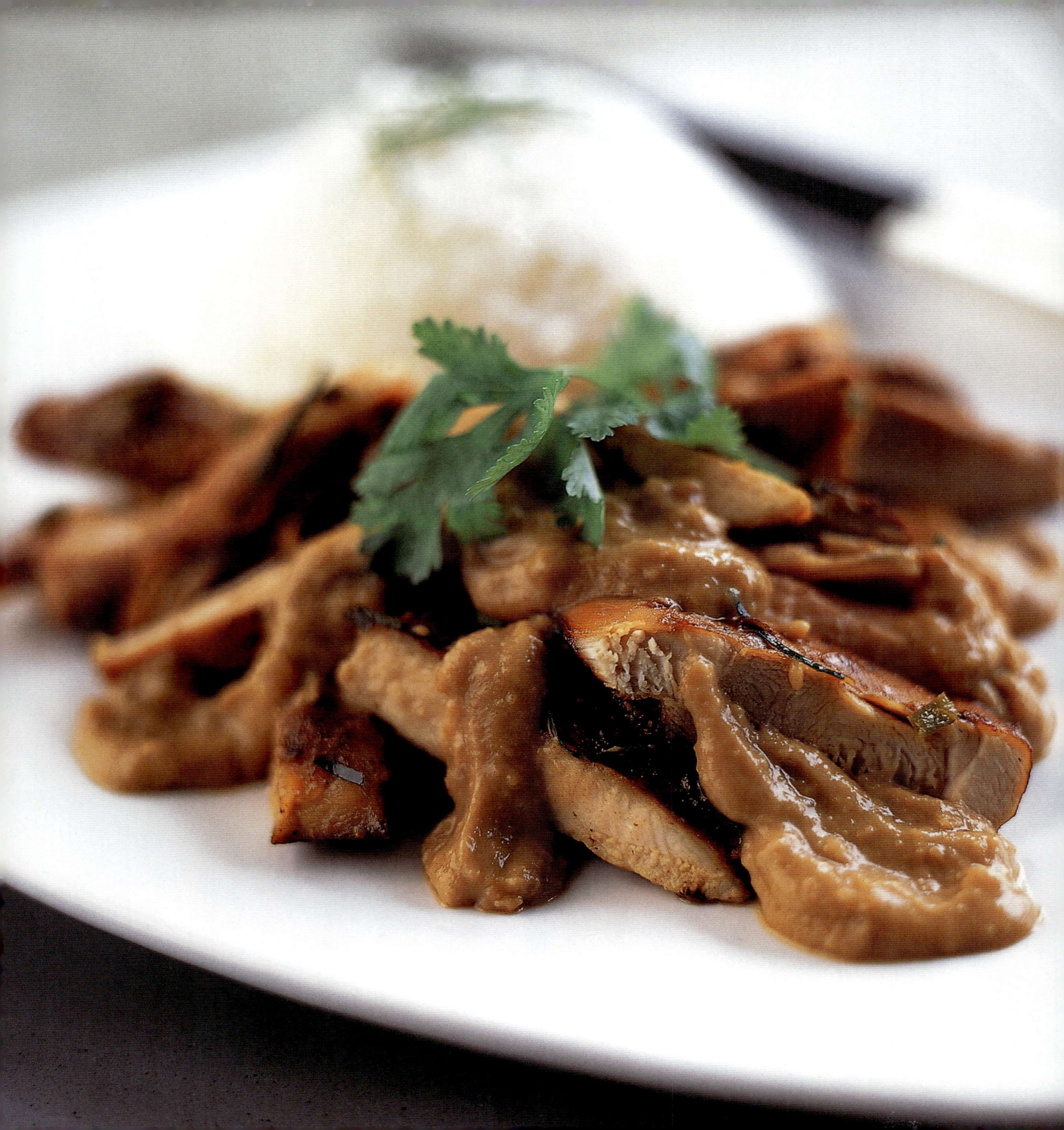

8 chicken thighs, total of 1kg (2lb), trimmed of all fat
½ cup lime juice, fresh
1 tablespoon ginger, minced
3 kaffir lime leaves, rib removed and finely shredded
1 green chilli, large, seeded and chopped
1 tablespoon sugar
2 x ½ cups peanut sauce (see recipe below)
1 tablespoon peanut oil
8 sprigs coriander (cilantro)
Spray oil

Peanut Sauce
6 tablespoons peanut butter (smooth or crunchy)
1 cup water
1 clove garlic
2 teaspoons palm sugar
1 red chilli, de-seeded and roughly chopped
2 tablespoons soy sauce, light
1 tablespoon lemon juice
1 tablespoon fish sauce
½ cup coconut milk

CHICKEN & LIME MARINADE WITH PEANUT SAUCE

For the Peanut Sauce

Put peanut butter and water in a saucepan and stir over moderate heat until mixed. Remove from heat and add all other ingredients. Return to moderate heat and stir for 5 minutes.

Cut the chicken thighs in half so you have 16 pieces.

Mix the lime juice, ginger, lime leaves, chilli and sugar. Pour onto the chicken thighs and move the meat through the marinade so it coats evenly. Refrigerate for 30 minutes.

Spray medium-hot plate and add the chicken thighs which have been drained from the marinade and cook the chicken for 2 minutes on each side, adding a little of the remaining marinade, if any.

With a sharp knife and a set of tongs, cut the chicken thighs into strips about 1cm wide. Bring all the chicken pieces to a concentrated area on the plate and pour over ½ cup peanut sauce. Lift and coat the chicken with the sauce. Cook and coat with sauce until done.

Lift the chicken onto a serving plate and pour over the other half cup of peanut sauce. Decorate with the coriander sprigs and serve with boiled rice or cooked rice noodles.

Serves 4

4 x 150g (5oz) chicken breasts, boneless
Spray oil
1 large cob corn, husk and silk removed
1 cup unpeeled tomatoes, diced and lightly cooked
1 cup mango flesh, diced
1 very small red onion, peeled and finely diced
1 small banana chilli, deseeded and minced
1 tablespoon parsley, chopped
Salt and ground black pepper to taste
2 tablespoons sherry vinegar
3 tablespoons olive oil
20 asparagus tips

CHICKEN, BARBECUED CORN SALSA & ASPARAGUS

Slice each chicken breast, on the diagonal, into three even pieces. Flatten slightly.

Spray the corn cob with oil and cook on a hot grill, turning regularly to lightly brown the corn. When done and the corn is cool enough to handle, cut the kernels from the cob into a bowl. Add the tomato, mango, onion, chilli, parsley, salt and pepper. Stir in the vinegar and oil.

Grill the oil-sprayed asparagus tips over medium heat and lightly cook. Watch them because they burn very easily.

Cook the oil-sprayed chicken slices on a medium-hot plate to start and turn to seal both sides. You can finish these on the grill to get the grill marks if you like.

To serve, spoon equal amounts of salsa onto each plate, top with three chicken pieces on each plate and then top with the asparagus tips.

SERVES 4

1–2kg (2–4lb) chicken
2 teaspoons Australian Native BBQ spice mix
 (see note below)
½ cup vegetable oil
1 tablespoon lemon juice
Salt

Chicken & Australian Native Baste

There are any number of these unique spice mixes in supermarkets or delis. The one I use is from Herbies which can be purchased online and posted to you. See www.herbies.com.au

Pre-heat barbecue to 150°C (300°F).

Cut the chicken into halves (through backbones and breast—remove the breast bone) and slice two deep cuts into the skin side of each half to allow for quicker cooking. Insert a long metal skewer into each of the chicken halves from neck and under thigh bone.

Sit the chicken halves on a cake cooling rack on a baking tray.

Mix the Australian Native spices with the oil, lemon juice and salt. Using a pastry brush, baste the skin side of each chicken half.

Cook the chicken in the barbecue with the burners at each end on medium. Sit the baking tray in the middle of the plates with no direct heat under it. Drop the lid and baste twice during the 45 minutes it takes to cook the chicken halves.

Remove and allow to rest for 5 minutes before quartering to serve on individual plates with salads of your choice.

Serves 4-6

1kg (2lb) free range chicken
Spray olive oil
Salt

Bread stuffing
150g (5oz) day-old bread, broken into small pieces (I leave the crust on)
60g (2oz) onion, finely diced
1 tablespoon each parsley, rosemary and thyme, roughly chopped
1 teaspoon nutmeg, freshly grated
Zest of one orange
1 egg
2 tablespoons oil (I used macadamia because I like that nutty essence)

CHAR-ROASTED CHICKEN WITH OLD-FASHIONED BREAD STUFFING

Small meat thermometers are inexpensive and are so helpful in letting you know the internal temperature of the item being cooked. For the chicken, test (insert thermometer) between the thigh and the body of the bird. Also test the centre of the stuffing. If you have too much stuffing, put it into the neck cavity of the chicken and secure by wrapping the skin around the stuffing and skewer into place.

Preheat barbecue to 180–200°C (350–400°F). Have a maximum of only two burners on at one time.

Wipe out the inside of chicken. Mix all the stuffing ingredients together. Put inside the gut cavity and push firmly. Do not overfill as it will burst out during cooking. Tie or skewer the legs around the opening and spray with oil.

Put into an aluminium roasting tray or sit on a cake cooling rack (or you can use a rotisserie or the roasting tray that hangs from the lid). Sprinkle with salt and cook for 50 minutes. Baste twice and turn to ensure even cooking.

Internal temperature of chicken must be at least 75°C (167°F). Use small meat thermometer. Remove from barbecue, rest for 5 minutes and cut into quarters to serve with vegetables or salad.

Serves 4

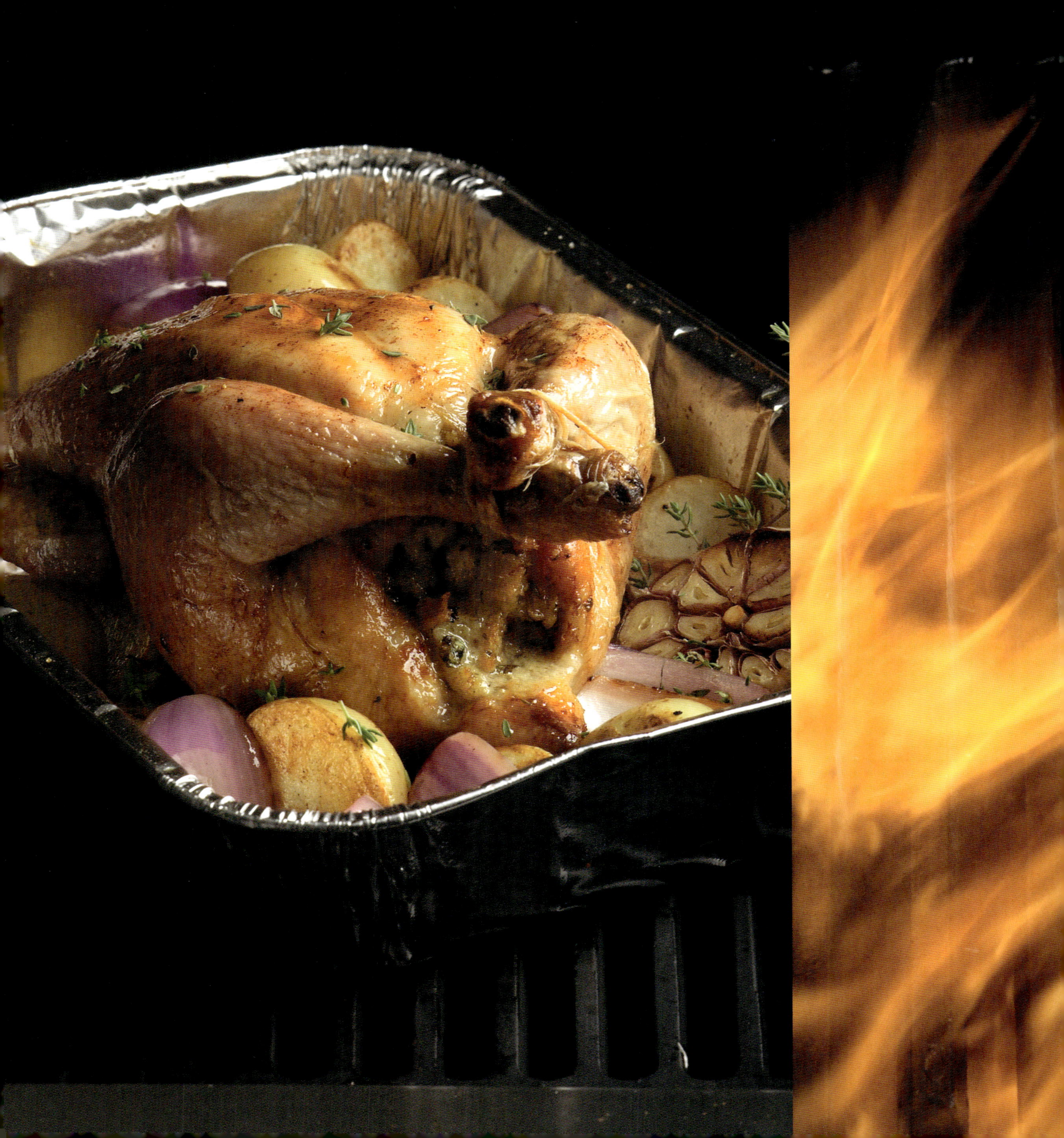

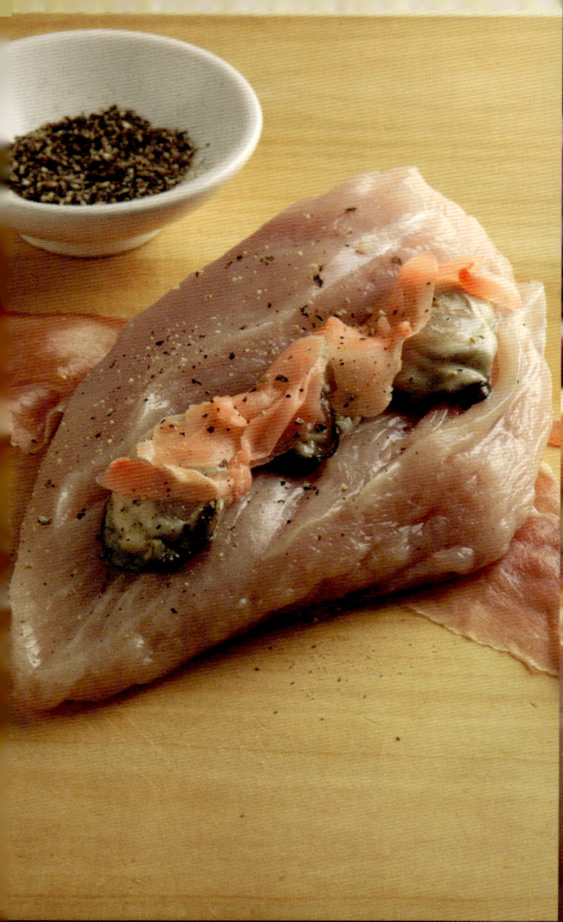
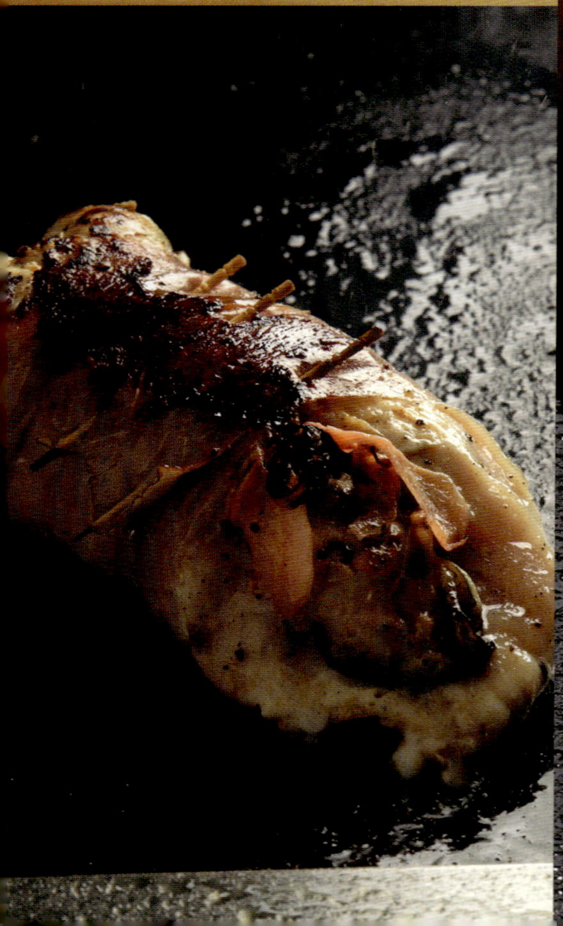
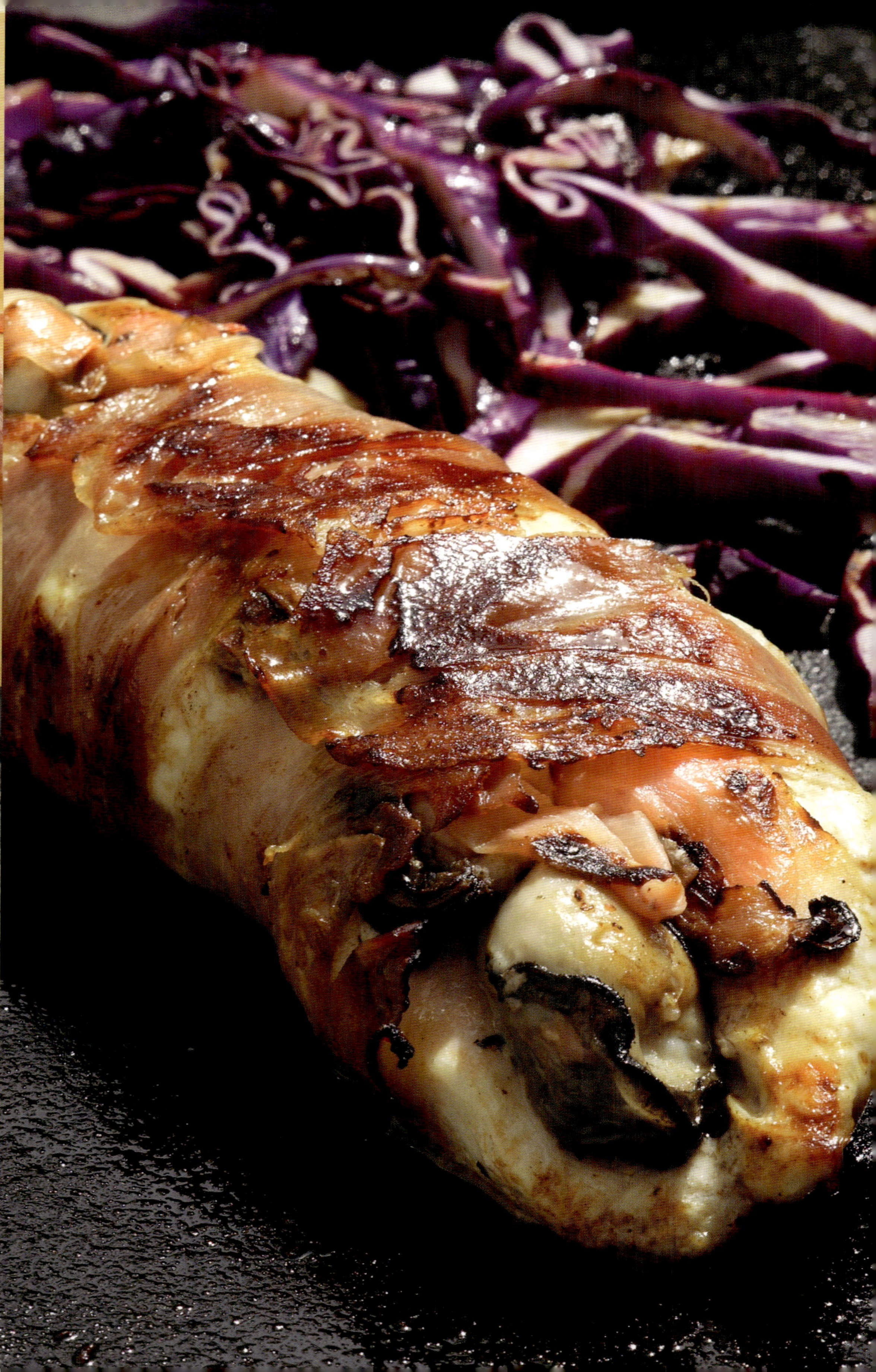

4 x 150g (5oz) boneless chicken breasts
16 natural oysters, removed from the shell
8 slices Japanese pink pickled ginger
Black pepper
4–8 slices proscuitto
Toothpicks
Spray oil
1 tablespoon vegetable oil
400g (14oz) red cabbage, finely sliced
1 tablespoon lemon juices
Salt and pepper to taste

CARPETBAG CHICKEN BREAST & RED CABBAGE

Butterfly the chicken breast by laying each one on a cutting board and then slicing almost through. Lift out one side to make the rough shape of a butterfly. Lay 3–4 oysters down the centre of each breast. Top with equal amounts of the pickled ginger and sprinkle on black pepper to taste. Fold the chicken meat around the oysters to form a neat parcel.

Wrap the breasts well in proscuitto. Pin into place with toothpicks and refrigerate until ready for use.

Spray a medium-hot plate with oil and add the chicken breasts. Seal for 2 minutes each side. Drop the lid and cook until done, turning every now and then, for around 10 –15 minutes depending on the size of the breasts.

Heat the oil to smoking point in a wok. Tip in the cabbage and move around the wok quickly. Add the lemon juice and salt and pepper and cook until softened.

Serve the chicken with the toothpicks removed and cut in half on the diagonal to sit on top of the cabbage in the middle of individual plates.

Serves 4

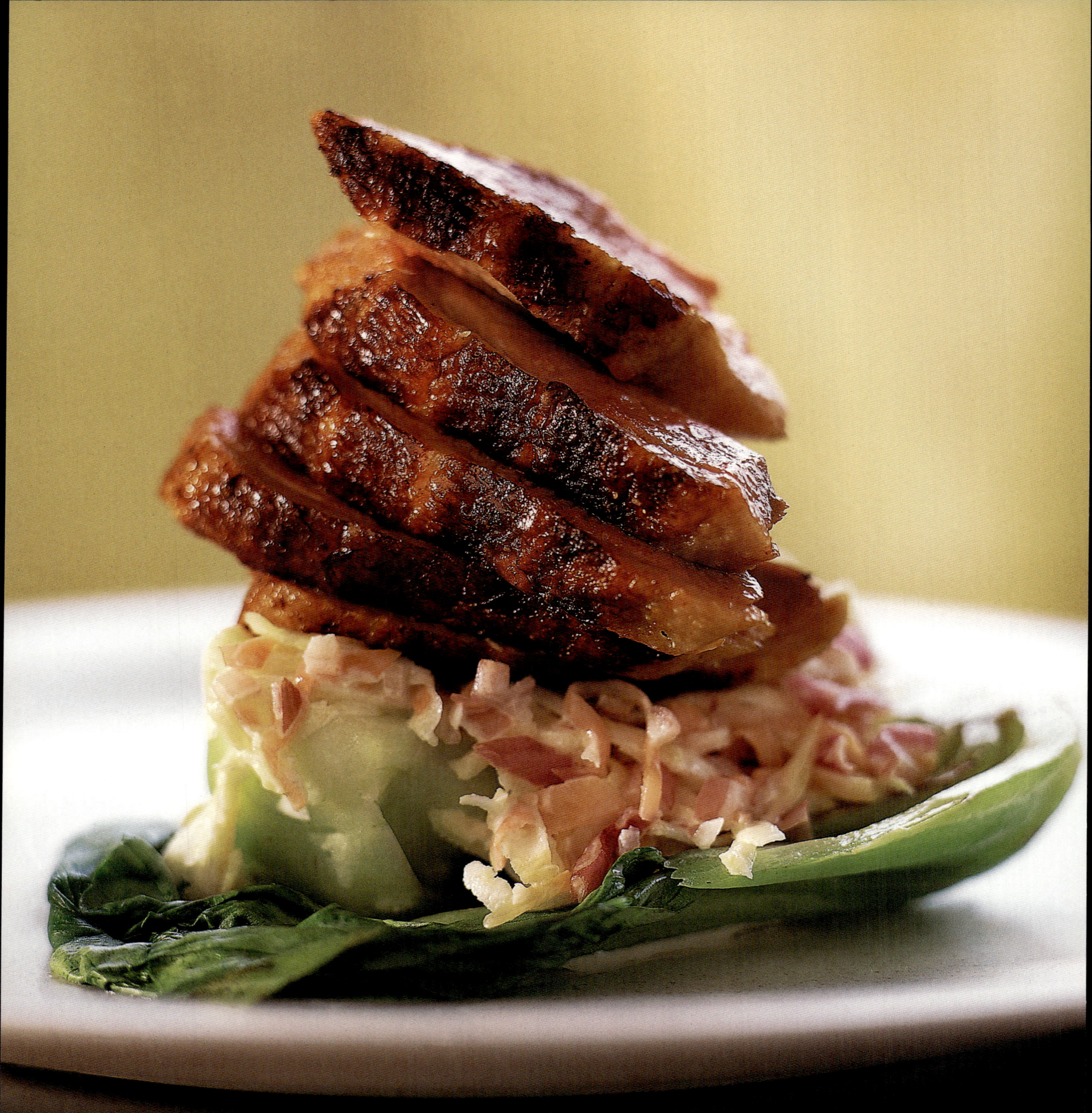

4 x 120g (4oz) duck breast, Muscovy is the best
200g (7oz) celeriac, peeled and roughly grated
2 medium eschallots, peeled and finely diced
1 tablespoon Japanese pickle ginger, finely sliced
½ cup mayonnaise
1 tablespoon pickled ginger juice
4 medium bok choy, trimmed, washed and halved

DUCK BREASTS WITH BOK CHOY & CELERIAC SALAD

THE COOKING OF THE DUCK BREAST IS DEPENDENT ENTIRELY UPON THE DEPTH OF FLESH. IF YOU ARE UNABLE TO GET MUSCOVY DUCK BREASTS, YOU WILL MORE THAN LIKELY END UP WITH QUITE THIN FLESH. MUSCOVY DUCK BREASTS HAVE AN EXCELLENT DEPTH OF FLESH, GENERALLY AROUND 2-3CM (1IN) THICK AND SOMETIMES LARGER. THE COOKING TIME THAT I HAVE RECOMMENDED WILL BRING THE DUCK BREASTS OUT TO MEDIUM TO RARE SO YOU WILL NEED TO COOK THEM LONGER IF YOU PREFER WELL DONE—WHICH I WOULD HEARTILY DISCOURAGE.

Trim the duck breasts if necessary and cut two slashes into the skin.

Combine the celeriac, eschallots, ginger, mayonnaise and ginger juice. Stir well and cover to refrigerate for 1 hour before use.

Take the duck from the refrigerator 10 minutes before use; place it onto a hot grill, skin-side down and cook for 2 minutes. Do not move the duck as you are looking for really good crisp marks on the skin. Turn the duck breast onto where it has already been cooking so that the natural fat that is on the grill will be used for the bare flesh and stop sticking.

Cook for 4 minutes, remove from heat and allow to sit for 5 minutes before slicing.

Place the bok choy on a medium hot plate and cook for 1–1½ minutes, turning only the once; the time will vary depending on the thickness of the white part of the bok choy as it must be crunchy.

Place two halves of the bok choy in the centre of the plate, spoon over equal amounts of the salad. Slice the duck breast into rounds and place on top of the celeriac salad.

SERVES 4

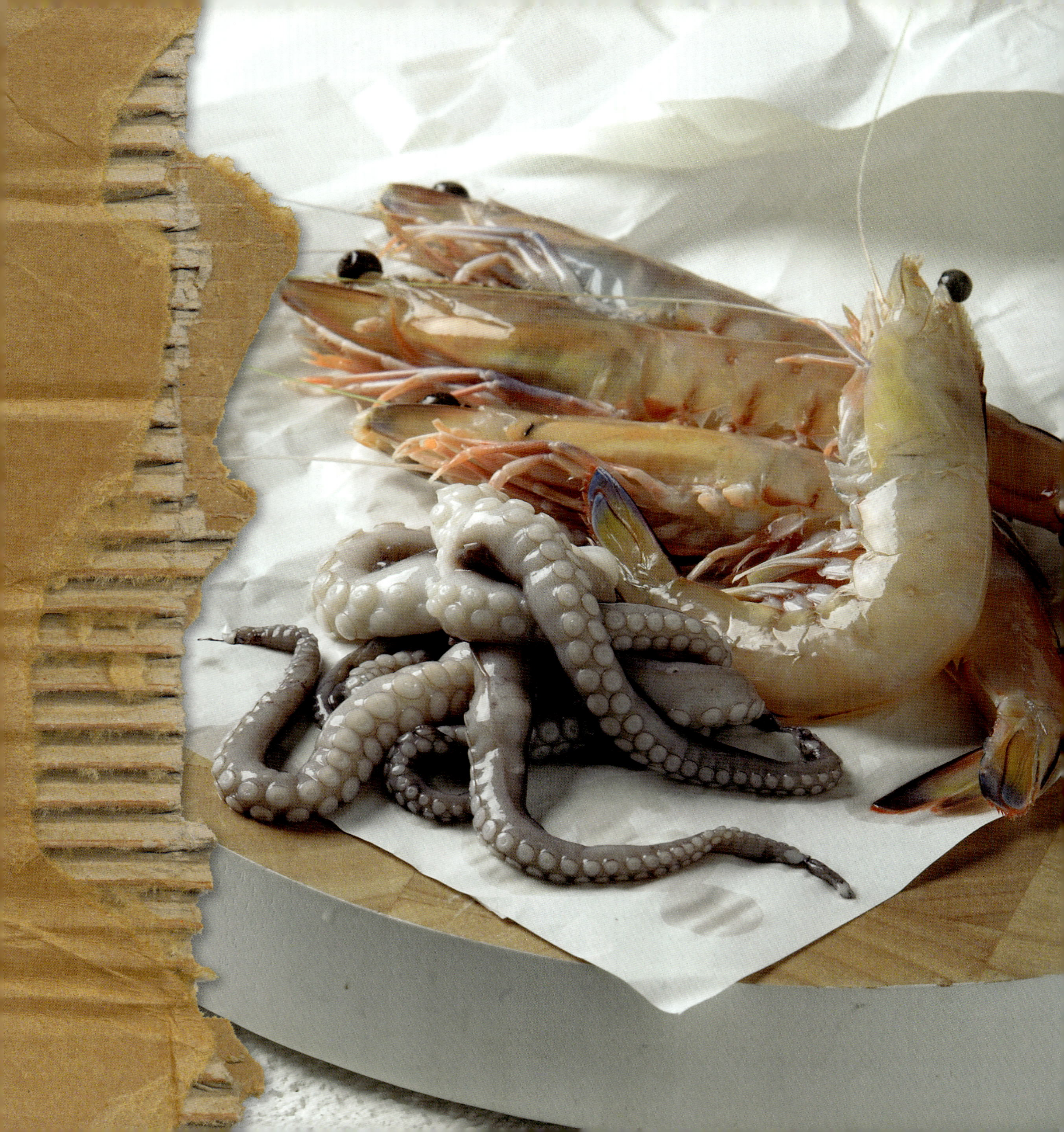

MAINS
SEAFOOD

600g (20oz) swordfish fillets, not broadbill swordfish
1 tablespoon sesame seeds
½ tablespoon sesame oil
1 tablespoon rice oil
¼ cup soy sauce
1 cup mango flesh, diced
½ cup lychees, deseeded and diced
¼ cup green spring onions, finely diced
¼ cup lime juice
8 coriander (cilantro) leaves, roughly chopped
1 teaspoon fish sauce
1 large green fruity chilli, minced
Coriander leaves for decoration

SWORDFISH KEBABS WITH MANGO & LYCHEE SALSA

I try to use stainless steel skewers as they conduct some heat through to the middle of fish pieces so they cook evenly.

Cut the swordfish into even pieces. Thread equal quantities onto oiled stainless steel skewers. Refrigerate until ready for use.

Make the sesame baste by pounding the seeds in a mortar and pestle and, when crushed, adding the oils and soy. Mix well and set to one side.

Make the salsa by combining the mango, lychees, green spring onion, lime juice, coriander, fish sauce and chilli. Gently toss. Refrigerate until ready for use.

Brush the swordfish kebabs with the sesame baste and place onto medium-hot plate. Turn regularly and carefully and baste as you go. Cook until just done because the fish cooks on when it has left the barbecue.

Spoon salsa into the middle of individual plates, top with swordfish and decorate with plenty of coriander leaves.

Serves 4

4 x 150g (5oz) tuna steaks
2 tablespoons black peppercorns, crushed
2 medium green mangoes or green apples
½ teaspoon salt
1 tablespoon fish sauce
1 tablespoon palm sugar, grated
1 tablespoon vegetable oil

3 tablespoon fried eschallots (called Fried Shallots and available in Asian supermarkets)
4 medium green spring onions, trimmed and sliced diagonally to bite-sized pieces
½ teaspoon ground white pepper
3 tablespoons roasted macadamia nuts, roughly crushed
Spray vegetable oil
1 large green chilli, deseeded and finely sliced

TUNA & GREEN MANGO SALAD

Lightly crust the tuna with the pepper and refrigerate until ready to cook.

Peel the mangoes and slice from the seed. Slice very finely into half moon shapes. If using apples, remove from the core, halve and slice very finely. Place the slices into a bowl and sprinkle with salt and toss together. Mix the fish sauce, palm sugar and oil together and pour over the mango or apple slices. Add the eschallots, green spring onions, pepper and macadamias. Toss gently to combine.

Spray the tuna with oil and cook on medium-hot plate for a minute. Spray oil, turn and cook for 30 seconds. You can continue cooking on the plate or at this stage move to the grill to get more flavour and to get the grill marks. You must not let the tuna overcook and it is best served medium.

Spoon the mango or apple salad into individual large Asian bowls, top with the tuna and sprinkle over the green chilli slices.

Serves 4

24 whole sardines, cleaned, gutted and butterflied
Sea salt
Spray olive oil

Huey's Aioli
½ cup good mayonnaise
3 tablespoons sour cream
1 teaspoon Dijon mustard
3 cloves garlic, crushed
1 tablespoon lemon juice

Carrot and Chickpea Salad
200g (7oz) baby carrots, peeled and cut on the diagonal
300g (11oz) canned chickpeas, drained and rinsed
1 teaspoon ground cinnamon
1 teaspoon ground cumin
1 small red chilli, deseeded and finely sliced
1 large lemon, zest
1 large lemon, juiced
2 tablespoons honey
½ cup olive oil

SPANISH-STYLE SARDINES WITH AIOLI & CHICKPEA CARROT SALAD

Iain Hewitson is a great bloke who adores his food and his influence on the Melbourne restaurant scene and Australian food at large is well recognised. His bar and restaurant, Barney's Bar, on Fitzroy Street in Melbourne's St Kilda is the place to go. He has let me use this recipe from Huey's Best Ever Barbecue Recipes.

Press some sea salt onto the sardines, spray with oil and cook on medium-hot grill until done. I do these in batches of 6–8 as they cook quickly. Cook until done.

Spoon the salad onto the sides of individual dinner plates, pile the sardines beside the salad and spoon a big dollop of aioli beside the sardines and serve immediately.

For the Carrot and Chickpea Salad
Cook the carrots in boiling water for a few minutes or until just tender. Mix the remaining ingredients, drain the carrots when ready and add to the chickpea mixture. Toss well to combine and leave to cool.

For Huey's Aioli
Whisk all the ingredients together for this quick, delicious version of aioli.

Serves 4

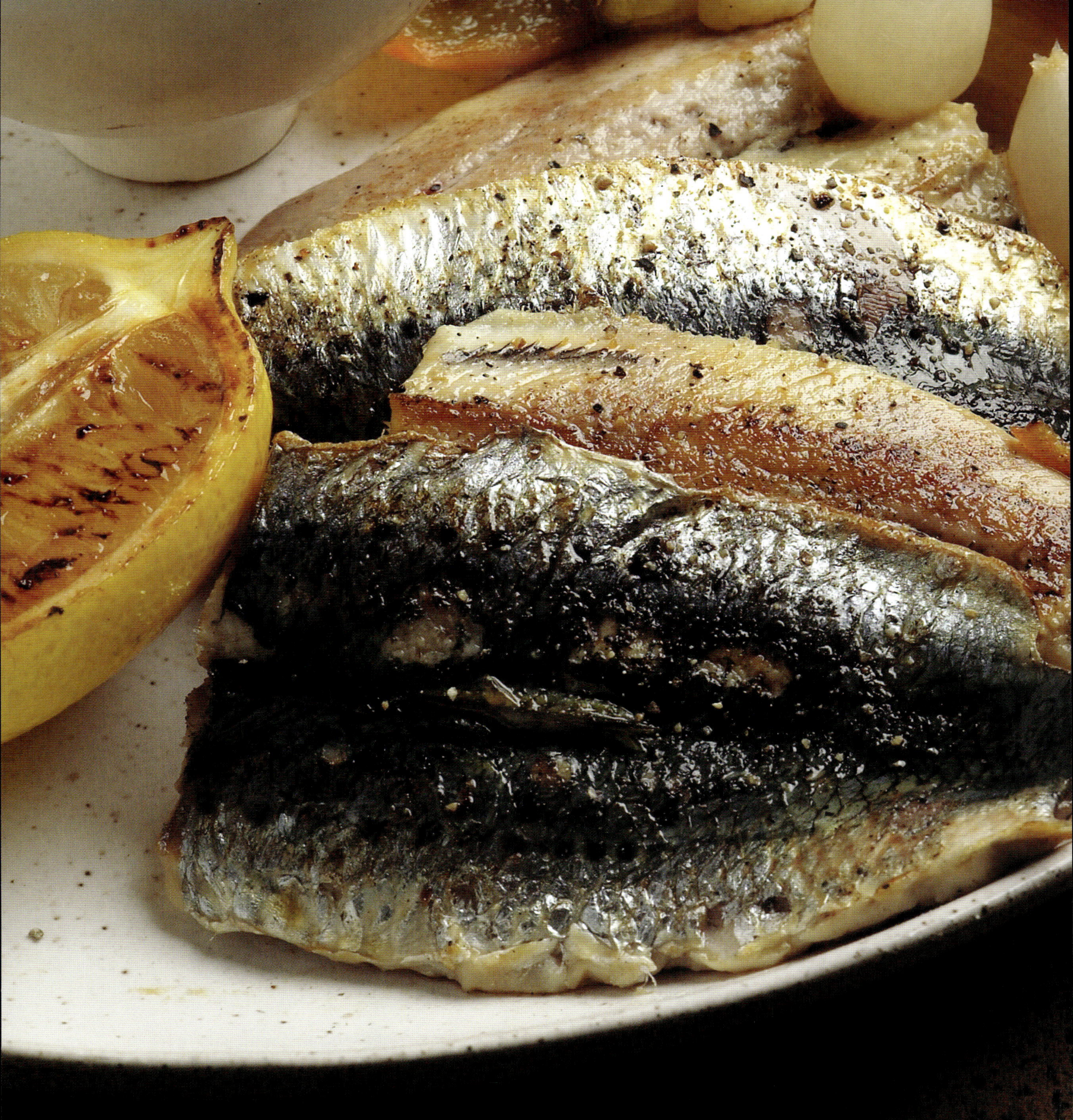

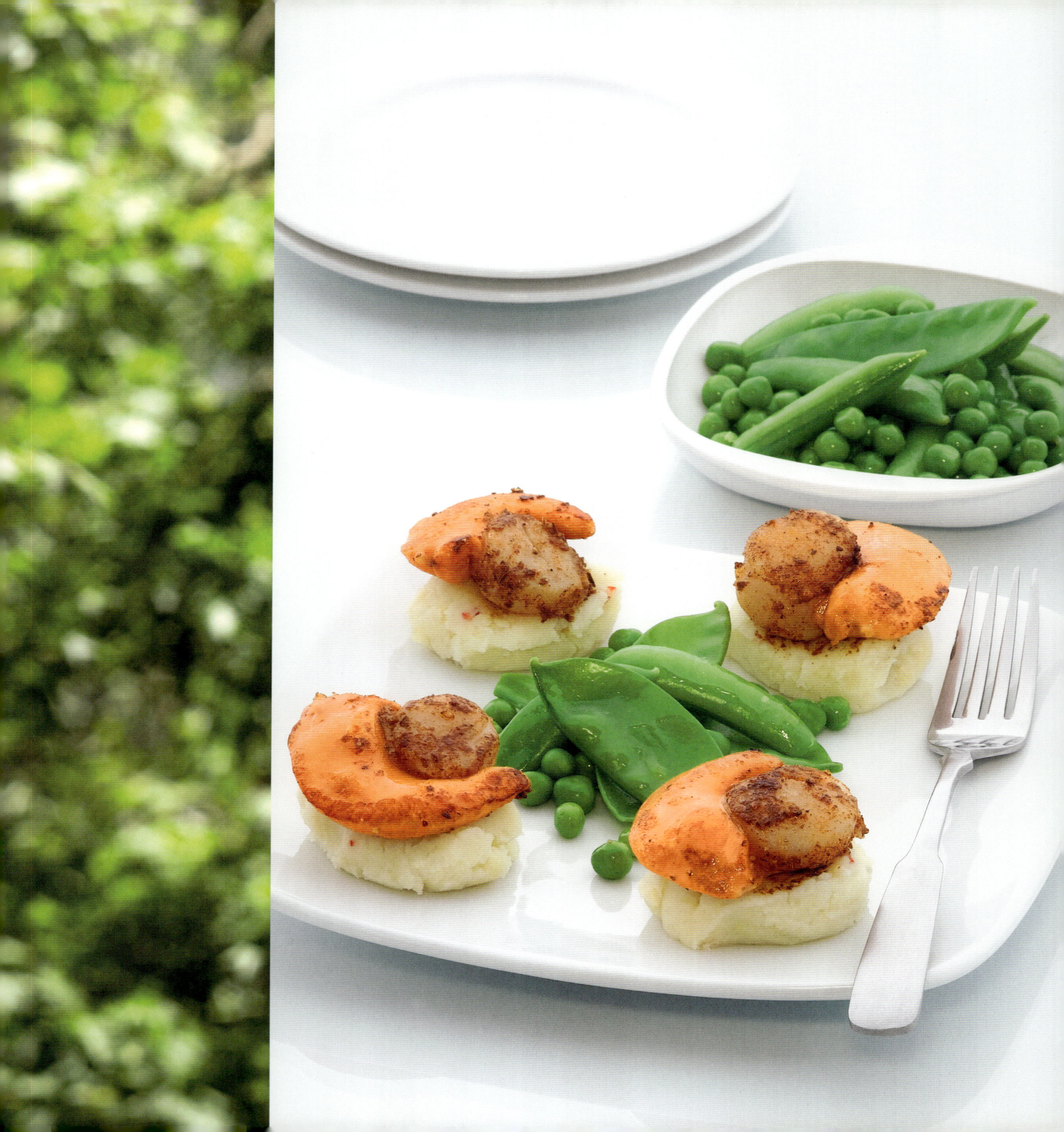

16 large sea scallops, roe on
1 teaspoon caraway seeds
½ teaspoon white peppercorns
½ teaspoon sea salt
½ teaspoon paprika
½ teaspoon allspice
100g (4oz) snow peas, trimmed
100g (4oz) honey snap peas, trimmed
100g (4oz) green peas, frozen
1 tablespoon butter
Spray olive oil

Mash
500g (18oz) pontiac potatoes, peeled and roughly chopped
60g (2oz) onion, finely chopped
1 teaspoon red chilli, finely chopped
4 tablespoons coconut milk, warmed

SPICE-CRUSTED SEA SCALLOPS WITH MASH & MIXED PEAS

Trim the scallops of the black membrane. Refrigerate until ready for use.

For the mash

Boil the potatoes until well done. Strain and return to saucepan with lid to sit for 3 minutes. Add the onion, chilli and milk and mash to a smoothish paste.

Dry roast the caraway seeds and peppercorns for 30 seconds. Tip into mortar and pestle and when cooled, add the salt and grind to a fine powder. Add the paprika and allspice and mix with the pestle.

Take the scallops from the refrigerator 10 minutes before use. Sprinkle both sides of the scallops liberally with the spice mix and pat it onto each scallop. Spray with oil and cook on a hot flat plate for 1–1½ minutes on this side. Spray with oil and turn to cook for 1 minute on the other side. Do not overcook these succulent beauties.

Boil the snow and honey snap peas for 2 minutes in salted water. Add the green peas and bring back to the boil. Cook for 1 minute, strain and toss with butter.

Spoon four equal amounts of mash around the perimeter of individual dinner plates. Top with a scallop and spoon the peas into the centre of each plate.

Serves 4

400g (14oz) ling fish fillets
½ cup soy sauce
2 tablespoons vegetable oil
1 clove garlic, crushed
1 tablespoon green ginger root, peeled and minced
1 teaspoon white sugar
2 tablespoons fresh pineapple juice
Spray vegetable oil
Coriander (cilantro) leaves for decoration (optional)

Glass Noodle Salad
125g (4oz) dried bean thread noodles
100g (4oz) daikon (Japanese white radish), peeled and finely shredded
½ telegraph cucumber (cut lengthwise), cut into half moons
1 very small red onion, peeled and sliced very finely
50g (2oz) Japanese pickled ginger, finely sliced
1 cup snow pea sprouts, washed and crisped

For the dressing
1 tablespoon palm sugar
100ml (4oz) coconut cream
2 limes, juiced
1–2 tablespoons fish sauce
Coriander (cilantro) leaves to garnish

SOY-SOAKED LING FISH STRIPS & GLASS NOODLE SALAD

I MAKE MY PINEAPPLE JUICE BY PULVERISING THE FLESH WITH A HAND PROCESSOR IN A LARGE JAR AND THEN STRAINING THE JUICE FOR THE PULP.

Cut the fish into even strips. Mix all the remaining ingredients together (except for the spray oil and coriander leaves) and add the fish strips. Coat well and marinate for 20 minutes.

FOR THE NOODLES AND DRESSING
Put the noodles into a large bowl and pour boiling water over to cover them. Let sit for 5–10 minutes then strain. Run under cold water to stop cooking. Ensure all the water is removed and tip the noodles into a mixing bowl and allow to cool for 10 minutes. Add all the other ingredients and toss gently using your hands. Make the dressing by combining all the ingredients and mixing well.
Pour over the assembled salad ingredients and toss. Top with the coriander leaves and serve as it is for a side salad or incorporate it as below.

Drain the fish and cook them on oil-sprayed medium-hot plate. Turn gently as they are fragile.

Serve equal amounts over the top of individual bowls of the noodles salad.

SERVES 4

4–8 flathead tails
Spray olive oil
3 cups chicken stock
1 cup yellow polenta
½ cup mushrooms, small and white as possible and finely chopped
Salt to taste
30g (1oz) butter

Mint Lemon Pesto
2 cups mint leaves, loosely packed
2 tablespoons lemon juice
1 clove garlic, roughly chopped
1 tablespoon pine nuts
1 tablespoon parmesan cheese, finely grated
125ml (4fl oz) olive oil
1 teaspoon ground black pepper

FLATHEAD TAILS, SOFT MUSHROOM POLENTA & MINT LEMON PESTO

THIS PESTO IS REALLY REFRESHING AND TANGY—IT DOES NEED TO BE MADE AS CLOSE TO SERVING AS POSSIBLE AS IT LOSES ITS COLOUR QUITE QUICKLY.

Trim the tails of the fin and refrigerate until ready to cook.

Spray the fish and cook, with the hood down, on a medium-hot plate until done. They will exude a white liquid from around the bone when ready to go—turn regularly as you cook.

Meanwhile, make the polenta by bringing the stock to the boil and tipping the polenta in slowly as you stir with either a wooden spoon or a whisk. Add in the mushrooms. Keep cooking over medium heat until the polenta is soft–about 5 minutes—remove from heat and stir in the salt and butter. Serve as soon as possible as it thickens. You may have to add more stock to keep it soft.

Spoon the polenta into the middle of individual plates and lean the fish tail against the polenta. Spoon a tablespoon or two of the mint pesto beside the fish and serve.

FOR THE MINT LEMON PESTO

Put the mint leaves, juice, garlic, pine nuts and cheese into a food processor. Start the motor and slowly add the oil in a steady stream. Season with pepper—mix well.

SERVES 4

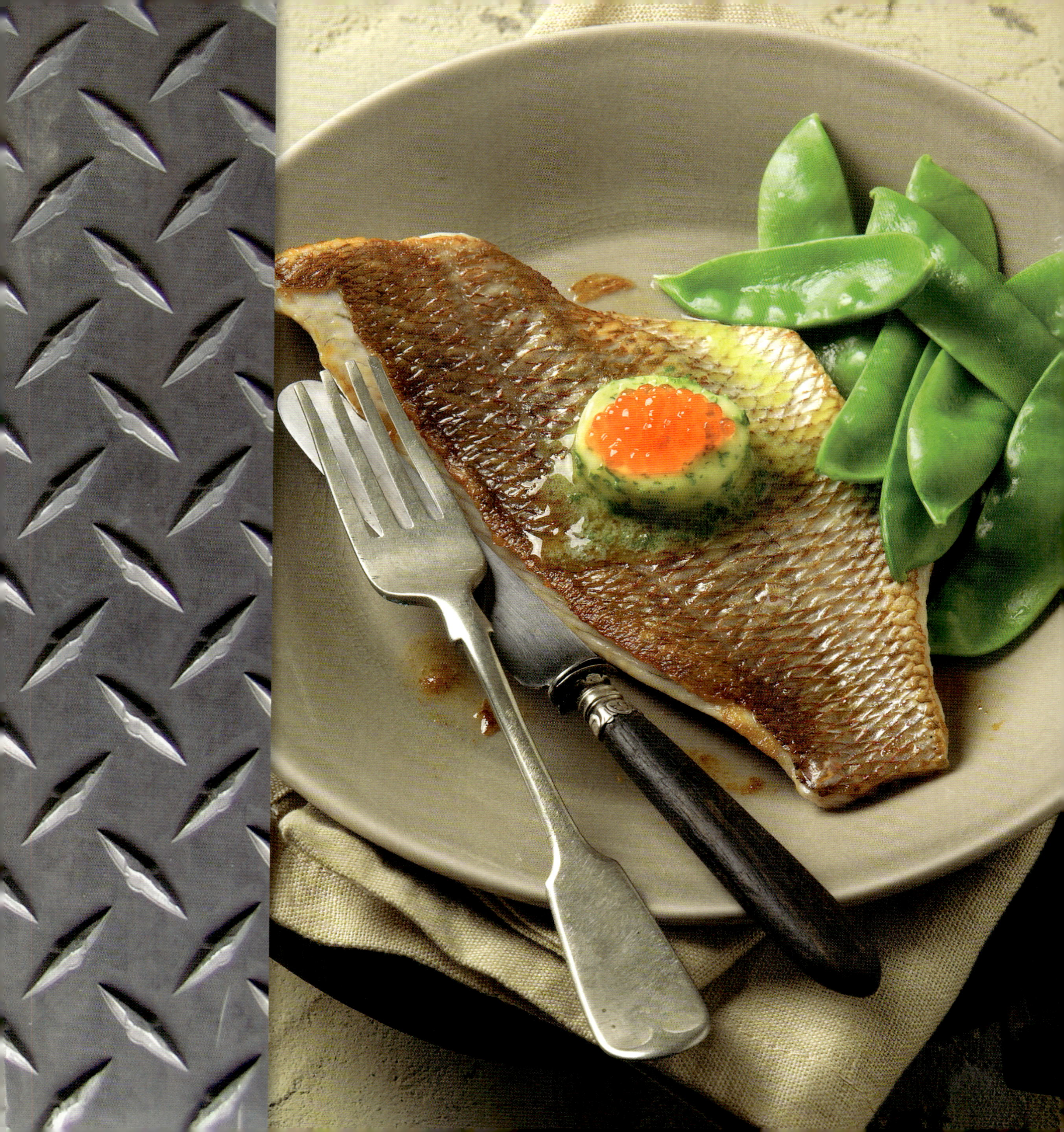

4 x 150g (5oz) snapper fillets
Spray olive oil
24 large snow peas, topped and tailed
4 tablespoons salmon roe

Chive Verjuice Butter
150g (5oz) butter, at room temperature
¼ cup chives, chopped
1 tablespoon verjuice
1 teaspoon ground white pepper

SNAPPER FILLETS WITH CHIVE VERJUICE BUTTER & SALMON ROE

For the Chive Verjuice Butter

Put the butter, chives, verjuice and pepper into a food processor and pulse until combined. Lift out with a spatula onto a piece of clingwrap or waxed paper. Shape into a log/roll and freeze to set for at least 30 minutes or longer so the flavours meld.

Trim the fish fillet and check for scales. Pat dry with towelling and spray with oil. Cook on medium-hot plate, starting with flesh side down. Spray the skin side of the fillet and turn after a couple of minutes. The thickness of the fish will determine how long they cook on this side. When you turn each fillet, put the spatula/flipper on top to stop the fillet curling.

Boil (or microwave) the snow peas until done.

Serve the fish on individual plates with the snow peas alongside and top with a good thick slice of the chive butter and with a tablespoon of roe on top of the butter.

Serves 4

4 x 160g (6oz) snapper fillets

For the salad
400g (14oz) canned cannellini beans, drained
2 large eschallots, finely chopped
¼ cup semi-roasted tomatoes, roughly chopped
1 tablespoon parsley, roughly chopped
½ cup olive oil
1 tablespoon prepared Dijon mustard paste
¼ cup cider vinegar
Salt and ground black pepper to taste
Spray olive oil
4 lime halves

SNAPPER FILLETS WITH CANNELLINI BEAN & ESCHALLOT SALAD

Trim the fish, if necessary, and refrigerate until ready to use.

Make the salad by tumbling the beans, eschallots, tomatoes and parsley together. Whisk the oil and mustard—dribble in the vinegar while whisking— and season with salt and ground black pepper to taste before spooning over the bean mix. Mix well and let sit for 2 hours, refrigerated, before serving.

Spray the fish with oil and cook on medium-hot plate until done. Cook the lime halves, cut-side down on a very hot grill to lightly brown and mark the cut flesh.

To serve, spoon the bean salad into the centre of individual flattish bowls, top with the snapper and put the lime half beside the fish with the cooked flesh-side up.

SERVES 4

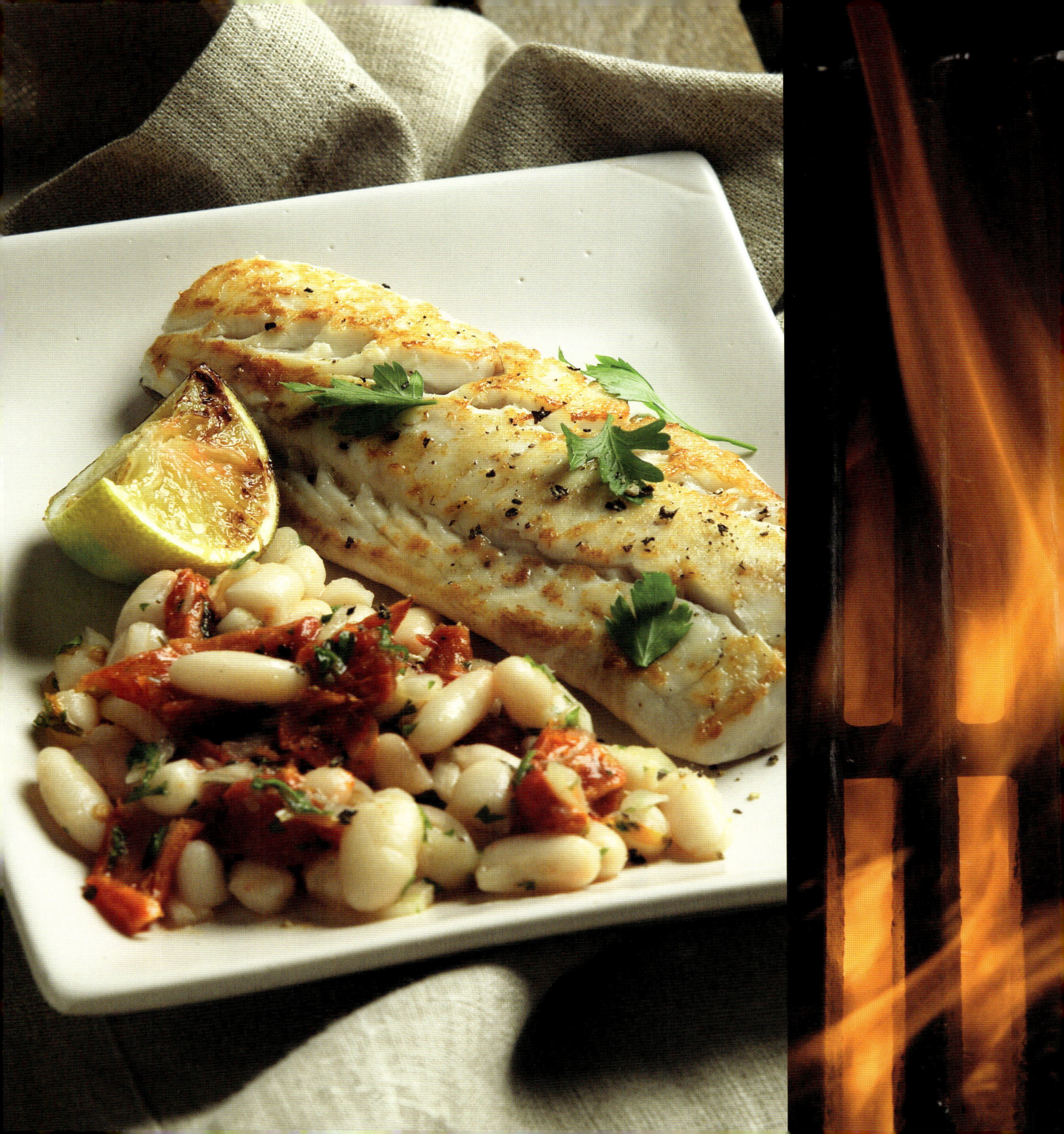

4 x 150g (5oz) ocean trout steaks
Spray olive oil
Salt
4 lemon cheeks

Apple, Fig, Walnut and Celery Salad
2 medium eating apples, cored, halved
　　and cut into half moon slices
2 dried figs, trimmed and cut into thin slices
1 cup celery, diced
1 cup celery leaves, washed and crisp, loosely packed
½ cup walnuts
½ cup mayonnaise
1 tablespoon Indian curry powder
1 tablespoon cider vinegar

SEARED OCEAN TROUT ON APPLE, FIG, WALNUT & CELERY SALAD

Trim the fish and refrigerate until ready to cook.

Spray skin with a little oil and sprinkle on a little salt. Cook the fish on a hot flat plate skin-side down for 1 minute. Lightly spray the flesh side with oil and turn and cook for 2 minutes. If the fish is sliced thinly, it will take less time.

Remove and serve on individual dinner plates with the lemon cheek and salad beside the fish.

For the Apple, Fig, Walnut and Celery Salad

Toss the apples, fig slices, celery, celery leaves and walnuts in a salad bowl. Mix the mayonnaise, curry powder and vinegar, pour over the apple mix and toss well.

It is important to do all this quickly as the apple will brown if allowed to sit without being coated with the dressing.

Serves 4

600g (5oz) cuttlefish, body only and with cuttlebone removed
Olive oil
250g (9oz) spicy Italian sausage, about 3cm (1in) in diameter
½ cup toasted pinenuts
1 x 100g (4oz) bag mesclun salad mix
20 grape tomatoes, halved
2 tablespoons zest of lemon, finely grated
¼ cup lemon juice
2 tablespoons Italian parsley, finely chopped
Salt
Extra virgin olive oil

SCORED CUTTLEFISH WITH SPICY ITALIAN SAUSAGE & PINE NUT SALAD

Cut the cuttlefish open to form one large flat piece. Trim and, with a very sharp knife, score the flesh into diamond shapes. Cut into bite-sized pieces and put into a bowl. Pour over some olive oil and toss the cuttlefish in it. Let sit for 15 minutes and if any longer, refrigerate.

Put the nuts, mesclun and tomato halves into the salad bowl and refrigerate.

Put the cuttlefish onto a hot plate with the scored side down. Toss once the scored side is lightly browned. Cuttlefish cooks quickly so do not overcook as this makes it tough. Lift from the barbecue and put into a bowl. Tip over the lemon zest, lemon juice, parsley and salt to taste. Toss to coat and cool the fish. Let rest.

Cook the sausage slices onto the grill. Allow to crisp and brown and remove from the barbecue when done.

Pour some olive oil over the salad mix and toss. Divide the sausage slices into equal amounts on individual plates. Add some salad on the top of the sausage slices and put pieces of the cuttlefish on top and around the salad.

SERVES 4

8 medium Rainbow Trout fillets
Spray olive oil
350g (12oz) red cabbage, finely shredded
½ green apple, cored and chopped finely
2 tablespoons vegetable oil
Sea salt and ground white pepper to taste
2 tablespoons red wine vinegar
2 cups green peas, cooked and kept hot
1 cup sour cream, at room temperature
1 tablespoon dill, chopped
¼ cup salmon roe

RAINBOW TROUT WITH PANFRIED RED CABBAGE & SALMON ROE CREAM

Trim the trout fillets if necessary and remove as many bones as possible. Refrigerate until ready to cook.

Tip the cabbage, apple and oil into a large bowl and toss to coat. Sprinkle with salt and pepper to taste. Cook on a medium-hot plate by lifting and tossing to keep the cabbage moving. Heap, pour on the vinegar and cover with hood or large stainless steel bowl and steam/cook for a minute. Lift from barbecue and keep warm. Alternatively, this can be done in a wok on the ring.

Cook the fish by spraying with fillets with oil and putting them onto a medium-hot plate, skin-side down. Cook for 1–2 minutes and turn. These fillets are generally quite thin and cook quickly so judge the cooking time by the thickness of the fillets.

Mix the sour cream, dill and roe together very carefully so as not to break the roe.

Serve by putting the cabbage into the middle of individual dinner plates, lean the fish against the cabbage, spoon the peas around and serve the cream on the side for everyone to take as much as they want.

SERVES 4

MAINS | SEAFOOD

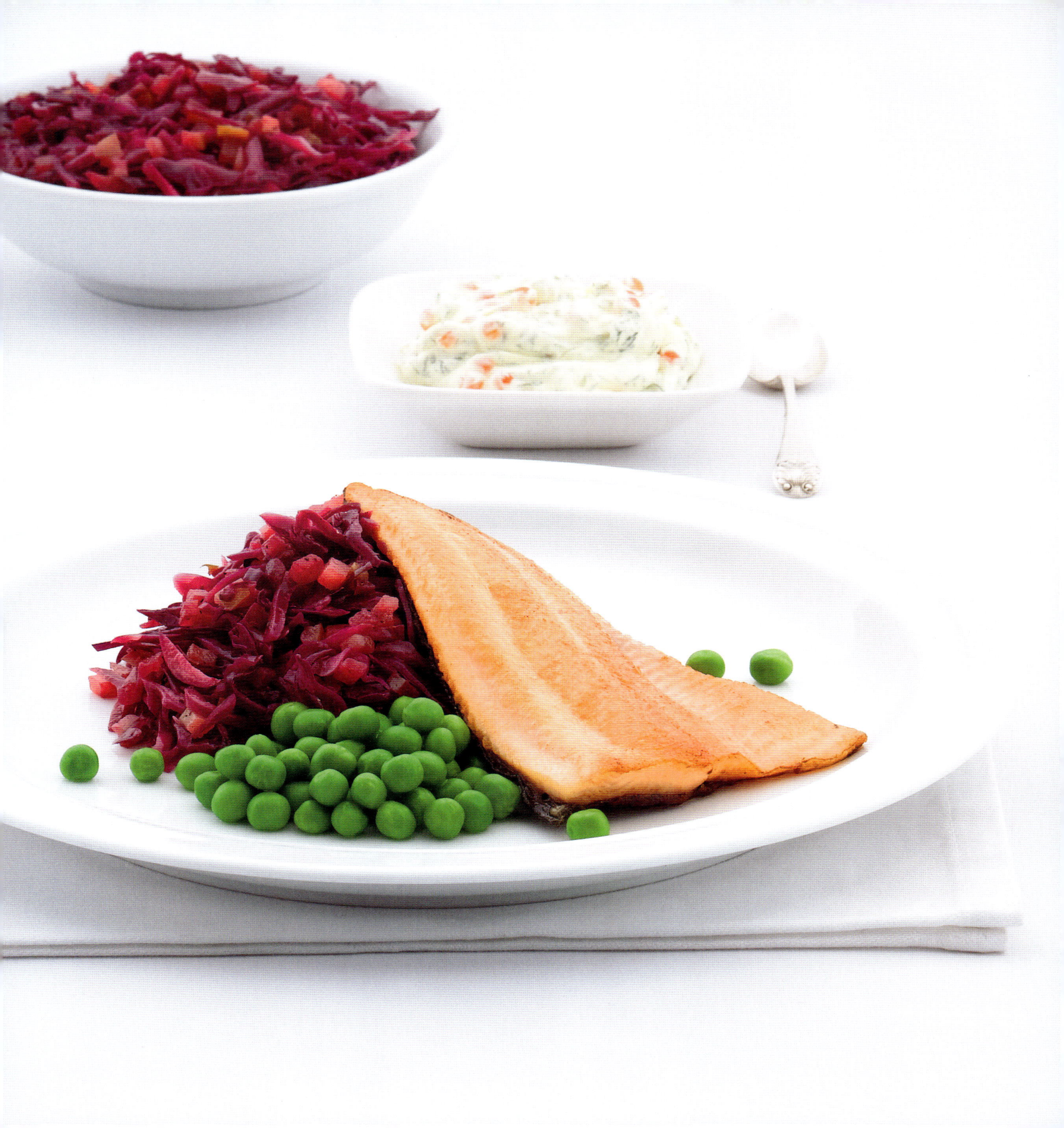

24 large green king prawns, with middle section peeled and de-veined
24 bamboo skewers, soaked in water for 30 minutes or metal skewers
12–24 slices prosciutto (this depends on how long each slice is. If really long, cut across to give two equal pieces. Larger prawns will require the whole piece)

Rocket Aioli
4 medium cloves garlic
½ teaspoon sea salt
2 egg yolks
½ teaspoon lemon juice
½ cup blanched and well drained rocket
125ml (4oz) olive oil

PROSCIUTTO PRAWNS WITH ROCKET AIOLI

Garlic varies in its intensity and you need to be aware of this. In testing this recipe twice with garlic from two different sources, I got two very different results. Go for large garlic cloves if they are not so powerful. How do you find out about the intensity? Cut a small piece off the end of the garlic you are using and eat. If it is strong, cut back on the amount used or blanch the garlic in boiling water for 30 seconds.

Take each prawn and thread it onto a skewer starting from the tail. Roll each prawn in prosciutto so as to cover all the prawn. Store on clingwrap-covered plate in the refrigerator until ready to use. The size of the slice of prosciutto will depend on the size of the prawns being used.

Cook the prawns on a medium-hot flat plate, turning regularly for even cooking. When the top (head end) of the prawns are completely white, they are ready to eat. The prosciutto wraps around the prawn very tightly as it cooks.

Serve with the aioli to one side and with lemon and olive oil-dressed rocket leaves.

For the Rocket Aioli
Put the garlic, salt, egg yolks, lemon juice and rocket into the food processor bowl and work for 30 seconds.

When this mixture is starting to thicken, slowly pour the oil down the feeder shoot. As it takes, you can add the oil a little more quickly until finished. Use immediately or store up to five days only.

Serves 4

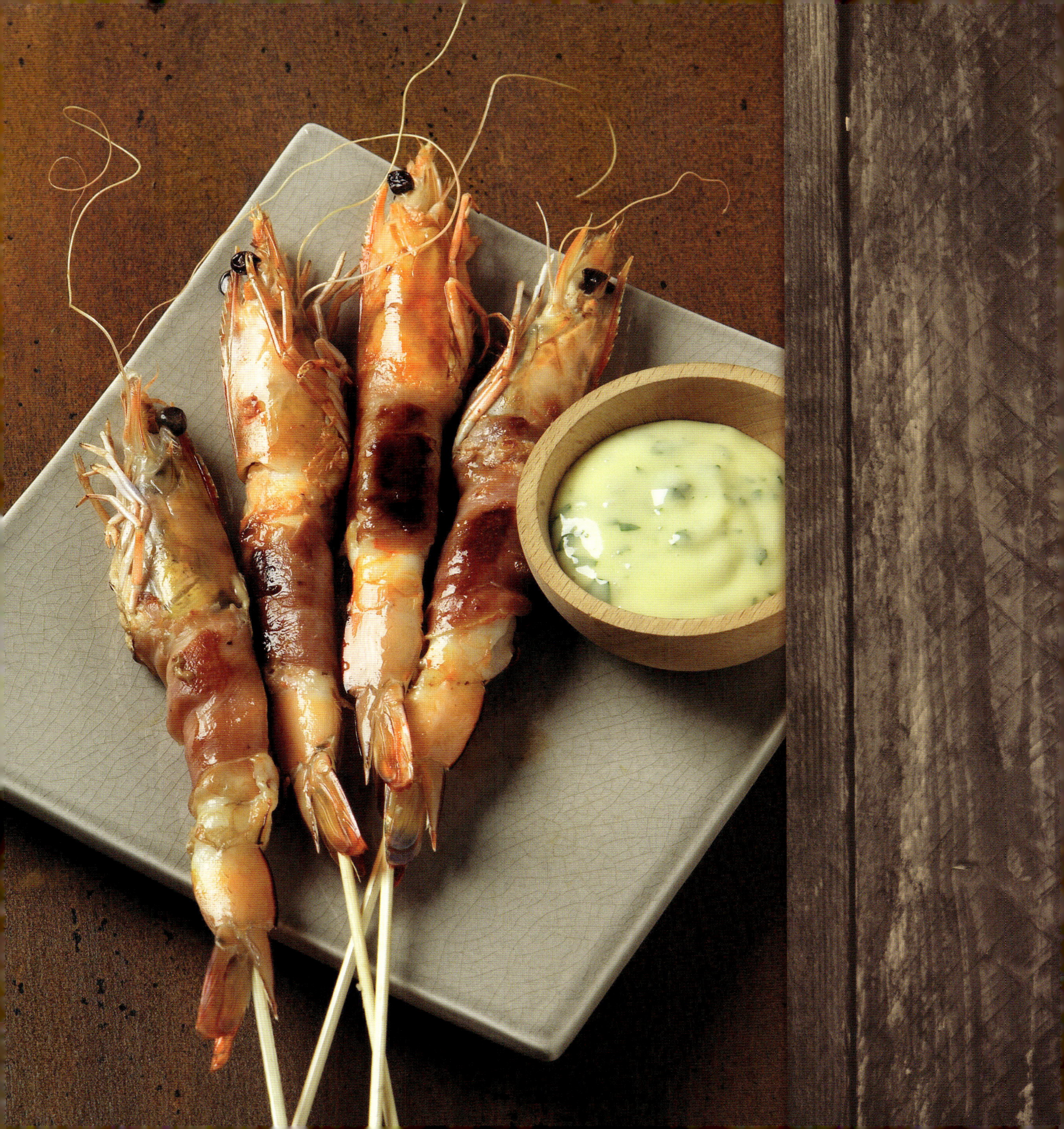

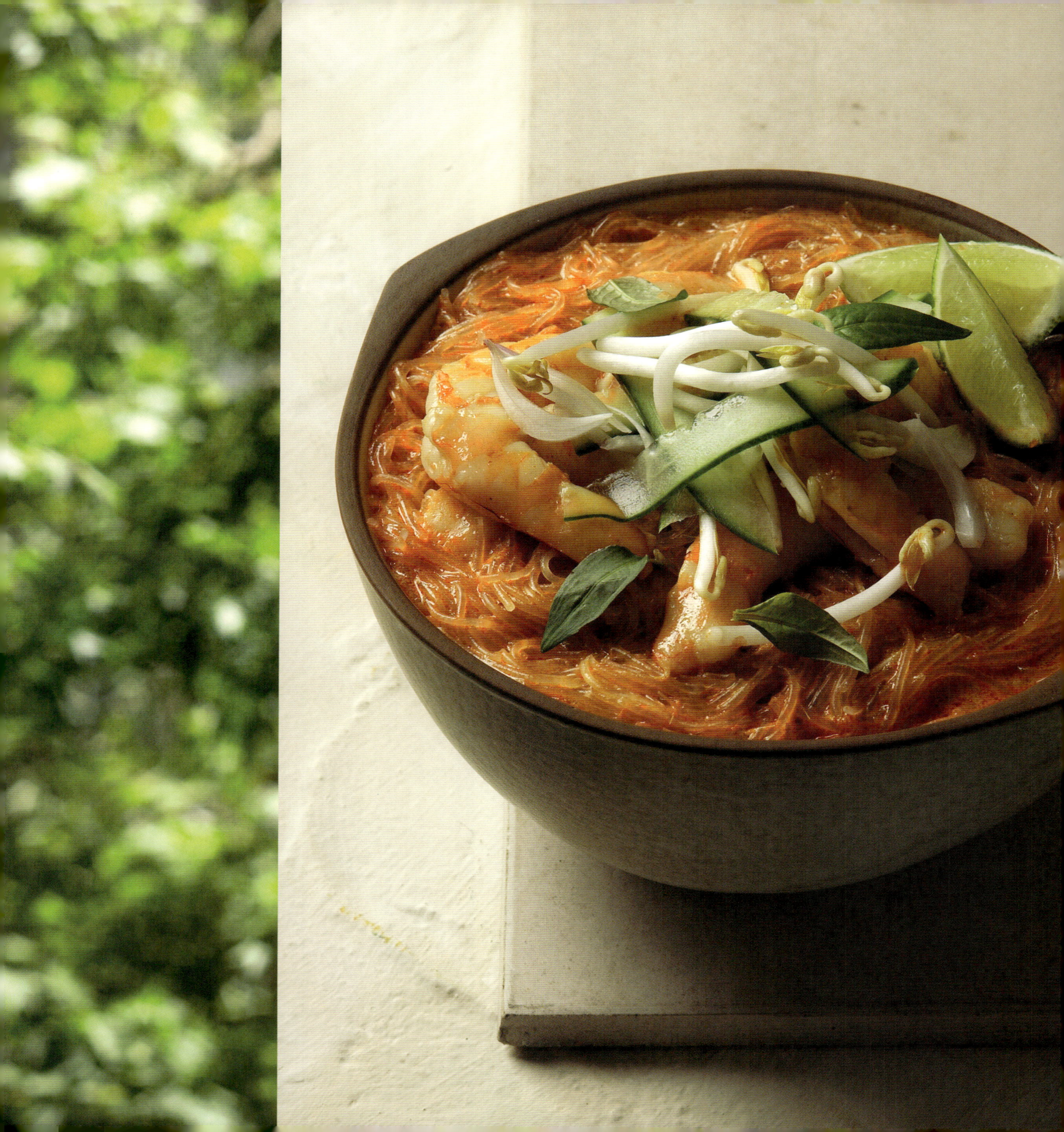

24 large green king prawns
Spray vegetable oil

Laksa
3 x 10cm (4in) stalks lemon grass, white part only and roughly chopped
3cm (1in) galangal, peeled and roughly chopped
3cm (1in) green ginger root, peeled and roughly chopped
2 small red chillies, seeds in and roughly chopped
2 tablespoons vegetable oil
1 tablespoon yellow curry powder
1 teaspoon chilli sauce or less/more to taste
2 teaspoons tamarind paste
1½ cups coconut milk
½ tablespoon fish sauce
Ground white pepper and white sugar to taste
2 tablespoons lightly browned desiccated coconut
3 cups cooked vermicelli noodles
Garnish with 2 sliced eschalots, 1 sliced lime, 1 shredded small Lebanese cucumber and 1 cup Vietnamese mint leaves

PRAWNS WITH LAKSA

Usually you would do this scrumptious, spicy Singapore soup in a wok in the kitchen but with modern barbecues, there is often a wok burner attached. Rice vermicelli noodles are easy to make because you simply soak them in boiling water for 5–10 minutes and drain to serve.

Completely peel and de-vein prawns and make a stock using heads and shells with 3 cups water; simmer to reduce to 1 cup. Barbecue prawns by spraying with oil and cooking on a hot grill.

For the Laksa
Put the lemon grass, galangal, ginger and chillies into a food processor and work into a paste (you may need to add a little water) or you can use a mortar and pestle.

Heat oil in a wok and fry lemongrass paste mixture for 2 minutes; add the 1 cup prawn stock, curry powder, chilli sauce and tamarind puree and bring to a simmer to cook for a 2 minutes. Pour in the coconut milk—season to taste with fish sauce. Ground white pepper can be used if you like and sugar can be used to taste to balance out the flavours.

Add the desiccated coconut to the coconut sauce mix to thicken it; simmer for 2 minutes and serve over equal amounts of cooked noodles in individual bowls.

Top with equal amounts of prawns and serve immediately. Serve the garnish of sliced eschallots, sliced limes, shredded cucumber and Vietnamese mint on a separate plate. This can be added to the prawn dish or eaten on its own.

Serves 4

Mains | Seafood

4 x 150g (5oz) ocean trout fillets
Spray olive oil
150g (5oz) Desiree potato slices, 2cm (1in) thick
    and boiled until cooked but firm
3 Roma tomatoes, trimmed and cut into wedges
200g (7oz) green beans, whole, trimmed and blanched
2 hard-boiled eggs, peeled and quartered lengthwise
3 tablespoons extra virgin olive oil
2 tablespoons white wine vinegar
8 anchovy fillets
20 kalamata olives
Cracked black pepper to taste

OCEAN TROUT ON NICOISE SALAD

Spray the fillets with a little oil and cook on hot plate of barbecue for 2 minutes; turn and cook a further 2 minutes. This fish is best cooked medium so the time cooking will depend on the thickness of your fish. Lift and let cool to room temperature.

Heap potatoes, tomatoes, beans and hard-boiled egg quarters into the centre of a large plate or platter. Scatter the olives around the vegetables and eggs.

Mix the olive oil and vinegar together and spoon over the ingredients on the plate.

Top with ocean trout, sprinkle with black pepper and serve.

Serves 4

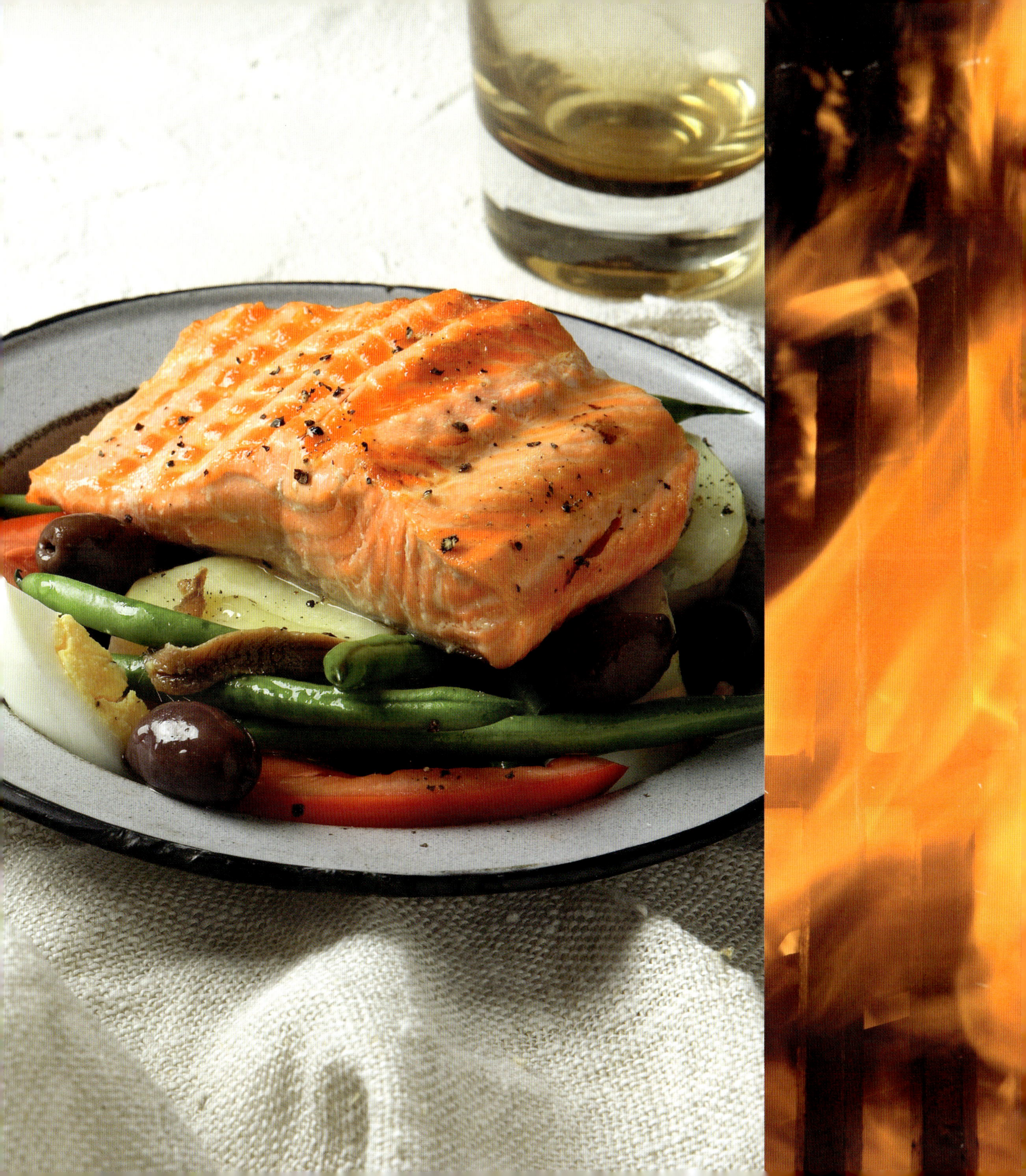

4 x 150g (5oz) pieces ocean trout
½ cup melted butter
300g (11oz) Pontiac potatoes (or similar), peeled and chopped
60g (2oz) mascarpone
Salt and cayenne pepper to taste
2 small radicchio, washed thoroughly and halved from root to top
Spray olive oil

Beurre Rouge
1 cup chicken or fish stock
½ cup red wine (Shiraz preferably)
1 tablespoon onion, finely chopped
200g (7oz) unsalted butter, very cold and in 3cm (1in) cubes

OCEAN TROUT & POTATO MASH WITH CHARRED RADICCHIO & BEURRE ROUGE

Trim the fish if necessary. Refrigerate until ready to use.

Boil the potatoes until really well cooked. Drain and put hood back on and leave to sit for 3 minutes. Mash with the mascarpone, salt and cayenne to taste.

Remove fish from refrigerator 10 minutes before use, brush with butter and put onto a medium-hot plate, flesh-side down and cook for 1–2 minutes. Brush skin side with butter and turn to cook until done to your liking. The cooking time depends on the thickness of your fish.

Spray the cut side of radicchios and flash them onto a very hot grill, then lift.

Put the radicchio cut-side down on outer part of individual dinner plates, spoon potato mash beside the radicchio base, then place the fish standing against the potato and radicchio base. Spoon the sauce around the base of all the ingredients and serve immediately.

For the Beurre Rouge
Make the sauce by simmering the stock, red wine and onion until the liquid has reduced by three quarters. Remove from the heat and swirl in each cube of butter to combine to a thickish red wine sauce. Serve as soon as possible. The base can be done beforehand and can then be reheated before swirling in the butter.

Serves 4

4 x 180g (6oz) pieces monk fish
Spray olive oil
200g (7oz) sugar snap peas, trimmed,
    blanched and refreshed
1 small red onion, finely diced
1 green apple, cored and finely sliced
150g (5oz) bacon pieces, 3cm long,
    rind removed and crisped on the barbecue
½ cup macadamia nuts, roasted and unsalted,
    roughly chopped
½ cup mayo mixed with 1 tablespoon lemon juice
¼ cup chervil leaves
Ground black pepper

Macadamia Mayonnaise
3 large egg yolks, room temperature
¼ teaspoon salt
Pinch white pepper
½ teaspoon prepared mustard (smooth Dijon is best)
1 teaspoon white vinegar
250ml (9fl oz) macadamia oil

MONK FISH WITH SUGAR SNAP PEAS, BACON & APPLE SALAD

IF YOU ADD THE OLIVE OIL TOO QUICKLY, THE MAYONNAISE WILL CURDLE. SHOULD THIS HAPPEN, TIP IN 1 TEASPOON OF HOT WATER AND CONTINUE TO ADD A LITTLE MORE OIL TO THE MIXTURE. WHEN USING EGG YOLKS IN COOKING, THEY COOK VERY QUICKLY SO IF YOU ARE DOING A WARM EGG YOLK SAUCE, SUCH AS A HOLLANDAISE, AND THE EGG YOLKS LOOK AS THOUGH THEY WILL CURDLE, DROP AN ICE CUBE INTO THE MIXTURE AND WHISK AWAY FROM THE HEAT.

For the Macadamia Mayonnaise

Place the egg yolks, salt, pepper, mustard and vinegar into a food processor. Work for 30 seconds or until the mixture in light in colour. Drip the oil in drop by drop until you have a third of the oil added and then slowly increase the flow of oil to a steady thin stream until all oil has been incorporated.

Trim the fish if necessary. Spray with oil and cook on medium-hot plate until done.

Toss the peas, onion, apple, bacon and nuts with the mayo and lemon juice. Add the chervil leaves as you do the final toss with ground black pepper to taste.

Pile equal amounts of bean salad into the centre of individual plates and top with fish. Serve with grilled sourdough bread.

Serves 4

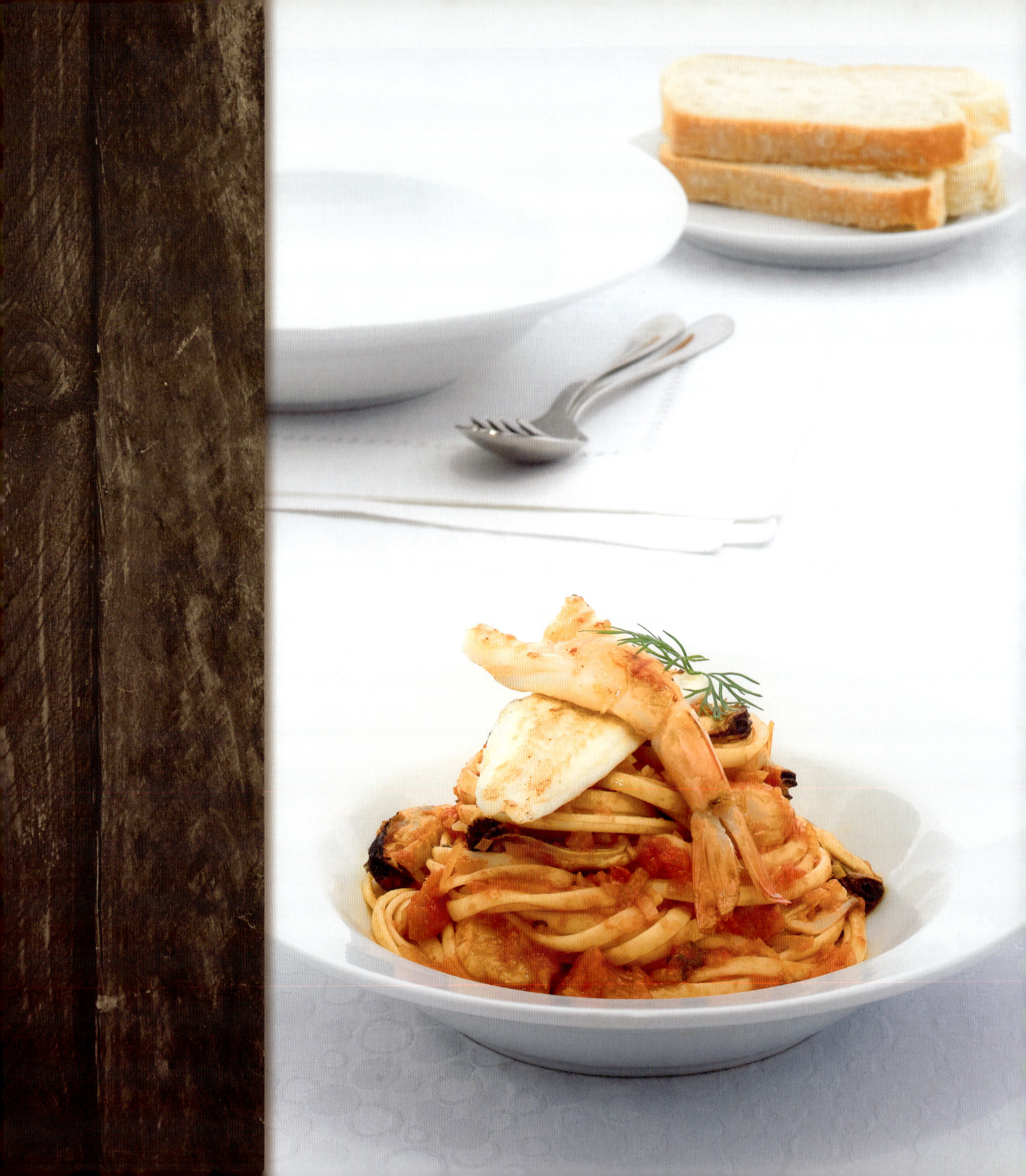

4 small fillets fish, such as whiting
8 medium king prawns, peeled and de-veined, tails left on
Spray olive oil
12 mussels, out of shell
8 small sea scallops, cleaned and black membrane removed
12 Pacific oysters, out of shell

For the sauce
2 tablespoons olive oil
2 tablespoons butter
1 small onion, finely chopped
400g (14oz) canned crushed tomatoes
1 cup white wine
2 cloves garlic, chopped
Oregano or marjoram to taste
Salt and pepper to taste
600g (1lb) linguine, cooked al dente
Ciabiatta bread, sliced

MIXED SEAFOOD LINGUINE

Make sure all the seafood is cleaned and ready to cook. Store covered in the refrigerator.

Make the sauce by heating the oil and butter in a saucepan (I use a wok). When foaming add the onion and cook, stirring, for 2 minutes. Pour in the crushed tomatoes, wine and add the garlic. Simmer for 30 minutes. Remove from heat and keep warm if using shortly; otherwise, cool, cover and refrigerate.

When ready to cook and serve, add the oregano or marjoram and salt and pepper to sauce and take it to the barbecue along with the linguine and raw seafood.

Heat the sauce on the wok ring. Stir and add the mussels and simmer. Cook the fish and prawns by spraying with a little oil and cooking on a medium-hot plate until done.

Meanwhile, add the scallops and oysters to the sauce and stir in. Carefully add the linguine and coat/reheat using tongs to lift and stir.

Take the cooked seafood from the barbecue and keep warm. Serve the pasta and sauce in large individual bowls. Place a cooked fillet on this and top with the prawns. Put the bread into the middle of the table and serve with a green salad.

SERVES 4

500g (18oz) ocean trout fillets, skin and pin bones removed
2 tablespoons corn oil (or light olive oil)
2 tablespoons white vinegar
1 teaspoon Mexican chilli powder
1 teaspoon ground allspice
½ teaspoon ground oregano
Spray olive oil
8 wheat flour tortillas
2 cups shredded lettuce
1 small red onion, finely sliced
1 cup grated carrot
Red tabasco (optional)

Mexican Spiced Ocean Trout Wraps

Cut across the fish into 2cm (1in) wide x 8cm (4in) long strips. Mix the oil, vinegar, chilli powder, allspice and oregano in a bowl and add the strips. Cover and refrigerate for 20 minutes.

To cook, spray a medium-hot flat plate with oil and add the strips. Spread them evenly and do only as many as you can control. As ocean trout does not like to be overcooked, I normally cook 10 strips at a time and turn them only once. Lift and keep warm.

Spray the tortillas with oil and heat very quickly, 30 seconds each side, on the hot grill. Remove and stack on plate.

Assemble fajitas by putting fish strips near the middle of each tortilla, then top with lettuce, onion and grated carrot. Roll and eat immediately. You can drizzle on some tabasco if you like.

Serves 4

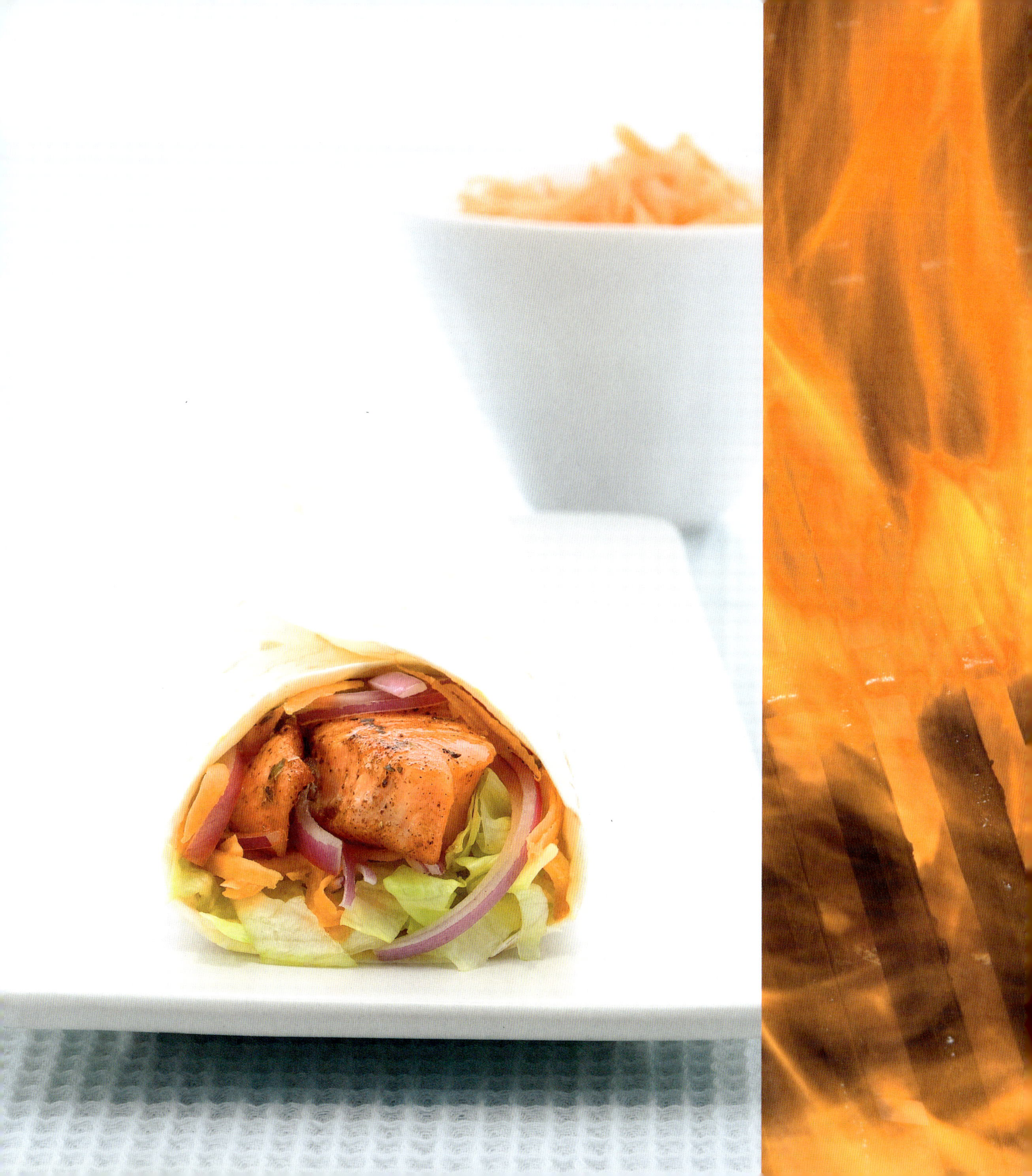

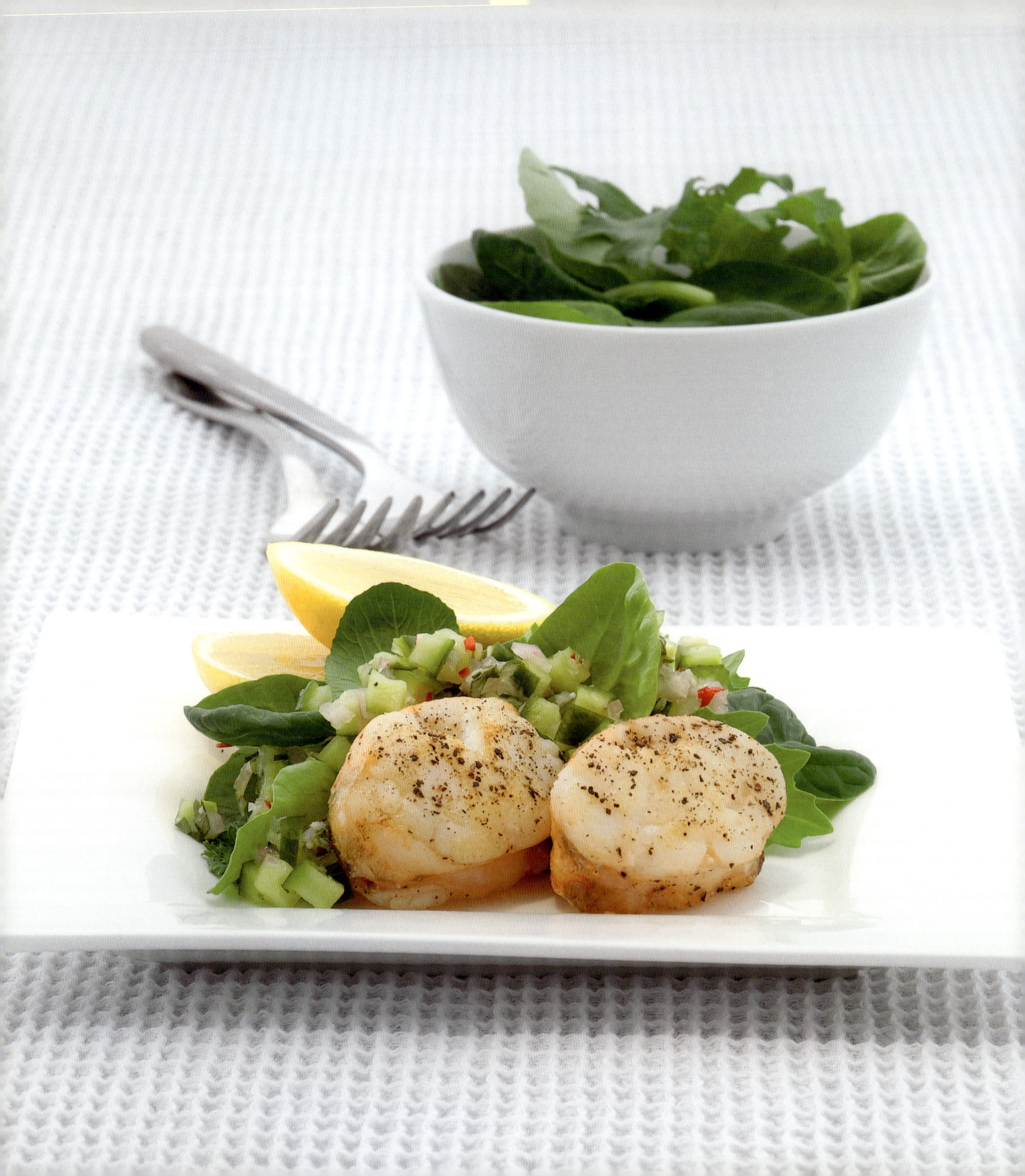

12 medium lobster medallions
¼ cup vegetable oil
¼ teaspoon sea salt
Ground black pepper to taste
1 x 100g (4oz) mixed Asian leaves

Thai-flavoured Cucumbers
4 tablespoons coconut/rice vinegar
3 tablespoon white sugar
1 small red chilli, deseeded and minced
1 large Lebanese cucumber, seeds removed and finely diced
1 red eschallot, finely diced
1 tablespoon green ginger root, minced
1 clove garlic, crushed
1 tablespoon coriander leaves, chopped
1 tablespoon vegetable oil
1 tablespoon fish sauce

LOBSTER MEDALLIONS WITH THAI CUCUMBER & ASIAN LEAVES

For the Thai-flavoured Cucumbers

Mix the vinegar and sugar together and stir to dissolve. Add all the other ingredients, toss and marinate for 1 hour before serving.

Pat the lobster dry and brush both sides with oil. Cook on medium-hot plate and sprinkle with salt and pepper as you cook. Turn when done and sprinkle with salt and pepper. Turn only once as they cook through quite quickly. Lift from the barbecue and keep warm.

Distribute the leaves into the centre of individual dinner plates. Drain the cucumbers and toss over the leaves. Serve the lobster beside medallions sitting beside the salad.

Serves 4

500g (18oz) green lobster meat, in 3 cm thick slices or chunks
1 teaspoon lime zest, finely grated
1 lime, juiced
¼ teaspoon sea salt
8 baby Pontiac potatoes, skin on, par-boiled for 5 minutes and cooled
2 tablespoons olive oil
Ground black pepper to taste
32 green beans, trimmed, blanched and refreshed
Spray olive oil
1 teaspoon fresh black pepper, finely ground
60g (2oz) butter, melted and lightly browned

LIME LOBSTER WITH CRUSTY POTATOES & GRILLED GREEN BEANS

Soak the lobster meat in the zest, lime juice and salt for no more than 10 minutes.

Squash or slightly flatten the potatoes using the palm of your hand or a potato masher.

Pour some olive oil onto a medium-hot flat plate and gently place the potatoes onto that part of the barbecue—I use a spatula. Sprinkle with pepper and drizzle with a little more oil and bring down the hood or cover with a stainless steel bowl. After 5 minutes turn the potatoes over gently—they can break easily.

Spray the beans with oil and cook on the grill—lay across the grill so they don't fall in. Turn regularly so they don't burn. Lift when ready along with the crisped potatoes. Keep both warm.

Drain the lobster pieces and pour a little more olive oil onto the flat plate—add the lobster and drizzle on lime juices from the soaking and half the butter. Turn and toss the lobster constantly until cooked through. Lift from barbecue and assemble dish by placing two potatoes into the centre of each plate, stand equal quantities of beans rampantly against them and spoon lobster pieces over the base of the beans. Spoon remaining butter over the lobster and serve immediately.

SERVES 4

4 x 160g (6oz) Jewfish steaks
2 tablespoons fresh thyme, minced
Ground black pepper to taste
Spray olive oil

Beetroot, Blood Orange, Mustard Dressing
500g (18oz) beetroot, medium size,
    cooked and skin removed
4 blood oranges
2 tablespoons fennel leaves, finely chopped
½ tablespoon fennel seeds, toasted
    and roughly crushed
2 tablespoons smooth French mustard
Reserved orange juice

JEWFISH STEAKS WITH BLOOD ORANGE & BEETROOT SALAD

Beetroot can be boiled in water that covers them through the cooking time. Leave to sit in cooking water to cool for around 10 minutes. Lift out and rub skin off with your hands in plastic gloves.

They can also be roasted in loosely wrapped foil which is then used to rub against the skin to remove it after the beetroot is cooked and cool enough to handle. Beetroot about the size of tennis balls take about 25 minutes to cook by boiling and around 45–60 minutes when roasting in foil.

Trim the fish if necessary and pat the thyme into each side with ground black pepper to taste.

Spray the fish with oil and cook on a medium-hot flat plate. This fish cooks very quickly and goes mushy if overcooked. The steaks go white along the side and when half way up the sides of each steak, turn to cook another minute. When the steak is firm to the press of your middle finger or tongs, lift from the barbecue.

Heap salad into the middle of dinner plates and serve the fish on top.

For the Beetroot, Blood Orange, Mustard Dressing

Cut the cooled beetroot into wedges; slice the skin and pith (white part of orange skin) from three of the oranges and cut into wedges. Do this on a plate so you capture the juices. Juice remaining whole blood orange and combine with any of the reserved juices; whisk in the mustard.

Combine the beetroot and oranges, add the fennel and fennel seeds; spoon the dressing over and tumble gently before serving.

Serves 4

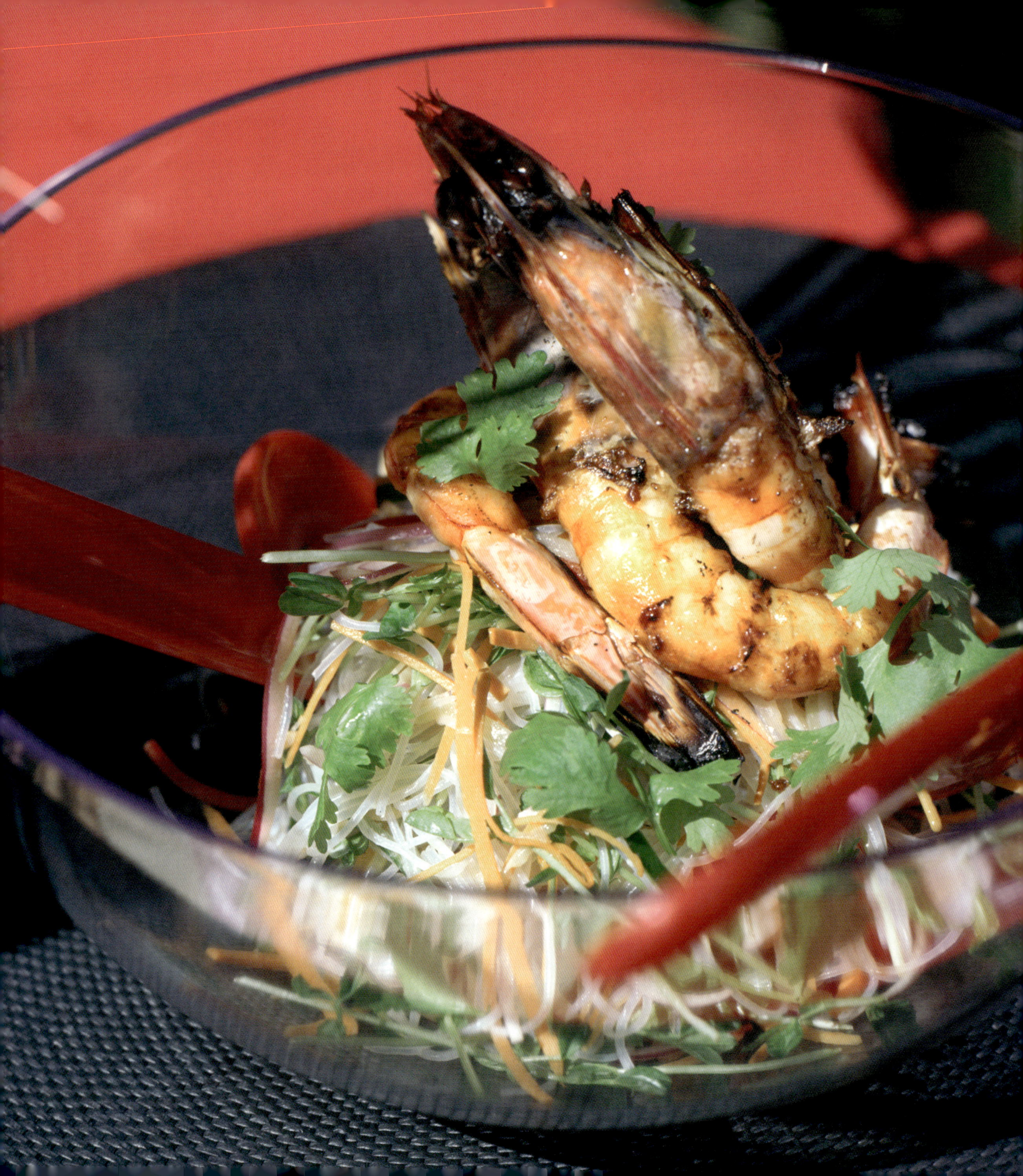

20 green king prawns, peeled except for heads and tails
2 tablespoons peanut oil
1 tablespoon fish sauce
1 clove garlic, crushed
1 tablespoon green ginger, peeled and minced
1 teaspoon palm sugar
2 tablespoons pineapple juice, preferably fresh

Glass Noodle Salad
125g (4oz) dried bean thread noodles
1 carrot, peeled and finely sliced
1 x 20cm (9in) Lebanese cucumber, cut lengthwise, deseeded and julienned
1 very small red onion, peeled and sliced very finely
30g (1oz) Japanese pickled ginger, julienned
1 cup snow pea sprouts, washed and crisped
1 red capsicum, finely julienne
½ cup coriander (cilantro) leaves

For the dressing:
1 tablespoon palm sugar
200ml (7fl oz) coconut cream
2 limes, juice of
1 tablespoon Nam Prik sauce (see recipe below)
1–2 tablespoons fish sauce

Nam Prik
3 tablespoons dried shrimps
1 teaspoon shrimp paste
4 cloves garlic
2 tablespoons soy sauce
2 tablespoons chilli sauce
2 teaspoons raw sugar or palm sugar
4 tablespoons water

KING PRAWNS & GLASS NOODLE SALAD

For the Nam Prik
Soak the shrimps in water for 20 minutes. Spoon the shrimp paste onto a small piece of foil and cover with a similar size. Cook on top of hot plate for 3 minutes or until slightly dried. Strain the shrimps and put them and all the ingredients into a blender and blend until smooth.

For the Glass Noodle Salad
Put the noodles into a large bowl and pour boiling water over to cover them. Let sit for 5–7 minutes and then strain. Run under cold water. Tip the noodles into a mixing bowl and allow to cool for 10 minutes. Add all the other ingredients except for the coriander leaves and toss gently using your hands. Make the dressing by combining all the ingredients and mixing well. Pour over the assembled salad ingredients and toss gently. Top with the coriander leaves and serve.

Mix all remaining ingredients together and add the prawns. Coat well and allow to marinate for 20 minutes. Cook the prawns on a hot plate, tossing for 3–5 minutes depending on the size.

Top the salad with the prawns and serve with coriander leaves (optional).

Serves 4

4 x 150g (5oz) reef fish fillets,
    for example; red emperor, coral trout or sweet lip
400g (14oz) potatoes (Pontiac or similar),
    peeled and chopped
100g (4oz) butter
60g (2oz) eschallots, finely chopped
½ teaspoon sea salt
¼ teaspoon cayenne pepper

Handmade Mayonnaise
3 egg yolks
1 teaspoon American mustard, prepared
1 cup olive oil, light or vegetable oil
1 tablespoon lemon juice
1 tablespoons caraway seeds, finely crushed
½ teaspoon salt

FILLETS OF REEF FISH WITH ESCHALLOT MASH & CARAWAY MAYO DRIZZLE

Trim the fish if necessary and pat dry. Refrigerate covered with cling wrap.

Cover the potatoes with water and bring to the boil, then simmer to cook until tender. Drain and return to the saucepan. Add the butter, eschallots and salt and pepper and return the hood. Allow to sit for 3 minutes and then mash roughly. Spoon mash into a microwave-proof bowl.

Spray the fish with oil and place on a medium-hot plate. Cook for 2 minutes. Spray with oil, turn over and cook for a further 3 minutes. The cooking time depends on the thickness of the fish, however you can tell by seeing the white juice beads come to the top of the fish. Spoon reheated mash into the centre of individual plates. Lean a piece of fish against the potato and drizzle over mayo to taste. Great served with steamed broccolini.

For the Handmade Mayonnaise

Make the mayo by putting the egg yolks, mustard and lemon juice into a food processor. Process for a minute. Dribble in the oil for the first half of it and then pour in at a slow and constant speed to form a thick mayonnaise. If the mixture gets too thick, pour in a tablespoon of warm water and then continue to add the oil.

Spoon mayonnaise into a bowl. Sprinkle in caraway seeds and salt and stir to combine.

The consistency of this dressing needs to be that of pouring cream and it can be thinned by adding more lemon juice or water—it depends on how much you like lemon flavours.

Serves 4

4 x 150g (5oz) Atlantic salmon fillets,
　　skinless and bones removed
Spray olive oil
1 cup Dukkah, purchased
　　or recipe below
4 lemon cheeks

Tabbouleh
1½ cups spiced bulgur mix
　　(I use Samir's Bulgur Feast mix)
1–2 cups warm water
3 cups parsley, chopped
1 cup ripe tomatoes, diced
1 tablespoon lemon zest,
　　finely shredded
3 tablespoons lemon juice
2 tablespoons extra virgin olive oil

Dukkah
100g (4oz) almonds, skin on
60g (2oz) pine nuts
4 teaspoons linseeds
1 teaspoon ground coriander
1 teaspoon ground cumin
1 teaspoon white sesame seeds
½ teaspoon chilli powder
1 teaspoon Szechuan peppercorns

DUKKAH-CRUSTED ATLANTIC SALMON WITH TABBOULEH SALAD

For the Dukkah

Dry roast the almonds; dry roast pine nuts and linseeds over medium heat. Cool and tip into a food processor. Add the coriander, cumin, sesame seeds, chilli and Szechuan pepper and work to a rough mixture—it should be granular/lumpy and not a paste. Store in an airtight container.

Evenly slice the fillets into pieces around 2–3cm (1in) thick. Spray flesh side lightly with oil and press into Dukkah on flat dinner plate. Lift and shake off excess. Spray medium-hot flat plate with oil and cook the fillets Dukkah-side down first. After a minute, spray the other side of the fish pieces and, with a long spatula gently flip the fish over. The cooking time will depend on the thickness of the pieces.

Put the salad onto individual plates, top with fish and serve with lemon cheeks to one side.

For the Tabbouleh

Make the salad first by soaking the bulgur mix in the water for 30 minutes. After that, add the other ingredients and mix thoroughly. I like to leave this mixture sit for at least 3 hours before use. Why do I use the Samir mix? All the spices are in the mix and it saves you time and having to shop for all the ingredients.

Serves 4

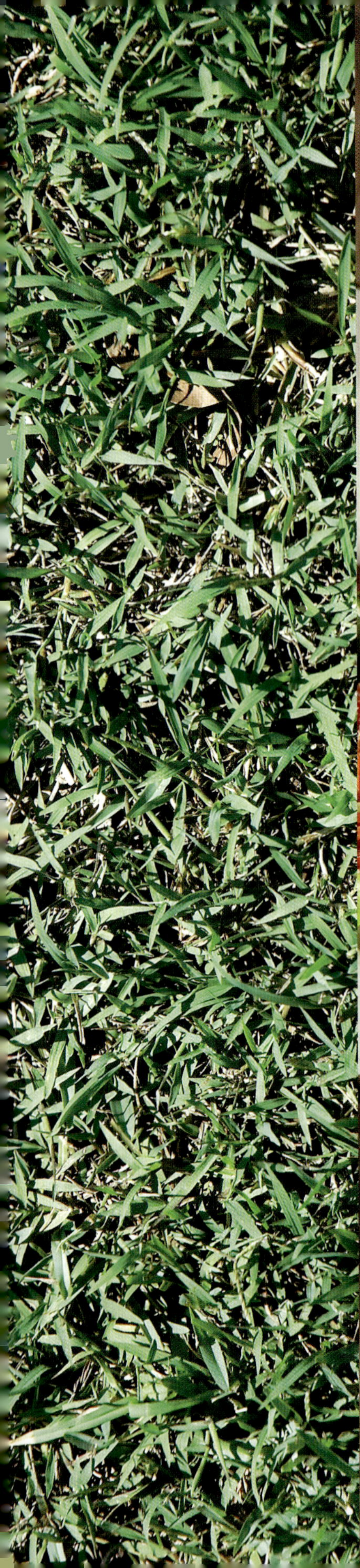
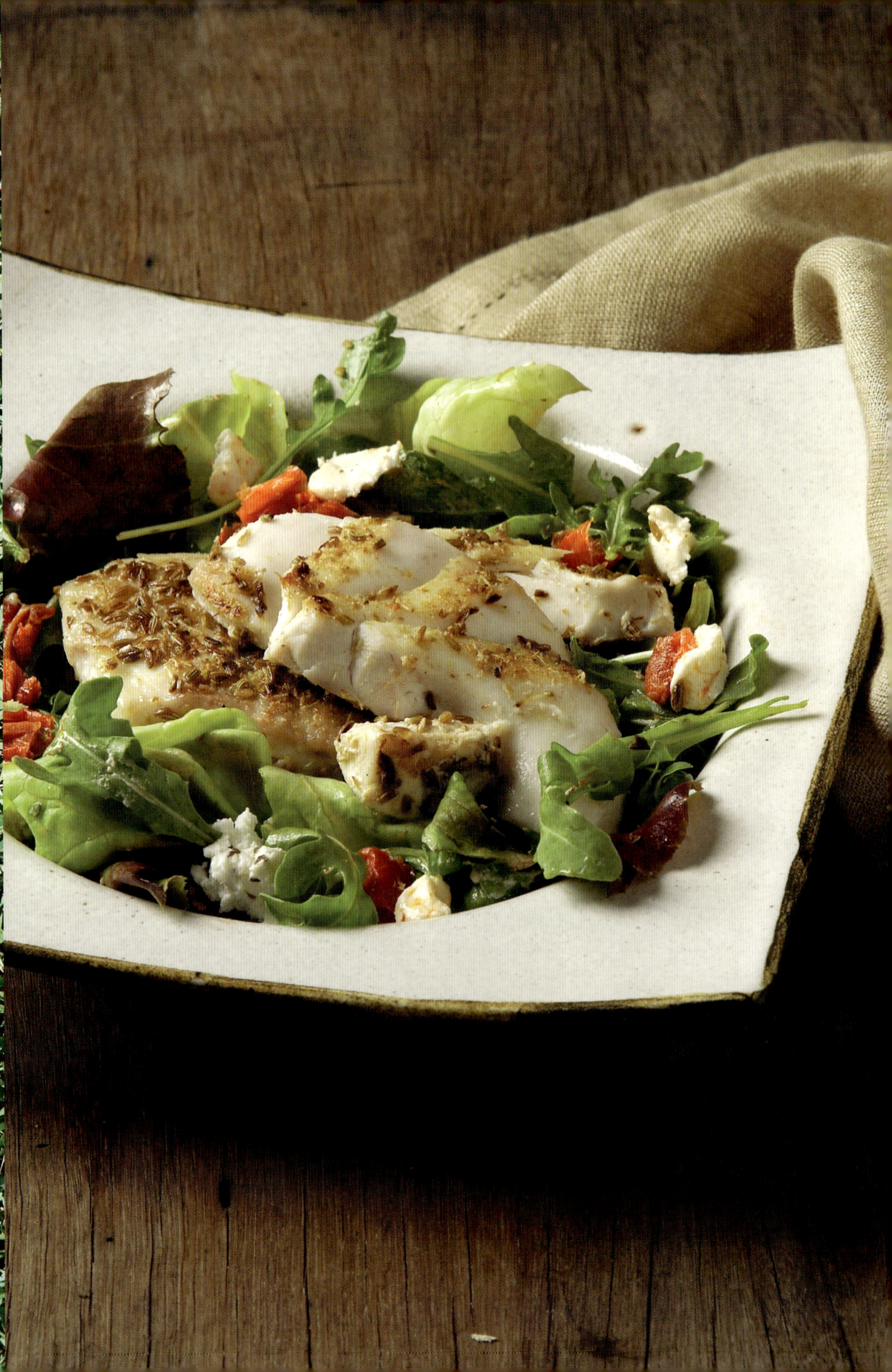

4 x 150g (5oz) blue-eye cod steaks
1 tablespoon fennel seeds
½ tablespoon white peppercorns
¼ teaspoon sea salt
Spray olive oil

Goat's Cheese Salad
150g (5.3oz) mixed salad leaves
100g (3.5oz) semi-roasted tomatoes, chopped
100g (3.5oz) dry goat's cheese, crumbled or cut into dice
3 tablespoons extra virgin olive oil
1 tablespoon balsamic vinegar

FENNEL & PEPPER CRUSTED BLUE EYE WITH GOAT'S CHEESE SALAD

Pat the fish dry. Roughly crush the fennel seeds, peppercorns and salt in a mortar and pestle. Sprinkle equal amounts onto each side of the fish and pat into each fillet.

Heat half the flat plate to high, spray fish with oil and cook on a medium plate—spray with oil and turn after a minute and cook through. The time will depend on the thickness of the fish which will be firm to touch but not breaking up when it is done.

Meanwhile, have the leaves, tomatoes and cheese in a bowl; toss with the oil and balsamic vinegar.

Serve the fish on individual plates with the salad into the middle of the table.

SERVES 4

400g (14oz) cuttlefish, body only
¼ cup good olive oil
250g (9oz) chorizo (Spanish sausage), cut into 1cm (½in) thick slices
150g (5oz) yellow capsicum, deseeded and cut into bite size pieces
½ cup pine nuts, toasted
20 grape tomatoes, halved
2 tablespoons zest of lemon, finely grated
¼ cup lemon juice
2 tablespoons Italian parsley, roughly chopped
Sea salt to taste
2 tablespoons good olive oil
100g (4oz) mixed salad leaves

CUTTLEFISH WITH CHORIZO, CAPSICUM & PINE NUT SALAD

Cut the cuttlefish open to form one large flat piece. Trim and with a very sharp knife score the flesh into diamond shapes. Cut into bite-sized pieces and put into a bowl.

Pour the first lot of olive oil in and toss the cuttlefish in it. Let sit for 15 minutes and if any longer, refrigerate.

Put the capsicum, pine nuts and tomato halves into the salad bowl; mix the lemon zest, juice and salt and pour over the capsicum mix. Add the chopped parsley and toss together—refrigerate until ready for use.

Put the cuttlefish onto medium-hot flat plate, scored side down. These pieces will curl so you need to move them around to ensure all the surfaces are exposed to the heat. Cuttlefish cooks quickly so do not overcook as it toughens. Lift from the barbecue and put into a bowl. Tip over the capsicum mixture and toss to coat and cool the fish. Let rest.

Put the chorizo slices on the hot grill; let crisp and brown and remove when done.

Pour the second lot of olive oil over the salad leaves and toss. Divide the sausage slices into equal amounts on individual plates. Add some salad onto the top of the sausage slices and put pieces of the cuttlefish and capsicum mixture on top and around the salad. Spoon any juices from the cuttlefish over if you like.

SERVES 4

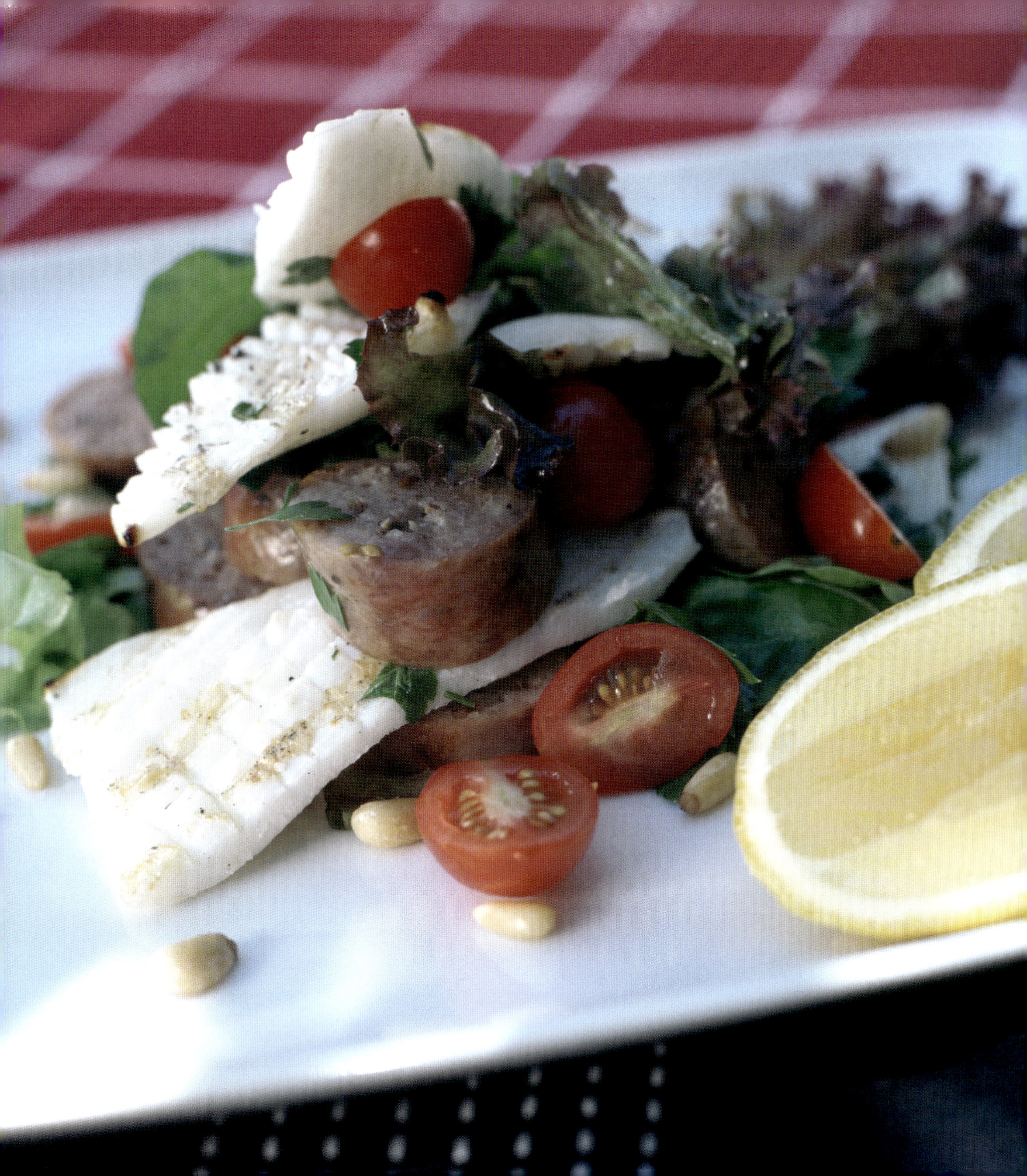

2 x 250g (4oz) green crayfish tails
2 tablespoons Szechuan peppercorns,
　　crushed in mortar and pestle
　　with 1 teaspoon sea salt
½ cup vegetable oil.
¼ cup orange juice, fresh or processed
1 tablespoon Vietnamese mint, minced
Finely grated zest of 1 small orange
Spray oil

CRAYFISH MEDALLIONS WITH SZECHUAN PEPPER & ORANGE DRESSING

Gently remove flesh from shell and cut, on the diagonal, into medallions 1–2cm (½–1in) thick. Coat the medallions with the peppercorn and salt mixture and let sit for no longer than 10 minutes before cooking.

Make the dressing by combining the oil, orange juice, salt and Vietnamese mint and orange zest. Mix well.

Spray the crayfish medallions with oil and cook on a medium-hot plate for 1 minute. Spray with oil and gently turn the slices. Cook a further 2 minutes, remove from the barbecue and put onto individual plates.

Spoon over the dressing; serve with cooked rice noodles and steamed Chinese greens.

SERVES 4

2 x 350g (12oz) green crayfish tails,
   cut in half lengthwise.
150g (5oz) unsalted butter, melted
1 lime, juice of
2cm (1in) lemongrass, white part only, finely minced
½ teaspoon pink peppercorns, crushed
¼ teaspoon sea salt

Potato Salad
1kg (2lb) Desiree potatoes, washed
1 small white onion, chopped
3 tablespoons white vinegar
2 hard-boiled eggs, roughly chopped
½ cup dill pickles, roughly chopped
5 tablespoons mint, roughly chopped or broken
1 cup good mayonnaise
Ground white pepper and salt to taste

CRAYFISH IN SHELL WITH LEMONGRASS & LIME FLAVOURS & POTATO SALAD

Gently lift the flesh from the tail and cut into bite-sized pieces. Retain the shell.

Put the meat, melted butter, lime juice, lemongrass, peppercorns and salt in a bowl and tumble. Pack the meat back into the shells and press down firmly. Refrigerate, covered, for 1 hour and the butter will set the meat in place; retain any of the butter and crayfish juices that may be left in the bowl.

To cook, place the crayfish tails on the plate flesh-side down. You can use your hand to hold the meat in place as you shoode it onto a medium-hot plate, however using a long spatula is safer.

Cook for 2 minutes. Very carefully shoode a long spatula underneath the cooking tails and lift onto the grill. Cook for 5 minutes and drizzle into the shells any of the retained butter and crayfish juices. Getting the tails to sit up is easily done by resting them against each other and it is important that the tails sit as upright as possible so the juices don't leak out.

The juices and butter will bubble up through the pieces of crayfish to let you know the tails are cooked. Lift gently to a serving platter or onto individual plates and serve with potato salad.

For the Potato Salad
Cut the potatoes into even 3cm (1in) cubes and boil until just done; strain and put into a large bowl with the onions and the vinegar—toss well.

Add the remaining ingredients and stir well to combine. Allow to cool or you can serve warm.

Serves 4

1 x 450g (16oz) Atlantic salmon tail (lower dorsil and tail fin removed)
2 cups prawn stock
3 star anise
1 cup green lentils
400g (14oz) kumara
Salt and pepper to taste
Spray olive oil

CHAR-ROASTED ATLANTIC SALMON TAIL WITH KUMARA, GREEN LENTILS & PRAWN STAR ANISE BROTH

Cut two incisions to the bone on each side of the tail. Refrigerate until ready to cook.

Simmer the prawn stock with the star anise to reduce to one cup. Barely simmer as the star anise will infuse into the reducing stock better this way. Keep warm or chill and then heat in small saucepan or in microwave when ready to serve.

Rinse the lentils and then cook covered with water for 10 minutes. Drain and run under cold water. Stir in salt and pepper to taste and place in microwave-proof container. Wash the kumara and puncture with a dinner fork over the skin and cook in the microwave at 70 per cent for 4 minutes. Remove and keep to one side.

Spray the kumara and salmon with oil; place the kumara on a hot grill and turn when it has browned/marked. Put the salmon on a medium-hot plate and cook for 1 minute on each side. The skin will crisp slightly. Lift both to the tray that sits above the plates and close the hood. Cook at 180°C (350°F) for 12–15 minutes. Remove the fish and kumara and let rest for 3 minutes.

To serve, spoon warmed lentils into the centre of deep-welled plate. Slice the kumara evenly and place to one side of the lentils. Divide the tail into four serves and place on top of the kumara and lentils; splash over the warmed prawn broth.

SERVES 4

4 x 160g (6oz) blue-eye cod steaks
Ground black pepper
Spray oil
4 medium zucchinis, trimmed and halved lengthwise
4 medium trussed tomatoes
Fresh thyme springs
Salt to taste
Prawn and Lime Butter (see recipe below)
20 kalamata olives
Trim the fish if necessary and sprinkle with ground black pepper.

Prawn and Lime Butter
250g (9oz) salted butter
60g (2oz) cooked prawn meat, finely chopped
1 tablespoon dill, finely chopped
1 tablespoon lime juice
1 teaspoon lime zest, finely grated

BLUE EYE WITH ZUCCHINI, TOMATO, PRAWN & LIME BUTTER

Spray the zucchini and tomato halves liberally with oil. Sprinkle with salt and cook on a medium-hot plate cut-side down. Turn onto skin side and cook for 3 minutes, adding the thyme leaves only to the cut side. Spray with a little more oil if necessary and turn once more and cook for a minute. Remove and keep warm.

Spray the fish with oil and cook on a medium-hot plate. When the fish is firm to the press of your middle finger or tongs, lift it carefully from the barbecue.

Place two zucchini halves onto the centre of each plate, top with two tomato halves and then the fish. Slice some prawn butter (to taste), add to the top of the fish and distribute the olives around the fish. Serve with a Watercress, Radish and Feta Salad (see recipe page 283).

For the Prawn and Lime Butter
Mash all ingredients together in a bowl and when well combined, spoon into a bowl to refrigerate, covered with cling wrap, until ready to spoon over the top of whatever you want.

Serves 4

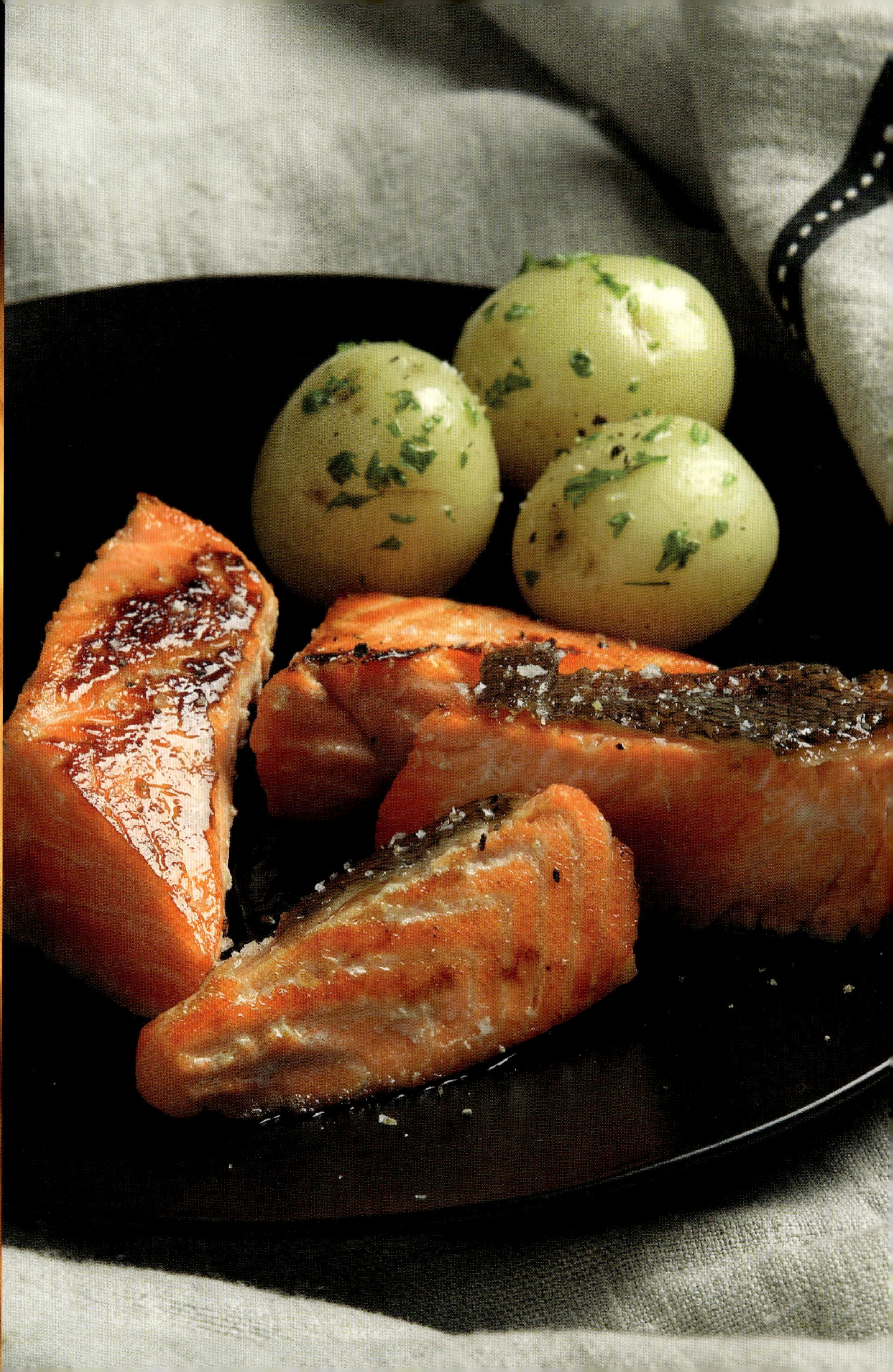

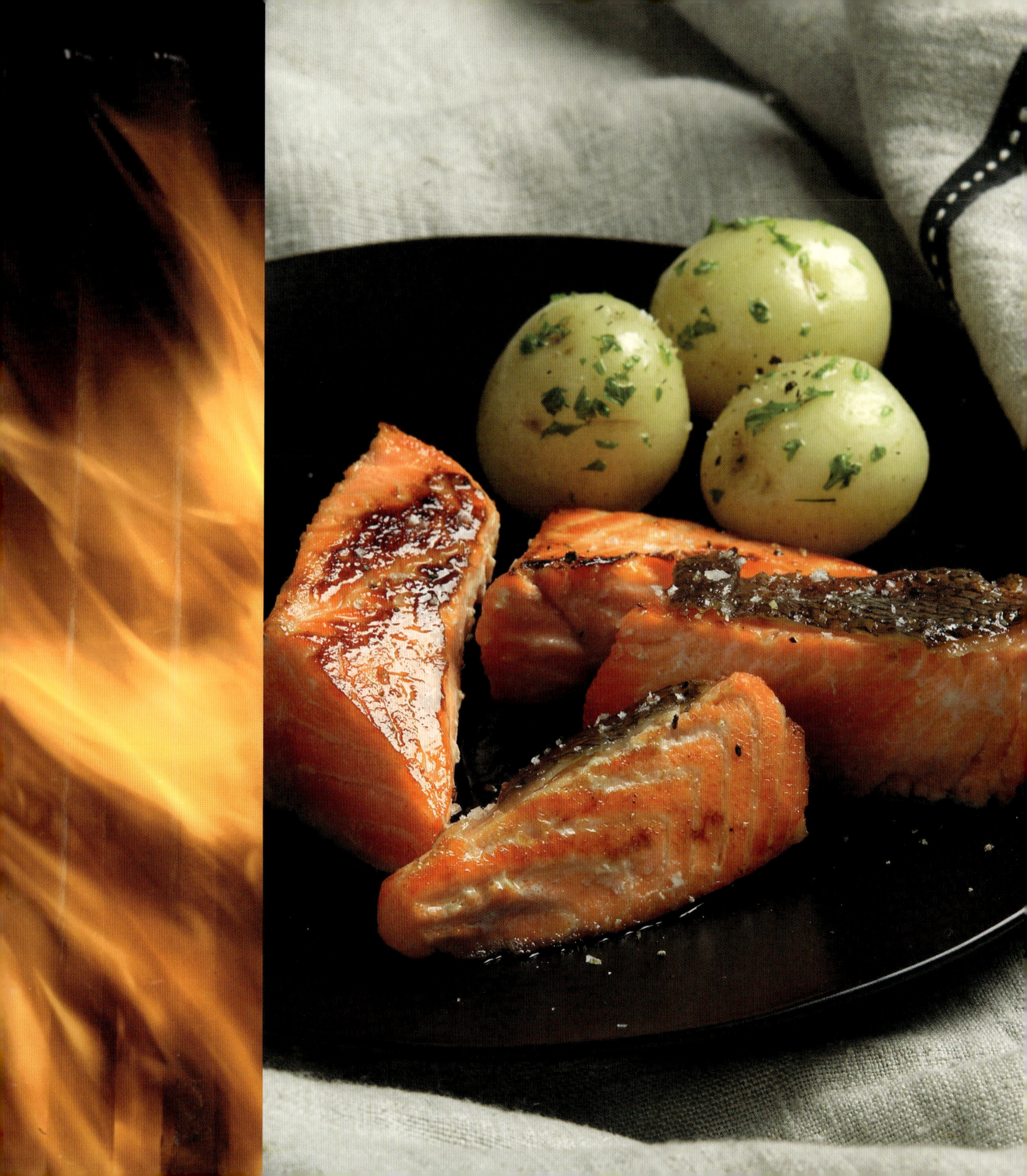

600g (1lb) ocean trout fillet skin on
4 teaspoons coarse sea salt
4 teaspooons white sugar
¼ cup fresh dill, finely chopped
4 teaspoons single malt scotch whisky
Spray olive oil

Buttered Chats, Parsley and Black Pepper
400g (14oz) chats (or small new potatoes)
60g (2oz) melted butter
2 tablespoons parsley, chopped
½ tablespoon ground black pepper

BARBECUED GRAVALAX OCEAN TROUT

Trim the ocean trout if necessary.

Mix salt and sugar together and sprinkle onto a large piece of plastic wrap in same shape as trout piece. Spread the dill over the top of this and drizzle over the whisky. Lay trout fillet skin-side up on mix and tightly fold in the cling wrap. Refrigerate skin-side up for 2 hours.

Unwrap, thoroughly brush off dill mix and cut into four pieces. Spray with oil on both sides.

Put the fish, skin-side down, on medium hot plate for 2 minutes or until skin is crisp and brown; turn spray oiled ocean trout over and cooked cured side for ½ minute.

Serve sitting beside the butter-drizzled new potatoes on individual plates and with a green salad.

For the Buttered Chats, Parsley and Black Pepper
Boil the potatoes in salted boiling water until done. Drain and return to saucepan. Put hood on and let sit for 2 minutes. Add the butter, parsley and pepper and replace the hood. Toss holding the hood on to coat the potatoes.

Serves 4

4 x 160g (6oz) pieces Monkfish
Ground black pepper
Spray olive oil
16 asparagus spears, trimmed

PEPPERED MONKFISH WITH ASPARAGUS & BRAISED BORLOTTI BEANS

I dry my own mandarin skin every year. It adds such a delicious flavour. You can buy it in Asian supermarkets. I also use it in stews and in ratatouille.

This fish is stunning to eat. If your pieces come from the top (head end) they will be very thick and so it is best to have them cut on the angle which gives you more surface to cook the fish. Otherwise, the thick piece does take a longer time to cook so you need to move it to a part of the barbecue plate that is lower in heat… generally around the edge of the plate. It does not dry out if it is 'just' cooked.

Trim the fish if necessary. Refrigerate until ready for use. Sprinkle both sides of the fish with pepper, spray with oil and cook on medium-hot plate until done.

Spray the asparagus spears with oil and cook on grill, turning regularly.

Serve by spooning equal amounts of the braised beans into the centre of individual flattish bowls, then top with equal quantities of asparagus and fish.

Serves 4

Braised Borlotti Beans

300g (11oz) rehydrated borlotti beans
100g (4oz) onion, finely chopped
3 cloves garlic, minced
400g (14oz) canned crushed tomatoes
¼ cup tomato paste
1 small piece dried mandarin skin
Sea salt and ground black pepper to taste
¼ cup parsley, finely chopped

For the Braised Borlotti Beans

Cover the beans with water and simmer for 45 minutes.

Put the onion, garlic, tomatoes, tomato paste and mandarin skin into a large saucepan and bring to the boil. Simmer and add the drained beans and continue simmering for at least 30 minutes. Season with salt, pepper and parsley and cook a further 5 minutes.

4 x 200g (4oz) rainbow trout, fresh,
   gutted and cleaned
½ cup onions, sliced into rounds
2 cups cous cous, hydrated
Salt and ground black pepper to taste
4 lemon cheeks
4 tablespoons Dukkah
   (see recipe page 243 or buy already
made)
Olive oil
Spray oil

Rainbow Trout with Onion Cous Cous & Dukkah

Wash the inside of the trout and dry with paper towelling and also pat dry the skin.

Lightly oil a medium-hot plate and cook the onions until lightly brown. At the same time, spray the trout and cook for 5 minutes on each side of a medium-hot grill.

Lift the onions and mix through the cous cous with salt and ground black pepper to taste. Cover and reheat in the microwave on medium for 2 minutes.

Serve the trout alongside the cous cous on individual plates. Decorate with lemon cheek and serve the Dukkah separately.

The trout flesh is eaten with Dukkah sprinkled over each mouthful.

Serves 4

4 x 160g (6oz) bream fillets—the best is silver, black or yellowfin
Spray oil
Salt
300g (11oz) snow peas, trimmed
4 lemon cheeks

Garlic Potato Bake
30g (1oz) butter
1 tablespoon olive oil
3 leeks, white only, cleaned and sliced thinly
4 cloves garlic, chopped
300ml (11fl oz) pouring cream
4 large potatoes, peeled and sliced thinly
Salt and pepper to taste
3 tablespoons chopped parsley

BREAM FILLETS, SNOW PEAS & GARLIC POTATO BAKE

Sea bream, sometimes called morwong, is on the overfished list of fish so beware of this when buying your bream.

For the Garlic Potato Bake

Pan fry leeks in foaming butter and oil until soft. Add garlic, stir, add cream and reduce until thick. Place potatoes in a bowl and pour over creamed leek. Season with salt and pepper and parsley and mix gently. Line a heavy round oven dish or ovenproof round frying pan with baking paper and press in potatoes.

Bake in a moderate oven for about an hour. When cooked, allow to settle and cool well before turning out and slicing into wedges. Cut into wedges and either reheat in the microwave, oven or on the flat plate of your barbecue with the hood down.

Trim the fish if necessary. Spray the skin side with a film of oil and sprinkle on a little sea salt. Put fish, skin-side down, onto a hot flat plate and hold each piece down with a spatula which prevents the fillet from curling. Repeat with all the fillets. Spray the flesh side with oil and turn after 1–2 minutes to cook through. The skin can go quite crispy and the cooking time will depend on the thickness of the fillets.

Drop the peas into boiling salted water and cook for 1–2 minutes depending on the size of the snow peas. Thinner ones take much less time to cook through. Drain and serve immediately.

Place a wedge of the potato bake with the point in the centre of individual plates, put a pile of peas around that point and place a piece of fish, skin-side up, on the peas and with the lemon to one side.

Serves 4

4 x 160g (6oz) Blue Eye pieces
Ground black pepper
Spray olive oil
250g (9oz) Pontiac potatoes, cooked and mashed
200g (7oz) green peas, cooked
2 tablespoons mascarpone
120g (4oz) extra green peas, cooked
100ml (3fl oz) cabernet jus, heated

Easy Cabernet Jus
2 tablespoons onion, finely diced
½ cup cabernet sauvignon wine
1 teaspoon ground sage
1 packet (165g/6oz) Gravox Red Wine and Garlic prepared liquid gravy
25g (1oz) unsalted butter

BLUE EYE WITH PEA MASH & EASY CABERNET JUS

Some people prefer not to use flour in the sauce; others like to use a thickening gel like arrowroot at the end to achieve the desired consistency. I like to see a fine film of sauce over the back of a dessertspoon. I freeze the original jus in 1 cup lots and it comes out very well, although I normally add a splash of cream to it when I am reheating. It brings back the consistency I like.

Trim the fish if necessary, spray with oil and cook on medium-hot flat plate. Sprinkle with ground black pepper. Cook until done, depending on the thickness of the fish.

Combine the hot mashed potatoes, peas and mascarpone and mash well.

Serve by spooning equal amounts of pea mash into the centre of individual flattish bowls, top with cooked fish and spoon jus around the base of the pea mash. Sprinkle the extra peas onto the jus and serve.

For the Easy Cabernet Jus
Simmer onion in the red wine until volume reduced to half. Add the sage, pour in the gravy and simmer for 5 minutes. When ready to use, swirl in the butter and serve.

Serves 4

Mains | Seafood

32 black mussels
4 medium zucchinis, halved lengthwise
4 red capsicum cheeks
8 asparagus spears, white part removed
Spray oil
3 tablespoons balsamic vinegar
2 tablespoons cup extra virgin olive oil
½ teaspoon salt
½ teaspoon ground black pepper

BLACK MUSSELS & BARBECUED VEGETABLES

When the mussels start to open they will emit steam, so be careful when lifting them. I put them onto a baking tray to let them cool before taking off the top shell.

Soak the mussels in cold water for a couple of hours; remove the beard and any extra hairy bits on the shell.

Put the mussels on a medium-hot grill. When they start to open, adjust them so they sit as flat as possible on the barbecue. The shells will start to open after one to two minutes of cooking. Lift carefully from the barbecue so as to retain as much of the juice as possible.

Whisk the balsamic vinegar, olive oil, salt and ground black pepper together and when the mussels have cooled sufficiently to handle, ease the orange-coloured flesh from the shell into the balsamic mix. Ensure the juices from the mussels go into the mix too. Let sit for 10 minutes and stir occasionally.

Spray the zucchini and capsicum with olive oil and cook on a medium-hot plate, turning regularly to brown. Add the oil-sprayed asparagus to cook as you turn them regularly.

Assemble by putting equal amounts of zucchini halves into the centre of individual plates. Sit a capsicum cheek on top with two asparagus spears on it. Sit equal numbers of mussels on top and spoon over the extra dressing. Serve with good crusty bread.

Serves 4

4 x 160g (6oz) pieces barramundi fillet
Spray vegetable oil
½ cup Thai green curry paste
1 cup coconut milk
300g (11oz) snake beans, trimmed

Quick Stir-fried Rice

2 tablespoons vegetable oil
2 eggs, beaten
3 rashers bacon, rind removed and diced
4 green spring onions, white part minced and the green tops reserved
2 cloves garlic, minced
4 cups long grain rice, cooked
3 tablespoons soy sauce

BARRAMUNDI FILLET WITH GREEN CURRY SAUCE & QUICK STIR-FRIED RICE

For the Quick Stir-fried Rice

Heat 1 tablespoon oil in a wok to smoking point. Tip in the eggs and move around very quickly so they set and separate into small pieces. Remove from wok and make sure they are in small pieces. Set to one side. Reheat wok, add the other tablespoon oil and cook the bacon. Stir-fry for 2 minutes or until it starts to crisp. Add the white part of the spring onions with the garlic. Stir and cook for another minute.

Tip in the rice and stir through to reheat. Pour in the soy, add the egg pieces and combine well. Remove from the heat and chop some of the reserved green tops of the spring onion and stir through. Serve immediately.

Trim the fish if necessary and refrigerate until ready to cook.

Mix the curry and coconut milk in a saucepan and simmer for 5 minutes, stirring occasionally.

Cut the snake beans into bite-sized pieces and boil until tender. Drain and keep warm.

Spray both sides of the fish with oil and cook on medium-hot plate. The time will depend on the thickness of each piece but barramundi cooks quickly, so do watch it carefully.

Spoon rice onto a plate and pile snake beans alongside the rice. Place fish on the rice and spoon over the green curry sauce to taste. I love it and have lots but it's up to you how much you serve.

Serves 4

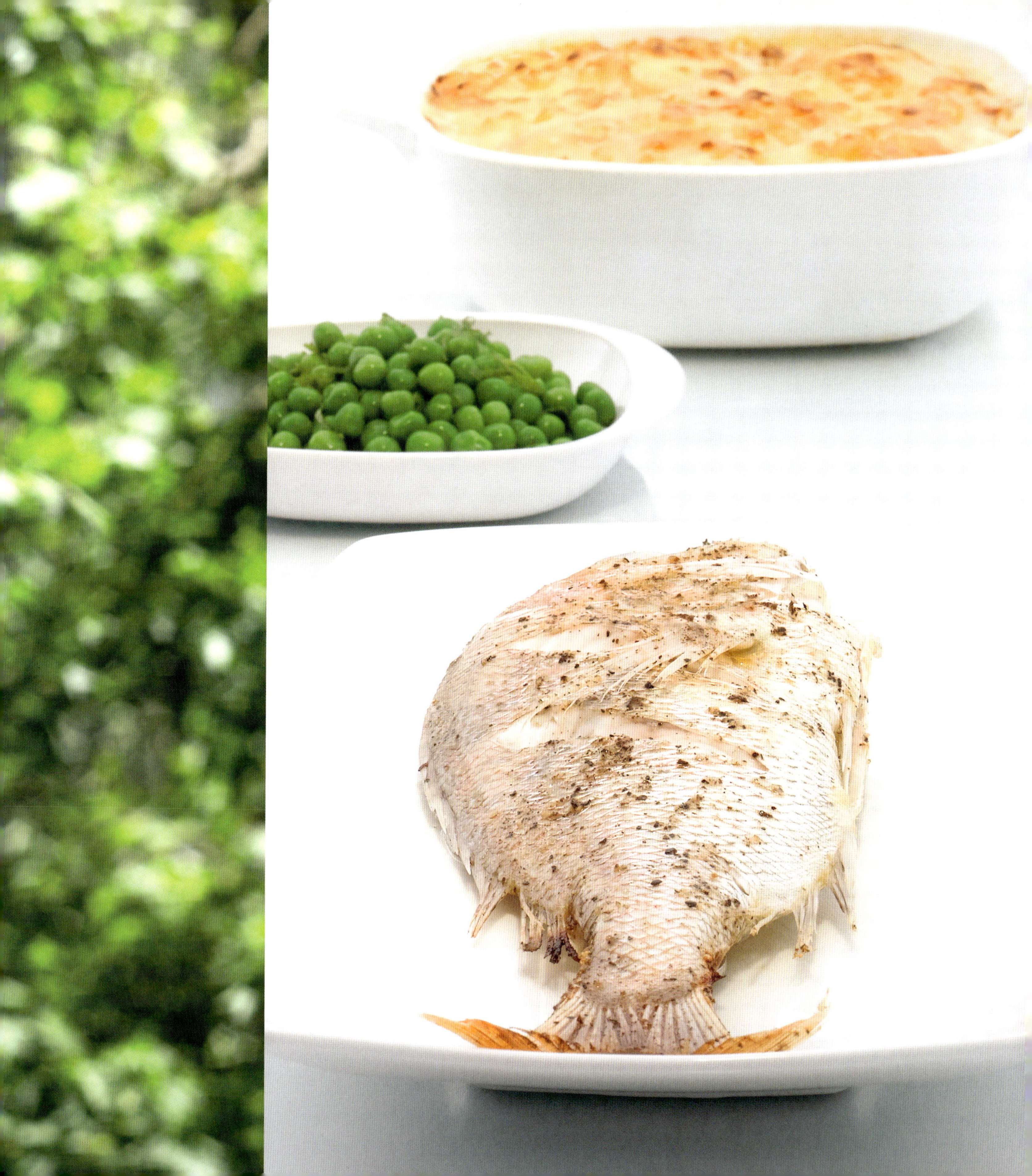

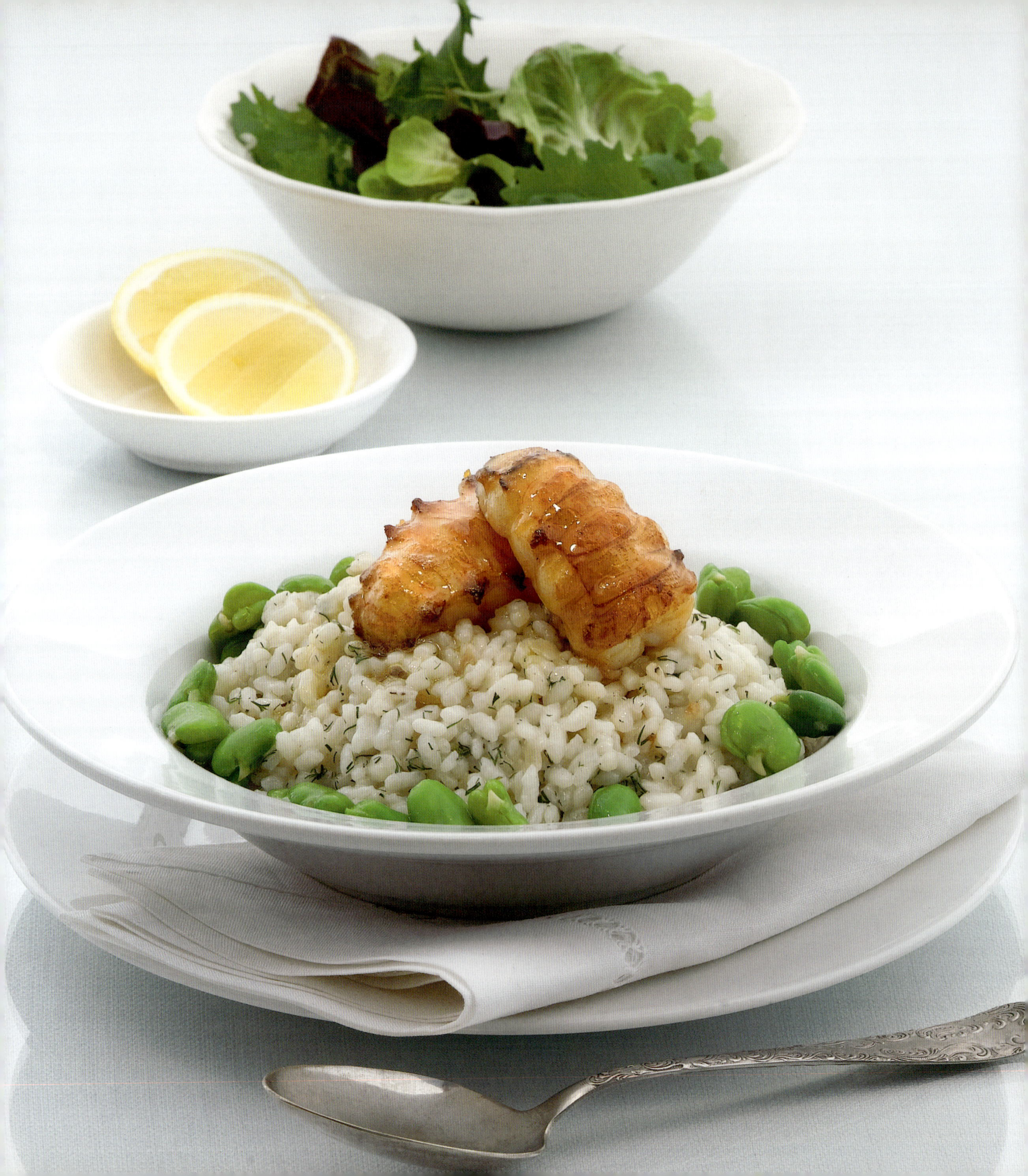

8 green bug tails, shell removed

Spray garlic oil

400g (14oz) fava/broad beans, removed from pod or frozen

1 teaspoon extra virgin olive oil

100g (4oz) butter, melted and browned over medium heat and kept warm

4 lemon cheeks

Dill and Lemon Risotto

2 tablespoons olive oil

2 tablespoons onions, finely chopped

1 clove garlic, chopped

1 cup Italian arborio rice

4 cups boiling fish/prawn stock

3 tablespoons chopped dill

½ teaspoon lemon essence

2 tablespoons parmesan cheese, finely grated

1 teaspoon sea salt

½ teaspoon white pepper

BALMAIN BUGS WITH DILL RISOTTO & BROWNED BUTTER

Make sure the vein is removed from the back of the bug tail. Refrigerate until ready to cook.

Boil the fava beans in salted water for 1 minute. Strain and cool under cold water. These can be eaten as they are but are better with the thick greyish skin removed. This will reveal brilliant emerald green beans and that is what you want. To remove this skin, pinch the bottom of each bean with your thumb and forefinger and the inner bean will pop out. It is best done as soon as they are cool enough to handle.

Make the risotto and keep warm. This risotto likes being a bit runny so you may like to add more stock. Spray the tails with oil and seal on hot plate. Move to medium-hot grill to cook through and slightly crisp. Reheat the beans in a microwave with the oil. Spoon risotto into the middle of flattish bowl, scatter the beans evenly around the base, top with two bug tails and spoon over some browned butter. Serve with green salad.

For the Dill and Lemon Risotto

Heat oil in a large heavy based saucepan over medium heat and fry onions and garlic until soft and golden. Lift the heat to high and add the rice. Stir for 1 minute. Add 1 cup boiling stock and cook, while stirring, until it is absorbed. Add stock a cupful at a time, stirring constantly, for 15–20 minutes or until rice is tender and all liquid is absorbed.

Stir in dill, lemon essence, cheese, salt and pepper. Cover with hood and leave risotto to sit for 3 minutes before serving.

Serves 4

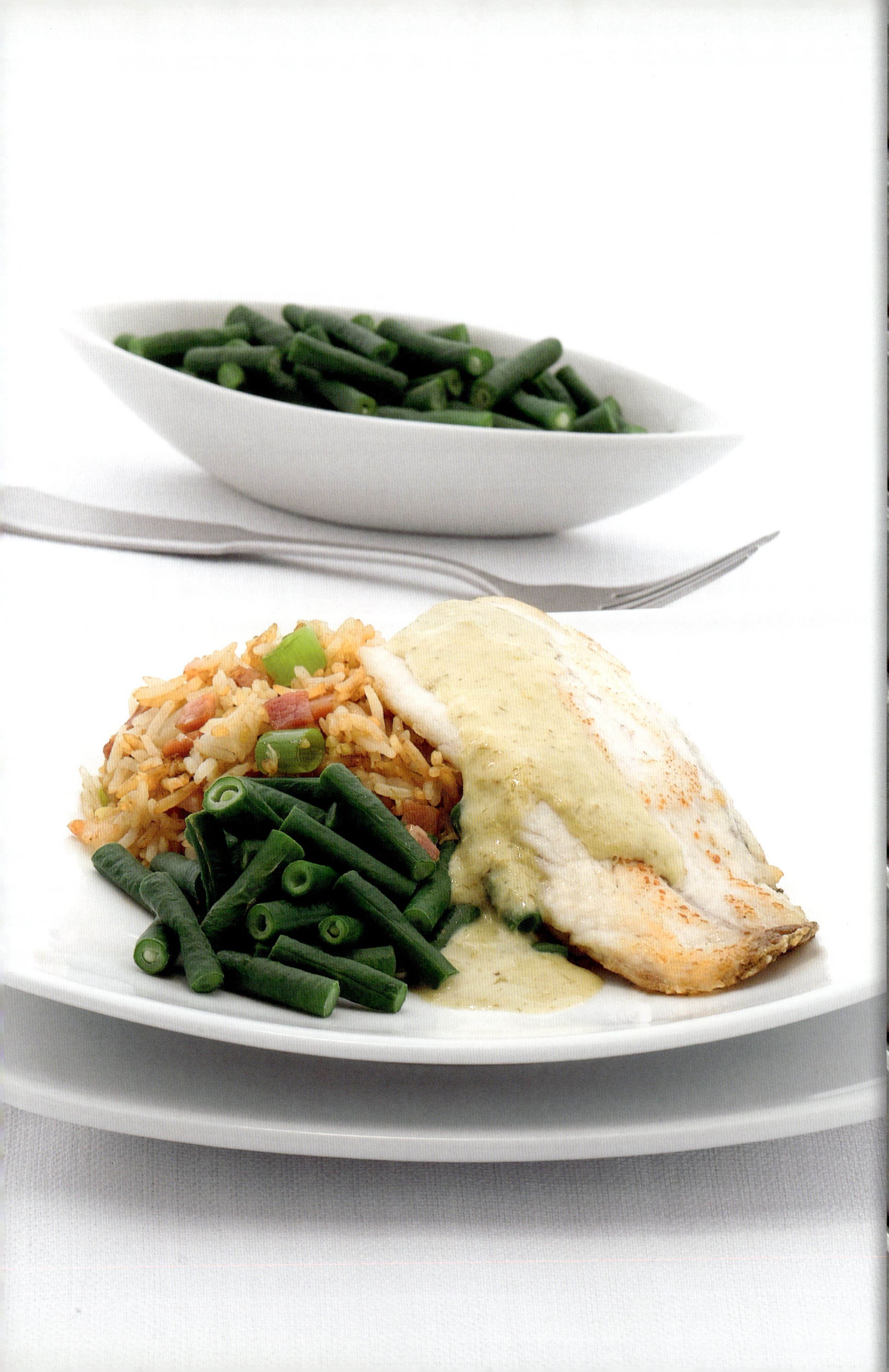

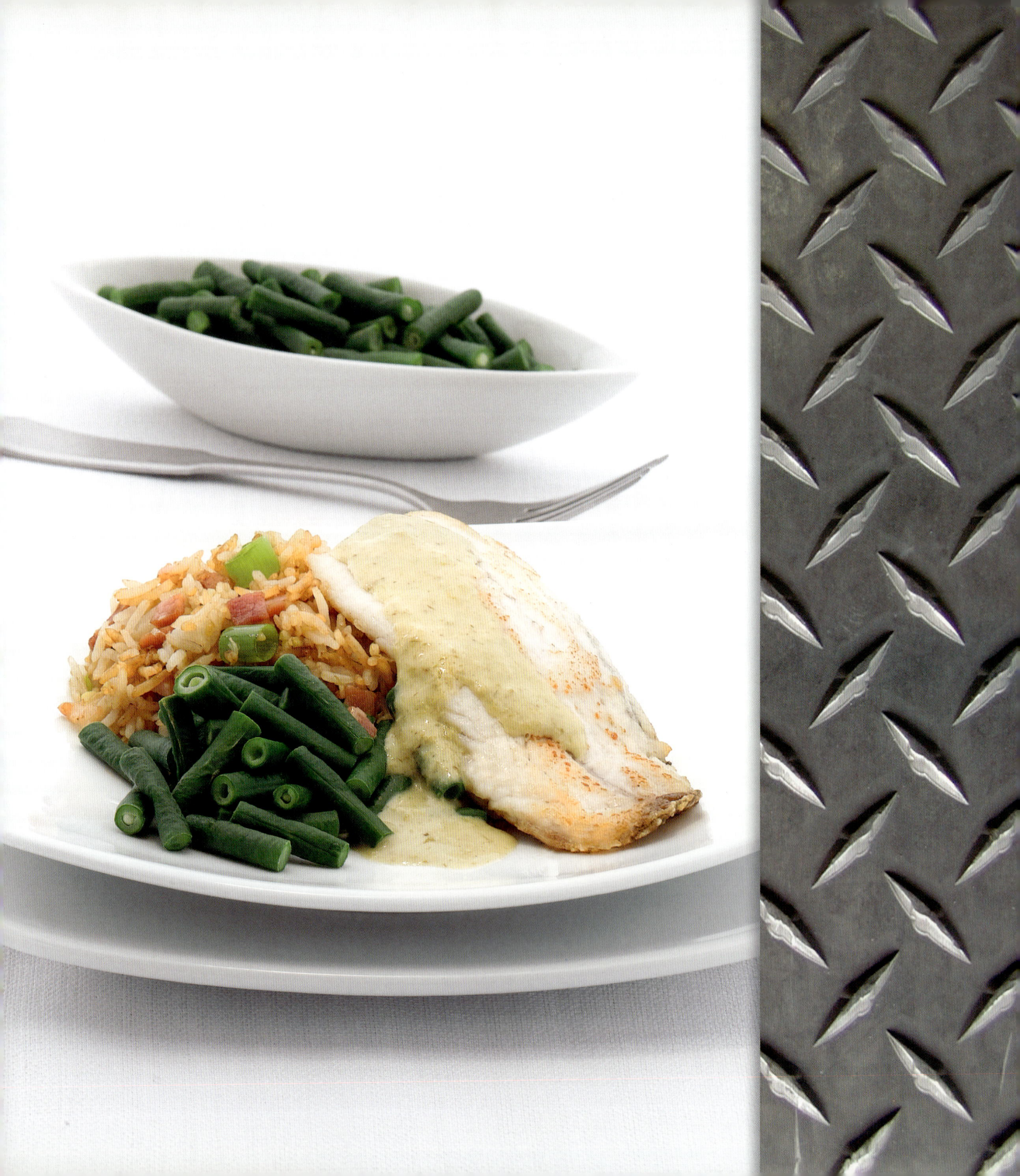

4 plate-size baby snappers
1 small lemon, cut into quarters
12 garlic chives
80g (3oz) butter, melted
1 teaspoon sea salt
1 teaspoon cracked black pepper
4 large sheets of aluminium foil, sprayed with oil
2 tablespoons vegetable oil
1 small onion, roughly chopped
1 x 100g (4oz) bag baby spinach leaves
1 tablespoon sage, finely chopped

Cheesy Creamy Potatoes
1kg (2lb) potatoes, washed (use Pontiac or regular ones)
1 tablespoon butter
125g (4oz) onion, finely chopped
100ml (4oz) cream whisked with 350ml (12fl oz) milk
Salt to taste
Ground white pepper to taste
125g (4oz) gruyere cheese, grated

BABY SNAPPER WITH CHEESY CREAMY POTATOES & SPINACH

Wash the fish cavity with cold water and dry with kitchen towelling. Cut two deep slashes into each side of each fish. Lay the fish on individual pieces of oiled foil. Stuff the cavity with the lemon quarter and three garlic chives, cut to fit the cavity. Spoon over the melted butter and sprinkle with salt and pepper. Wrap the fish in the foil and refrigerate for 30 minutes. Ensure foil is tight around the fish so the juices cannot escape.

For the Cheesy Creamy Potatoes
Slice the potatoes very finely and put into water to stop browning. Grease an ovenproof dish with the butter and sprinkle in a layer of onion. Layer in half the potatoes and pour in half the cream/milk mixture. Shake the dish so the liquid goes all the way through and sprinkle with a little salt and pepper. Add the last of the onion, potatoes, cream and milk. Sprinkle a little more salt and pepper, top with the cheese and cook at 180°C (350°F) for 50 minutes to 1 hour or until soft.

Bring the fish to room temperature for 10 minutes before placing them on a medium-hot flat plate and cooking for 6–7 minutes each side. Heat the oil to smoking point on the wok burner. Add the onions and move them around for 30 seconds. Tip in the spinach and sage and flip/toss it quickly for not much more than a minute.

Serves 4

4 x 150g (5oz) Atlantic salmon steaks, about 4cm (2in) thick.

For the rub
1 teaspoon lemon myrtle powder
½ teaspoon ground pepper berry
½ teaspoon coriander, ground
½ teaspoon paprika, ground

For the Cucumber Compote
2 cups of telegraph cucumber, peeled, de-seeded and sliced into half-moons
1 tablespoon vinegar
½ tablespoon sugar
1 teaspoon salt
½ teaspoon green tabasco
2 tablespoons dill, finely chopped

ATLANTIC SALMON WITH LEMON MYRTLE RUB & CUCUMBER COMPOTE

FOR PEOPLE WHO DON'T LIKE THE CRISP SKIN OF FISH, THE FLESH WILL SLIP EASILY FROM THE SKIN ONCE IT IS COOKED. BY THE WAY, IF YOU WANT YOUR FISH COOKED MORE THAN I HAVE SUGGESTED, THEN BY ALL MEANS DO SO.

Spray a medium-hot plate with oil, place fish flesh-side down and cook for 2 minutes. Spray the skin side of the salmon and turn onto a hot part of the plate. You may need to press firmly with a spatula to stop the fish from buckling. Cook for 1 minute so the skin of the fish will go crisp but not burn.

Serve the fish on individual plates with the cucumber compote on the side. Green salad is ideal with this summer lunch dish.

FOR THE RUB
Mix the dry rub ingredients together. Sprinkle and massage the desired amount of rub into the flesh side of the salmon. You decide the amount that you will use but the big flavour of the salmon will cope with the complex flavours of the rub.

FOR THE CUCUMBER COMPOTE
Combine all of the cucumber compote ingredients together, stir well, cover and refrigerate.

SERVES 4

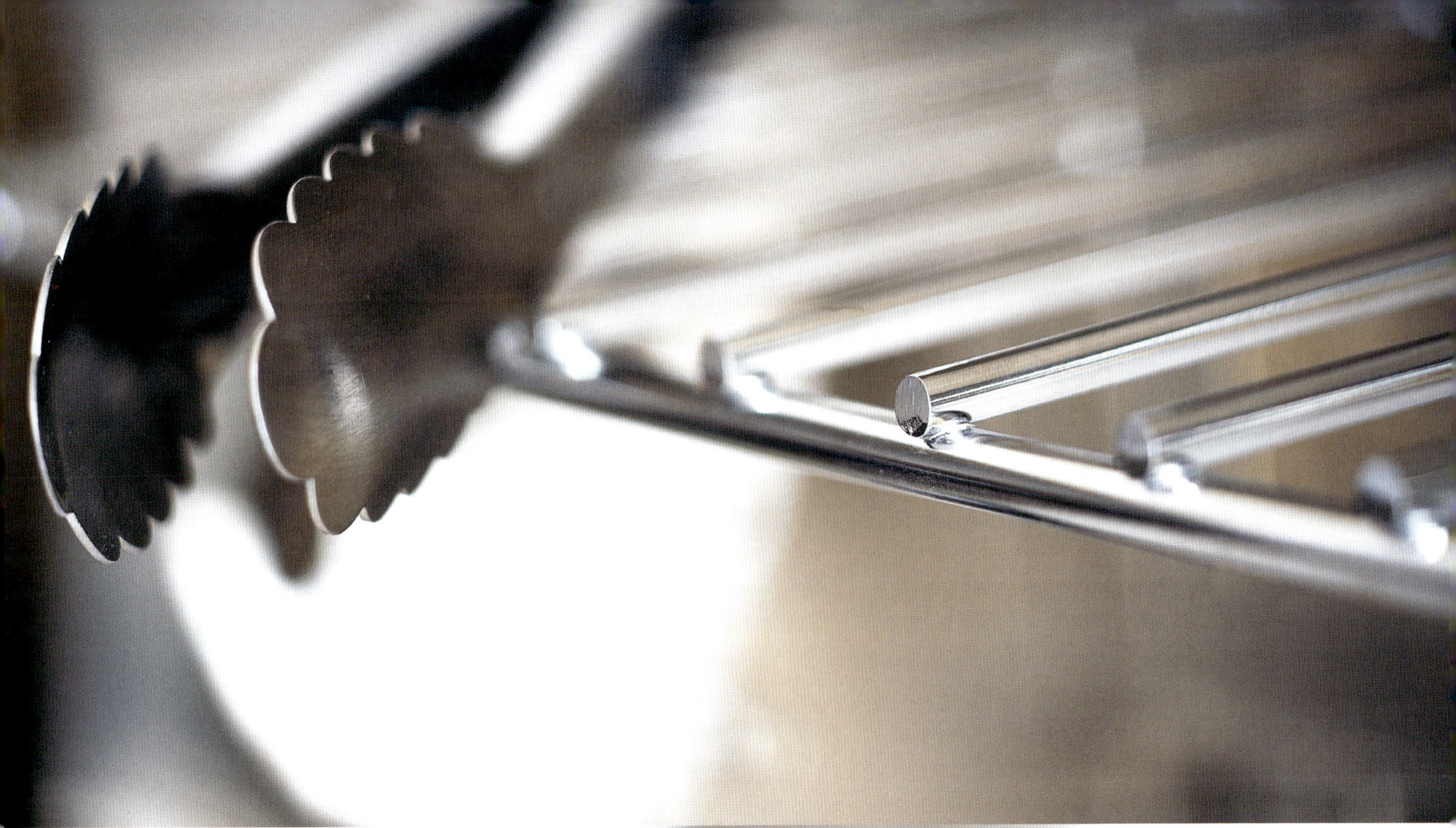

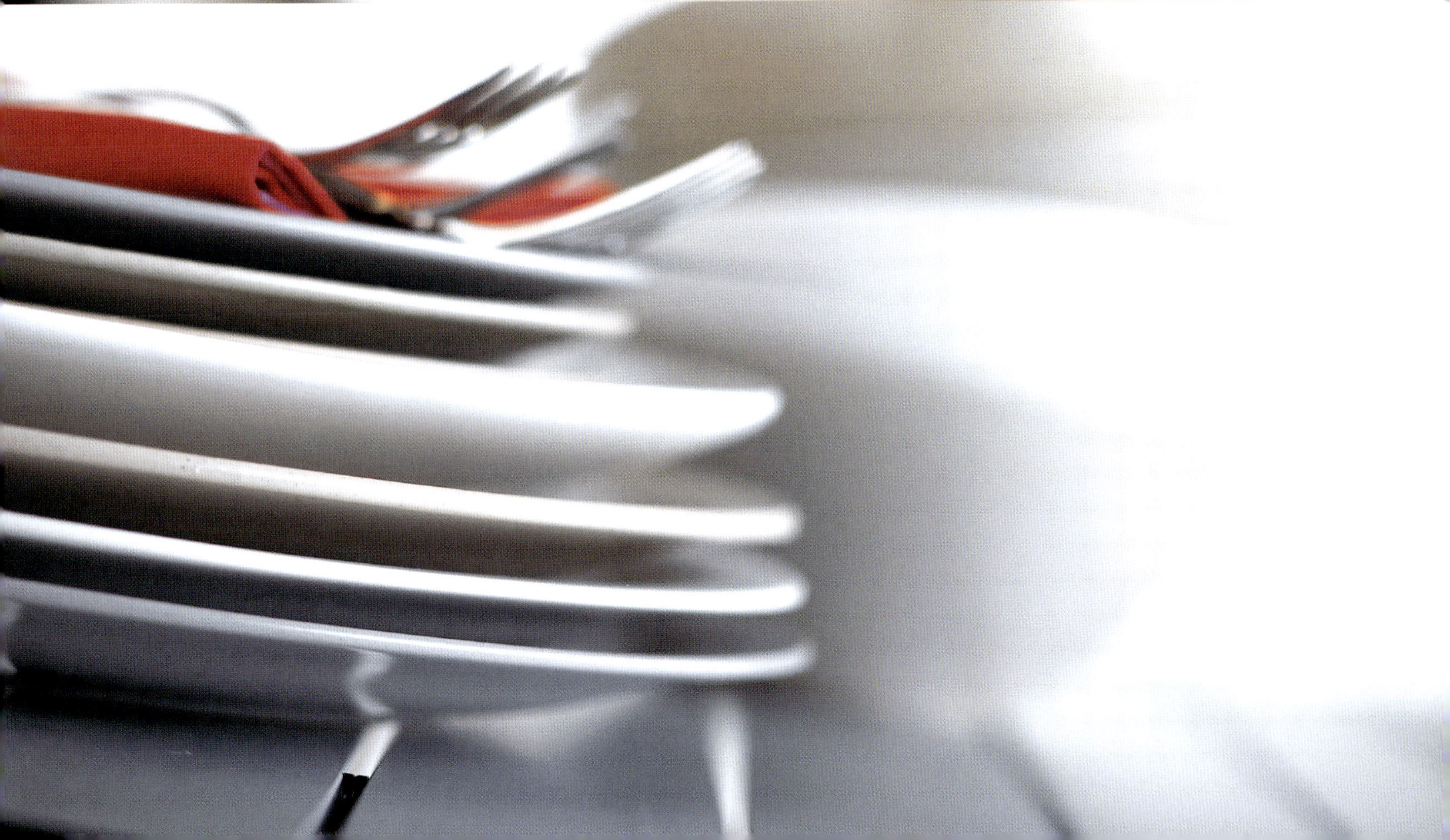

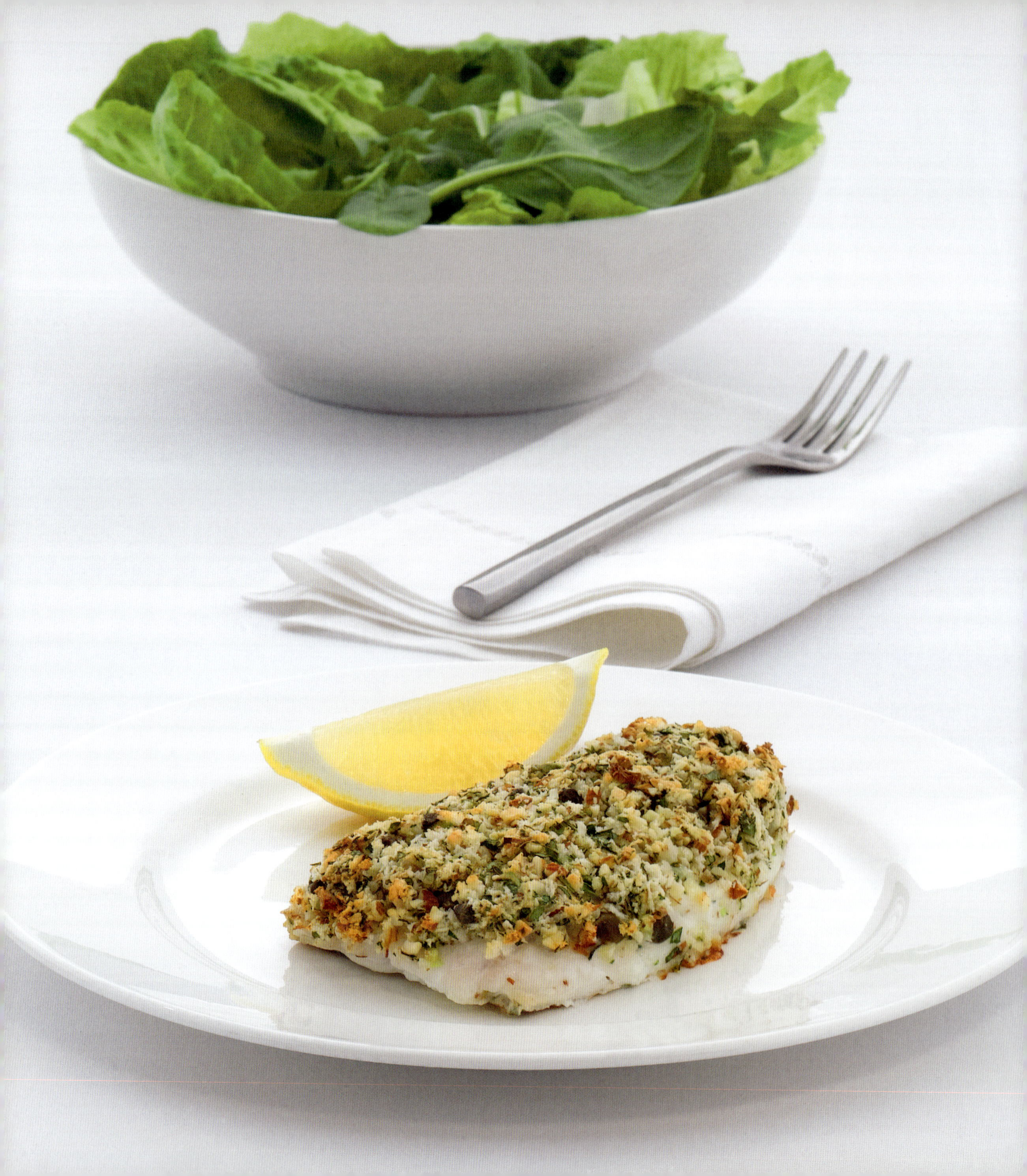

4 x 180g (6oz) snapper fillets
¼ cup flat leaf parsley, finely chopped
¼ cup green spring onions, finely chopped
¼ almonds, skin on and finely chopped
1 clove garlic, minced
1 tablespoon capers, rinsed
½ cup breadcrumbs, fresh
1 egg white
Spray vegetable oil
Baking paper
4 lemon wedges

ALMOND PARSLEY-CRUSTED SNAPPER FILLETS

For this fish dish I suggest you use the thinner tail end of the snapper fillets.

Trim the fish fillets if necessary and refrigerate until ready to cook.

Mix the parsley, spring onions, almonds, garlic, capers and breadcrumbs. Whisk the egg white with a fork and tip half into the crust mixture and tumble to combine well.

Pat the fish dry with paper towelling and brush with remaining half egg white. Spoon and pat a layer of the parsley mix onto each fish fillet. Spray a flat baking tray with oil, line with baking paper and spray the paper with oil. Carefully lift the snapper fillets onto the baking tray.

Put a cake cooling rack or similar onto the hot flat plate and sit the fish on that. Cook in moderately hot barbecue with the hood down for 6–8 minutes. Time depends on the thickness of the fish fillet.

Lift and serve with lemon wedge to one side and Potato Salad with Garlic Dressing (see recipe, page 310).

Serves 4

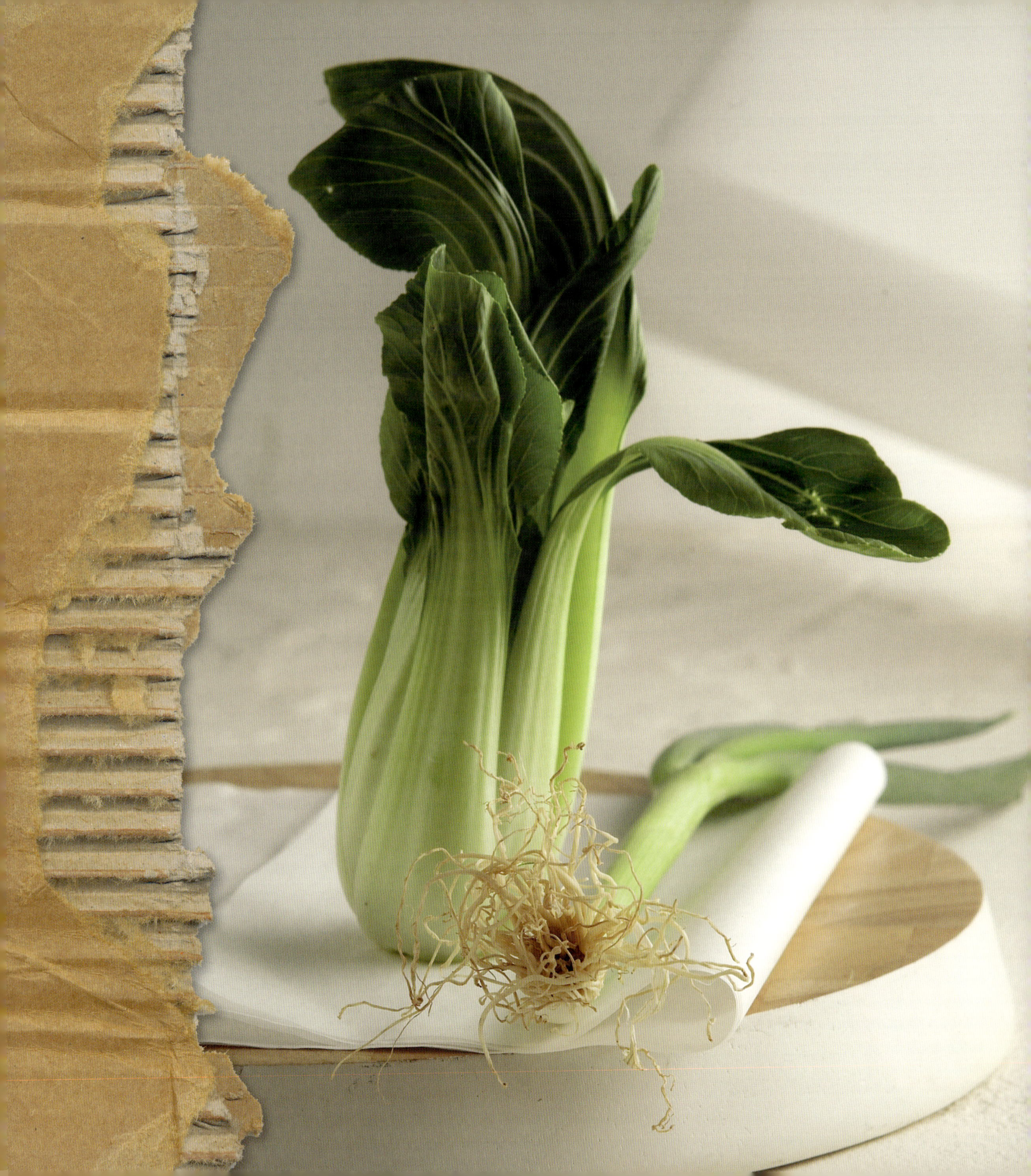

SALADS

2 small zucchinis, trimmed and cut in half lengthwise
2 small carrots, peeled and cut in half lengthwise
Spray vegetable oil
1 onion, coarsely chopped
1 cup cauliflower flowerettes, blanched
8 tear drop tomatoes, halved
1 cup tomato flesh, peeled and seeds removed
¼ cup olive oil
10 basil leaves, ripped
1 teaspoon green peppercorns, rinsed well
Salt to taste
2 cups spirali pasta, dry

CHARGRILLED VEGETABLES & PASTA SALAD WITH TOMATO BASIL DRESSING

Spray zucchinis and carrots with vegetable oil and cook on a medium-hot grill until just cooked. Insert a skewer into them when soft but firm, then lift and cool. Spray onion with oil and cook on medium grill for 1 minute.

Put the cauliflower, onion and tear drop tomatoes into a salad bowl. Cut the carrot and zucchini into bite-sized pieces and add to the pasta mix.

Make the tomato dressing by blending the tomato flesh, oil, basil, peppercorns and salt in a blender or processor. When pureed, pour over the pasta and toss well to combine flavours.

Cook the pasta in plenty of boiling water until done—around 6–7 minutes. Strain and rinse under cold water. Drain well and tip into the vegetable mix while still hot. Add the dressing and mix well.

For the best combination of flavours, prepare this salad 4–5 hours before use and toss hourly.

SERVES 4

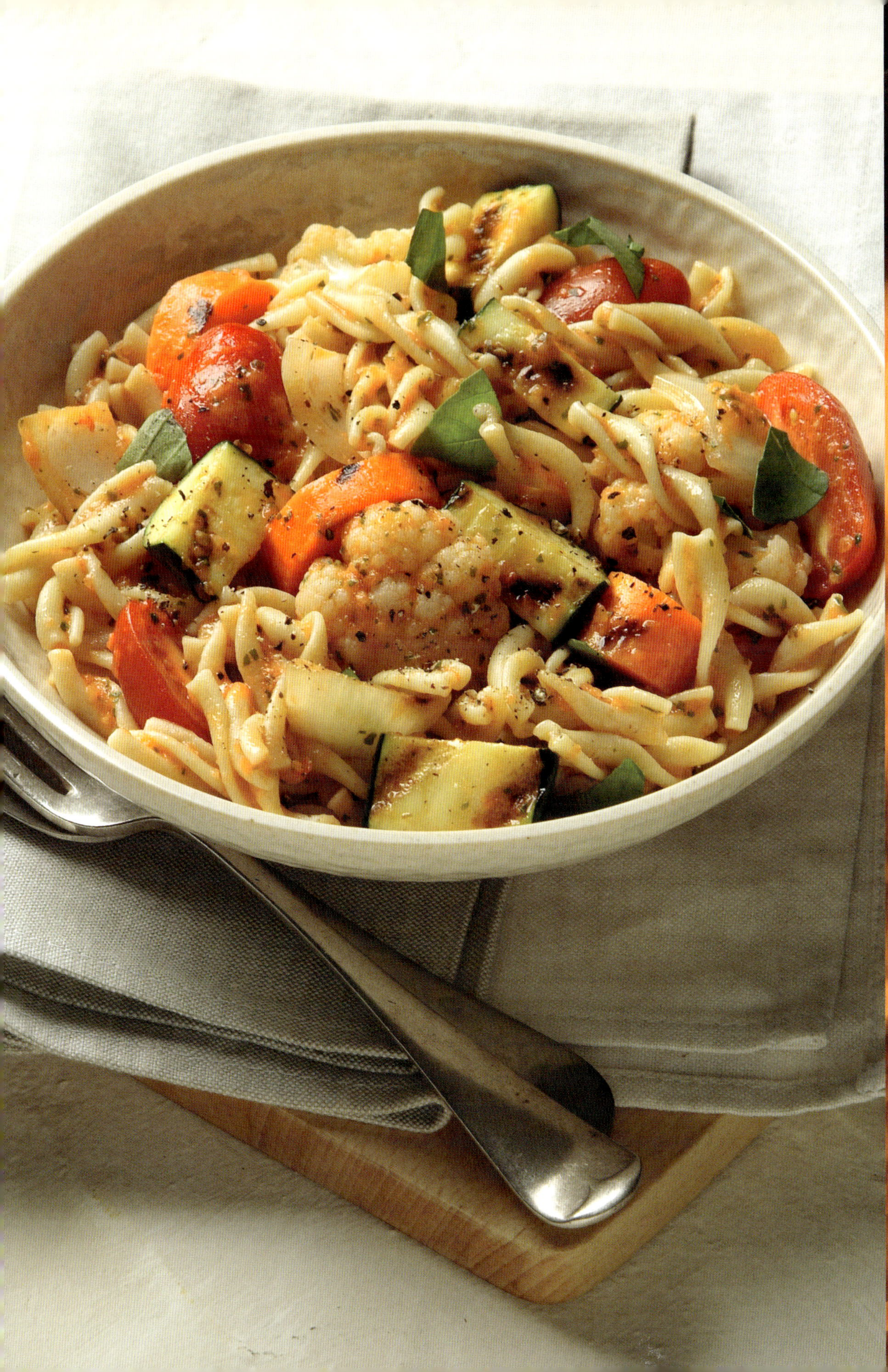

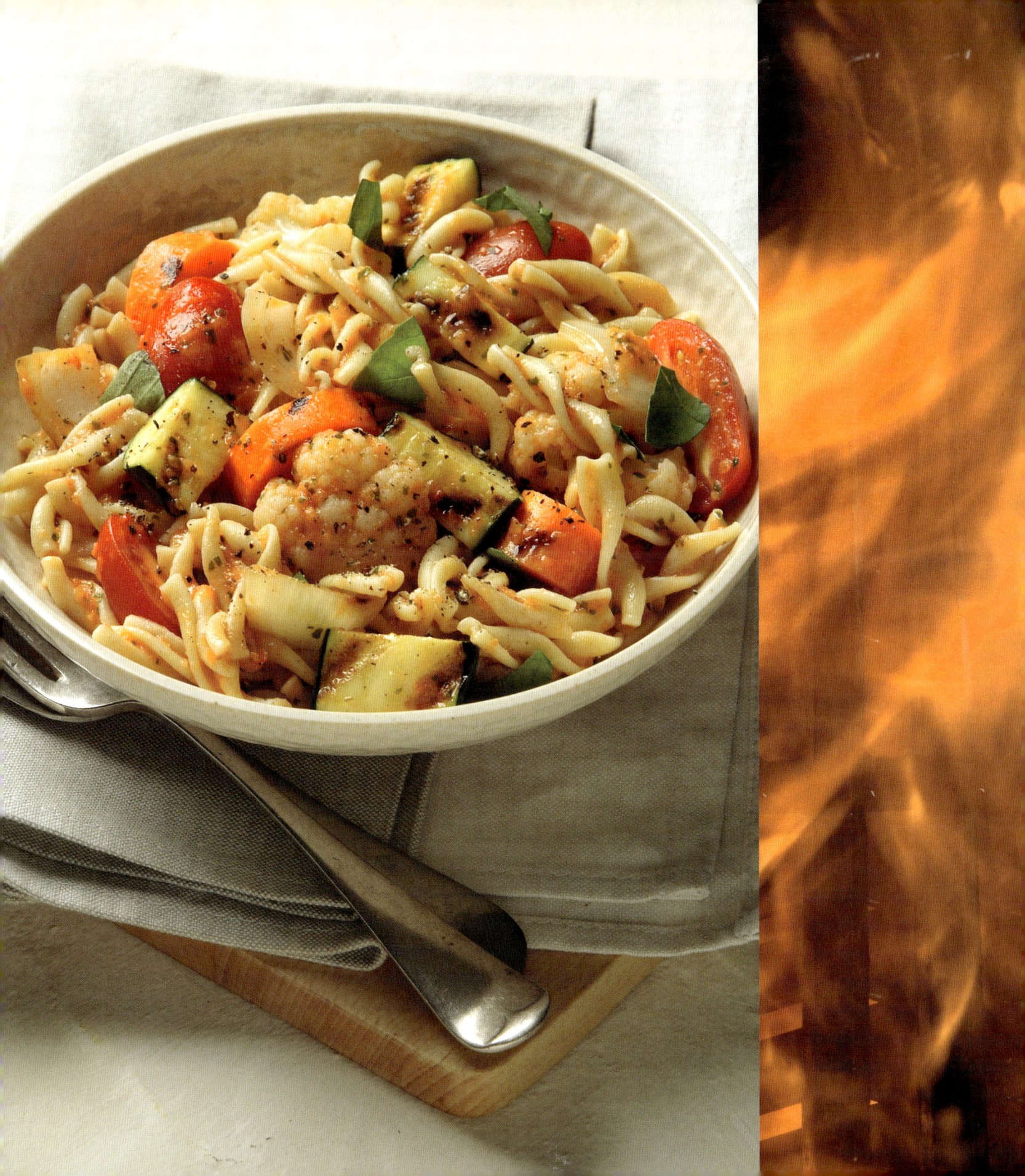

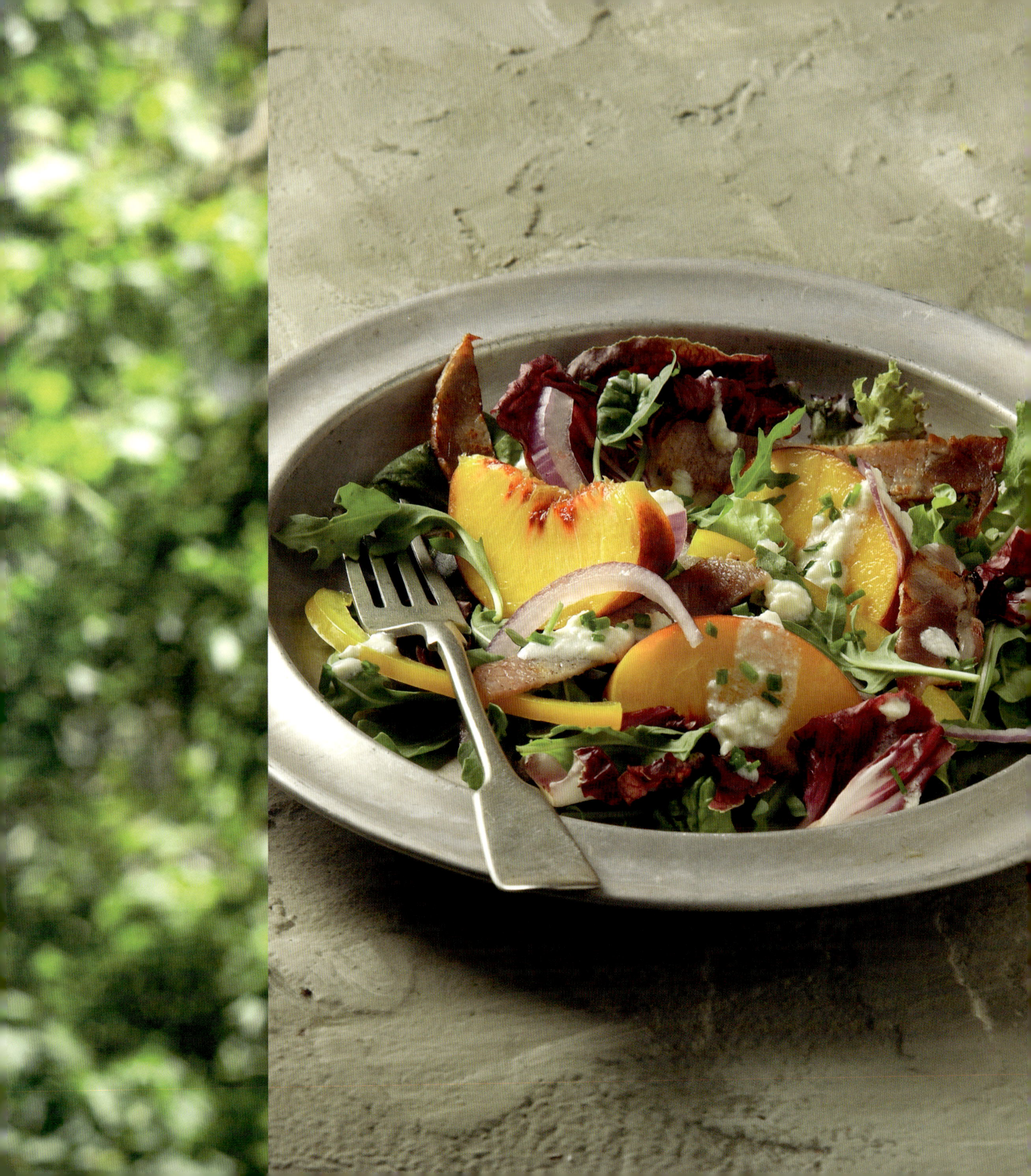

4 medium bacon rashers
2 firm peaches
Juice of 1 small lemon
1 x 100g (4oz) bag mixed lettuce leaves
1 small radicchio, core removed, washed, dried and chilled
1 yellow capsicum, cut in strips
1 small red onion, in rings
100g (4oz) creamy blue vein cheese
2 tablespoons white balsamic vinegar
Ground black pepper to taste
2 tablespoons chopped chives

BACON, PEACH & BLUE CHEESE SALAD

Cut the rind from the bacon and then cut into 3cm (1.2in) lengths cooked on hot plate until crisp. Drain on kitchen towelling.

Slice the peaches into wedges. Toss in the juice of the lemon.

Mash the cheese with the vinegar—leave quite lumpy.

Assemble the salad by layering various leaves, capsicum, onion, peaches and bacon into a salad bowl. Spoon over the cheese dressing and sprinkle over the chopped chives. Serve immediately.

SERVES 4

6–8 Kipfler potatoes, about 400g (14oz)
½ cup celery, finely diced
¼ cup white onion, finely diced
8 caper berries, halved
150g (5oz) canned tuna, drained
1 tablespoon fresh fennel leaves, finely chopped

For the dressing
4 anchovy fillets
1½ cups mayonnaise
1 tablespoon white vinegar
½ teaspoon salt
¼ teaspoon white pepper

BARBECUE POTATOES WITH TUNA & ANCHOVY DRESSING

Wash the potatoes, cut in half lengthwise. Cover with water and bring to the boil, then simmer for 5 minutes. Strain and cool.

Make the dressing by blending all ingredients to a smooth, creamy consistency.

Spray the cut side of potatoes with oil and cook on medium-hot plate. Cook for 2 minutes and turn for another 2 minutes of cooking.

When done, lift into a large bowl and spread the celery and onion over the potatoes. Equally distribute the caper berries around the potatoes and flake in the tuna.

Spoon the dressing over the top and shake the bowl well, making sure the dressing sinks down to the bottom. Cover with cling wrap and refrigerate for at least 4 hours before serving.

As you serve, scatter the fennel over the top.

SERVES 4

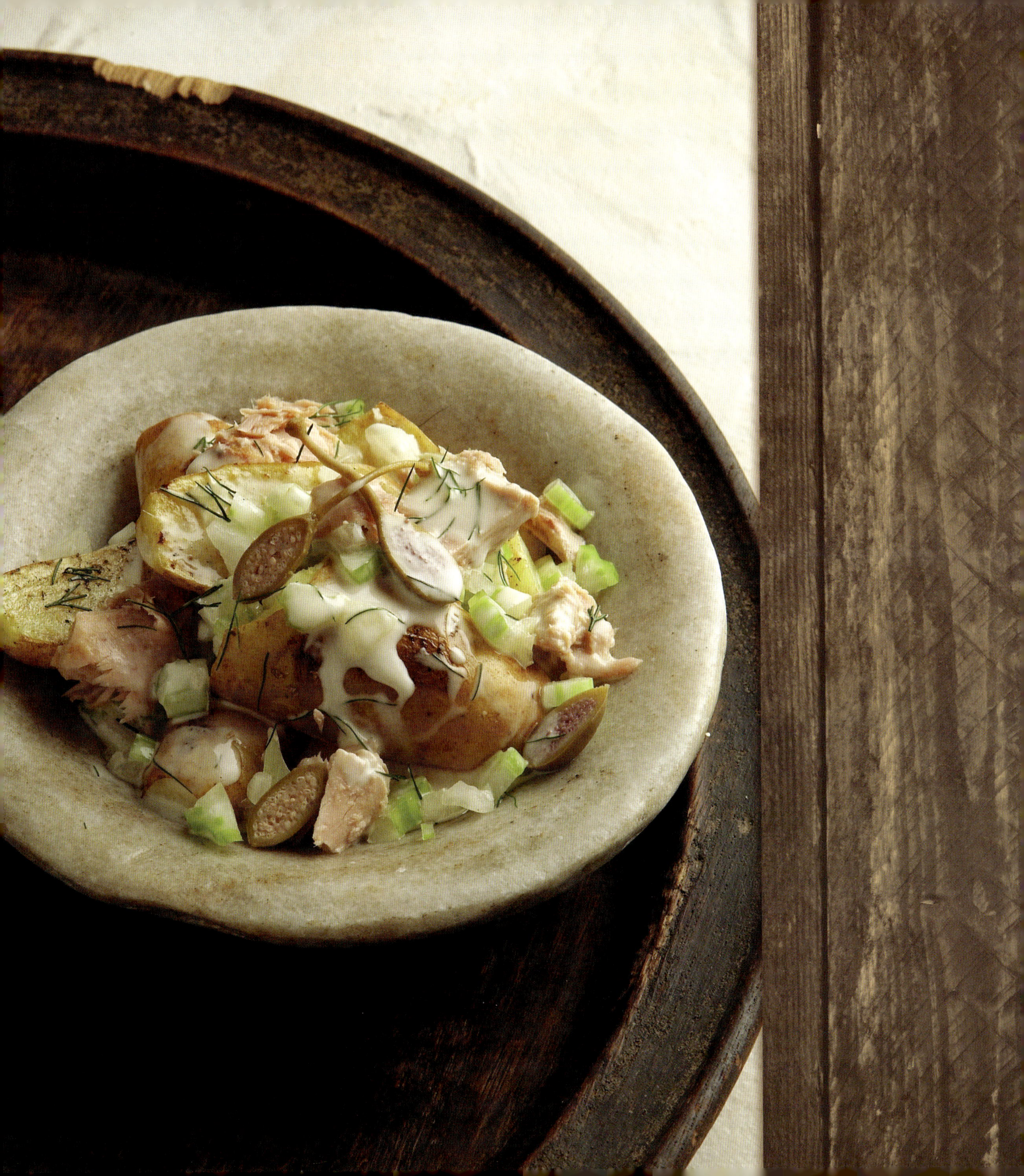

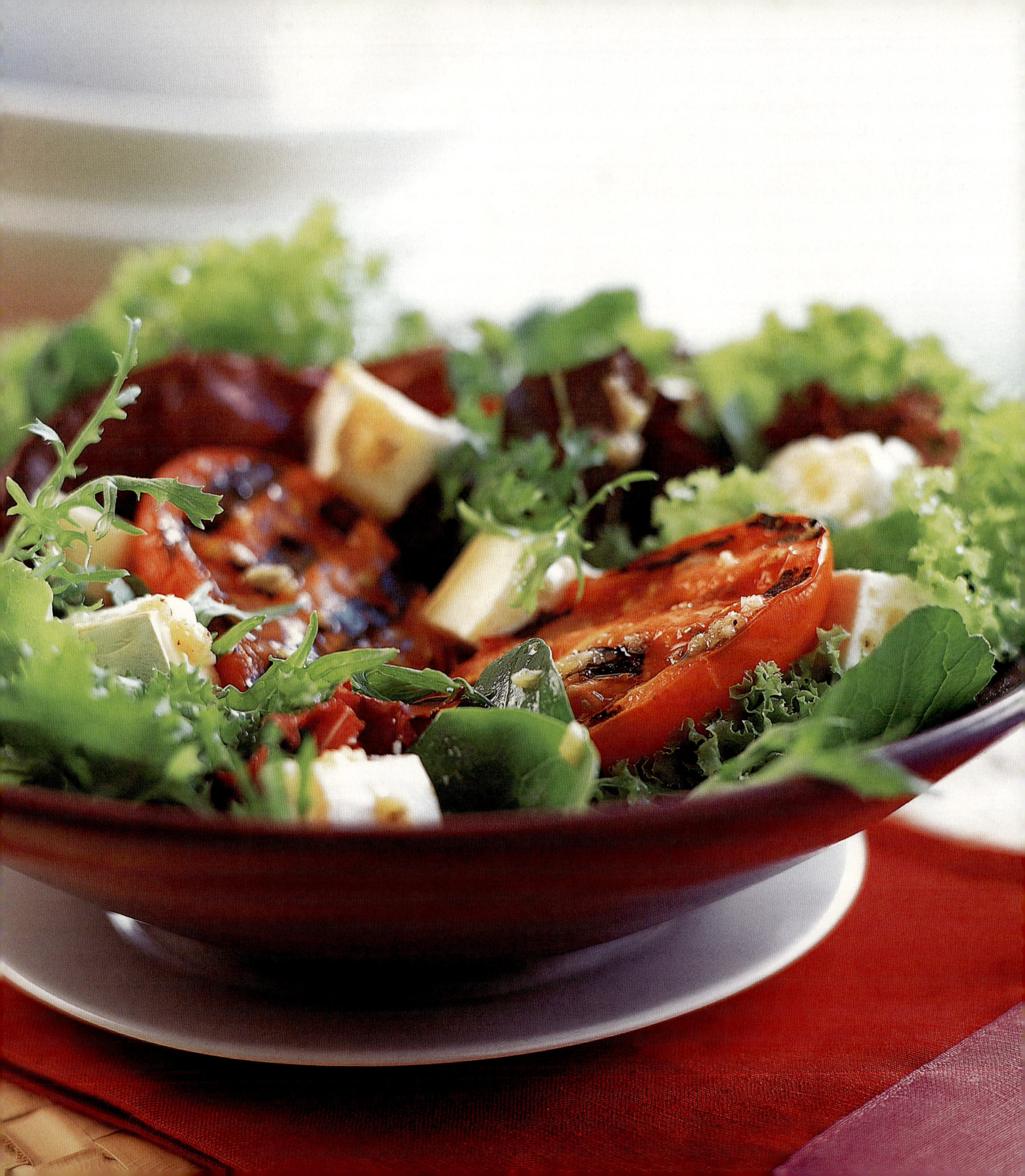

4 Roma tomatoes
1 x 100g (4oz) bag mesclun mix leaves
100g (4oz) dry goat's cheese, crumbled or cut into dice
½ cup Barbecued Garlic Dressing (see recipe below)
Spray olive oil

Barbecued garlic dressing
3 garlic cloves
½ cup light olive oil
½ teaspoon salt
¼ teaspoon ground black pepper
1 teaspoon sugar
2 tablespoons Spanish sherry vinegar

GOAT'S CHEESE & MESCLUN SALAD WITH BARBECUED GARLIC DRESSING

Cut the tomatoes in half. Spray the tomatoes with oil and cook, on a medium-hot plate, for 1½-2 minutes each side. Remove from barbecue to cool for 10 minutes.

Arrange the leaves in a salad bowl, top with the crumbled goats cheese and tomatoes.

Spoon dressing over and serve.

For the Barbecued Garlic Dressing

Spray a medium-hot plate with oil, add the garlic and cook for 4 minutes, turning it regularly to allow it to lightly brown. Put the garlic, oil, salt, pepper and sugar into a blender/food processor and blend until smooth and a light creamy colour.

Pour the vinegar through the feeding shute and when combined, pour this rich dressing into a sealable jar.

Serves 4

24 peach slices, fresh and cut from the stone or canned and drained

Spray oil

1 x 100g (4oz) mixed lettuce leaves

200g (7oz) feta cheese, diced

1 tablespoon extra virgin olive oil

3 tablespoons fresh lime juice

60g (2oz) lychee flesh, in 1cm (½in) dices (canned and drained)

1 teaspoon dill, chopped

1 teaspoon green peppercorns, crushed

4 large slices prosciutto, grilled on the barbecue to crisp, cooled and crumbled

PEACH, FETA & PROSCIUTTO SALAD WITH LIME & LYCHEE DRESSING

Lightly spray the peach slices with oil and lightly brown them on a hot grill; the canned slices cook very quickly while the fresh ones take a little longer. Do 6 slices at a time to have better control. Leave to cool before adding to the leaves and cheese.

Make the dressing by whisking the oil for a few seconds. Whisk in lime juice slowly and stir in the lychee dices, dill and pepper.

Pour the dressing onto the peach and salad ingredients and toss gently. Sprinkle crumbled prosciutto over and serve.

SERVES 4

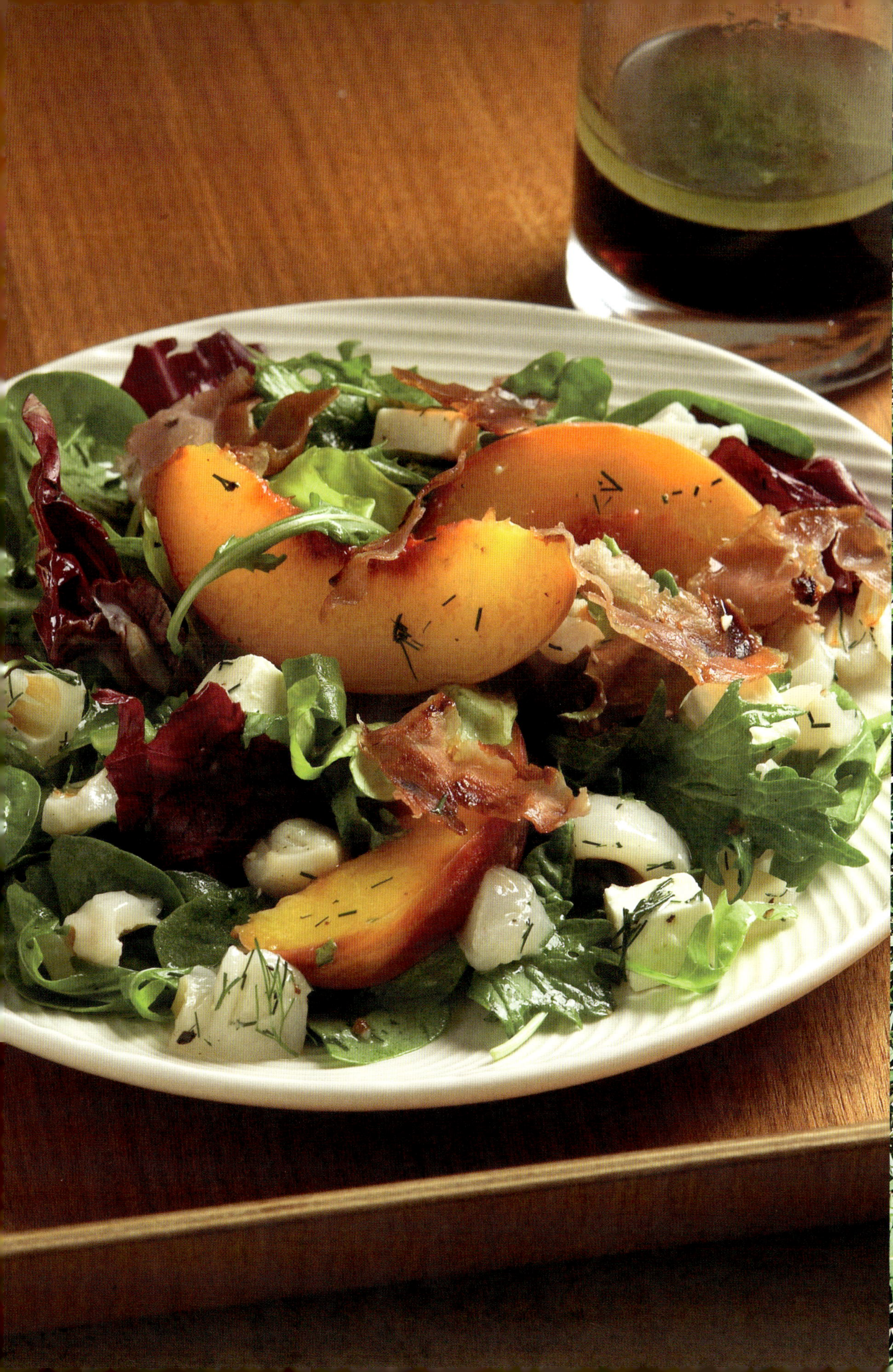
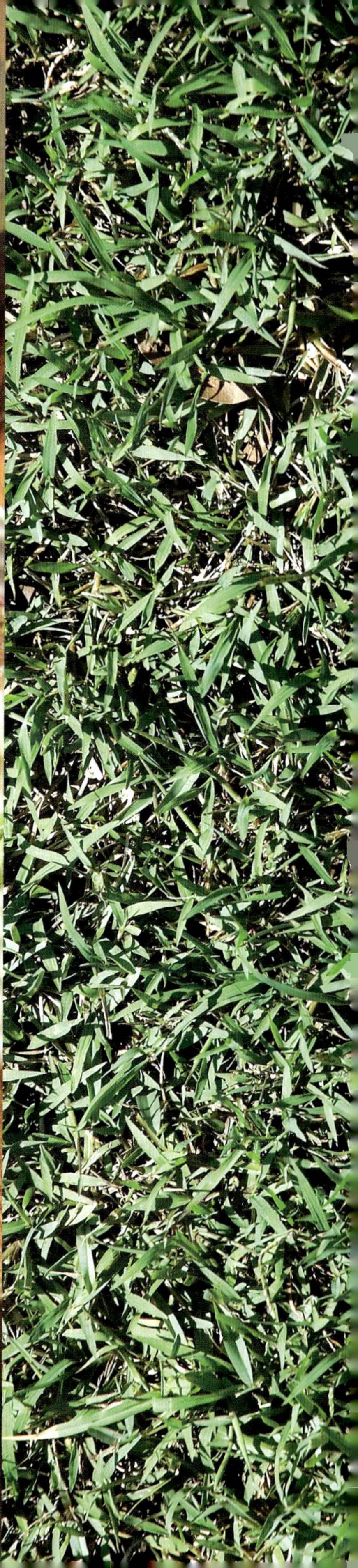

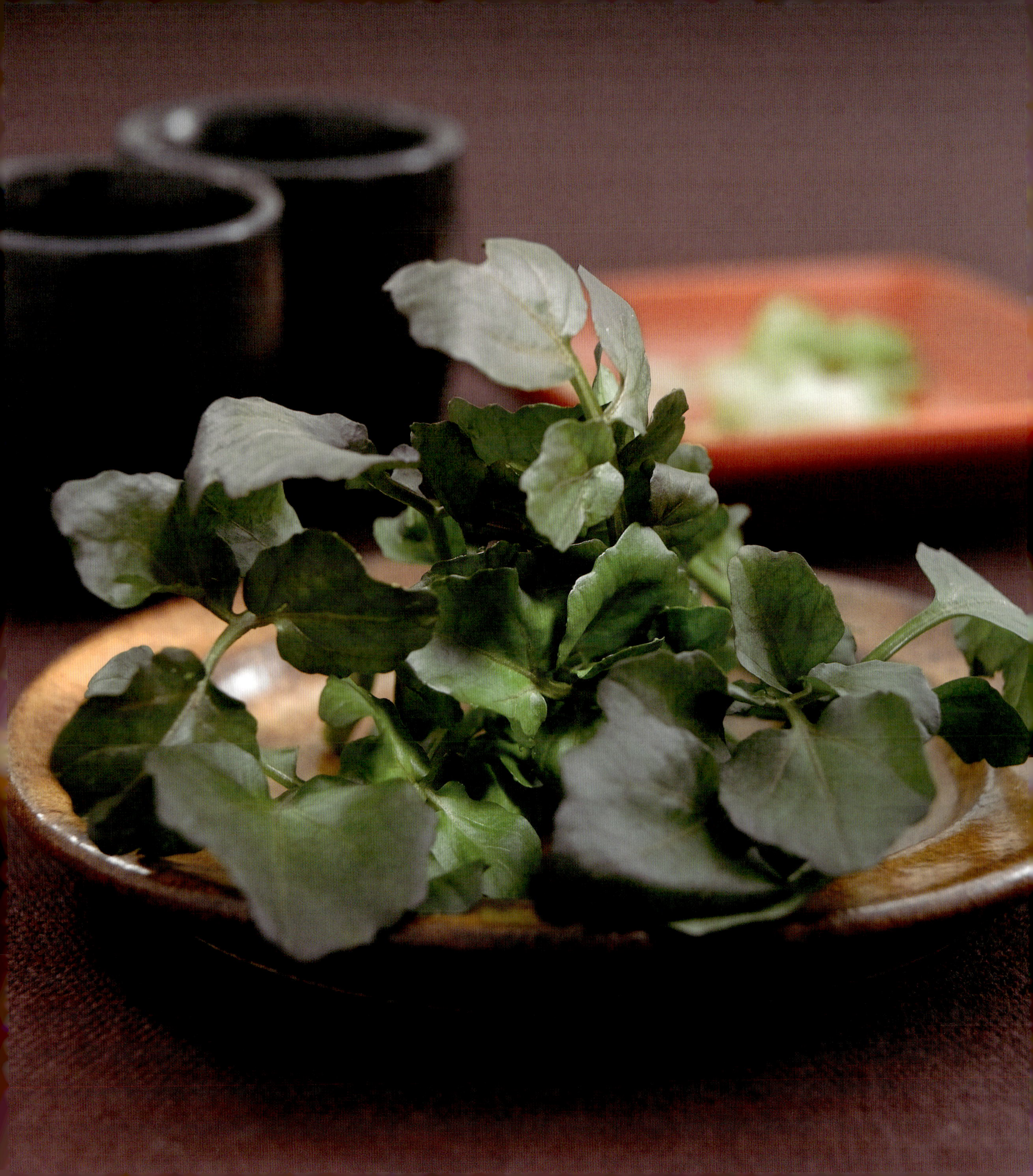

4 cups watercress, sprigs only, washed
  and loosely packed
4 medium red radishes, trimmed
125g (4oz) firm feta cheese
1 tablespoon lemon juice
2 tablespoons raspberry vinegar
2 tablespoons olive oil
3 tablespoons tarragon, fresh and finely chopped
1 teaspoon pink peppercorns, rinsed and crushed

WATERCRESS, RADISH & FETA SALAD WITH RASPBERRY & TARRAGON DRESSING

Tip the watercress into the salad bowl. Finely slice the trimmed radish and add. Crumble or cut the cheese into the salad bowl.

Whisk the lemon juice, vinegar, oil, tarragon and peppercorns together well. Pour over the salad when ready to use and toss well.

Serves 4

8 baby bok choy, halved, washed and well drained
Spray vegetable oil
250g (9oz) rice vermicelli noodles, rehydrated
60g (2oz) green spring onions, roughly chopped
120g (4oz) carrots, peeled and shredded
120g (4oz) yellow banana capsicum, deseeded and in fine strips
2 tablespoons sesame seeds, toasted

For the dressing
2 tablespoons green ginger root, minced
2 tablespoons red chilli, minced and with seeds left in
1 clove garlic, minced
1 cup soy sauce
1 tablespoon honey
½ teaspoon sesame oil

RICE NOODLES & BOK CHOY SALAD WITH GINGER CHILLI SOY DRESSING

Make sure the bok choy has been washed thoroughly and drained well. Spray cut side with oil and quickly cook (mark) on very hot grill. I do this by putting the stalk part onto the grill but let the leaves hang over the edge—in that way, the softer green leaves do not get dried out and burnt.

Lift from the grill and place around a large round platter.

To make dressing, whisk all ingredients together or blend in a processor or blender.

Mix the noodles, spring onions, carrots and capsicum with half the dressing. Tip onto the platter so that the noodles overlap some of the bok choy. Spoon the remaining dressing around and over the bok choy. Sprinkle with sesame seeds and serve immediately.

SERVES 4

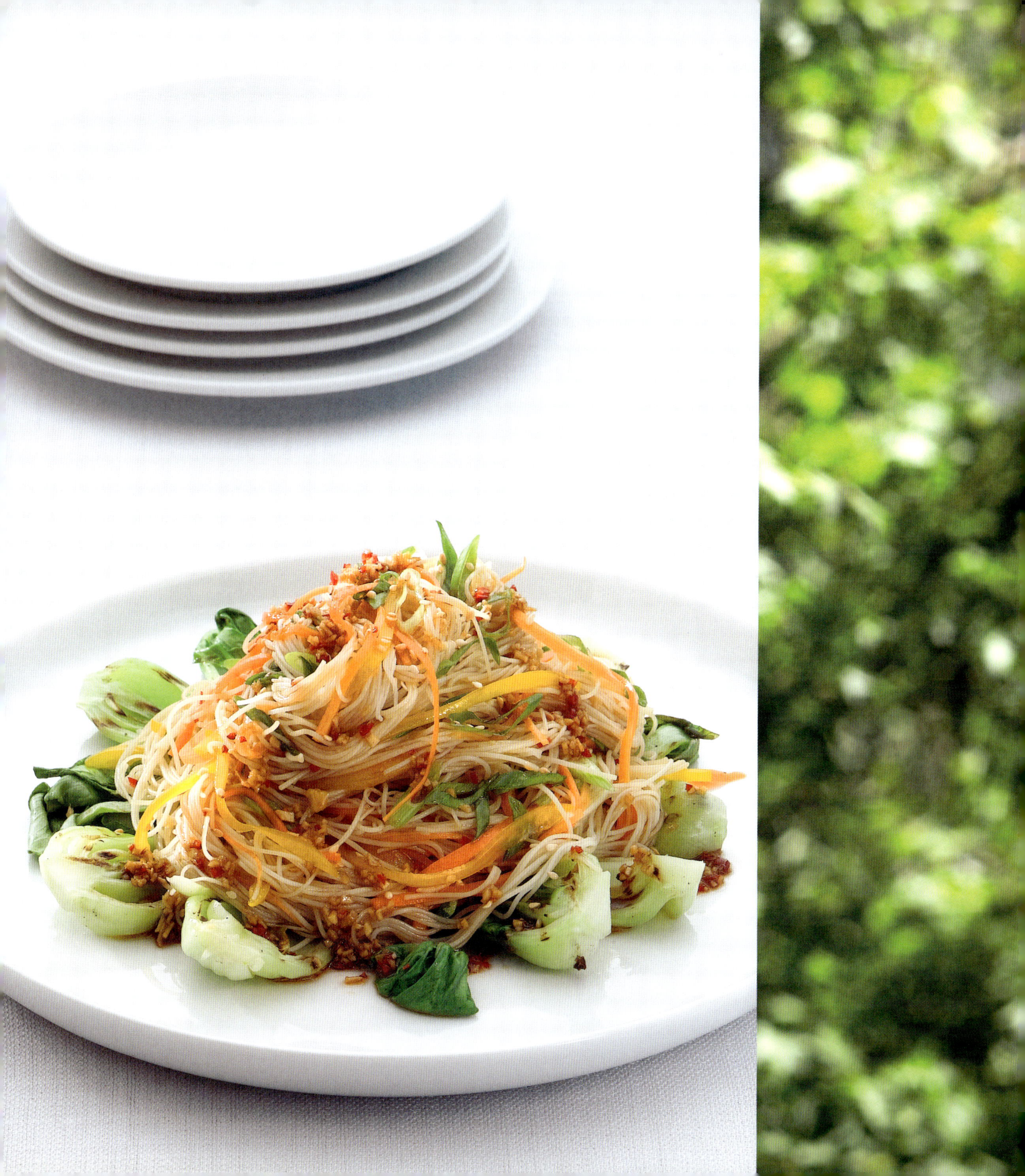

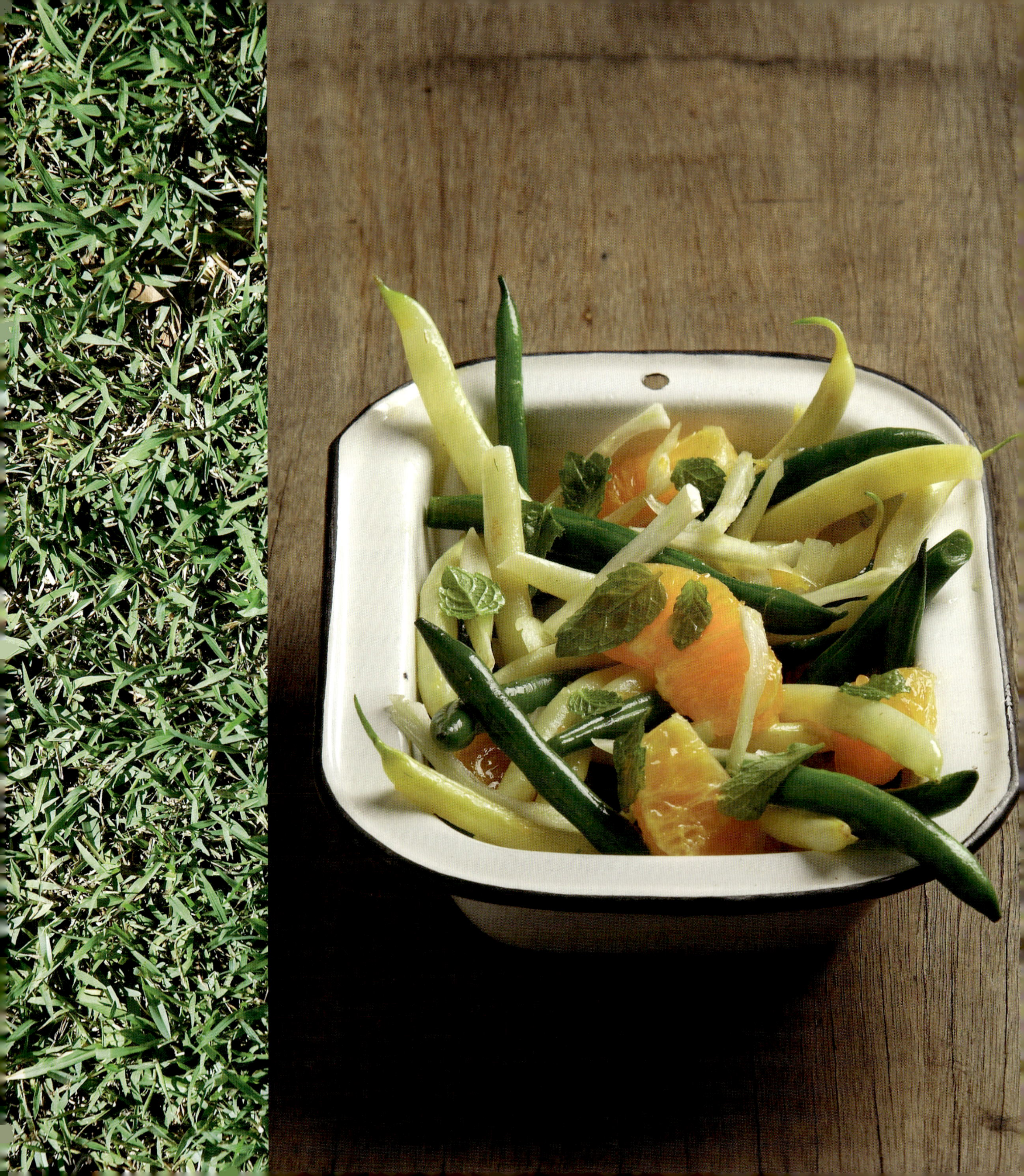

100g (4oz) fennel bulb
150g (5oz) butter beans, tails removed
150g (5oz) green beans, tails removed
2 medium oranges, peeled and segmented (capture juice)
¼ cup mint leaves, loosely packed
½ cup orange juice, incorporating captured juices
2 tablespoons olive oil
Salt and ground white pepper to taste

FENNEL, BEAN & ORANGE SALAD

Slice the fennel very finely.

Blanch and refresh the beans. Sit in large salad bowl. Add the fennel, orange segments and mint.

Whisk the oil until aerated, continue whisking in the juice, salt and pepper and pour over the bean ingredients. Toss well and serve.

Serves 4

300g (11oz) carrots, peeled, halved lengthwise
½ cup orange juice
¼ cup walnut oil
½ teaspoon powdered cumin
½ teaspoon powdered smoky paprika
¼ teaspoon powdered chilli
Salt to taste
½ cup garlic chives, in 4cm (2in) long pieces
4 x 2cm (1in) thick haloumi slices
Spray olive oil

Chargrilled Haloumi, Carrot & Chive Salad

Cut the halved carrots into half-moon shapes on the diagonal and boil for 2 minutes. Drain and keep warm.

Whisk the orange juice with oil, cumin, paprika, chilli and salt. Add the carrots and chives and toss well. Tip into salad bowl.

Spray the haloumi with a little oil, then cook on medium grill until lightly browned each side. Spread around the top of the carrots and serve while warm.

Serves 4

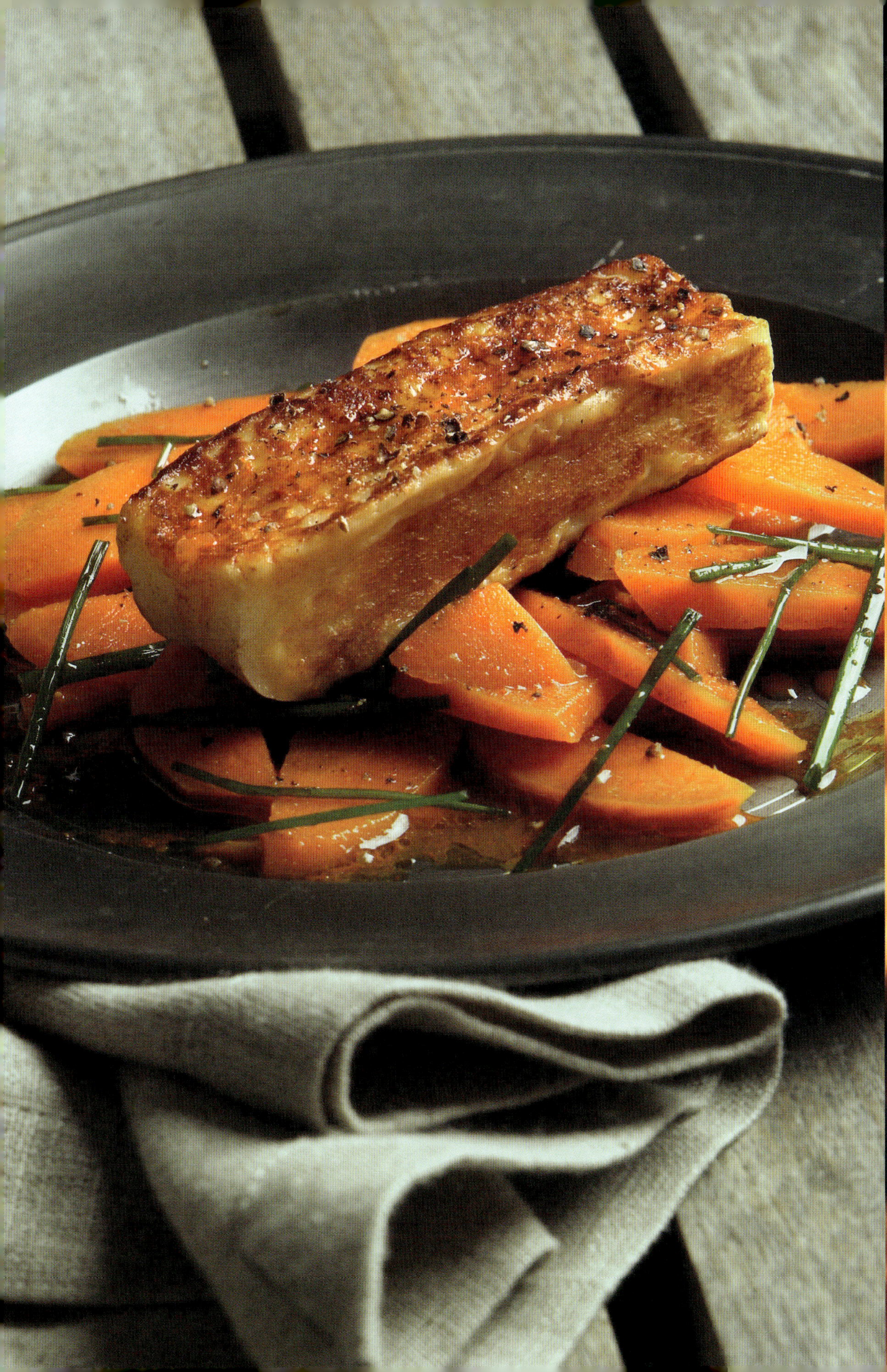

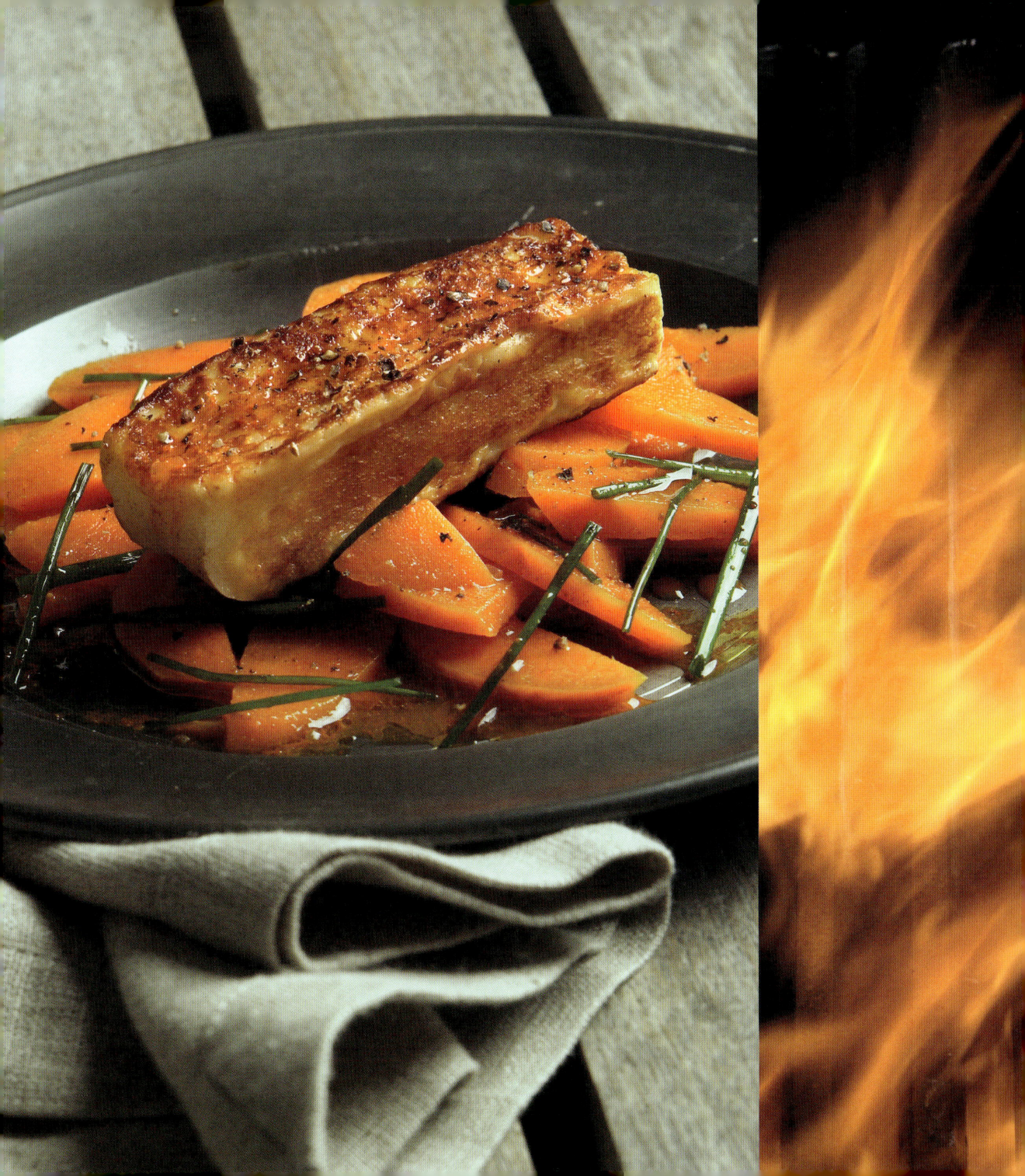

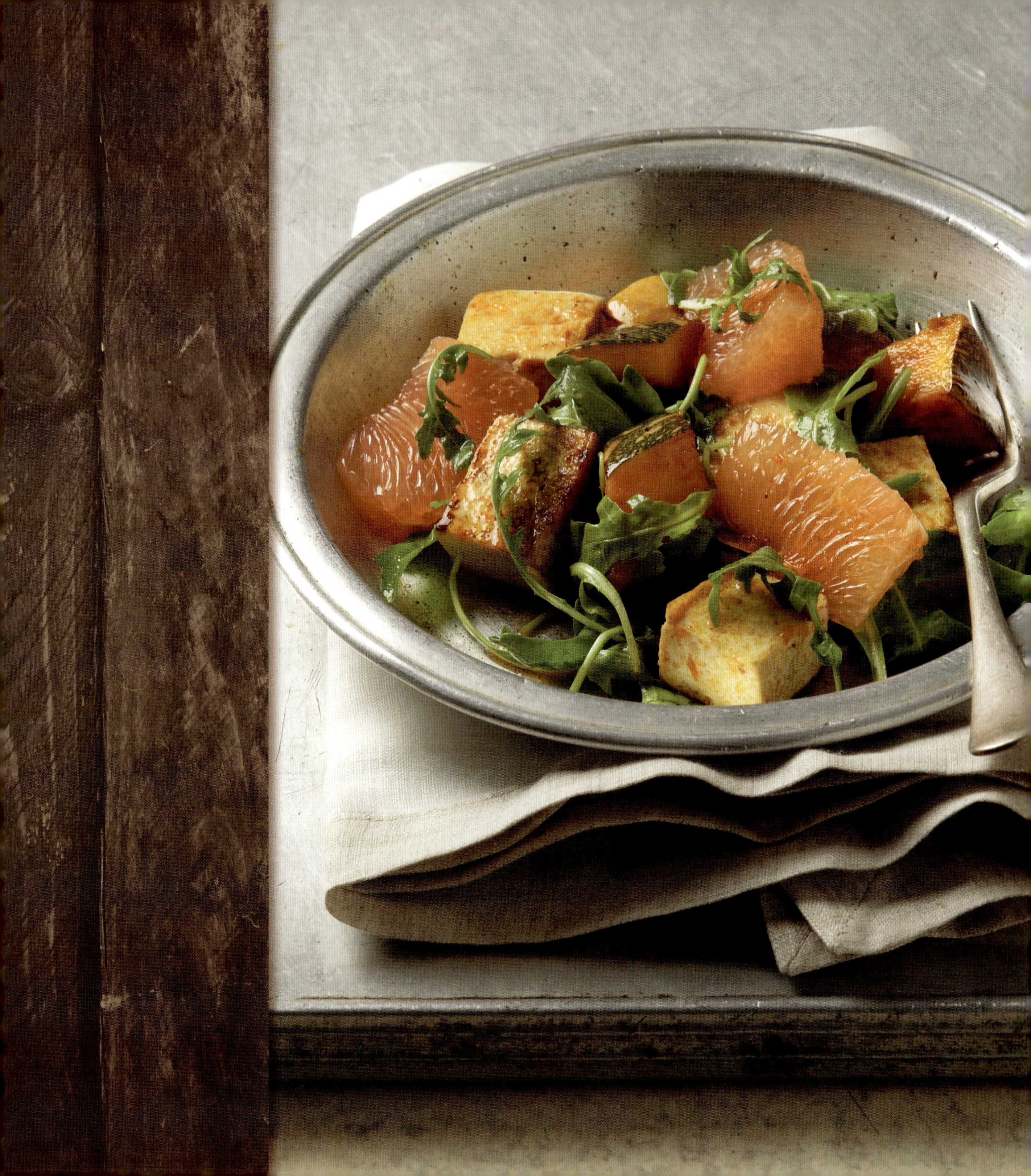

300g (11oz) Japanese pumpkin, skin on
    and cut into bite size pieces
Spray olive oil
200g (7oz) firm tofu, drained and cut
    into pieces around the same size
    as the pumpkin
2 pink grapefruit
½ cup olive oil
½ teaspoon honey
¼ teaspoon smoky paprika
Sea salt and ground black pepper to taste
1 x100g (4oz) bag baby rocket leaves

PUMPKIN, TOFU & PINK GRAPEFRUIT SALAD

Spray the pumpkin with oil and cook on medium-hot plate with the hood down or covered with large bowl, until done. Do the same with the tofu and cook on the flat plate as well.

Remove all the skin from the grapefruit on a plate so you capture all juices. Cut the segments out of the membrane over a bowl so you capture those juices too and put the segments into a separate bowl.

Take the pumpkin and tofu from the barbecue and cool on kitchen paper.

Whisk the grapefruit juice, oil, honey, paprika, salt and pepper together. It is good to have at least twice as much juice as oil. Put the pumpkin and tofu into the salad bowl and pour the grapefruit dressing over the cooling pumpkin and tofu and gently toss with your hands. Allow to sit for 20 minutes.

When ready to serve, put the leaves in with the pumpkin and tofu, toss to coat leaves and mix. Clean down the inside of the bowl, spoon over the grapefruit segments and serve.

SERVES 4

2 cups green paw paw, finely shredded
½ cup mint leaves
½ cup coriander leaves
¼ cup garlic chives, sliced
1 tablespoon Kaffir lime leaf, rib removed finely sliced
1 tablespoon red chilli, sliced
Nam Jim Dressing (see recipe below)

Nam Jim Dressing
3 cloves garlic
3 green chillies, de-seeded and roughly chopped
2 coriander roots, washed and trimmed (about 4cm/2in long)
1 tablespoon palm sugar
150ml (5fl oz) lime juice
2 tablespoons fish sauce (Nam Pla)

GREEN PAW PAW SALAD WITH NAM JIM DRESSING

This dressing goes extremely well with barbecued meats like chargrilled chicken breasts and quail.

Combine all ingredients and add Nam Jim to your liking. Mix well and serve immediately.

For the Nam Jim Dressing

Combine garlic, chillies, coriander roots and palm sugar. Work into a rough paste either in a food processor or better still, in a mortar and pestle. Tip in the juice and fish sauce and combine. This dressing is best used immediately it is made.

Serves 4

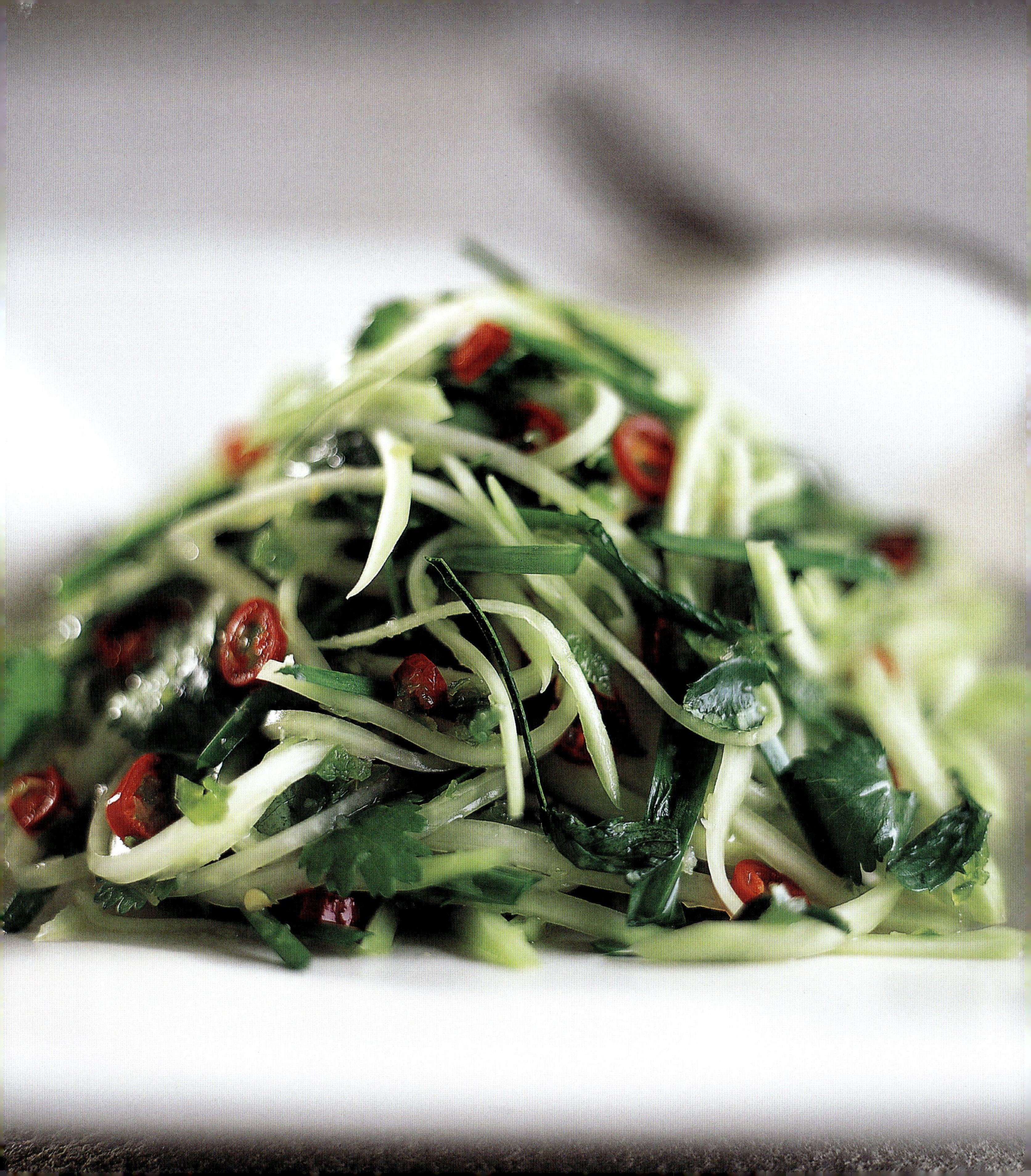

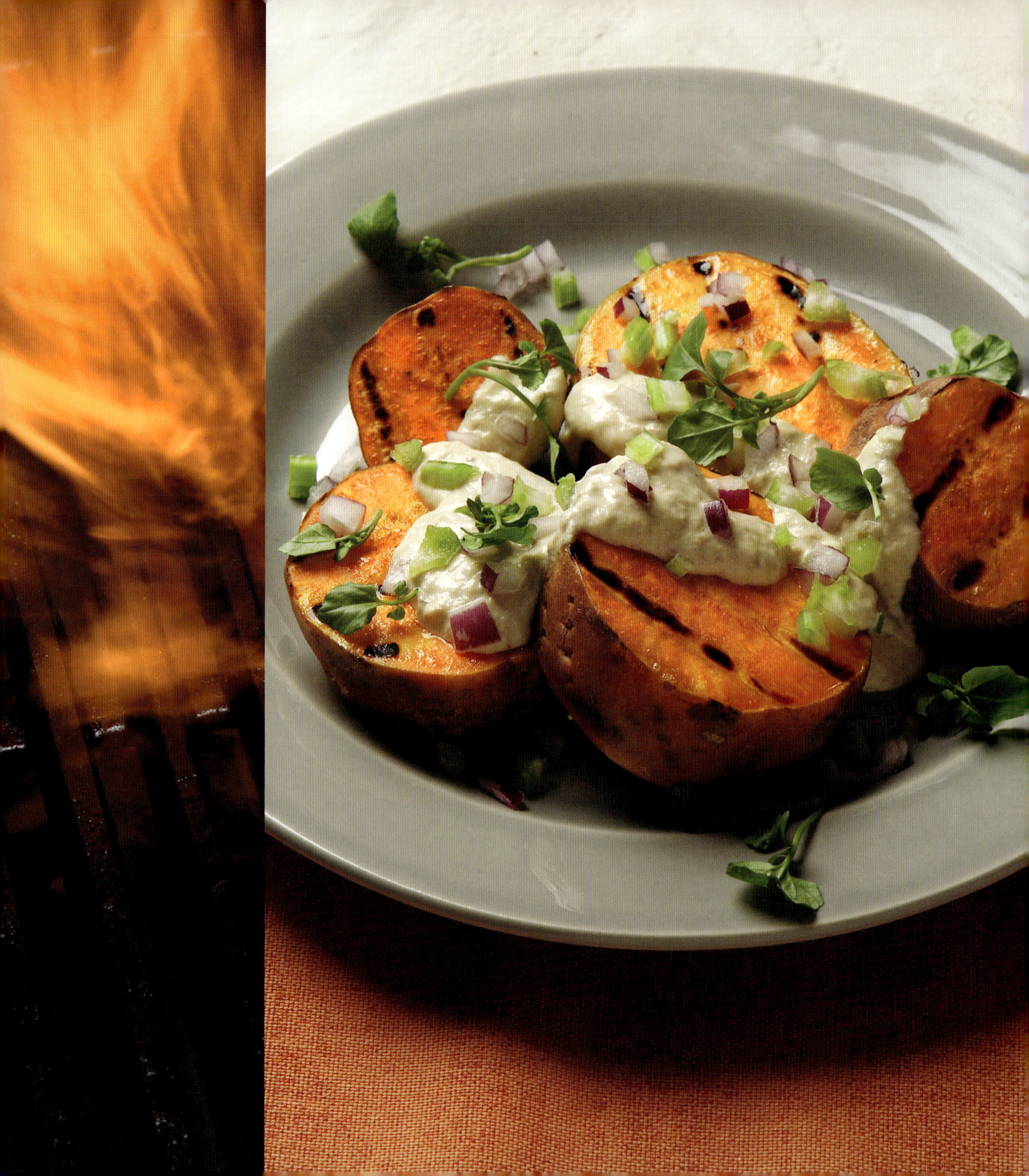

2 x 300g (11oz) whole kumara
Spray oil
100g (4oz) red onion, finely chopped
1 cup celery, finely diced
½ cup mustard cress leaves, loosely packed

For the dressing
180g (6oz) canned tuna, drained
1½ cups mayonnaise
1 tablespoon white vinegar
½ teaspoon sea salt
¼ teaspoon white pepper

KUMARA, RED ONION, CELERY & TUNA DRESSING

Prick the kumaras all over with a dinner fork and cook in the microwave at 70 per cent for 3 minutes. Remove and cool. Cut into 2cm (1in) thick rounds, spray the flat surfaces of the kumara with oil and cook on a medium hot plate for 2 minutes each side. If you like, you can crisp them on the open grill but beware they 'caramelise' very quickly here. Lift and cool on kitchen paper.

Make the dressing by blending or processing all ingredients to a smooth, creamy consistency.

Spread the kumara slices around a flat plate so they overlap, spoon on enough dressing, sprinkle with the onion, celery and cress then serve.

Serves 4

4 medium zucchinis
4 x 1cm ($^1/_2$ inch) thick slices haloumi cheese
1 x 100g (4oz) bag mixed lettuce leaves
1 tablespoon lemon juice
1 tablespoon mushroom oil (see recipe below)
spray oil

Mushroom Oil
200g (7oz) mushroom caps
250g (9oz) light olive oil
Slice the mushrooms into pieces around 5mm ($^1/_4$in) thick.

Zucchini, Haloumi & Mushroom Oil Salad

The haloumi needs to be served warm as it can toughen if left to cool too much.

Trim and cut the zucchinis in half lengthwise, sprinkle with a little salt, spray both sides with oil and cook on a hot grill until softened and marked. Start with cut side down and cook on both sides.

Spray the plate with oil and add the haloumi. Cook for 1 minute on each side.

Lift the zucchini and haloumi onto kitchen towelling lined plate and keep warm.

Pile equal quantities of leaves into the centre of individual plates. Top with the equal amounts of haloumi and zucchini and sprinkle over the lemon juice. Spoon the mushroom oil over the combined ingredients and serve.

For the Mushroom Oil

Slice the mushrooms into pieces around 5mm ($^1/_4$in) thick.

Spray a medium hot plate with oil and cook the mushrooms for 3 minutes without adding more oil. Lift mushrooms into an airtight storage container and pour the olive oil onto the mushrooms. Stir, close and keep in a cupboard for two days (do shake regularly or stir) before use and then use as soon as possible.

Serves 4

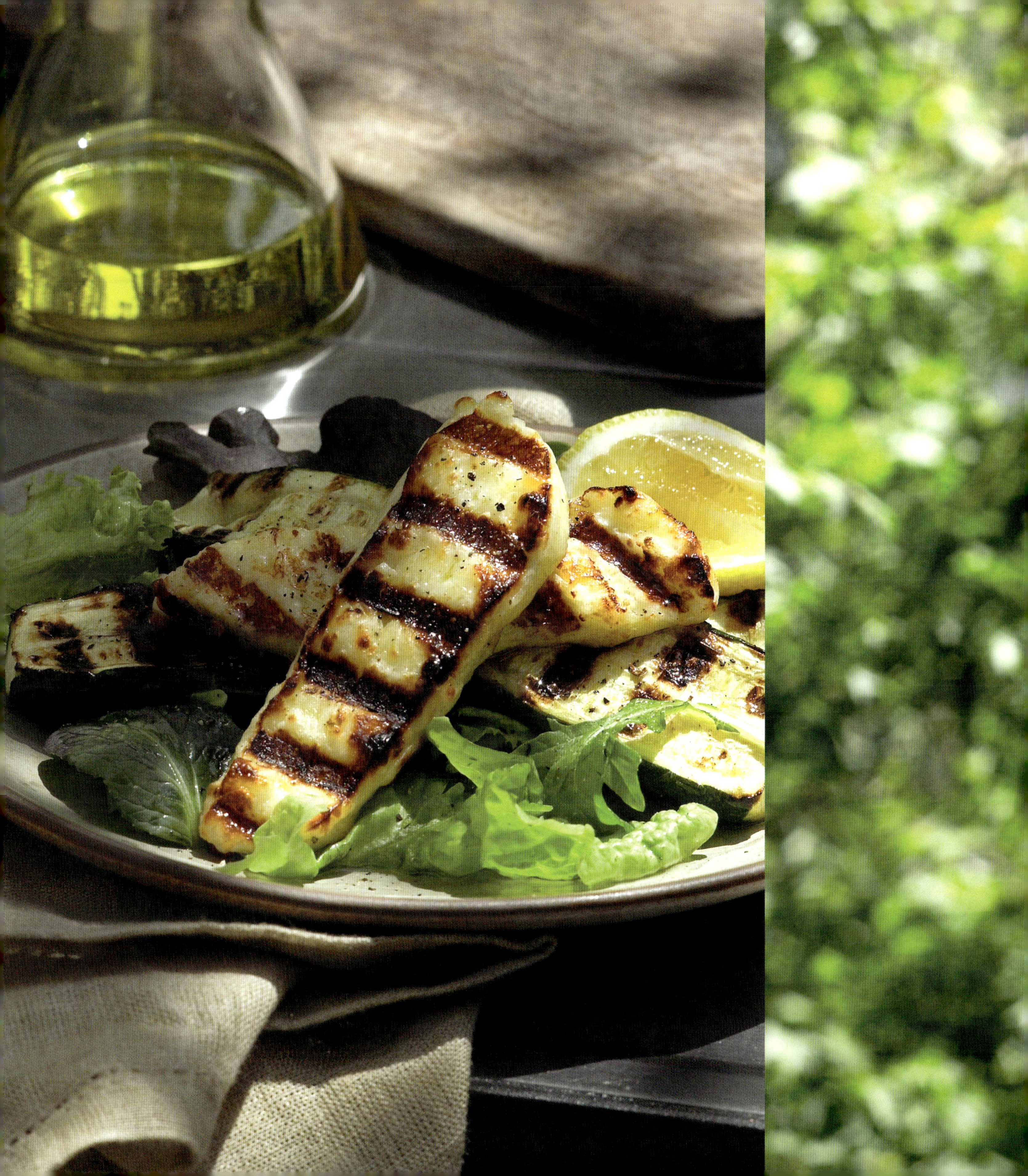

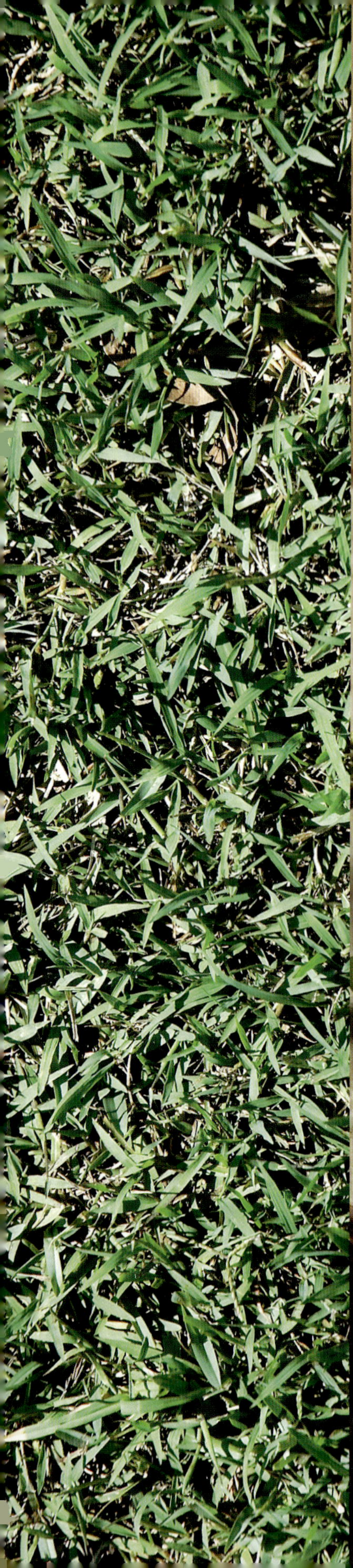

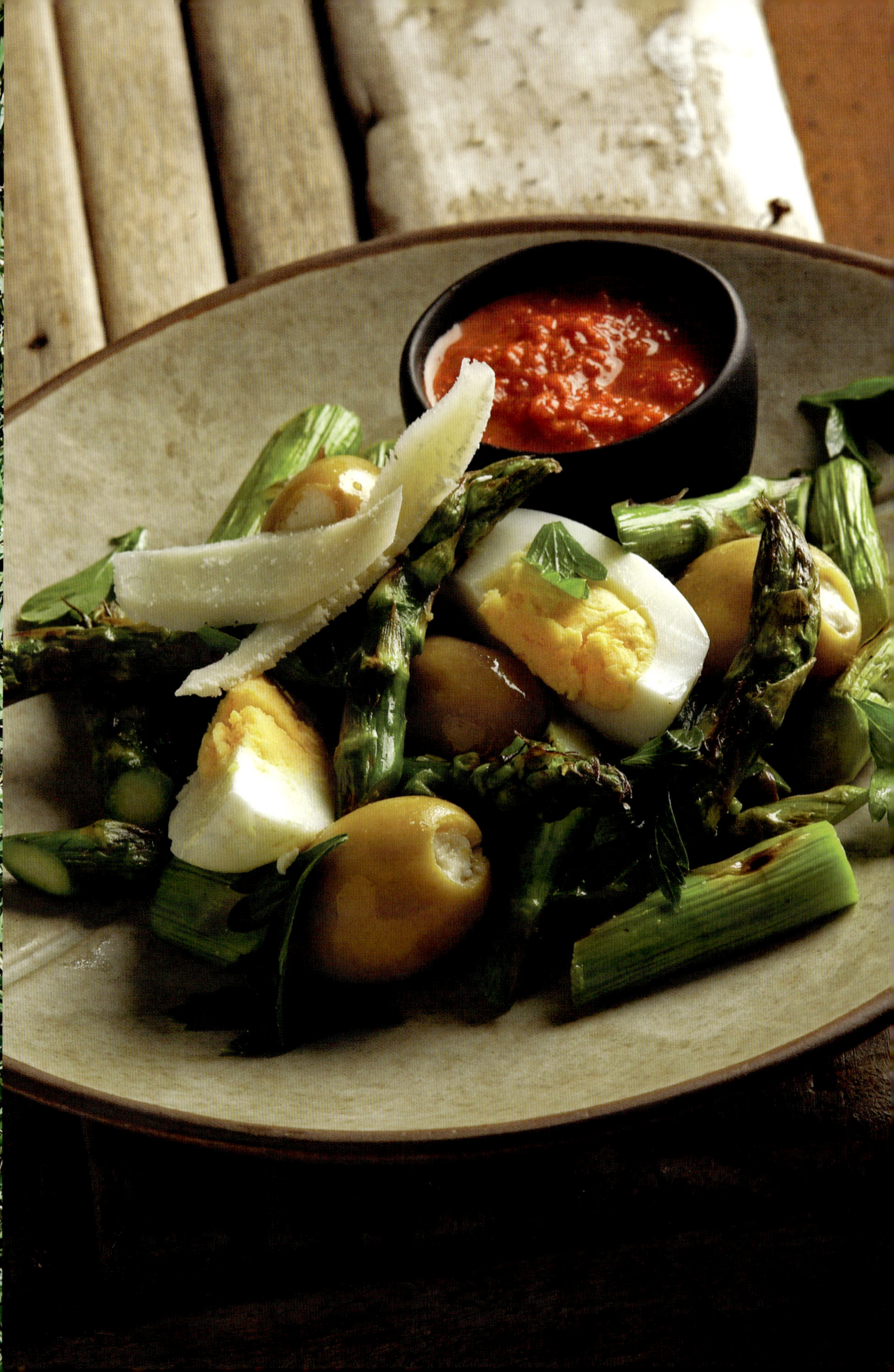

20 green asparagus spears
Spray vegetable oil
2 eggs, hard boiled
12 large green olives, stuffed
1 cup flat leaf parsley (Italian), loosely packed
¼ cup Romano cheese, shaved

For the dressing
2 medium red capsicums
Spray olive oil
2 tablespoons red wine vinegar
2 tablespoons extra virgin olive oil
Sea salt and ground black pepper to taste

ASPARAGUS, EGGS, OLIVES & RED CAPSICUM DRESSING

Trim the asparagus of the white part and spray with oil. Cook on a medium-hot grill and turn regularly for 2–3 minutes. Remove and cool.

Peel the eggs and cut into quarters. When the asparagus is cooled enough to handle, cut into bite side pieces on an angle. Place asparagus into a salad bowl with the eggs, olives and parsley. Spoon over capsicum dressing to your taste, scatter the cheese over and serve.

Make the dressing first by cutting the cheeks of the capsicum away from the seed core. Spray the skin side with oil and cook on a very hot grill to blister the skin. Turn only once and cook for 1 minute on flesh side. Pop the cheeks into a plastic bag and let sit for 20 minutes so the skin lifts. Remove cheeks and peel away the skin. Run under water to remove all skin.

Chop capsicum and place in a food processor or blender with the other dressing ingredients and blend to a puree.

Serves 4

2 large just ripe nectarines
Spray oil
8 slices pancetta
200g (7oz) feta cheese, crumbled
1 x 100g (4oz) bag mixed salad greens
½ cup olive oil
1 teaspoon Dijon mustard
2 tablespoons balsamic vinegar
8 slices cinnamon zucchini bread (see recipe below)

NECTARINE, PANCETTA & FETA SALAD WITH CINNAMON ZUCCHINI BREAD

Wash the nectarines and halve, then cut the halves into wedges. Spray the wedges well with oil and mark on a hot grill. The wedges will cook quickly so turn regularly and remove when well marked.

Cook the pancetta at the same time on a hot plate. When crisped and browned, lift onto a plate lined with kitchen towel.

Make the dressing by whisking the oil and mustard in a bowl. When combined (the mixture looks as though it has curdled), whisk in the Balsamic vinegar and set to one side but do not refrigerate.

Spray the bread and brown both sides on a medium hot grill.

Place the salad greens into a large bowl, top with the room temperature nectarine wedges, feta cheese, crumble the crispy pancetta over the salad and dress. Serve, in the middle of the table with the bread alongside.

SERVES 4

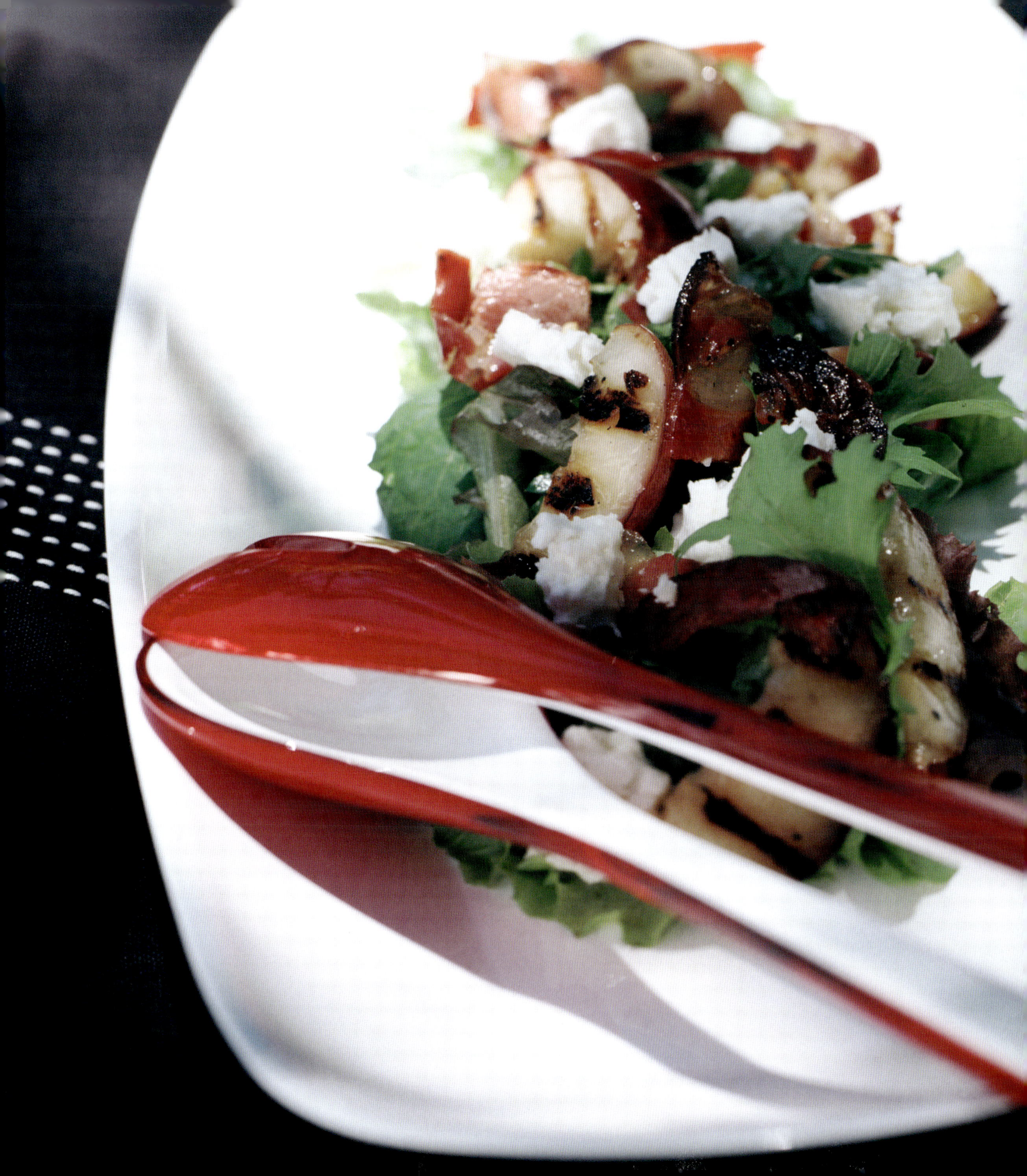

Cinnamon Zucchini Bread

375g (13oz) small zucchinis (courgettes), washed, trimmed and grated
1 egg beaten with 2 egg whites and 1 tablespoon olive oil
1 tablespoon honey
1 teaspoon ground cinnamon
3 cups self raising wholemeal flour
1 teaspoon baking powder
½ cup walnuts, crumbled
spray olive oil

For the Cinnamon Zucchini Bread

Preheat oven to 170°C (340°F).

Mix the zucchinis, eggs and oil, honey and cinnamon, stirring to combine well.

Fold in the flour and walnuts and leave to sit for 5 minutes.

Spray two bread tins 21cm long x 11cm wide and 6cm deep (8 x 4 x 2in) with olive oil. Spoon equal amounts of the zucchini mixture into the tins and cook in the oven for 1 hour or until a skewer comes out clean.

Leave in tin for 10 minutes to cool and turn onto a cooking rack to cool before slicing.

The zucchini keeps the bread moist during the cooking.

Makes 2 loaves

400g (14oz) kangaroo strip loins
1 clove garlic, peeled
1 trimmed coriander root (cilantro), washed and chopped
1 medium-hot green chilli, roughly chopped
1 lime, juiced
1 teaspoon fish sauce
2 teaspoons palm sugar (or brown sugar)
100g (4oz) mixed Asian lettuce leaves or similar
1 small Lebanese cucumber, washed and roughly diced
1 snow pea shoots, small packet
4 tablespoons chopped coriander (cilantro)
1 cup tightly packed fresh mint leaves
Spray oil

THAI KANGAROO SALAD

Trim the meat of all sinew and refrigerate until ready to use.

Make a paste with the garlic, coriander root, chilli, juice, fish sauce and sugar in a food processor or in a mortar and pestle. Tip into a flattish dish.

Remove the kangaroo from the refrigerator 10 minutes before use, spray the kangaroo with oil and sear on a hot plate. Cook for a couple of minutes only as the meat must be served rare. When done, remove from heat and let sit for 5 minutes to set juices.

Put the lettuce leaves, cucumber and pea shoots into a large mixing bowl. Slice the cooked meat and toss in the garlic coriander root mix to coat it and then put in with the lettuce. Rip the coriander and mint leaves and add the meat.

Toss the salad gently and then serve on a large platter or individual plates.

Serves 4

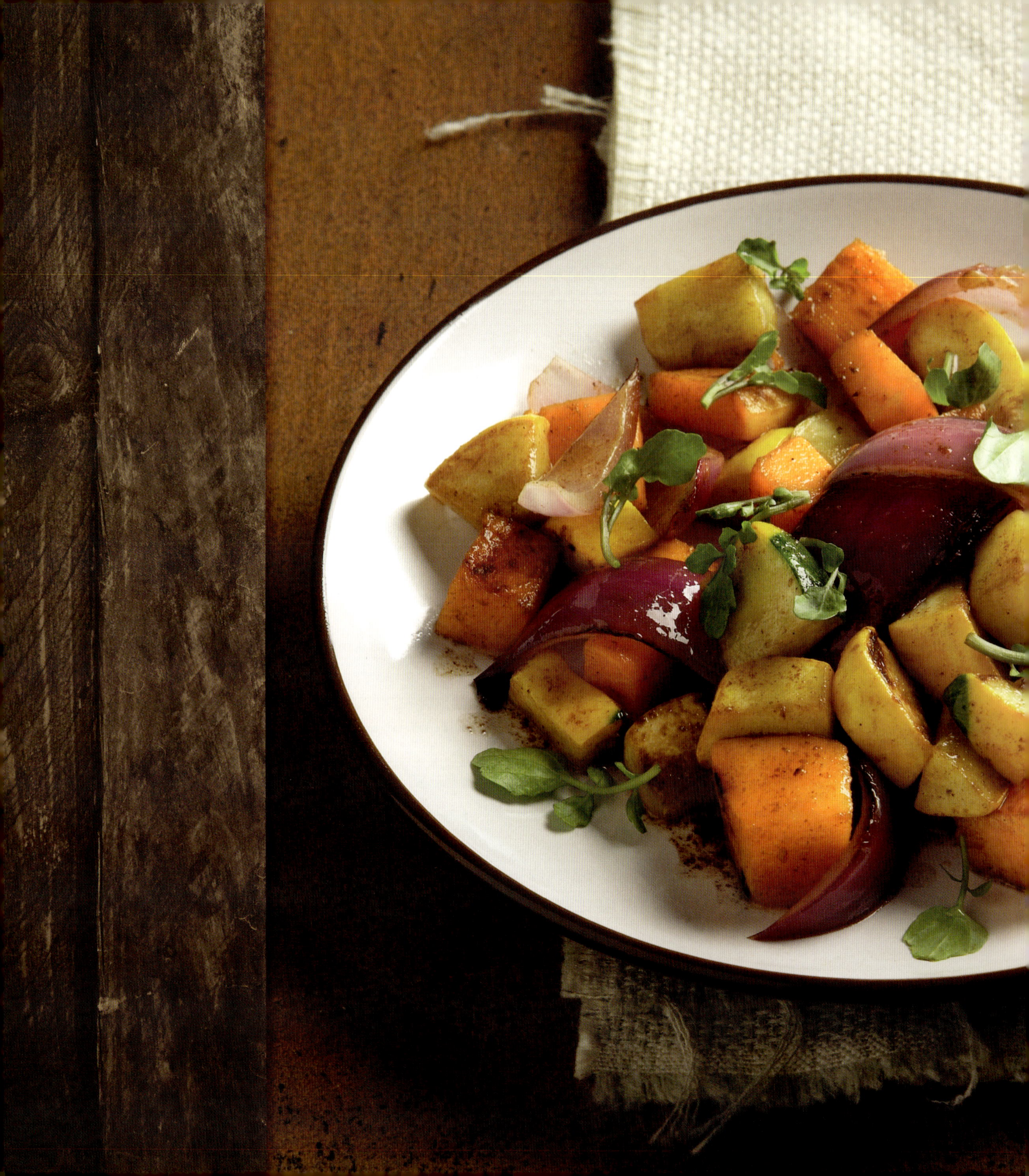

¼ cup olive oil
1 tablespoon ground cumin
½ tablespoon ground rosemary
½ teaspoon ground white pepper
400g (14oz) butter nut pumpkin, peeled and cut into 2 cm dices
200g (7oz) yellow squash, trimmed and cut into 2 cm dices
1 medium red onion, skin and roots on and cut into 8 wedges
8 toothpicks
Spray olive oil
2 tablespoons extra virgin olive oil
1 tablespoon balsamic vinegar
½ cup baby watercress sprigs

CUMIN PUMPKIN, YELLOW SQUASH & RED ONION SALAD

Mix the oil, cumin, rosemary and pepper in a large bowl. Add the pumpkin and squash and toss to coat the pieces. Let rest for 20 minutes.

Put a toothpick through the onion wedges lengthwise to hold them in place when cooking Leaving the root on also helps here.

Spoon the pumpkin mix onto a medium-hot plate and cook, turning often, for around 5–7 minutes or until softened and browned.

Spray the onion wedges and cook on the same plate for 5 minutes. The wedges need to be cooked but still holding their structure. Lift from the heat and cool. Peel the skin away, remove the toothpick and cut the root off.

Drain the pumpkin mix on kitchen towelling and tip into a large bowl. Add the onions, oil and balsamic vinegar. Tumble to coat and mix flavours. Let cool before serving. Decorate with watercress.

Serves 4

4 x 100g (4oz) banana eggplant
1 teaspoon salt
4 red capsicum cheeks
1 tablespoon sesame seeds
2 tablespoon balsamic vinegar
1 tablespoon extra virgin olive oil
1 teaspoon black pepper, freshly cracked
Spray oil

EGGPLANT, CAPSICUM & SESAME SEED SALAD

Remove the stem from the eggplant, cut in half lengthwise and sprinkle the cut side with salt. Leave to sit cut side up for 30 minutes.

Spray the capsicum cheeks on both sides and cook on a medium–hot grill for 2 minutes on the cut side, then 2 minutes on the skin side. Put into a plastic bag, tie and let sweat for 10 minutes. Wash the capsicum under cold water to remove skin, pat dry with paper towelling.

Toast the sesame seeds by placing them in a very small frying pan and sit over medium heat to let lightly brown. Shake regularly and tip onto kitchen towelling when done.

Rinse the eggplant and pat dry with kitchen towelling. Spray with oil and cook on medium hot plate for 3 minutes or until soft. Serve onto platter.

Cut the capsicums into strips, 1cm ($^1/_2$in) thick, and spread evenly over the eggplant. Sprinkle with the toasted sesame seeds. Mix the olive oil and balsamic vinegar and drizzle over both. Sprinkle the cracked pepper over the top and serve.

SERVES 4

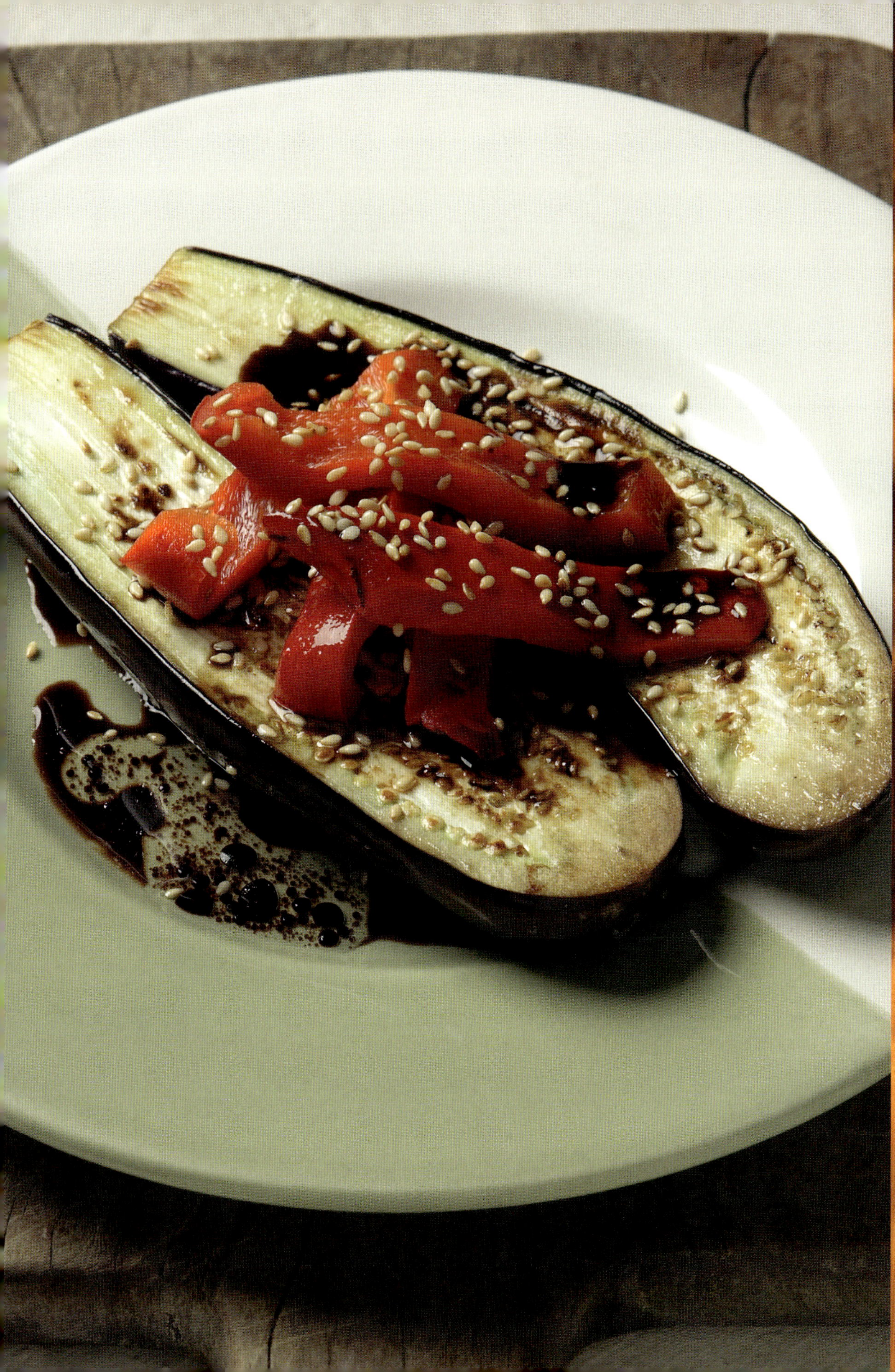

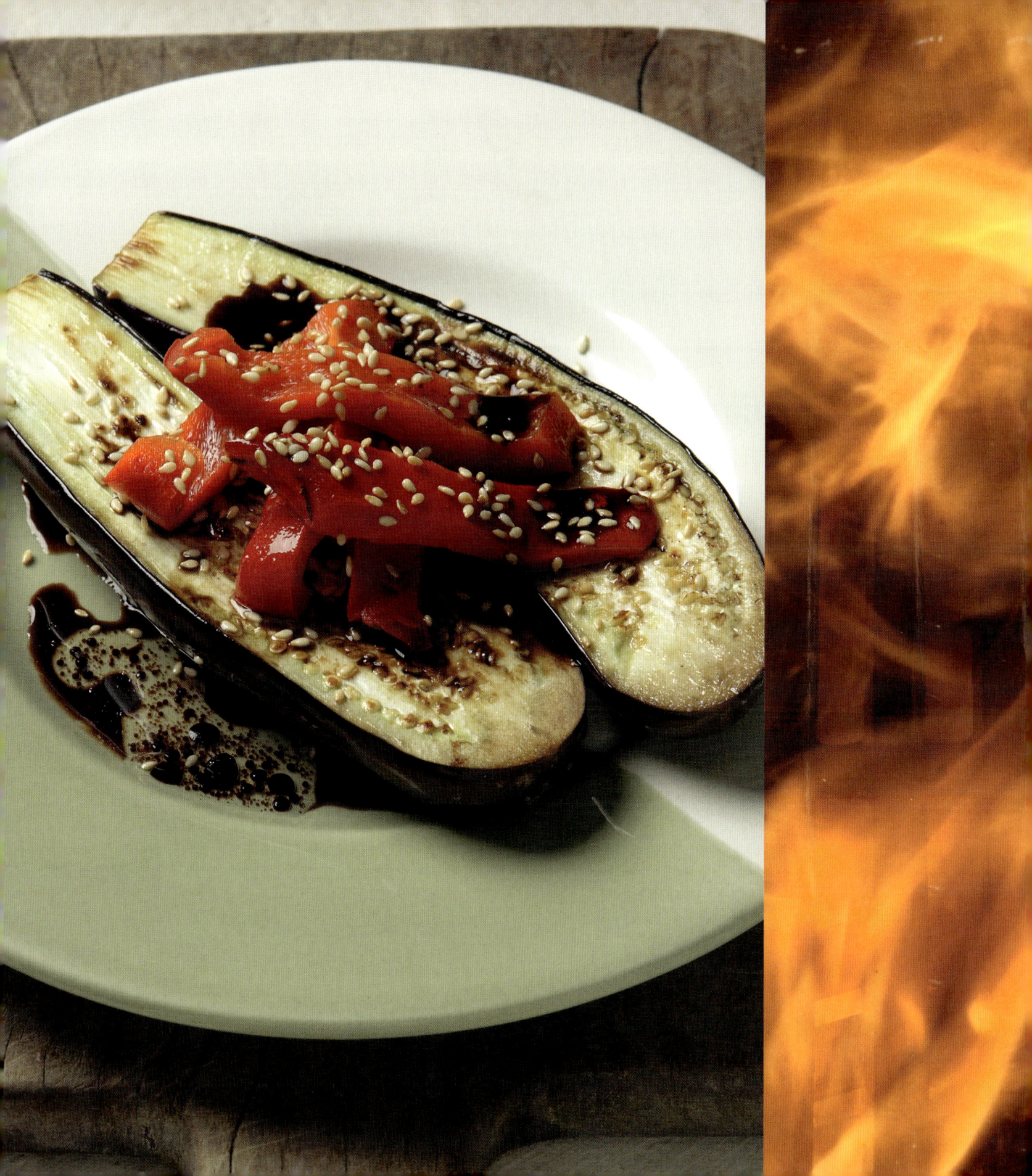

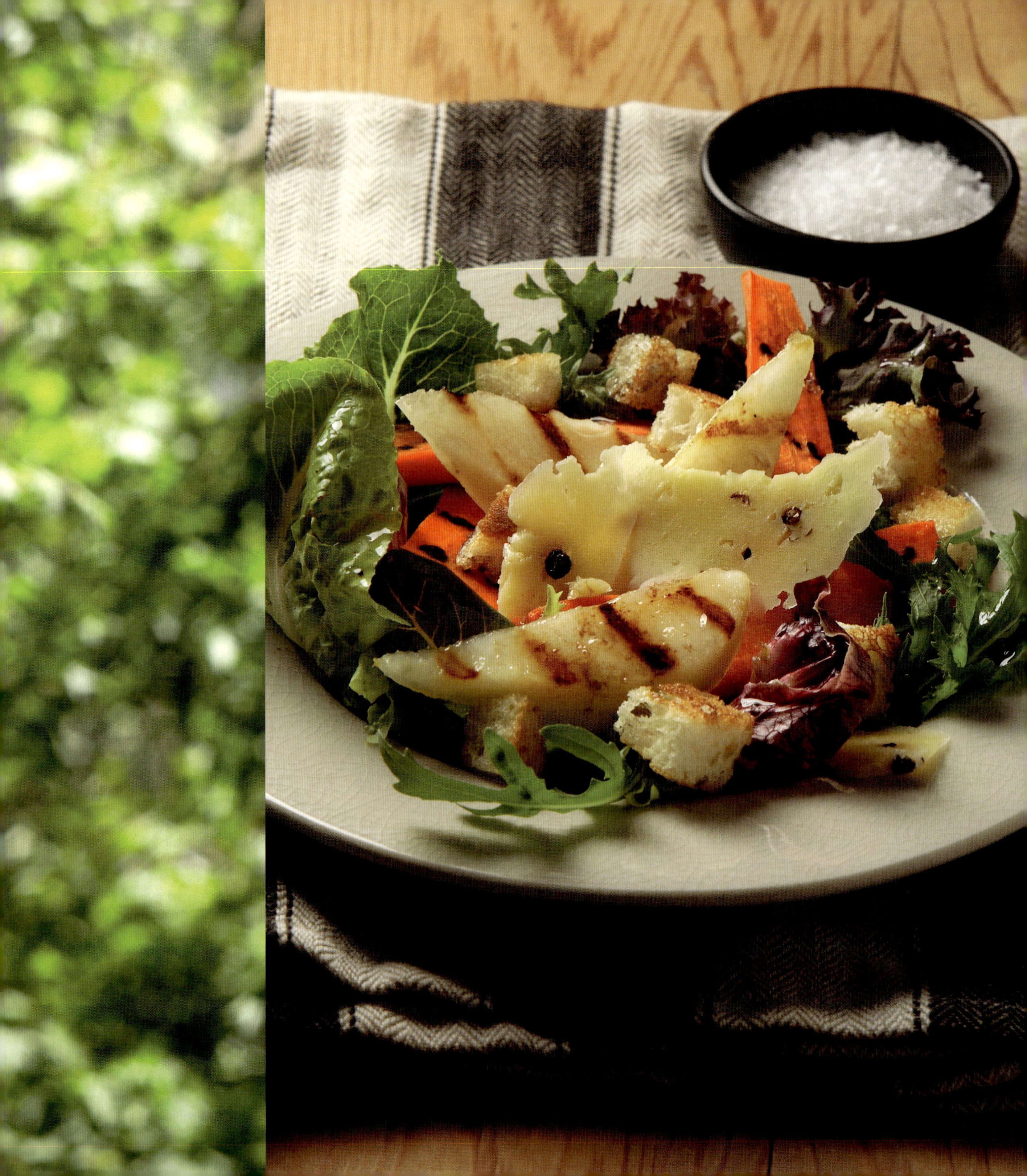

2 large semi-ripe pears, cored and halved
4 medium carrots
2 slices day-old bread
spray oil
200g (7oz) pecorino cheese, cubed or sliced
1 x 100g (4oz) bag mesclun mix leaves
½ cup olive oil
2 tablespoons balsamic vinegar
1 tablespoon marjoram, minced
Salt and pepper to taste

PEAR, CARROT & PECORINO CHEESE SALAD

Cut the pear halves into wedges and toss with lemon juice if not using immediately.

Trim the ends from the carrots and cut into halves lengthwise (or even quarters for quicker cooking if larger than needed).

Cut the crusts from the bread and cut into cubes to be able to make fresh croutons.

Make the dressing by whisking the oil until aerated, then whisk in the balsamic vinegar, marjoram, salt and pepper to taste. Set to one side but do not refrigerate.

Spray the pear wedges with oil and put onto a medium–hot grill. They will mark and cook quickly. To retain the crunch, turn regularly and remove when well marked.

Cook the oil sprayed carrots quickly on a medium–hot grill. Do not lose the crunch. Spray the bread cubes with plenty of oil and put onto hot plate, turning regularly until browned and crisp.

To assemble the salad, put the greens into a large bowl, top with the room temperature pears, carrots and cheese. Drizzle over the dressing and toss the salad. Top with the croutons and serve immediately.

SERVES 4

400g (14oz) Kifler potatoes (pink fir apple or baby desiree)
Spray olive oil
3 green spring onions, white only and finely sliced
2 hard boiled eggs, shells removed and roughly chopped
2 tablespoons crisp bacon pieces
3 tablespoons mint, roughly chopped
4 cloves garlic, poached for 5 minutes
½ cup good mayonnaise
¼ cup cider vinegar
1 teaspoon dried mustard
½ teaspoon ground black pepper

POTATO SALAD & GARLIC DRESSING

Cut the potatoes on the diagonal to give bite size pieces. Boil in salted water for 5 minutes. Drain well and let cool. When cool enough to handle, spray with oil and cook until tender on a medium–hot grill.

Remove from the barbecue and tip into a large mixing bowl. Add the spring onions, eggs, bacon and mint.

Mash the garlic and whisk in mayonnaise, vinegar, mustard and ground black pepper to taste and pour over the hot potato mixture.

Toss to coat the ingredients and leave to cool. Refrigerate to use when needed and this salad is best done when the potatoes are warm and made the day before use.

Serves 4

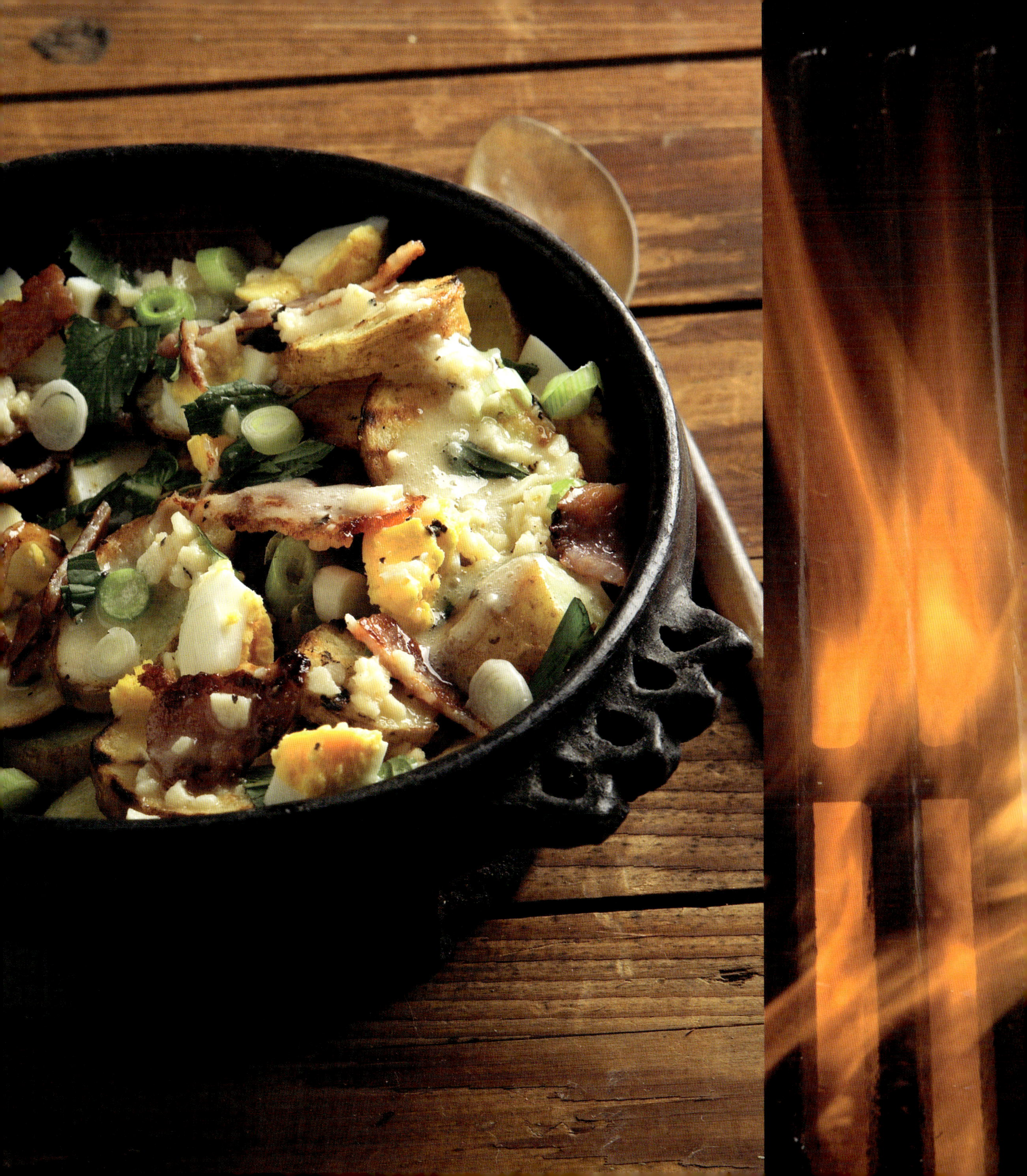

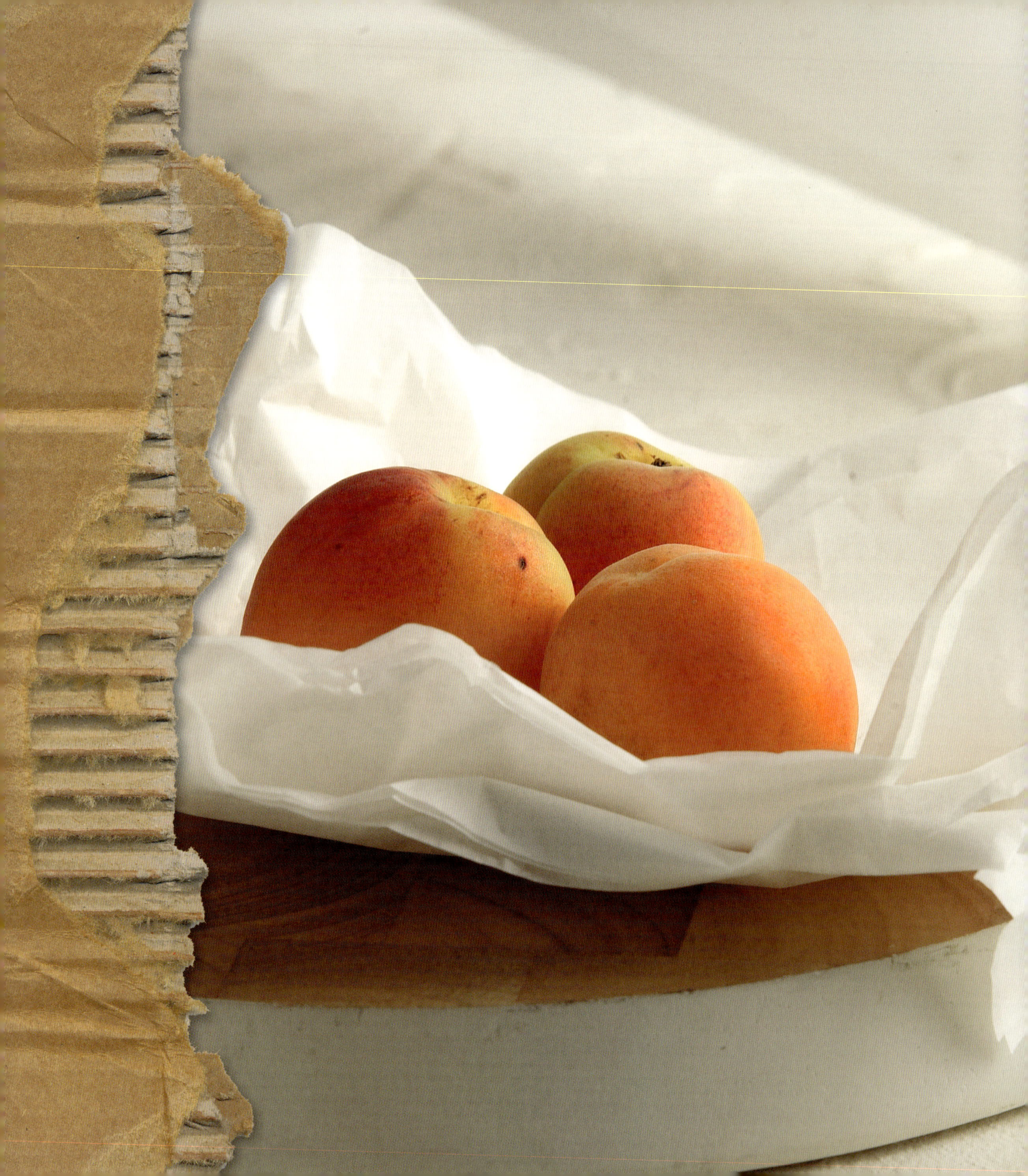

DESSERTS

2 cups milk
1 teaspoon lemon zest, finely grated
2 tablespoons almond meal
¼ teaspoon almond essence
4 tablespoons cornflour
4 tablespoons castor sugar
12–16 apricots, just ripe
4–8 small skewers, depending on the size of the apricots and skewers
½ cup Drambuie

APRICOT BROCHETTES & ALMOND BLANCMANGE

For the blancmange

Reserve a quarter cup of milk and pour the rest into a non-stick saucepan. Place over medium heat and add the lemon zest and almond meal. Stir until near boiling. Remove from heat.

Mix the cornflour and sugar with the reserved milk and stir to a paste. Stir in a cup of the heated milk and then stir cornflour mixture into the warm milk. Add the almond essence and return saucepan to heat. Stir until the mixture is at simmering point, then simmer for 3 minutes.

Pour into wet moulds, cool and refrigerate to set. Allow at least 4 hours but these are best made the day before use.

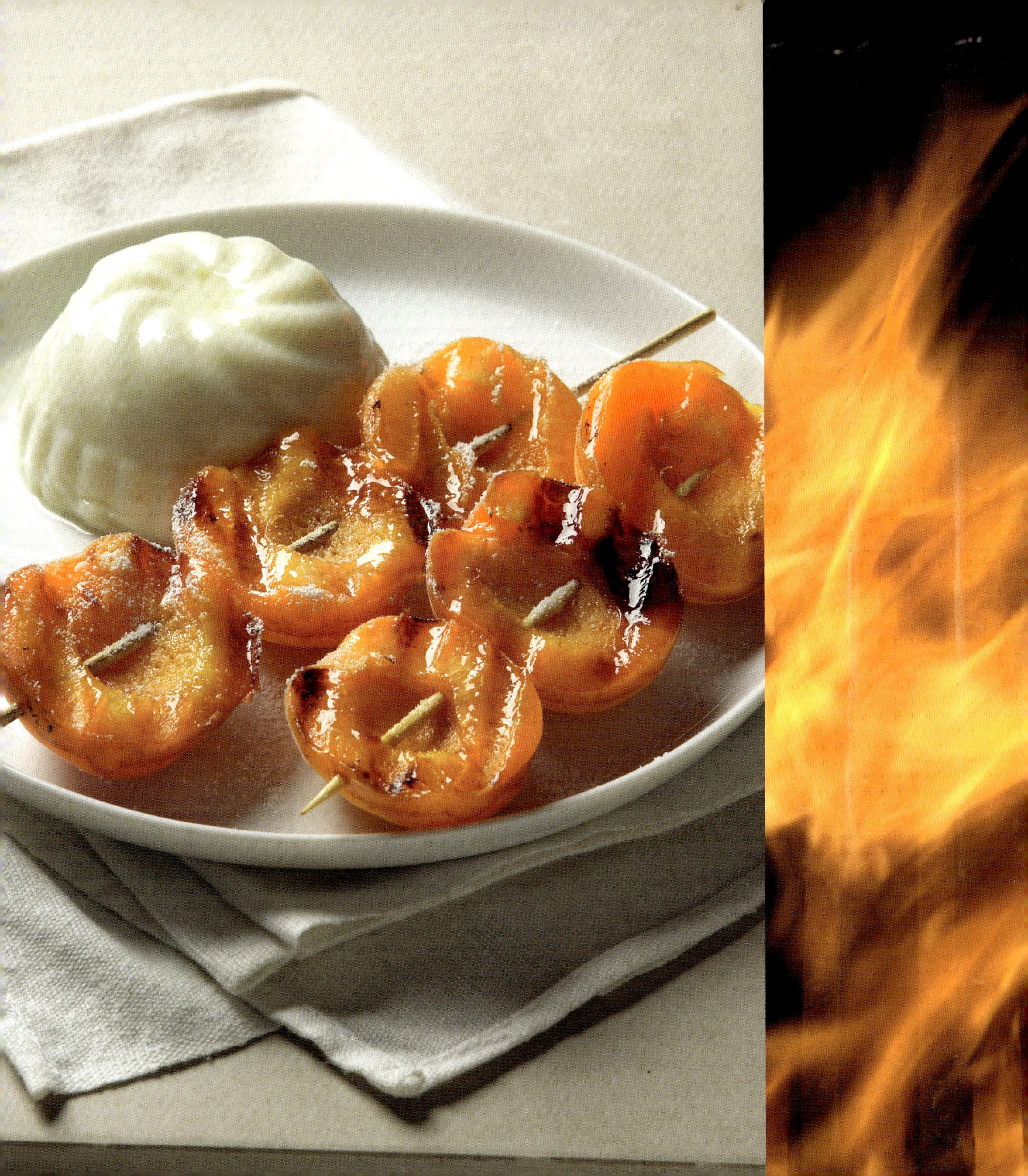

For the brochettes

Cut the apricots in half and discard the stones. Thread equal amounts of the halves onto skewers so they are sitting to look like joined circles with the cut sides aligned. Lay them on a plate and sprinkle with half the Drambuie and leave to sit for one hour.

Sprinkle the cut sides of the apricots with sugar and place the skewers cut side down on a medium–hot grill and only just heat through. The apricots should have the strips, which should occur quickly due to the added and natural sugar of the apricots.

Turn over onto the skin side and leave for around 30 seconds. The idea is to just heat the apricots through and get the marks on the cut side. Remove and put onto a large plate cut side up and sprinkle with the remaining Drambuie.

To serve, remove the blancmange from the moulds by putting the moulds into very hot water. When you can see just the smallest amount of liquid forming around the inside of the mould, invert onto individual plates and place a skewer of apricots along side or resting on top of the blancmange. Drench with a good dusting of icing sugar.

Serves 4

30g (1oz) butter, melted
1 tablespoon castor sugar
3 egg whites, at room temperature
1/3 cup castor sugar for the egg whites
1 (170g/6oz) can passionfruit in syrup
Icing sugar
Vanilla ice-cream or whipped cream

PASSIONFRUIT SOUFFLE

Make sure you have plenty of room on the rack for the soufflé dishes (or tea cups in my case) so you can move them. You can open the lid and move the soufflés very gently if they are not getting even heat and are tending to look lopsided. Through experience, I have found the tops will brown very quickly if the sugar is not incorporated into the egg whites properly.

Sometimes you may need an extra soufflé bowl depending on how much volume you develop.

Preheat barbecue to 180°C (350°F).

Brush four 250ml (1 cup) ovenproof dishes or teacups with butter to lightly grease. Sprinkle with the sugar, shaking off any excess and refrigerate for 5 minutes.

Beat egg whites with an electric beater in a large, clean bowl until soft peaks form. Sprinkle in the extra castor sugar slowly, so it may dissolve and become incorporated into the egg whites. It is important that the sugar be dissolved into the whites. You do not need really firm peaks in the beaten whites.

Fold passionfruit into egg whites using a sharp-sided metal spoon. Gently spoon the mixture into the cups and use a flat edge spatula to smooth the tops.

Run a thumb around inside rim of dishes or cups and place on a baking tray.

Sit on the dishes on a baking tray, and place on a cake cooling rack (for ease of handling) in the centre of the barbecue, not over direct heat. Cook for 8–10 minutes or until risen.

Dust with icing sugar and serve immediately with ice-cream or cream on the side.

Serves 4

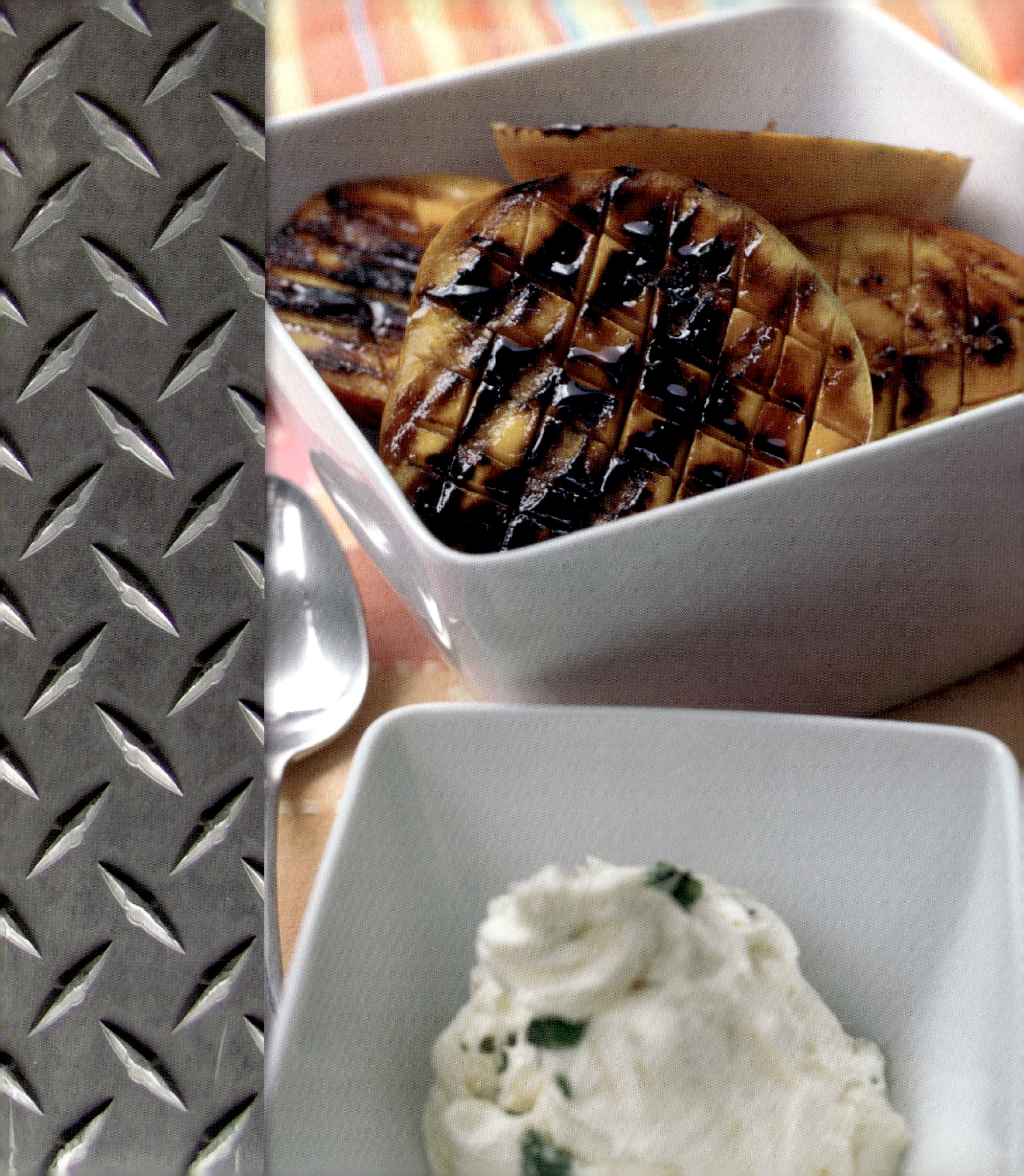

4 medium ripe mangoes
1 tablespoon icing sugar
1 cup crème fraiche
2 tablespoons honey
2 tablespoons ripped mint leaves
   (spearmint if possible)
¼ cup white Sambucca

SAMBUCCA MANGO CHEEKS & MINTED CRÈME FRAICHE

Mix the crème fraiche with the honey and mint leaves at least 3 hours before use. Refrigerate until ready to serve.

Cut the cheeks from the mangoes and cut diamond shapes into the cheek without cutting through the skin.

Sprinkle the cut sides of the mango cheeks with equal amounts of the icing sugar and leave to sit until the sugar melts. Put the cheeks onto a clean hot grill to cook for a minute or so. The cheeks will brown very quickly, so turn them gently, as you want to retain the marks of the grill. Leave the cheeks, skin-side down, for 30 seconds and remove.

Serve the two cheeks on individual plates, sprinkle with Sambucca and add the crème fraiche to one side.

SERVES 4

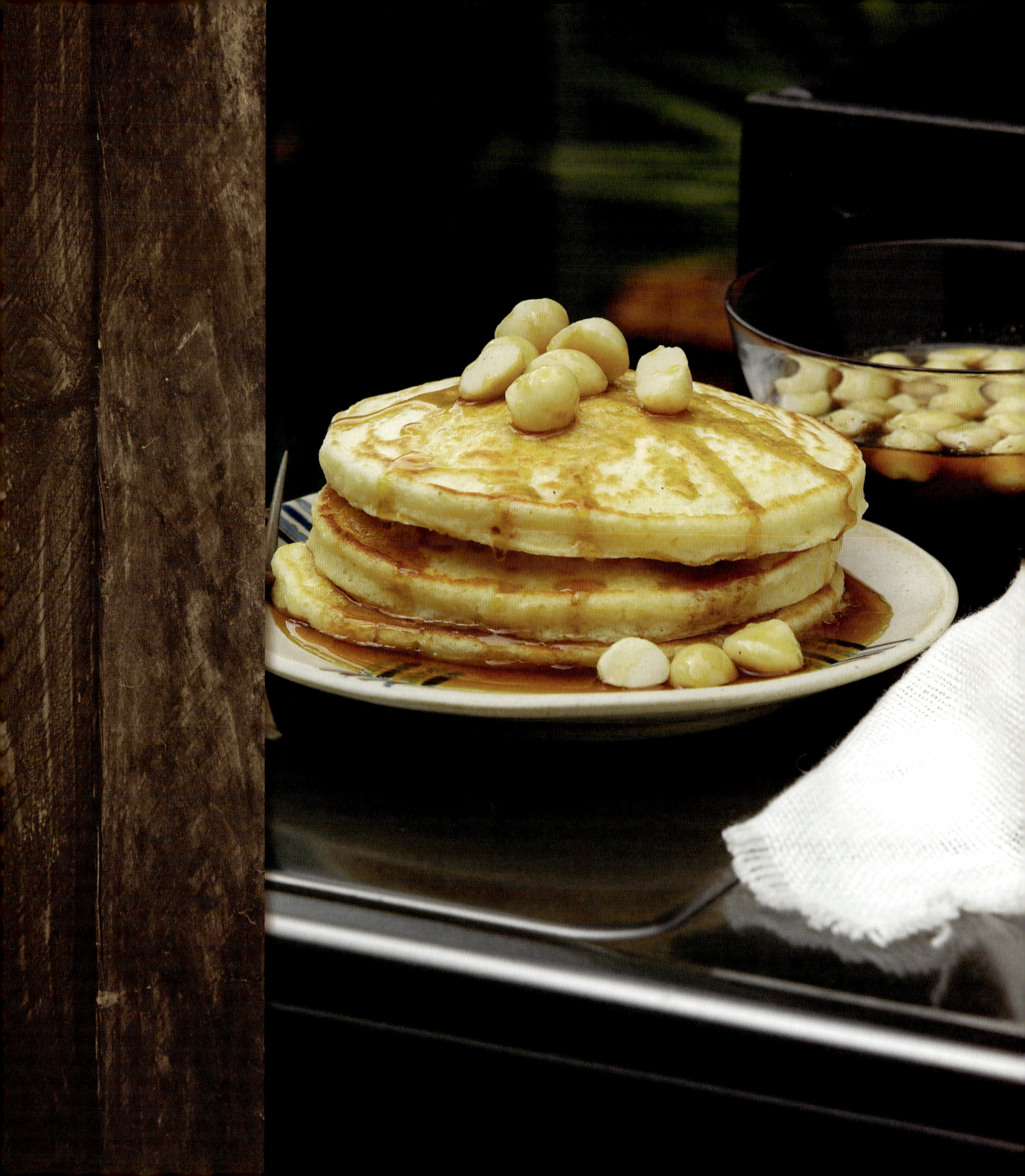

2 cups self-raising flour
¼ teaspoon salt
1 tablespoon sugar
3 eggs
1–2 cups milk
3 tablespoons unsalted butter, melted

1 cup golden syrup
1 cup roasted unsalted macadamia nuts
¼ cup dark rum
1 cup pouring cream
1 tablespoon castor sugar
¼ teaspoon vanilla essence
2 tablespoons oil with 1 tablespoon butter melted in it

FLAPJACKS, GOLDEN SYRUP MACADAMIA NUTS

DON'T OVERHEAT YOUR BARBECUE PLATE AS THE FLAPJACKS WILL BURN BEFORE THEY COOK IN THE MIDDLE.

Sift the flour into a bowl, then add the salt and sugar. Whisk in the eggs and half the milk. Add more milk as you go to get the desired thickness for the flapjacks. Add the butter and stir in. Leave to sit for 30 minutes before use.

Over medium heat, pour the syrup into a saucepan with the nuts and rum and stir to combine.

Whip the pouring cream with the castor sugar and vanilla essence until very thick.

Test a medium–hot clean plate with a few drops of water. When they dance and sizzle, the plate is ready. Spoon on a little of the oil/butter and pour a tablespoon of the batter (or a little more if you like, depending on the size you want) onto the plate. A tablespoon will give approximately a 15cm (6in) diameter flapjack. Do no more than four at a time. When there are bubbles across the top of the flapjack, flip over and cook through. Repeat until all the batter is used.

On individual plates, layer the flapjacks with a little of the golden syrup spooned over each one as you go. When the layers are complete, distribute equal amounts of the nuts and the remaining syrup over the top and serve the cream separately.

MAKES ABOUT 12 FLAPJACKS

16 medium strawberries, hulls removed and halved lengthwise
1 tablespoon castor sugar
¼ cup Grand Marnier
1 large mango, very ripe
1 cup pouring cream, very cold
4 pre-made crêpes (see recipe below)
Icing sugar

Crêpe Batter
1¼ cups flour
Pinch salt
3 eggs, beaten
1½ cups milk
1 tablespoon brandy
2 teaspoons butter, melted
Extra butter for pan frying

STRAWBERRY-STUFFED CRÊPES & MANGO CREAM

These freeze very well. Make sure you interleave them with plastic wrap, as this makes them easy to separate. I normally freeze 4 or 8 per batch.

Macerate (soak) the strawberries in the sugar and the Grand Marnier. Tumble gently and let sit for at least one hour before use.

For the Crêpe Batter

Sift flour and salt into a bowl. Make a well in the centre and whisk in the eggs and milk, drawing in flour from the sides of the bowl. Beat well and stir in brandy and melted butter.

Cover and stand one hour. Strain batter to remove lumps if necessary. Heat a little butter in a crepe pan, pour off excess and keep for reuse. Pour about 1 tablespoon batter into an 18cm (7in) pan. Rotate the pan quickly to coat the bottom thinly and evenly, then pour off any excess batter.

Heat gently and when small bubbles appear (after about one minute) use a spatula to flip crêpes over. Cook for 1 minute on other side. Repeat to use up all the batter.

Remove the skin from the mango and slice away the flesh from the seed. Puree very finely in a food processor. Whip the cream to a very stiff stage, and stir in the mango.

Lift the strawberry halves from the liquid with a slotted spoon and place on a low hot plate. Turn often and cook for no longer than one minute. Remove and spoon equal amounts down the centre of each crêpe. Loosely fold the crepes around the strawberries.

Spoon the remaining Grand Marnier over the strawberry crêpes, dust with icing sugar and serve with the mango cream.

Serves 4

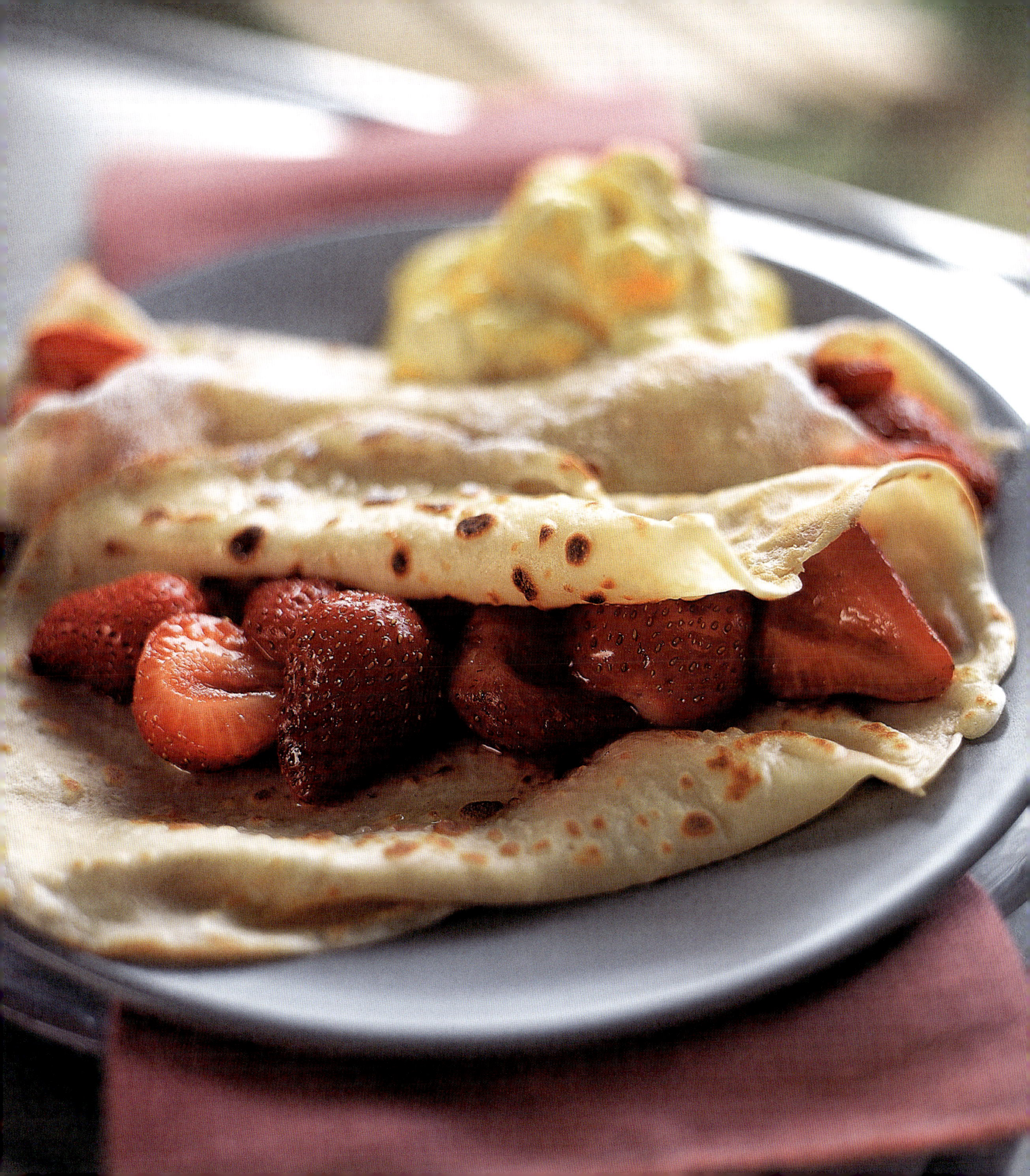

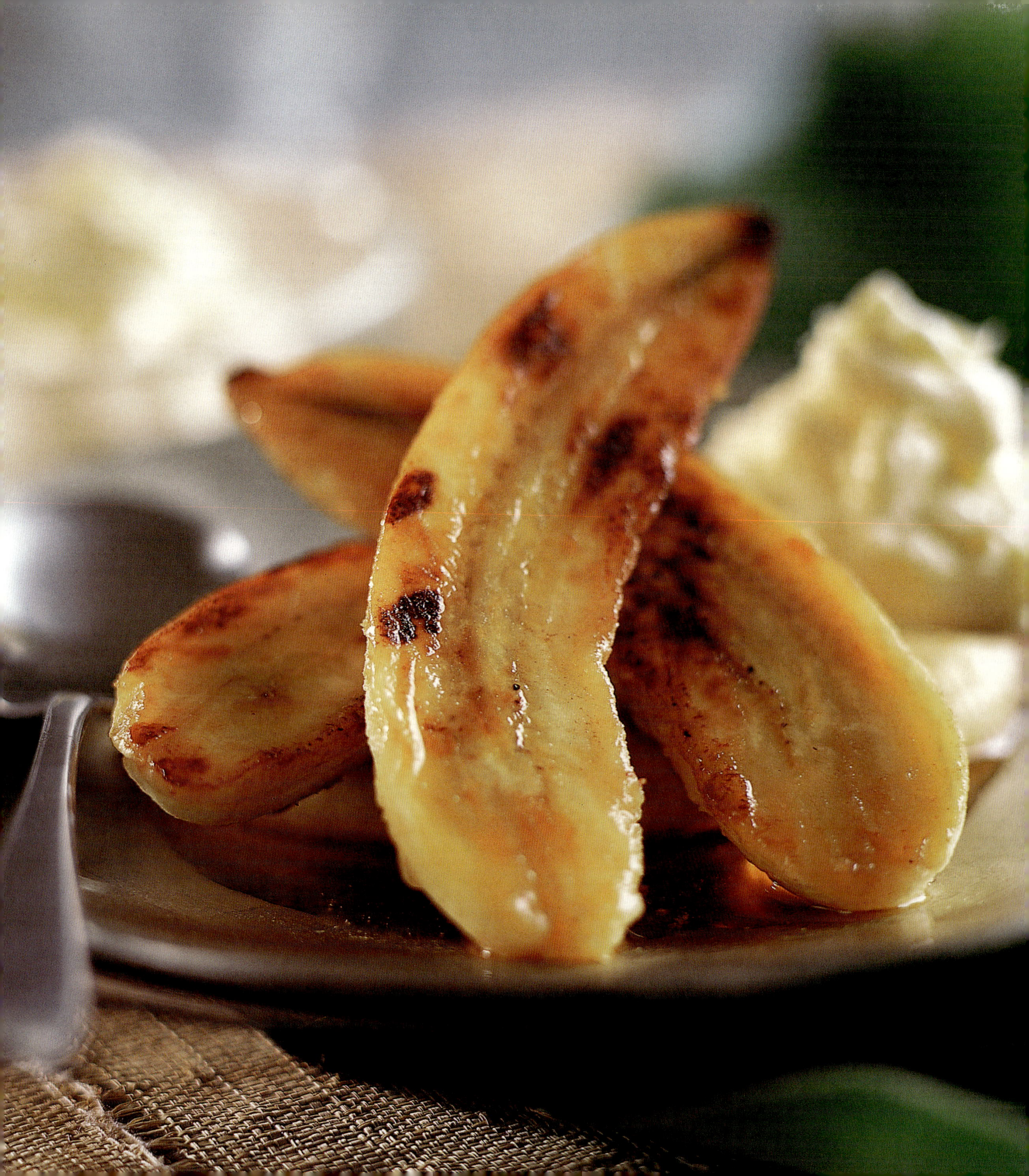

200ml (7fl oz) mascarpone
50ml (2fl oz) pouring cream
2 tablespoons vanilla sugar
8 lady finger bananas, peeled, not too ripe
2 tablespoon butter, melted
60ml (2fl oz) rum

BANANAS, RUM & WHIPPED MASCARPONE

You can buy vanilla sugar at the supermarket, but it is so easy to make. I always have my castor sugar with a whole vanilla pod stuck in it. You can use a vanilla bean to infuse milk for custards. After the milk has been infused, remove the bean from the milk, wash it and dry it, then return it to the castor sugar.

Whip the mascarpone with the cream and the vanilla sugar.

Place bananas onto a low-heat plate and spoon over the melted butter. Turn the bananas gently using a long spatula and a set of tongs. Cook for four minutes and lift onto a serving plate.

Pour the rum over the bananas and serve with the whipped mascarpone spooned over as you serve.

Serves 4

4 x 1½ cm (½ in) thick slices raisin bread
   or good fruit bread
3 eggs, lightly beaten
1 cup milk
1 teaspoon powdered cinnamon
200ml (7fl oz) pouring cream, stiffly beaten
60ml (2fl oz) Cointreau
2 tablespoons butter, melted
Icing sugar

CINNAMON FRENCH TOAST & COINTREAU CREAM

Cut the crusts from the bread if you like. Combine the eggs, milk and cinnamon.

Mix the whipped cream and Cointreau together and refrigerate.

To cook, dip the raisin toast in the egg mixture and place onto a hot, lightly oiled plate. Cook for one minute and turn onto a lightly oiled part of the plate that has not been used. Cook for 1–2 minutes and lift from the plate onto individual plates and spoon over the melted butter and dredge with icing sugar.

Serve a slice of this special French toast with a really good dollop of the Cointreau cream.

You can serve almost any stewed fruit with this raisin toast, but one of my personal favourites is stewed rhubarb and apple which has a lovely bite to it to counteract the sugar rush in this dessert.

SERVES 4

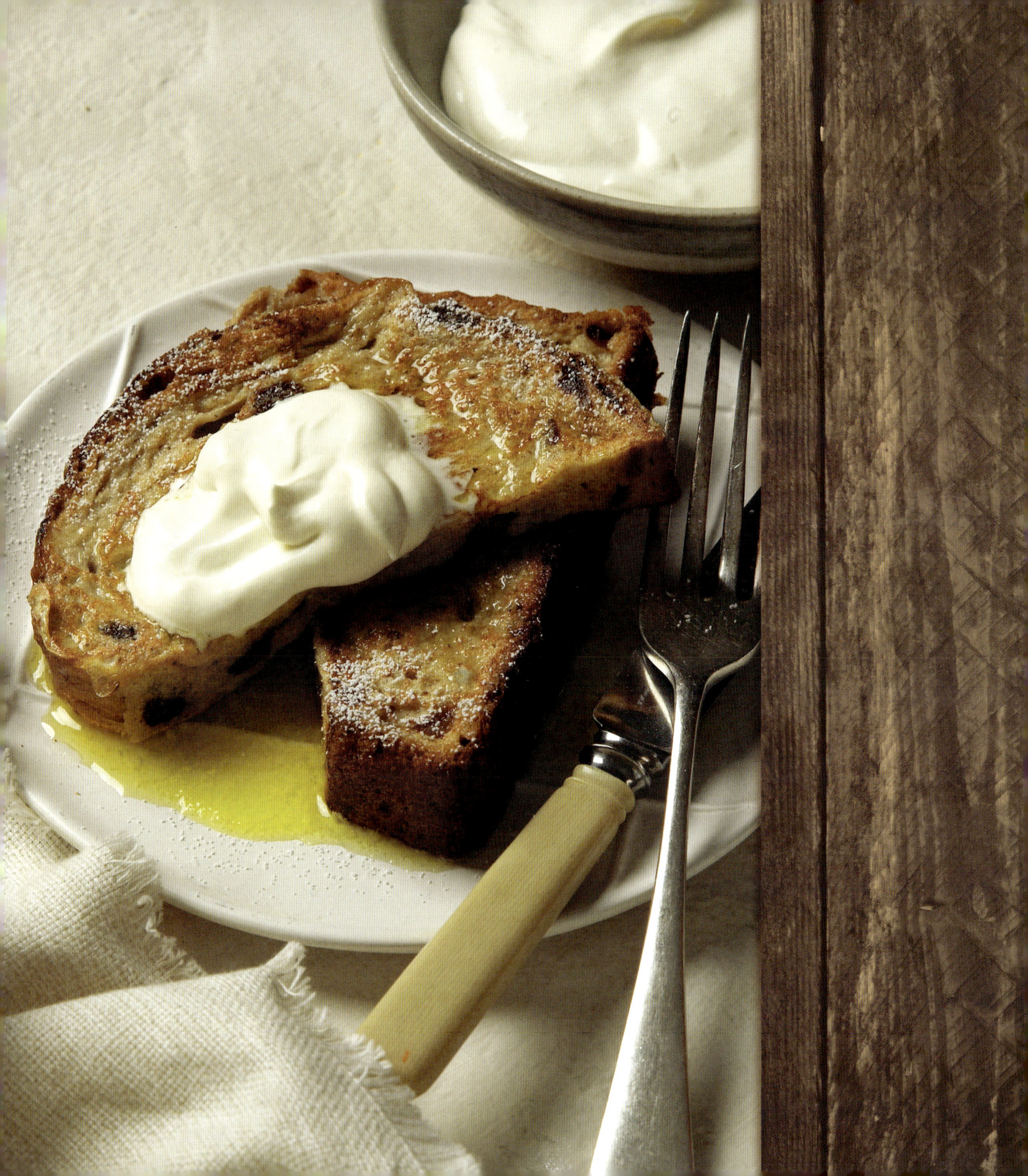

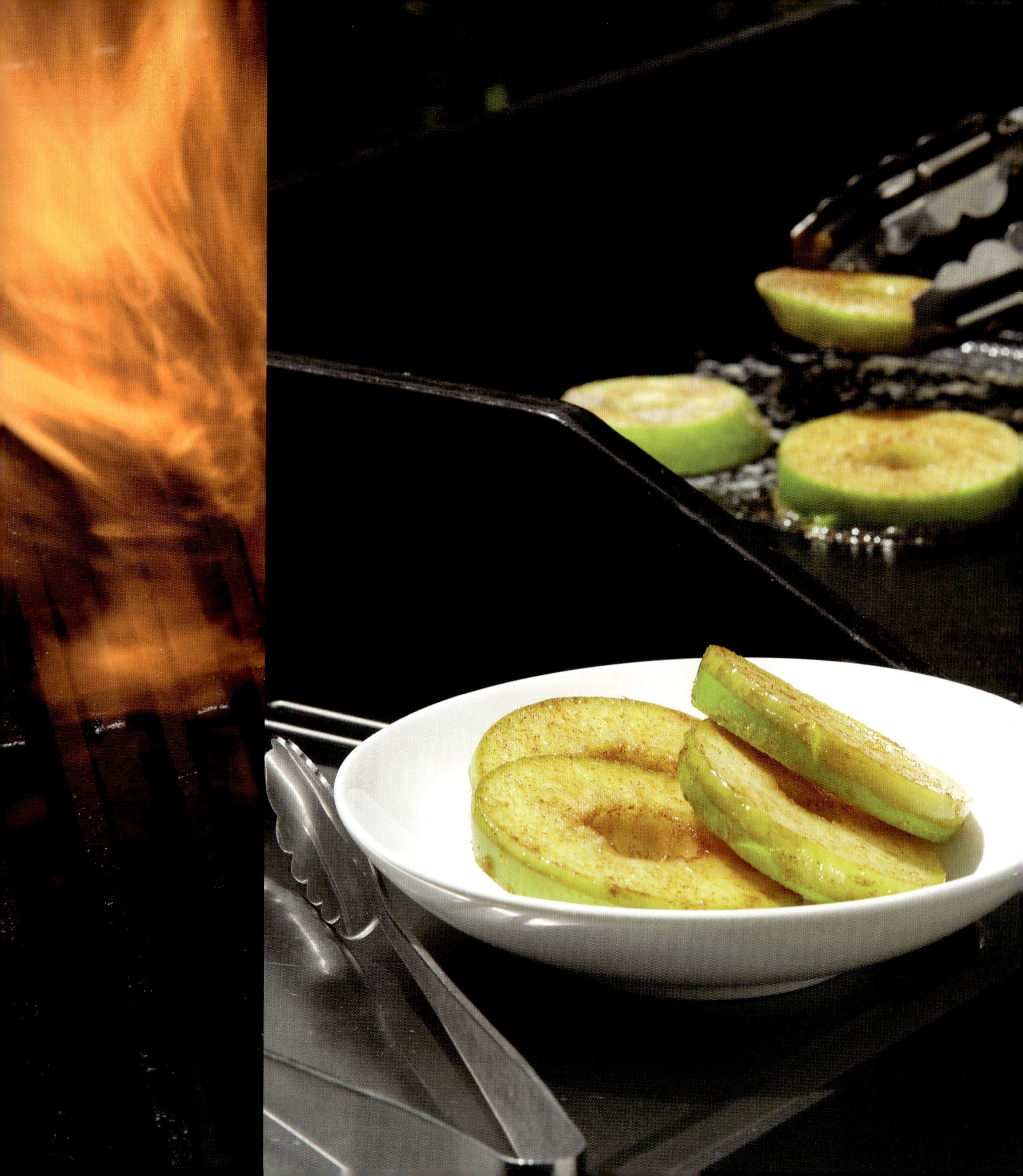

2 granny smith apples, large
½ tablespoon nutmeg, ground
1 tablespoon castor sugar
2 tablespoons butter, melted
30ml (1fl oz) Calvados (substitute with brandy)
Vanilla ice-cream

NUTMEG APPLE SLICES, CALVADOS & VANILLA ICE CREAM

Core the apples and slice into rounds approximately 1cm (½in) thick.

Mix the nutmeg and sugar and sprinkle on both sides of the apple slices.

Spread half the melted butter onto a low heated plate. Add the apple slices and cook for 1 minute. Spoon over the remaining butter and turn, cooking for two more minutes. Remove onto a service platter.

Spoon over the Calvados and serve with balls of vanilla ice cream.

SERVES 4

For the Cakes
½ cup plain flour
⅔ cup yellow polenta
1 teaspoon salt
½ teaspoon bicarbonate of soda
1 teaspoon baking powder
¼ cup self-raising flour
2 tablespoons butter, melted
1 cup milk
1 egg, beaten
4 medium bananas
Icing sugar for dusting

For the Caramel Sauce
1 cup brown (soft) sugar
300ml (10fl oz) pouring cream
spray oil
extra butter

POLENTA GRIDDLE CAKES, BANANA & CARAMEL SAUCE

Mix the flour, polenta, salt, bicarbonate of soda, baking powder and self-raising flour together in a bowl. Make a well and stir in the well combined butter, milk and egg. Stir well and use immediately, as the polenta soaks up the liquid very quickly. If the batter gets too thick at the barbecue, add a little milk.

Spray a medium-hot plate well. Add a little butter and when foaming spread over the part of the plate to be used and spoon some of the cake mixture onto the plate. Make only 3 or 4 at a time and when browned on one side, flip over to cook the cakes through. Repeat until all the batter is used. If the batter thickens while waiting to be cooked, add a little more milk.

Make the caramel sauce by putting the sugar into a small saucepan and start to melt over medium heat. Remove from the heat and stir in the cream. Return to the heat and stir to combine.

Keep the cakes warm. Put a little butter in between each of the cakes and pile at least two-high. Slice peeled banana over the cakes and pour on some caramel sauce. Dust with icing sugar to serve.

SERVES 4

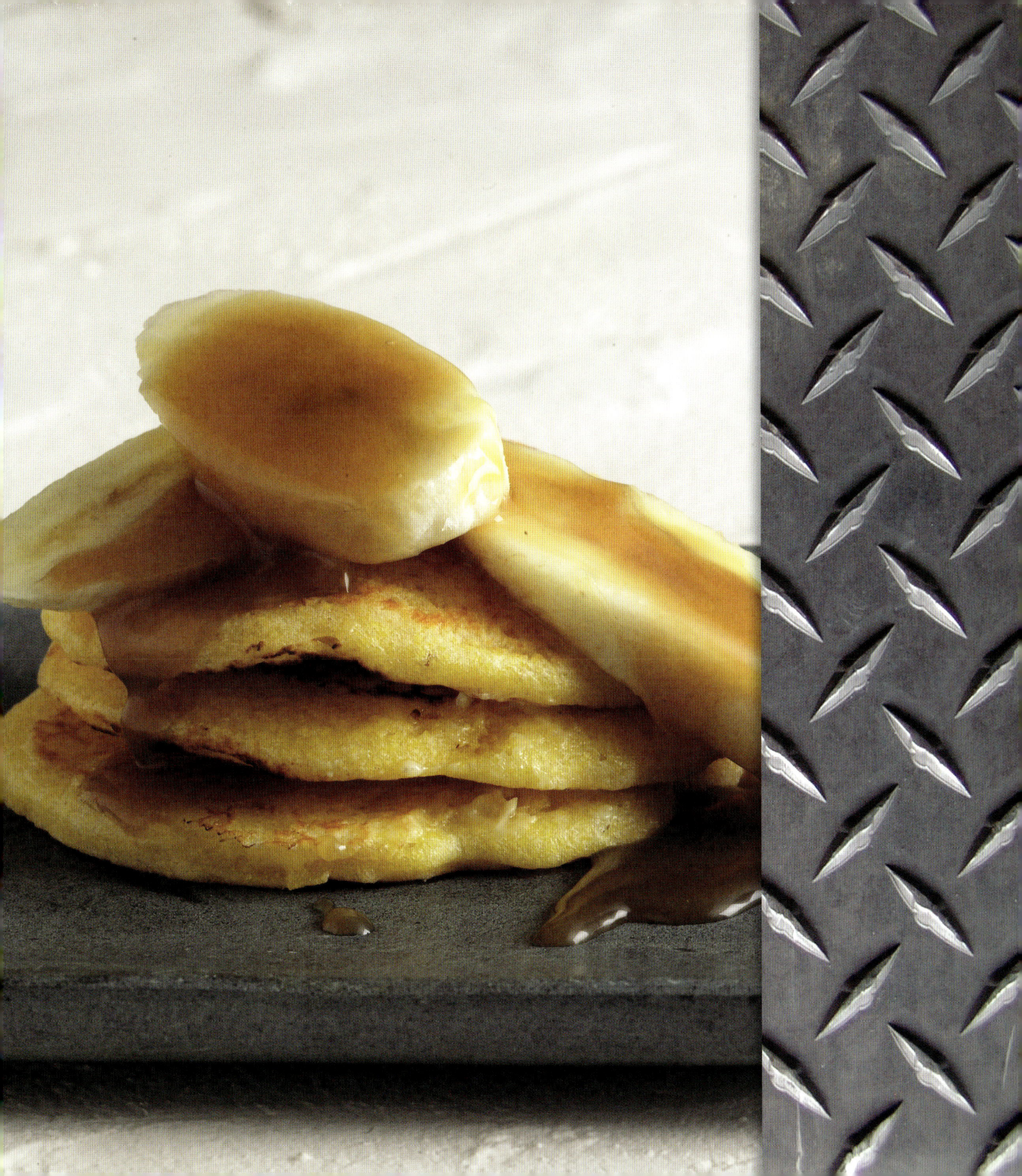

INDEX

A

Abalone Strips with Vietnamese Dipping Sauce 23
Almond
   Almond Parsley-crusted Snapper Fillets 69
   Apricot Brochettes & Almond Blancmange 14
Anchovy
Angels on Horseback 16
Apple, Fig, Walnut and Celery Salad 220
Anchovy
   Barbecue Potatoes with Tuna & Anchovy Dressing 290
   Bug Tails & Dill Risotto Cakes With Garlic, White Wine & Anchovy Cream 125
Apricot Brochettes & Almond Blancmange 314
Asian-flavoured Sea Scallops 19
Asparagus, Eggs, Olives & Red Capsicum Dressing 299
Asparagus in Prosciutto 36
Atlantic Salmon with Lemon Myrtle Rub & Cucumber Compote 266
Atlantic Salmon Risotto Cakes 92

B

Baba Ganoush 25
Baby Snapper with Cheesy Creamy Potatoes & Spinach 265
Bacon, Chilli Jam & Peanut Butter Rolls 33
Bacon, Peach & Blue Cheese Salad 275
Balmain Bugs with Dill Risotto & Browned Butter 262
Bananas, Rum & Whipped Mascarpone 325
Barbecue Lamb Sandwich with Chilli Chive Mayo 126
Barbecued Beef & Mushroom Kebabs with Homemade Barbecue Sauce 132
Barbecued Garlic Dressing 279
Barbecued Gravalax Ocean Trout 253
Barbecue Sauce 132
Barbecued Sirloin & Green Curry Dressing 129

Barramundi Fillet with Green Curry Sauce & Quick Stir-fried Rice 260
Basic Handmade Mayonnaise 128
Basic Pizza Dough 122
Beef
   Barbecued Beef & Mushroom Kebabs with Homemade Barbecue Sauce 132
   Barbecued Sirloin & Green Curry Dressing 129
   Beef, Onion & Chive Pancakes with Tomato Relish 118
   Beef Sausages & Barbecue Vegetable Stirfry 135
   Chilli Beef Strips Tacos 140
   Perfect Barbecue Steak, the 177
   Rissoles & Ratatouille 162
   Stir-fried Beef & Prawns 168
Black Mussels with Garlic & Red Wine Butter 104
Black Mussels & Barbecued Vegetables 259
Blue Eye
   Blue Eye with Pea Mash & Easy Cabernet Jus 258
   Blue Eye with Zucchini, Tomato, Prawn & Lime Butter 251
Boneless Leg of Lamb with Rosemary Rub 136
Boston Bay Clams with Basil & White Wine 87
Braised Borlotti Beans 255
Bream Fillets, Snow Peas & Garlic Potato Bake 257
Bug Tails & Dill Risotto Cakes with Garlic, White Wine & Anchovy Cream 117
Buttered Chats, Parsley and Black Pepper 267
Butterflied Loin Lamb with Grilled Potato & Caesar Spinach Salad 141

C

Calamari
   Calamari With Green Lentil & Mint Salad 114
   Calamari with Lime Juice & Coriander 109

Calve's Liver with Skewered Onions & Cashew & Mustard Butter 174
Caraway Pork Cutlets with Basil & Tomato Slaw 139
Carpetbag Chicken Breast & Red Cabbage 203
Chardonnay Butter Oysters 39
Chargrilled Vegetables & Pasta Salad with Tomato Basil Dressing 272
Chargrilled Haloumi, Carrot & Chive Salad 288
Chargrilled Baby Octopus with Mango Salsa 53
Char-roasted Atlantic Salmon Tail with Kumera, Green Lentils & Prawn Star Anise Broth 250
Char-roasted Chicken with Old-fashioned Bread Stuffing 200
Char-roasted Goat Rack with Garlic Thyme Baste, Barbecued Onions & Broccolini 181
Cheese
   Cheesy Creamy Potatoes 265
   Pear, Carrot & Pecorino Cheese Salad 309
   Pork Chops with Blue Cheese Mayo & Sweetcorn Potato Cakes 150
Chermoula Rub Atlantic Salmon Salad 107
Chicken
   Carpetbag Chicken Breast & Red Cabbage 203
   Char-roasted Chicken with Old-fashioned Bread Stuffing 200
   Chicken Breast Saltimbocca 195
   Chicken Breast with Asian Parsley Salad 188
   Chicken Breast with Tzatziki & Greek Salad 192
   Chicken Fajitas 190
   Chicken Livers, Lemon & Marjoram Baste 119
   Chicken Pattie & Sourdough Sandwich 189
   Chicken & Australian Native Baste 199
   Chicken & Lime Marinade with Peanut Sauce 197

Chicken, Barbecued Corn Salsa
    & Asparagus   198
  Chicken Koftas   110
Chilli
  Barbecue Lamb Sandwich with Chilli
    Chive Mayo   126
  Chilli Beef Strips Tacos   140
  Chilli Lamb Skewers & Asian Slaw   143
Chived Eggs, Smoked Salmon
    & Brioche   113
Chorizo, Mediterranean Vegetables
    & Goat's Curd Pizza   120
Cinnamon
  Cinnamon French Toast & Cointreau
    Cream   326
  Cinnamon Zucchini Bread   302
Corn on the Cob with Parsley Pesto   95
Crab Omelettes with Spicy Cucumber
    Salsa   58
Crayfish
  Crayfish Medallions with Szechuan Pepper
    & Orange Dressing   248
  Crayfish in Shell with Lemongrass & Lime
    Flavours & Potato Salad   249
Crispy Focaccia with Spicy Black Eye Bean
    Spread & Rocket   62
Cumin Pumpkin, Yellow Squash & Red
    Onion Salad   305
Cumin, Ginger & Coriander Rub Goat Rack
    with Roma Tomatoes, Asparagus
    & Butternut Pumpkin   180
Cuttlefish with Salsa Verde
    & Baby Rocket   100
Cuttlefish with Chorizo, Capsicum
    & Pine Nut Salad   246
Curried Zucchini Pappadum Stack   103

D

Dill Risotto   262
Duck
  Duck Breasts with Bok Choy & Celeriac
    Salad   205
  Duck Quesadillas & Semi-roasted Tomato
    Salsa   186
  Duck Sausages with Parsnips, Fava Beans
    & Orange Dressing   184

Dukkah-crusted Atlantic Salmon
    with Tabbouleh Salad   243
Drunken Oysters   57

E

Eggplant
  Eggplant, Capsicum & Sesame
    Seed Salad   306
  Spicy Eggplant & Lentil Puree
    with Chapatis   178

F

Fennel & Pepper Crusted Blue Eye
    with Goat's Cheese Salad   245
Fennel, Bean & Orange Salad   287
Fillets of Reef Fish with Eschallot Mash
    & Caraway Mayo Drizzle   242
Flapjacks, Golden Syrup Macadamia
    Nuts   321
Flathead
  Flathead Tails, Soft Mushroom Polenta
    & Mint Lemon Pesto   215

G

Goat
  Char-roasted Goat Rack with Garlic
    Thyme Baste, Barbecued Onions
    & Broccolini   181
  Cumin, Ginger & Coriander Rub Goat
    Rack with Roma Tomatoes, Asparagus
    & Butternut Pumpkin   190
Goat's Cheese
  Goat's Cheese Salad   245
  Goat's Cheese & Mesclun Salad
    with Barbecued Garlic Dressing   279
Green Curry Paste   131
Green Paw Paw Salad with Nam Jim
Dressing   292
Grilled Pide & Beetroot Hummus   54
Grilled Asparagus Rolls   80

H

Haloumi
  Chargrilled Haloumi, Carrot & Chive
    Salad   288
  Zucchini, Haloumi & Mushroom Oil
    Salad   296

Ham
  Ham, Cumin & Cous Cous Cakes   45
  Veal & Ham Burger with Beetroot
    Relish   171

J

Jewfish Steaks with Blood Orange
    & Beetroot Salad   239

K

Kaffir Lime Prawns with Sweet
    Chilli Sauce   81
King Prawn Caesar Salad   66
King Prawns & Glass Noodle Salad   241
King Prawns, Mint & Chervil Sauce   77
Kumara, Red Onion, Celery & Tuna
    Dressing   295

L

Lamb
  Barbecue Lamb Sandwich with Chilli
    Chive Mayo   126
  Boneless Leg of Lamb with Rosemary
    Rub   36
  Butterflied Loin Lamb with Grilled Potato
    & Caesar Spinach Salad   141
  Chilli Lamb Skewers & Asian Slaw   143
  Lamb Chops with Green Bean Salad
    & Kumera   144
  Lamb Burgers with Minted Yoghurt
    & Mint Pesto   147
  Lamb Koftas with Pita Bread, Yoghurt
    & Mint   32
  Pepper-crusted Lamb Rump with Lentil,
    Sugar Snap Peas & Chervil Salad   158
Ling
  Soy-soaked Ling Fish Strips & Glass
    Noodle Salad   214
Lobster
  Lime Lobster with Crusty Potatoes
    & Grilled Green Beans   238
  Lobster Medallions with Thai Cucumber
    & Asian Leaves   237

M

Mandarin Vodka Chervil Oysters   84

Mango
  Pork Cutlets & Mango Mint Sauce   153
  Swordfish Kebabs with Mango
    & Lychee Salsa   208
  Tuna & Green Mango Salad   209
Meatballs & Homemade Barbecue Sauce   50
Mexican Spiced Ocean Trout Wraps   234
Mixed Seafood Linguine   233
Monk Fish with Sugar Snap Peas, Bacon
  & Apple Salad   231
Mussels & Tandoori Dressing   29

N

Nectarine, Pancetta & Feta Salad
  with Cinnamon Zucchini Bread   300
Nutmeg Apple Slices, Calvados & Vanilla
  Ice Cream   329

O

Ocean Trout Brochettes with Satay Dipping
  Sauce   40
Orange-scented Meatloaf & Mushroom
  Ragout   146
Oysters, Garlic Oil & Preserved Lemon   43
Oysters & *Café de Paris* Butter   46
Oysters in Prosciutto   69

P

Passionfruit Souffle   317
Peach, Feta & Prosciutto Salad with Lime
  & Lychee Dressing   280
Pear, Carrot & Pecorino Cheese Salad   309
Pepper-crusted Lamb Rump with Lentil,
  Sugar Snap Peas & Chervil Salad   158
Peppered Monkfish with Asparagus
  & Braised Borlotti Beans   254
Perfect Barbecue Steak, the   177
Pesto-infused Prawn Skewers   49
Polenta Griddle Cakes, Banana
  & Caramel Sauce   330
Pork
  Caraway Pork Cutlets with Basil
    & Tomato Slaw   139
  Pork Chops with Blue Cheese Mayo
    & Sweetcorn Potato Cakes   150
  Pork Cutlets & Mango Mint Sauce   153

Pork Fillet with Zucchini & Herb Spaghetti   154
  Pork Sausages with Spiced Apple
    & Red Currant Jelly   157
  Pork, Green Apple & Vermicelli Noodle
    Salad   167
Potato
  Butterflied Loin Lamb with Grilled Potato
    & Caesar Spinach Salad   141
  Potato Salad & Garlic Dressing   310
  Potato, Tarragon & Pea Cakes
    with Smoked Salmon & Salmon Roe   44
Pumpkin, Tofu & Pink Grapefruit Salad   291
Prawns
  King Prawns & Glass Noodle Salad   241
  Prawns, Asparagus & Mint Hollandaise   88
  Prawn Kebabs with Pineapple
    Coriander Salsa   61
  Prawns with Laksa   227
  Prosciutto Prawns with Rocket Aioli   224
  Stir-fried Beef & Prawns   168
Prosciutto Sage Lamb Cutlets with Pea
  & Tomato Linguine   160
Pumpkin & Parmesan Souffle   78

R

Rice Noodles & Bok Choy Salad with Ginger
  Chilli Soy Dressing   284
Rissoles & Ratatouille   162
Roasting Chart   08

Q

Quail & Pineapple Scented Cous Cous   83

S

Salads
  Bacon, Peach & Blue Cheese Salad   275
  Chargrilled Haloumi, Carrot & Chive
    Salad   288
  Chargrilled Vegetables & Pasta Salad
    with Tomato Basil Dressing   272
  Chicken Breast with Tzatziki
    & Greek Salad   192
  Cumin Pumpkin, Yellow Squash
    & Red Onion Salad   305
  Eggplant, Capsicum & Sesame
    Seed Salad   306

  Fennel, Bean & Orange Salad   287
  Goat's Cheese Salad   245
  Goat's Cheese & Mesclun Salad
    with Barbecued Garlic Dressing   279
  Green Paw Paw Salad with Nam
    Jim Dressing   292
  Jewfish Steaks with Blood Orange
    & Beetroot Salad   239
  King Prawns & Glass Noodle Salad   241
  Kumara, Red Onion, Celery
    & Tuna Dressing   295
  Monk Fish with Sugar Snap Peas, Bacon
    & Apple Salad   231
  Nectarine, Pancetta & Feta Salad
    with Cinnamon Zucchini Bread   300
  Ocean Trout on Nicoise Salad   228
  Peach, Feta & Prosciutto Salad with Lime
    & Lychee Dressing   280
  Pear, Carrot & Pecorino Cheese
    Salad   309
  Pine Nut Salad   246
  Potato Salad & Garlic Dressing   310
  Pumpkin, Tofu & Pink Grapefruit
    Salad   291
  Rice Noodles & Bok Choy Salad
    with Ginger Chilli Soy Dressing   284
  Soy-soaked Ling Fish Strips
    & Glass Noodle Salad   226
  Tabbouleh Salad   243
  Thai Kangaroo Salad   317
  Watercress, Radish & Feta Salad with
    Raspberry & Tarragon Dressing   283
  Zucchini, Haloumi & Mushroom
    Oil Salad   310
Salmon
  Atlantic Salmon with Lemon Myrtle Rub
    & Cucumber Compote   280
  Dukkah-crusted Atlantic Salmon
    with Tabbouleh Salad   257
  Snapper Fillets with Chive Verjuice Butter
    & Salmon Roe   217
Sambucca Mango Cheeks & Minted
  Crème Fraiche   319
Sardines
  Spanish-style Sardines with Aioli
    & Chickpea Carrot Salad   210

Scallops, Blood Sausage, Prawn
    & Lime Butter   22
Sea Scallops
  Scallop & Bacon Kebabs   96
  Sea Scallops, Parlsey & Macadamia
    Pesto   74
  Spice-crusted Sea Scallops with Kumera
    Mash & Mixed Peas   213
  Seared Ocean Trout on Apple, Fig, Walnut
    & Celery Salad   220
  Seared Tuna Slices on Cucumber with
    Salmon Roe   14
Scallops & Anchovy Sauce   26
Scallops, White Bean Puree & Panini
    Bruschetta   70
Semillon Sauvignon Blanc Oysters   12
Skewered Prawns, Barbecued Lemon   35
Skewered Tuna & Wasabi Cream   65
Snapper
  Almond Parsley-crusted Snapper
    Fillets   269
  Baby Snapper with Cheesy Creamy
    Potatoes & Spinach   265
  Snapper Fillets with Cannellini Bean
    & Eschallot Salad   218
  Snapper Fillets with Chive Verjuice Butter
    & Salmon Roe   217
Soy-soaked Ling Fish Strips & Glass
    Noodle Salad   214
Spanish-style Sardines with Aioli
    & Chickpea Carrot Salad   222
Spicy Eggplant & Lentil Puree with
    Chapatis   188
Spice-crusted Sea Scallops with Kumera
    Mash & Mixed Peas 213
Strawberry-stuffed Crêpes
    & Mango Cream   322
Swordfish Kebabs with Mango
    & Lychee Salsa   208

T

Thai-inspired Fish Patties   99
Thai Kangaroo Salad   303
Tomato
  Caraway Pork Cutlets with Basil
    & Tomato Slaw   139

Duck Quesadillas & Semi-roasted
    Tomato Salsa   186
Prosciutto Sage Lamb Cutlets with Pea
    & Tomato Linguine   160
Thai Chicken Cakes   20
Tiny Arancini   30
Tiny Sausages & Red Bell Pepper Sauce   73
Trout
  Barbecued Gravalax Ocean Trout   253
  Mexican Spiced Ocean Trout Wraps   234
  Ocean Trout & Potato Mash with Charred
    Radicchio & Beurre Rouge   230
  Ocean Trout on Nicoise Salad   228
  Rainbow Trout with Onion Cous Cous
    & Dukkah   256
  Rainbow Trout with Pan-fried Red Cabbage
    & Salmon Roe Cream   222
  Seared Ocean Trout on Apple, Fig, Walnut
    & Celery Salad   220
Tuna
  Kumara, Red Onion, Celery & Tuna
    Dressing   295

V

Veal
  Veal & Ham Burger with Beetroot
    Relish   171
  Veal Cutlets with Olive, Parsley
    & Lime Pesto   172
Venison Sausages & Parsnip Mash
    with Cumberland Sauce   174

W

Watercress, Radish & Feta Salad with
    Raspberry & Tarragon Dressing   283
Whole Sardines, Capers & Pine Nuts   91

Z

Zucchini
  Blue Eye with Zucchini, Tomato, Prawn
    & Lime Butter   251
  Nectarine, Pancetta & Feta Salad
    with Cinnamon Zucchini Bread   300
  Pork Fillet with Zucchini & Herb
    Spaghetti   154
  Zucchini, Haloumi & Mushroom
    Oil Salad   296

First published in Australia in 2009 by
New Holland Publishers (Australia) Pty Ltd
Sydney • Auckland • London • Cape Town

1/66 Gibbes Street Chatswood NSW 2067 Australia
218 Lake Road Northcote Auckland New Zealand
86 Edgware Road London W2 2EA United Kingdom
80 McKenzie Street Cape Town 8001 South Africa

Copyright © 2009 New Holland Publishers (Australia) Pty Ltd
Copyright © 2009 in text Peter Howard
Copyright © 2009 in photographs New Holland Publishers (Australia) Pty Ltd

All rights reserved. No part of this publication may be reproduced, stored in a retrieval system or transmitted, in any form or by any means, electronic, mechanical, photocopying, recording or otherwise, without the prior written permission of the publishers and copyright holders.

A record of this book is held at the National Library of Australia

ISBN 9781741107968

Publisher: Fiona Schultz
Publishing Manager: Lliane Clarke
Senior Project Editor: Joanna Tovia
Designer: Hayley Norman
Photographers: Graeme Gillies, R&R Photo Studio, Joe Filshie
Stylist: Georgina Dolling
Assistants: Ashlea Wallington and Ishbel Thorpe
Production Manager: Olga Dementiev
Printer: SNP/Leefung Printing Co. Ltd (China)

10 9 8 7 6 5 4 3 2 1

Special thanks to speciality butcher Springbok Delights in Lane Cove for their support.